The Human Right to Water: Justice . . . or Sham?

The Human Right to Water: Justice . . . or Sham?

The Legal, Philosophical, and Theological Background of the New Human Right to Water

Evelyne Fiechter-Widemann

TRANSLATED BY
Andrene Everson

FOREWORD BY
Asit K. Biswas
AND
Cecilia Tortajada

⌒PICKWICK Publications • Eugene, Oregon

THE HUMAN RIGHT TO WATER: JUSTICE . . . OR SHAM?
The Legal, Philosophical, and Theological Background of the New Human Right to Water

Copyright © 2017 Evelyne Fiechter-Widemann. All rights reserved. Except for brief quotations in critical publications or reviews, no part of this book may be reproduced in any manner without prior written permission from the publisher. Write: Permissions, Wipf and Stock Publishers, 199 W. 8th Ave., Suite 3, Eugene, OR 97401.

Pickwick Publications
An Imprint of Wipf and Stock Publishers
199 W. 8th Ave., Suite 3
Eugene, OR 97401

www.wipfandstock.com

PAPERBACK ISBN: 978-1-4982-9406-5
HARDCOVER ISBN: 978-1-4982-9408-9
EBOOK ISBN: 978-1-4982-9407-2

Cataloguing-in-Publication data:

Names: Fiechter-Widemann, Evelyne, author | Biswas, Asit K., forward | Tortajada, Cecilia, foreword | Everson, Andrene, translator.

Title: The human right to water: justice . . . or sham? : the legal, philosophical, and theological background of the new human right to water / Evelyne Fiechter-Wideman ; Foreword by Asit K. Biswas and Cecilia Tortajada ; translated by Andrene Everson.

Description: Eugene, OR: Pickwick Publications, 2017 | Includes bibliographical references and index.

Identifiers: ISBN 978-1-4982-9406-5 (paperback) | ISBN 978-1-4982-9408-9 (hardcover) | ISBN 978-1-4982-9407-2 (ebook)

Subjects: LCSH: Human rights | Water Ethics—Developing countries.

Classification: K3498 F54 2017 (print) | K3498 (ebook).

Manufactured in the U.S.A.   04/11/17

To Eric, Jean-Rodolphe, and Gwendoline

Do to others as you would have them do to you.
—Luke 6:31

Contents

List of Images | x
Foreword | *Asit K. Biswas and Cecilia Tortajada* | xi
Synopsis | xiii
Acknowledgments | xv
List of Abbreviations | xxi
General Introduction | xxv

    Breaking the Vicious Circle of Unequal Access to Water Is an Ethical Imperative | xxv

    Method | xxix

Part I   Water Inequality: A Global Challenge for Humanity | 1

Chapter I: The Concept of "Globality" | 3

Chapter II: "Thinking" Water in Terms of Its Vulnerability, through Case Studies | 9

Chapter III: "Thinking" the Human Relationship to Water: The Phenomenology of Vulnerability | 15

Chapter IV: "Thinking" the Human in Need | 27

Chapter V: "Thinking" Human Beings in Terms of Their Dignity | 34

Part II   Normative Solutions to Water Inequality: Many Rational Units for Water | 43

    Introduction: *Two Areas of Focus* | 43

    A New Role for Civil Society | 44

Chapter I: Is The Human Right to Water an Ethical Normativity or a Legal One? | 47

Chapter II: Scientific Normativity for Water | 52

Chapter III: Economic/Political and Legal Normativities for Water | 61

Part III   A Changing Water Ethic: Moral Causes and Motives for the New Human Right to Water | 79

Introduction: *Thinking and Conceptualizing Mobilization for Potable Water* | 79

Section I   Is Natural Law a Justifiable Cause or Basis for the New Human RIght to Water? | 83

Introduction | 83

Possible Bases | 84

Creating a Space for Dialogue about the Human Right to Water | 85

Chapter I: A Theological Inquiry Into *Natural Law* from ABRAHAM through the Apostle Paul and the Church Fathers to Calvin | 89

Chapter II: A Philosophical Inquiry Concerning *Natural Law* from Grotius to the *Human Right to Water* via Kant and Bonhoeffer | 114

Section II   Motives for Actions that are in Conformity With Duty, Good, and Useful for Universal Access to Potable Water | 139

Chapter I: Deontological Motives for Action, or "Thinking" Water Philosophically with Immanuel Kant | 141

Chapter II: Eudaemonist and Anti-Eudaemonist Motives for Action, or How to "Think" Water Emotionally | 156

Chapter III: Empirical and Utilitarian Motives for Action, or How to "Think" Water for the Well-Being of All | 176

Part IV   Justice and Responsibility: From a Logic of Normativity to One of Implementation | 191

Introduction: *Justice for the "Other" Human Being, the One Who Thirsts* | 191

Does the Reality Affect Us and Make Us Responsible? | 192

Chapter I: Responsibility: A Problematic Concept | 195

Chapter II: Intergenerational Ethics | 201

Chapter III: Intragenerational Ethics | 211

CONTENTS

Part V   **The Theological Structure of Potable Water's Challenges** | 247

Introduction: What Kind of Justice Should Apply to Universal Access to Potable Water? | 247

Chapter I: Solicitude and Love as a Means to Supererogatory Justice: The Golden Rule Concept | 249

Chapter II: "Thinking" Water Differently—Theologically | 262

Part VI   **Strategies for Mitigating Water Poverty: Some Original Testimonies** | 283

General Conclusion | 330

Appendix—Looking for Water with EPER/HEKS | 341
Bibliography | 361
Translator's Bibliography | 383
Subject Index | 389
Scripture Index | 393

Images

Appendix Photos

Lady with white hat in Zimbabwe looking for water under the sand | 341
Dry garden in Zimbabwe (Vilakalidli garden) | 348
Lady with hat pointing her finger | 349
Community meeting in Zimbabwe at Makhasa Dam | 350
Guesthouse in Zimbabwe without running water | 352
Three hosts and two visitors | 352
Woman working in the fields | 353
Woman carrying water in a basket | 353
Windmill | 353
Hoses and baskets | 354
Manual water pump | 354
Field | 354
Author and statue of Mandela at Johannesburg airport in March 2012 | 355
Termit nest under a big tree | 358
Municipal secretary in Maruleng, South Africa | 359
Three women in a greenhouse in Maruleng | 359
Ashes in greenhouse in Maruleng | 359

Foreword

THE CONCEPT THAT WATER is a human right is not new. Throughout history, it has been recognized that water is essential for human survival. The well-preserved Babylonian code of King Hammurabi, dating back to around 1754 BC, notes that water is a human right. Clear rules about water rights can be found in the Hebrew Bible and the Koran. Both give rights first to human beings for drinking, followed by domestic animals.

Discussions in the United Nations on this issue have a somewhat checkered history. Analyses of resolutions and declarations in the various United Nations fora during the post-1970 period indicate that these vacillated between have water as basic human need and as a human right. In fact, the concept that water is a basic human need or a human right has often been used interchangeably during various international fora, without clear understanding or appreciation of either the concepts or their operational implications.

This changed with the General Comment No. 15 of the Committee on Economic, Social and Cultural Rights of November 2002. It reinterpreted Articles 11 and 12 of the Covenant on Economics, Social and Cultural Rights and concluded that water can be considered to be a human right under this Covenant. The United Nations General Assembly, on July 2010, explicitly recognized that clean drinking water and sanitation are essential to realize all human rights.

While globally now it is almost universally accepted that water is a human right, there is considerable disagreement as to how this principle should be put into practice, especially in terms of defining an appropriate balance between efficiency and equity considerations.

If human rights to water are to become more than a principle and a concept, as Evelyne Fiechter-Widemann has cogently and eloquently argued in this book, governments and the international organizations must fully appreciate what these rights mean and, further how these can be achieved with good water governance. Regrettably, at present, proper approaches to water governance are often mostly missing in developed and developing countries.

As the author has correctly noted, the "outcome of actions taken over the past 30 years has turned out to be totally inadequate, despite seemingly optimistic Millennium

Foreword

Development Goals statistics". Almost all international organizations have been using over the past several decades terms like improved sources of water, clean water and safe water interchangeably. Consequently, when WHO, UNICEF or other organizations say "only" 663 million people do not have access to "improved sources of water", people automatically assume that besides these 663 million, the rest of 6.83 billion people in the world now have access to clean water. Nothing is further from the truth. Improved sources of water is a meaningless term. It has absolutely no relation to clean water which is safe to drink. Globally, now at least 2.5 to 3 billion people do not have access to safe drinking water. We have a very long way to go before overwhelming majority of the people have access to it . Thus, as the author again correctly notes, humankind is facing major challenges to ensure safe drinking water is available to all. She further rightly questions whether water as a human right "will lead to greater justice in the matter of access to potable water; or whether humanity risks tearing itself apart over the cause in the name of a human right doctrine that is understood by the members of the international community in so many different ways . . ."

Throughout the entire book, the author makes numerous similar objective and refreshing statements which are mostly missing from the existing literature on water as human right.

Equally impressive is the author's multidisciplinary approach to the issue. She successfully blends legal, ethical, moral, philosophical, theological, social and economic analyses to the issue which makes the book unique. Also, of special interest to readers will be her virtual dialogues with the Dutch jurist Hugo Grotius (1583–1645) and the German philosopher Immanuel Kant (1724–1804). These virtual dialogues and discussions across time span centuries. They show the author's mastery of knowledge and understanding over law, philosophy, theology and religion.

When we were first invited to write this Foreword to the book, we had expected it to be a somewhat "normal" treatise on water as human right. We were totally wrong. It is a much broader, more comprehensive and a totally interdisciplinary approach to the issue which everyone interested in the subject must read and learn from.

In our view Evelyne Fiechter-Widemann has made a seminal contribution to the topic. Her enthusiasm for the issue is infectious. The water and development professions have a great deal to learn from this excellent treatise.

Asit K. Biswas	Cecilia Tortajada
Distinguished Visiting Professor	Senior Research Fellow
Lee Kuan Yew School of Public Policy	Institute of Water Policy
National University of Singapore	Lee Kuan Yew School of Public Policy
Singapore	National University of Singapore

Synopsis

WATER IS A MATTER of life and death.

Advanced technology and engineering enable humans to gain better access to it.

Nonetheless, the conditions and endeavor required to reach this goal remain colossal in many countries. Building a lasting infrastructure including for adequate treatment before and after use is costly.

Therefore, I do believe that a radical change of thinking among people around the world, from the domestic to the large scale users, becomes a priority.

Even if the United Nations entitles them to *justice* for water, more responsible and ethical use of it by all interested parties is more important than the spreading of promises, which, in practice, may turn out to be a sham.

Only a better understanding that access to water rests on efforts of all, without exception, will reduce overuse, waste and pollution of the indispensable resource.

My essay, while written from a theological, philosophical, and legal perspective (focusing on John Calvin, Immanuel Kant, John Rawls, and Paul Ricoeur), demonstrates that water cannot be merely understood as a human right (see chart, Part VI), but also has to be dealt with from an economic point of view as well as under the authority of the Golden Rule.

Evelyne Fiechter-Widemann

Acknowledgments

IT IS SAID THAT water brings together the most widely varied collection of beings in the unfathomable universe.

Having been alerted to the challenges potable water faces in today's world while serving on the board of the foundation called EPER,[1] a diaconal ministry of the Federation of Swiss Protestant Churches, I chose to undertake a study on the human relationship to water. It was the starting point for an experience that gave me new insights into the creation as "the Glory of God,"[2] and into the task of respecting it that each of us has been assigned. I offer my warm thanks to this ecclesiastical ministry, its president Claude Ruey, and its director Ueli Locher, which also extend to Part VI, where I interview one of its employees.

My guide throughout has been François Dermange, a Professor of Theology and Ethics at the Autonomous Faculty of Protestant Theology in Geneva, who is very aware of today's challenges and the issues associated with them. This project could never have been completed without him. The scientific material with which he supplied me through his courses in Geneva, especially those on environmental ethics, and his participation in the first MOOC[3] distance learning course on John Calvin, which I was able to take while in Hong Kong, Singapore, and Australia, turned out to be of incalculable value. I owe him my deep gratitude.

I would like to further note that all of the other professors on the Faculty of Theology at this academy founded by John Calvin were excellent mentors to me in one way or another, especially because of their excellent contributions to the MOOC mentioned above, offered in the fall of 2013.

I would also like to point out that my dissertation director encouraged me to organize public sessions, each of which represented an important stage of my journey. He attended each of these three colloquia[4] and enriched them by his striking syntheses.

1. EPER is the French acronym for Swiss Church Aid (also known by its German acronym HEKS).
2. Calvin, *Instit.*, I, V, 5.
3. MOOC is the acronym for Massive Open Online Course.
4. For the *Proceedings of the W4W Interdisciplinary Colloquia* held from 2011 to 2013, see http://www.fiechter.name/w4w.

Acknowledgments

Conference participants included leading figures who have been working on water's challenges for decades. Their presence not only enhanced the deliberations, but also engendered much productive discussion. I would like to personally thank each of them; their names are listed in the colloquium proceedings (Appendixes). Among them were three professors from the Faculty of Law in Geneva who played a special role. These were Anne Petitpierre-Sauvain, Laurence Boisson de Chazournes, and Mara Tignino. Not only did each of these women present an important aspect of water's challenges from a legal and ethical standpoint; they also helped expand my own "water platform," especially in Singapore, through the water specialists to whom they referred me.

The magnificent setting for these colloquia, which were supported by the Geneva Faculty of Theology, IRSE,[5] and CUSO,[6] was Geneva's History of Science Museum on the shores of Lake Geneva. I offer my heartfelt thanks to its manager, Laurence-Isaline Stahl Gretsch, for hosting us, which allowed a large group of researchers, students, and friends to launch the Workshop for Water Ethics (W4W) project. This seven-member informal group, consisting of Annie Balet, Benoît Girardin, Laurence-Isaline Stahl Gretsch, Christoph Stucki, Renaud de Watteville, Gary Vachicouras and me, set six goals for itself.[7] The first was to

> conceptualize and explain the ethical dimension—essential for identifying and implementing solutions—of fair and sustainable water management in a globalized world.

I think this interdisciplinary group has the potential to expand on the considerations I propose in this dissertation[8] and even act as a catalyst on the world stage. This role involves promoting increased awareness of all the very real challenges potable water faces today.

One can never say thank you enough, as Pastor Max Dominicé, the father of International Museum of the Reformation president Françoise Demole, likes to mention.

Knowing that, even against my will, I am going fail to mention one person or another who supported me throughout the project, I beg pardon in advance.

I am enormously grateful to all those who opened their doors to me and granted me interviews, especially at the very beginning of my research, like Géza Teleki, lawyer in Basel.

---

5. IRSE is the French acronym for Switzerland's French-Language Institute of Systematics and Ethics.

6. CUSO is the French acronym for the University Conference of Western Switzerland, Doctoral School of Theology.

7. For the Proceedings of the W4W Interdisciplinary Colloquia held from 2011 to 2013, see http://www.fiechter.name/w4w.

8. Summarized in a table in Part VI.

Acknowledgments

Among these preliminary interviews, I would like to mention the one at FEPS[9] headquarters in Bern in September 2010, during which I met with theologian Otto Schäfer and pastor Albert Rieger. The latter took an active part in drawing up the 2005 Ecumenical Declaration on *Water As a Human Right and a Public Good*.[10]

In Geneva, Reverend Martin Robra and his colleague Maike Gorsboth of the World Council of Churches informed me of the existence of another ecumenical statement[11] dating from 2006. I note that Nicole Fischer, former president of the Geneva Protestant Church[12] and an AMIDUMIR[13] board member, facilitated access to these distinguished persons.

It was in southern Africa that I saw first-hand some of potable water's challenges, especially the extreme poverty associated with this resource when it is not well managed. A key factor in this discovery was the hour granted to me by EPER's director, Ueli Locher. It was he who made possible my trip to these distant lands, under the guidance of Esther Oettli and Valentin Prélaz.

As work on my dissertation progressed, I met Philippe Roch, the former director of the Swiss Federal Office for the Environment. He called my attention to the holistic aspect of the water issue, focusing on the need to protect wetlands—the subject of the Ramsar Convention,[14] which has its headquarters in Gland, Switzerland.

Professor Adolfo Bondolfi also honored me with an interview and gave examples that reminded me of water as a source of conflict, and its complex nature.

Shortly thereafter, my sister Christiane Chanson steered me to a fascinating conference arranged by Services Industriels de Genève (SIG) and held in Geneva on Monday, November 22, 2010. The topic was "the water war," addressed by speakers Anne Le Strat, the deputy mayor of Paris in charge of water and president of Eau de Paris, and Peter Brabeck-Letmathe, Nestlé's chairman of the board.

It was upon this occasion that I met those who were later to participate in the first W4W colloquium in 2011: Anne Petitpierre-Sauvain, a professor of law at the University of Geneva, and François Münger, who is responsible for water issues at the Department of Development and Cooperation in the Swiss Federal Department of Foreign Affairs. The latter was introduced to me by attorney and biologist Susanne Lauber Fürst.

This was the real beginning of my exciting quest to learn more about water in general, and potable water in particular. Even the UN's former Special Rapporteur for

---

9. FEPS is the French acronym for Federation of Swiss Protestant Churches.

10. Ecumenical Declaration on Water As a Human Right and a Public Good. Appendix 2 hereafter.

11. Statement on Water for Life.

12. Known at the time of her presidency as the ENPG, the French acronym for National Protestant Church of Geneva.

13. AMIDUMIR is the French acronym for Friends of the International Museum of the Reformation.

14. Ramsar (Iran). See Convention on Wetlands.

Acknowledgments

water, Catarina de Albuquerque, and a representative of the Water Supply and Sanitation Collaborative Council (WSSCC),[15] Tatiana Fedotova, graciously accorded me a few moments of their valuable time.

Upon the recommendation of Lise Berthoud, an active member of the Protestant parish of Chêne, in Geneva, I was also kindly received by Victor Ruffy, a former member of the Swiss federal parliament. At the third W4W colloquium in March 2013, he vibrantly expressed his passion for ensuring that young people are educated about the challenges of water in the twenty-first century. Like him, I believe in the rising generation, especially as represented by the young women who supported my project, including Angelina Burri, Ana-Maria Pavalache, and Valérie Sturm, as well as Chiara von Gunten and Lydia Tazi Kusongi, former students at Collège de Genève.

In addition to the dynamic "Water" platform team at the Faculty of Law, led by Professor Laurence Boisson de Chazournes and currently consisting of Dr. Mara Tignino and Mr. Komlan Sangbana, the University of Geneva also boasts a group of high-level scientific experts. On the advice of Professor François Dermange, I attended one of the interdisciplinary conferences put on in the fall of 2012 by Professors Martin Beniston, a former member of the IPCC,[16] and Rémi Baudouï, on the topic of water. They had invited Dr. Herbert Oberhänsli, an economist and vice-president of Nestlé, to speak. I was able to hear him again in Singapore during Water Week in June 2014. It was during an interview with him that I learned of Oman's *aflaj* system for shared management of water, which I mention in my study.

Among all these tireless water researchers, I would especially like to mention Professor Géraldine Pflieger, the author of *Eau des villes*,[17] who also allotted me some much-appreciated time. Other welcome encouragement was received from Rajna Gibson, a Professor of Finance in Geneva, and Mario von Cranach, a Professor emeritus of Economics at the University of Bern.

In September 2012, I was invited by Professor Klaus Mathis of the University of Lucerne's law faculty to attend an interesting adversarial debate in which Maude Barlow and Franklin Frederick opposed legal scholar Christian Hofer of SECO[18] on the thorny question of water privatization.

Through the good offices of Rosmarie Gerber of Bern, I was also able to meet author Marianne Spiller-Hadorn, known for her efforts to mobilize citizens against extreme poverty and hunger.

Because of his important role in my decision to conduct this research, I would like to pay special tribute to someone who has left us far too soon. This was Professor François Bovon, who was the pastor of the Protestant parish of Chêne for several months in the 1990s. He led evening Bible studies that I attended. Twenty years later,

---

15. www.wsscc.org.
16. IPCC is the acronym for the Intergovernmental Panel on Climate Control.
17. Pflieger, *L'eau des villes*.
18. SECO is the acronym for the Swiss State Secretariat for Economic Affairs.

in the summer of 2010, I had the very great privilege of seeing him again, along with his sister Monique Bovon, on a magnificent Black Sea cruise arranged by the Swiss-Greek Jean-Gabriel Eynard Association and the Hellas et Roma Association. Being in my sixties, I told him that I was still a little hesitant to start preparations for writing a dissertation, despite the encouragement of Professor Dermange, whom I had already contacted. François Bovon invited me and my husband Eric to his table on deck one evening so I could meet Jean-Marie Brandt, who had just published his second doctoral dissertation,[19] which he had defended in 2009 at the University of Lausanne's Faculty of Theology. And he was about my age!

So I dared to do it, and I should say that no one around me tried to dissuade me from taking my chances on this adventure. Quite the opposite, in fact: I was encouraged by some very old friends—Anne-Marie Boillat, Elsa Flego, Elisabeth Philipps-Slavkoff, Jacqueline Kaempf, Marie-Laure Sturm, Christian Häberli, Frédéric Riehl, Frédérique Schwab, Catherine Voutsinas, Rachel Lellouche, Nicole Helfenberger, Adriana D'Addario, and Miguel Vidal. Many others had to lay in a store of patience to see me through this work, as couples Jelena and Thierry Rochat and Anne-Christine and Jean-Michel Oneyser will attest, along with my former teachers Jean Eigenmann from primary school and Georges Ottino from secondary school, with whom I have been lucky enough to keep in contact.

I hope that even after the defense, I will be able to continue to start a discussion with anyone—young or old, Christian or not, Swiss or foreigner—on the value of the water that binds us together as human beings. Water is not only an existential and vital "given"; but also a mysterious natural entity that can dissolve into a multitude of delicate *fanfreluches*,[20] to use Calvin's word, or tiny particles like sprays of translucent bubbles, and is to be cherished and protected for abundant life.

For while it is generally confined to the narrow role of "natural resource," in accordance with a concept that arose only about a century ago, it is much more than that. It rules our lives, enveloping us in love from our conception to our death, if we care for it.

I am grateful to have experienced this immeasurable gift of life, especially in the company of the participants in the three W4W colloquia of 2011, 2012, and 2013. Since their names are given in the proceedings, I will not list them again here except for four people. How could I have continued writing without input from W4W members Laurence-Isaline Stahl Gretsch and Annie Balet, attentive readers of my prose? How could the work have come to look so attractive without sustained attention from Gary and Georgia Vachicouras, who introduced me to Théodora Nicolopoulos, an

---

19. Brandt, *L'obsolescence de l'offre religieuse*.

20. Calvin indicates, "Que les épicuriens me répondent, vu qu'ils imaginent que tout se fait selon que les petites fanfreluches, qui volent en l'air semblables à menue poussière, se rencontrent à l'aventure . . ." [Let the Epicurians give me an answer, since they imagine that everything happens depending on whether tiny particles floating through the air like dust motes encounter each other by chance . . ." Calvin, *Instit.*, I, V, 4.

artist at laying out text in this twenty-first-century digital age? I owe her my warmest thanks for her endless supply of patience.

For this present English version of my dissertation, I owe many thanks to quite a number of persons, first of all to a very good friend of mine, Dorothea Benes and her daughter Nadia Yagüe-Beneš. They facilitated my discovery of Marc Woodward Services. Marc Woodward himself, originally from New Zealand but based in the international city of Geneva, Switzerland, created a team of translation expertise with Andrene Everson, based in Oregon in the United States. What a globalized world indeed! To both of them, I would like to express my gratitude for the quick advancement of the translation work and for the real interest they showed in the substance of the thesis. I should note that except as otherwise indicated, all translations of quoted material are by Andrene Everson. All biblical quotations are from the New Revised Standard Version (NRSV).

Before I close the guest book I would also like to mention Cornelio Sommaruga, the former president of both the ICRC and Initiative of Change.[21] He lent me his unfailing support by participating in all three W4W colloquia and encouraging me via e-mail during the times between.

The time has now come to say that I owe to my dear husband, Eric Fiechter, the privilege of having been able to write part of my dissertation in Singapore. Our home on Mount Sophia, an ideal location if ever there was one, was just across from Orchard Road Presbyterian Church, which we chose to attend regularly. This corner of Southeast Asia turned out—especially during Singapore International Water Week (SIWW) in June 2014—to be a source of additional high-quality information on this difficult topic that I so wanted to study using an interdisciplinary approach, as Geneva's Faculty of Theology allowed me to do.

Without the daily support of my family, whether virtually by Skype and the Internet as from my children Jean-Rodolphe and Gwendoline, and my sister, brothers- and sisters-in-law, aunt and uncle, cousins, nieces and nephews, and grand-nieces and grand-nephews, or in Eric's warm real presence, I could not have finished this project, which seemed rather overwhelming at the outset. His loving patience and comments as the work progressed were invaluable and I owe him a very big THANK YOU.

Once more, I would like to express my very sincere gratitude to everyone.

---

21. www.iofc.org.

Abbreviations

ACSEP	Asia Centre for Social Entrepreneurship and Philanthropy
ADR	Alternative Dispute Resolution
AEC	ASEAN Economic Community
AGLEAU	Alerte Générale Sur L'eau [association]
AMIDUMIR	Friends of the International Museum of the Reformation
ANC	African National Congress
AoA	WTO's Agreement on Agriculture
ASCC	ASEAN Social and Cultural Community
ASEAN	Association of Southeast Asian Nations
CAS	Certificate of Advanced Studies
CNRS	Centre national de la recherche scientifique [National Science Research Center]
CoE	Council of Europe
CSR	Corporate social responsibility
CUSO	Conférence Universitaire de Suisse Occidentale [University Conference of Western Switzerland]
DDC	Department of Development and Cooperation (Switzerland)
DWAF	Department of Water Affairs and Forestry (South Africa)
EPER	Entraide protestante [Swiss Church Aid] (also known as HEKS, *q. v.*)
EPFL	Ecole Polytechnique Fédérale de Lausanne [Swiss Federal Institute of Technology in Lausanne]
EU	European Union
FBW	Free Basic Water

Abbreviations

FEPS	Fédération des Eglises protestantes de Suisse [Federation of Swiss Protestant Churches]
FOEN	Federal Office for the Environment (Switzerland)
GATS	General Agreement on Trade in Services (cf. WTO)
GDP	Gross domestic product
GRD	General Resource Dividend
GSM	Global System for Mobile communication
HDB	Housing Development Board (Singapore)
HEKS	Hilfswerk des Evangelischen Kirchen Schweiz [Swiss Church Aid, also known as EPER, *q. v.*)
HKS	Harvard Kennedy School of Government
HRBA	Human Rights Based Approach
ICBL	International Campaign to Ban Landmines
ICC	International Chamber of Commerce
ICCPR	International Covenant for Civil and Political Rights
ICESCR	International Covenant for Economic, Social and Cultural Rights
ICRC	International Committee of the Red Cross
ICWE	International Conference on Water and Environment
IDEP	Itireleng Development and Educational Project (South Africa)
ILO	International Labour Organization
IPCC	Intergovernmental Panel on Climate Change
IRSE	Institut Romand de Systématique et d'Ethique [Switzerland's French-Language Institute of Systematics and Ethics]
ISO	International Standardization Organization
IWRM	Integrated Water Resources Management
MDG	Millennium Development Goal
MENA	Middle East and North Africa
MOOC	Massive Open Online Course
NGO	Non-governmental organization
NUS	National University of Singapore
OECD	Organisation for Economic Cooperation and Development

Abbreviations

OXFAM	Oxford Committee for Famine Relief
PERL	Prix Entreprendre Région Lausanne [Lausanne region entrepreneurship prize]
PPP	Public Private Partnership
PPPA	People's Participatory Planning and Action
RIAE	Réseau International Acteurs Emergents [International Network of Emergent Actors]
SECO	State Secretariat for Economic Affairs (Switzerland)
SFW	Swiss Fresh Water
SIG	Services Industriels de Genève [Geneva Industrial Services utility company]
SIWI	Stockholm International Water Institute
TNC	Transnational Corporation
UDHR	Universal Declaration of Human Rights
UN	United Nations
UNDP	United Nations Development Programme
UNICEF	United Nations Children's Fund
W4W	Workshop For Water Ethics
WHO	World Health Organization
WMO	World Meteorological Organization
WSSCC	Water Supply and Sanitation Collaborative Council
WTO	World Toilet Organisation
WTO	World Trade Organization
WWF	World Wildlife Fund

General Introduction

Breaking the Vicious Circle of Unequal Access to Water Is an Ethical Imperative

EMOTIONAL IS WITHOUT A doubt the adjective that best describes the current discussion about the challenges associated with potable water.

The rapid development of communications has contributed to global awareness of a division in the world that has exposed a new kind of poverty: water poverty. We have heard the terrible news that 800 million people on our planet have no access to a distribution service for potable water,[1] and nearly two and one-half billion have no access to basic sanitation services.[2]

In light of these alarming statistics major efforts have been undertaken, in which the UN has played a leading role with support from civil society, including Christian churches.

While the United Nations proclaimed water a human right in 1979 and 1989 in international conventions protecting women[3] and children,[4] it decided to accord this right a special place in a universal declaration in 2010.[5] It had been anticipated in this area by the Ecumenical Declaration on *Water As a Human Right and a Public Good*[6] in 2005 and the World Council of Churches' Statement on *Water for Life*[7] in 2006. Another important international document alerting the public to the water issue was

---

1. WHO/UNICEF indicate, "An estimated 768 million people did not use an improved source for drinking water in 2011 and 185 million relied on surface water to meet their daily drinking water needs." WHO/UNICEF, *Fast facts 2013*.

2. WHO/UNICEF indicate, "However, by end of 2011 2.5 billion people lacked access to an improved sanitation facility." WHO/UNICEF, ibid.

3. Convention on the Elimination of All Forms of Discrimination against Women, 13.

4. Convention on the Rights of the Child, 3.

5. Resolution A/RES/64/292, The Human Right to Water and Sanitation.

6. Ecumenical Declaration on Water as a Human Right and a Public Good.

7. Statement on Water for Life.

the May 21, 1997 UN Convention on the Law of the Non-navigational Uses of International Watercourses,[8] which went into effect on August 17, 2014.

It must be noted that the outcome of the actions taken over the past thirty years has turned out to be totally inadequate in 2014,[9] despite seemingly optimistic Millennium Development Goal (MDG)[10] statistics.

There is no doubt that this is an extremely complex issue, and that water inequality is a problem that cannot be run to ground overnight.

Why, though, have the many legal, political, economic, social, and environmental interventions not yielded better results to date? Worse yet, monthly bulletins published by many scientific societies report that the environmental condition of our planet, and in particular of potable water, is worsening.

So what can be done? Most especially, how can we do things *right*?[11]

Unable to remain indifferent to these questions, I felt a pressing need to ask another question—a very pointed one perhaps—about the relevance of a human right to water. Are we not in fact making the weakest of the weak a laughingstock, under cover of an ideal or a human-rights ethic?

Do not misunderstand me: in no way am I suggesting that when the UN General Assembly added potable water to the long list of human rights[12] on July 28, 2010, it did not wish to work toward greater justice in the world. I am convinced that it did. Rather, I am wondering whether the UN's members were not sending out a distress call motivated by a feeling of panic in the face of unacceptable water poverty.

And as everyone knows, fear is a bad adviser.

These gnawing doubts arise from my worry that neither I, my fellow humans, nor even Christian churches or the 193 countries bound by this Universal Declaration conferring a new status on potable water, have truly understood the document's full meaning and scope.

Should we not feel perplexed to see that suddenly, today, good local water management is becoming problematic, and that it must be understood—as it was in 2010—at the global level? For have not human beings known since time immemorial how to meet their water needs in a way appropriate to where they live, and properly

---

8. Convention on the Law of the Non-navigational Uses of International Watercourses.

9. WHO/UNICEF indicate, "Even though progress towards the MDG target represents important gains in access for billions of people around the world, it has been uneven. Sharp geographic, sociocultural and economic inequalities in access persist and sometimes have increased. This report presents examples of unequal progress among marginalized and vulnerable groups." WHO/UNICEF, *Updates report 2014*. WHO/UNICEF, indicate also: "The world remains off track to meet the MDG sanitation target, which requires reducing the proportion of people without access from 51 percent to 25 per cent by 2015.Great strides have been made in East Asia, where sanitation service coverage has increased from 27% in 1990 to 67% in 2011. This means that in 21 years, 626 million people gained access to improved sanitary facilities." WHO/UNICEF, *Fast Facts* 2013.

10. Millennium Declaration.

11. Fuchs, *Comment faire pour bien faire?*

12. Resolution A/RES/64/292, The Human Right to Water and Sanitation.

and even very ingeniously managed the vital resource of water? Think of Oman's *aflaj* irrigation systems and the ancient canals in Valais[13] known as *bisses*.

Led by a feeling that any possible answers were not to be found solely in the law, in general, or public law in particular (national constitutional law and international law), I wanted to investigate other disciplines to try and discern which of the intellectual tools available to twenty-first century humans would allow us to better meet the new challenges we face, among the most pressing of which is the issue of access to potable water for all.

Indeed, how can we talk about such a sensitive topic without multidisciplinary intellectual tools? How can we understand the central issue, the injustice of unequal access to water, without them?

So was I to turn to politics, geopolitics, sociology, economics, or history, or even leave to the world of science the task of appeasing my conscience?

There, I have said it. My conscience. Or to go even further... our conscience? Here is where skepticism comes into play: do the disciplines named above bother to examine what goes on in individual hearts?

Certainly not, or at least, not often enough.

So could ethics, philosophy, or even theology bring order to the hearts and minds of global citizens? Will these erudite and unfathomable subjects help me understand whether the new human right to water has any specific message to help humanity solve its potable water problems?

At the very least, there are some famous names sounding in my ears, names of men and women who have turned to these disciplines as a means of reflecting on the human condition, on good and evil, and especially on how people behave toward one another, a notion called "alterity" (otherness).

Let us not try to hide the fact: we are dealing with ethics and morals, the realms of thought where concepts simmer.

Of course it is true that the concepts we forge and hand down to posterity are often born of controversy in the throes of an eventful and violent history. So in my view, they will remain simple tools for understanding and can never be considered dogma. The same applies to the new concepts that have arisen in connection with potable water, some of which I will discuss. In the interest of simplification I will group them together under the concept (yet another!) of a global water ethic.[14]

I let myself be guided not only by Western thinkers, but also—though not enough—some from the Eastern world, in an attempt to find some answers to my questions. With regard to the serious issue of global water injustice, I will try to learn not only whether I have a responsibility, but also whether my neighbor has one, along with the most underprivileged persons; and finally, whether countries that have

---

13. Valais is one of Switzerland's 26 cantons.
14. See Part II, Chapter I and Part VI, last interview.

been duly urged to adopt methods for taking responsibility[15] will in fact equip themselves with the necessary means of facilitating universal access to potable water and sanitation.

Too many questions, probably with too few concrete answers.

Still, let us begin this voyage of discovery and try to move closer to the mystery of a responsibility that Dostoyevsky summed up as follows: "Everyone is really responsible to all men for all men and for everything."[16]

So what will be the guiding principle behind my remarks?

The dialectic apparent in the title of this work should be surprising, since I am contrasting *justice* with a *sham* as the new concept of a human right to water is being shaped. In doing so, I wish to open a dialogue on two points. First, it is important to examine the contemporary vocabulary of human rights, which has become such a part of us that some call it a vernacular.[17] This raises the question of whether the concept of a human right to water is a valid one. Second, in my opinion it is necessary to investigate whether this right will lead to greater justice in the matter of access to potable water; or whether, on the other hand, humanity risks tearing itself apart over this cause in the name of a human rights doctrine that is understood by the members of the international community in so many different ways, as I have had occasion to see in Asia.

Of course I appreciate that these human rights, especially the human right to water, potentially have the capacity to bring humanity together in a plan for world peace, in which all human beings would enjoy natural conditions appropriate for meeting their potable water needs, or could use the necessary infrastructures to quench their thirst and ensure their well-being under conditions conducive to good health.

Yet every human activity, even those favoring peace, has its downside, as attested by historic events from every era.

Does this mean that the promising momentum of the human right to water cannot escape the problem of good and evil? Or that wanting to bring all of the shocking inequalities of human access to potable water under one umbrella is not without dangers? How many times have attempts at unity failed? How many times have the passionate defenders of a cause come to blows over it?

In my opinion, without wanting to paint too bleak of a picture, it would be wise to pay close attention to the almost daily development of new theories, the effects of which can go beyond their authors' best intentions. They should be analyzed with enough distance so they can be read critically and constructively.

---

15. Genard, *La grammaire de la responsabilité*, 39, which mentions the duty to have the desire *(devoir vouloir)* and the desire to accept the duty *(vouloir devoir)*, and even the knowledge to gain the ability *(savoir pouvoir)* and the ability to acquire the knowledge *(pouvoir savoir)*!

16. Dostoyevsky, *The Brothers Karamazov*, 301.

17. Moyn, *The Last Utopia*.

General Introduction

My reason for taking up my pen is that I can see what shrewd Czech author Jure Vujik[18] calls secular irenicism sneaking in. Originally, irenicism was both the blessing and the bane of Christian men and women of various beliefs,[19] because even while irenic doctrines were extolling unity, they did not fail to form opposing factions.

This five-part dissertation, with a sixth section devoted to interviews, is my attempt to avoid this pitfall of a pointless and damaging confrontation between contradictory stances on the values surrounding issues related to potable water, which is vital to everyone.

Initially, I will set out the general problem of the global challenge that water inequality poses to humanity. I will focus on human beings in all their vulnerability, a condition that arises because men, women, and children are dependent on fulfillment of their potable water needs.

Next I will seek out some of the normative tools—whether legal, scientific, economic, or political—with which humanity has provided itself to date. Third, these beginnings will allow me to ask how these concepts arose and on what bases. We must seek these foundations in order to evaluate our current choices of direction based on known ethics such as deontology, eudaemonism, and utilitarianism.

In a fourth section, I will examine their validity as applied to responsible action in space and time, carried out under the authority of a justice that must be brought to life, the kind that can separate the just from the unjust and corresponds to Aristotle's description of the mean.

This is where theology invites itself in as a sort of grand finale, to help make the connection between justice, love, and repentance as expressed toward "the other": someone other than myself with his questioning, even challenging face expressing the expectation—never to be met on this earth—of a supererogatory kind of justice, that of love.

This will be a long journey, with stops along the way for interviews concerning areas where the challenge of potable water can be felt. Will it manage to convince us that the challenge is far too serious to continue treating it as a concern of civil society alone, even if the latter is represented in the forum of the UN and by Christian churches; and that in order to serve humanity, governing authorities from all countries are not only invited but enjoined to reconsider their mode of governance? It will be up to the reader to decide.

Method

Beyond a quest to reveal the enigma that in my opinion lurks behind the new *human right to water*, should I not be undertaking the even more crucial quest to drink at the fountain of life? Is this not what philosopher Paul Ricœur suggests by giving us tools

---

18. Vujik, *Democracie globale*.
19. Lechot, "Irénisme", 633–34.

for hermeneutics in his book *From Text to Action*[20] and inviting us to see beyond written works, whether they be theological, philosophical, or legal?

I will work to find the right keys among the enormous bunch available to me—contemporary texts, of course but also records that may have guided humanity in the past, and which I feel have the potential to direct humankind yet today; because they not only bear the indelible stamp of history, they also represent some of humankind's gems, manifested at countless points like bright flashes of freedom.

This beautiful metaphor was inspired by Wilhelm Dilthey, a German philosopher and defender of history who, in his *Introduction to the Human Sciences*, exclaimed with regard to the "realm" of history, "[t]hus from the realm of nature he distinguishes a realm of history, in which, amidst the objective necessity of nature, freedom is manifested at countless points."[21]

Through the miracle of writing, we ought to be able to connect texts as crucial to today's globalized world as the Universal Declaration of Human Rights (1948) and United Nations Resolution 64/292 The Human Right to Water and Sanitation (July 28, 2010) with founding documents from the Judeo-Christian world, such as the Bible, itself supplemented by the seminal sources of Western intellectual thought, such as Aristotle's *Nichomachean Ethics*.[22]

As Paul Ricœur says, the interpretation (or hermeneutics) of human works is indeed an aporia, or dead end! However, this French philosopher sees Wilhelm Dilthey as someone who

> has perfectly perceived the crux of the problem; namely, that life grasps life only by the mediation of units of meaning that rise above the historical flux. Here, Dilthey glimpsed a mode of transcending finitude without absolute knowledge, a mode that is properly interpretative.[23]

The method of thought used by these two masters consists of bringing out "not *what* a text says, but *who* says it."[24]

I wish to take my inspiration from them in two ways: first in the traditional way through various quotations, but also by devoting significant attention at the end of my investigation to leading figures with experience in the area of potable water and the strategies likely to provide solutions to the challenge it presents, which is vital to everyone.

In order to gain a better understanding of the twenty-first century world and the ultimate nature of human beings when faced with their necessary physical and moral constraints, I will draw mainly from that magnificent and fertile source, the history of

---

20. Ricœur, " La tâche de l'herméneutique", 96.
21. Dilthey, "Introduction à l'étude des sciences humaines", 200.
22. Aristotle, *Ethique à Nicomaque*.
23. Ricœur, "La tâche de l'herméneutique", 96–97.
24. Ibid., 95.

ideas and Western intellectual history. This inexhaustible well actually reminds us that there have been men and women who have used their talents to examine themselves in light of the historical realities with which they have had to grapple, with courage and determination and—who knows?—under grace.

Still, reporting on accounts from the present seems to me to be just as essential, even in a dissertation, because the men and women who agreed to the interviews I requested can play a prophetic role, in the sense given to the word by the apostle Paul: "those who prophesy speak to other people for their upbuilding and encouragement and consolation."[25]

May the ancient and modern voices that reach our ears be duly heard as by a servant who listens[26] and guide twenty-first century humanity, even redirecting it toward a better life together.

Will these voices be able to contribute to the emergence of a sort of global water ethic that will serve justice and dam the tide of any suspicions of a sham? I sincerely hope so.

25. 1 Cor 14:3.
26. Isa 50:4–5.

Part I

Water Inequality

A Global Challenge for Humanity

Introduction

THERE IS NO DOUBT that the last quarter of the twentieth century was a time for rethinking how human beings live. The warnings sounded by Hans Jonas[1] and the Club of Rome,[2] as well as the UN Declarations briefly mentioned earlier, helped open discussion, including the discussion about water.

Since this discourse has become a global one, I felt that understanding what globalization means should be a priority.

Though the chapter I am now dedicating to this concept should be considered as something of a digression, I feel that the time spent on it will not be wasted. It should provide a better understanding of why civil society, including the churches, wants to make its voice heard on a worldwide platform as a globalized civil society.[3]

It is true that we who are both Christians and world citizens are used to letting "water specialists" manage this vital resource. Perhaps we now need to share this responsibility, in our own way. But how?

I note that for me, the 2005 Ecumenical Declaration on *Water As a Human Right and a Public Good* is one possible answer to this question. It is a call to be aware that potable water is a high-priority challenge for humanity.

In Part II I will come back to this important document which, I will say right away, contains both an ethical focus pertaining to mankind's relationship to water, and an operational focus pertaining to methods for meeting humanity's water needs.

Now we will take a look at how globalization came into our lives.

---

1. Jonas, *Le principe responsabilité*.
2. Meadows, et al., *The Limits to Growth*.
3. Al Jayyousi, "Water as a Human Right," 121–31.

Chapter I

The Concept of "Globality"

The Intellectual Space Reshaped by Globalization

SHOULD THE CONCEPT OF globalization give cause for fear, or hope?

Everyone knows that globalization began a very long time ago, with commercial exchanges between Europe and Asia in the sixteenth century.

The concept was relegated to the back burner during the atrocities of the two World Wars, but again came to the fore, especially economically, at the end of the 1990s. It drew special attention when Thomas L. Friedman's famous slogan proclaimed in 2005, "The world is flat."[1]

It now has an impressive number of definitions. Miroslav Jovanovic, a UN economist and professor in Geneva, has counted more than six hundred.[2]

It is impossible to discuss the human right to water without referring to this concept, since the potable water question does not touch solely on local issues but also on the whole world, which has become more interdependent.

It is not my purpose here to find the best definition of the concept, or to describe globalization's advantages and disadvantages. On the other hand, I would like to note that in 2014, more and more philosophers are trying to move beyond the narrow scope of the economy to envision a human world that is more interconnected, not only in a technological sense but also mentally.

That is how a former Harvard professor, economist Pankaj Ghemawat, came to begin travels in Asia in 2011, in particular visiting Indonesia, Vietnam and the Philippines. There he discovered the importance of getting past prejudice and opening oneself to the culture and beliefs of populations other than those in America and Europe. He reached the conclusion that we need to give up the "caveman" mentality and work to create more empathy among the people of our planet.

> The key to banishing the caveman mentality [. . .] is to build empathy or [. . .] improve people so that they improve the world. [. . .] We just need to

---

1. Friedman, *The World Is Flat.*
2. Jovanovic, "Does Globalization Take Us for a Ride?," 501–49.

reduce by half the ratio of people who do not care about helping foreigners to those who do.[3]

Is it not significant that we can read in the work of Ghemawat,[4] a man of Indian heritage but American by adoption, about this philosophical notion of "care" that is so much in fashion these days and as we shall see later was already anticipated, in a way, by Emmanuel Lévinas and Paul Ricœur?

Another important work along these lines that attempts to "humanize" globalization is one by Mireille Delmas-Marty,[5] published in 2013, to which we will come back a number of times.

The Intrusive and Paradoxical Concept of "Globality"

How could we fail to be surprised at seeing how many familiar concepts have been labeled "global" since the end of the twentieth century? The phenomenon has become so common that it passes almost unnoticed.

And yet... there is more and more talk of global poverty, global justice, global democracy, and global responsibility.

It was actually the fact of the "global" poverty concept's appearance on the international political scene in the 1990s that made me wonder about the origin of this strange concept, this pair of mismatched morphemes that do not seem to grate on anyone's ears.

I believe I have found one of the potential keys to answering this question.

So, swept along on the wave started by the slogan "think globally, act locally" (attributed to French theologian Jacques Ellul), I too began to "dare to think" globally, referring to Immanuel Kant and his famous *"sapere aude."*[6]

"Globality": The Winds of Neoliberalism

One plausible explanation for the new semantic intrusion of "globality" into everyday language is given by Antoine Garapon in *Raison du moindre Etat*,[7] which is based on the works of Michel Foucault and his neologism, "governmentality." Most importantly, not content to settle for defining "global," he tries to explain its origin as well.

---

3. Ghemawat, "Shed caveman mentality," D9.
4. Ghemawat, *World 3.0*.
5. Delmas-Marty, *Résister*.
6. Kant, *Qu'est-ce que les Lumières?*, 43.
7. Garapon, *Raison du moindre Etat*.

Of course "global" can have two meanings, the first pointing to the world's geographic dimension (the globe) and the second covering the epistemological meaning of "cross-disciplinary" or "considered as a whole."[8]

The phenomenon of a "generalized breaking down of barriers"[9] is deeper and more complicated, however, and cannot be summed up in simple definitions.

Garapon and Foucault see a real paradigm shift, namely the transition from liberalism to neoliberalism. French legal expert Garapon is quick to add that this is not ultraliberalism, but a true break with liberalism on three key points, namely: the market is no longer considered natural, but "artificially created by the State";[10] the market goes beyond the scope of the economy itself to affect other sectors of human activity, such as schools and hospitals; and finally, competition has been substituted for trade.[11]

According to Foucault, this change implies a change in "governmentality," where the citizen would no longer be part of a sovereign State of which he would be a subject, but part of a State in which "general law is evaluated according to private interests."[12]

It is interesting to note that this would not be an ideology, but a kind of logic, a phenomenon which would seem quite impossible to resist:

> Neoliberalism hides its power behind the appearance of a simple technique of governance. In this way it sets itself apart from all ideologies because an ideology demands power while assigning it an end, from which, in contrast, neoliberal governmentality refrains—limiting itself (it claims) to returning power to the subjects and serving reason alone. While ideology is the logic of an idea, in contrast, neoliberal reason is the idea of a [kind of] logic.[13]

Yet I cannot help but react by noting that a concept such as "global poverty" gives us something to think about. I will explain.

They "Dared To Think Up 'Global Poverty'."

Immanuel Kant invites everyone to dare to think,[14] as I mentioned above.

Now to my mind, we also need to equip ourselves with the means for measuring the consequences of this drive, this daring, as it were. This implies that it behooves us to hold back somewhat in formulating our thoughts, according to the principle or well-known virtue of prudence.

---

8. Ibid., 204.
9. Ibid., 203.
10. Ibid., 15–16.
11. Ibid., 16.
12. Ibid., 193.
13. Ibid., 225.
14. Kant, *Qu'est-ce que les Lumières?*, 43.

To me, the World Bank's 1990 initiative to launch the concept of "global poverty" on the international scene, which involved classifying individuals having less than 1 dollar per day as the poorest in the world,[15] seems unusual, even untimely.[16]

> A new language has formed at the global level based on a new social construct of poverty—a representation that, as a silent instrument in the hands of unequaled power, has not failed to contribute to the unprecedented colonization of all parts of the vernacular and to the reduction of an uncountable variety of individuals to a single model: that of the "global" poor, defined by an income of less than 1 dollar per day![17]

Over forty years earlier, President Truman's semantic separation of developed countries from underdeveloped countries in his 1949 inaugural address had been equally daring. In this respect, the uneasiness felt by Daniel Noumbissié Tchamo of Cameroon in a stirring plea for global justice is meaningful.[18] In his book, as we shall see, he criticizes the stigmatization of poor countries by the use of disturbing expressions:

> [. . .] this gradation of nature—of disturbing semantic and conceptual import—evoked by the concepts of "developed countries" and "underdeveloped countries," "emerging countries" [. . .].[19]

The objection will be raised that of course this way of looking at things is a simplification, but it is so very practical and useful for politicians and economists of all countries as they draw up annual statistics likely to guide decision-makers' choices.

Let us not forget the attempt by Nobel economics laureate Amartya Sen to temper Westerners' zeal and their indicators[20] such as the GDP, and his concern that the "human" take center stage with his "Human Development Index." Of course he, too, incorporated the term "development" into his concept, Truman's old idea having become de rigueur!

---

15. Tchamo, *Justice distributive ou solidarité à l'échelle globale?*, 168.

16. Petters-Melo indicates, "According to Gustavo Esteva, 'underdevelopment' began then, on January, 20 1949: 'On that day, two billion people became underdeveloped. In a real sense, from that time on, they ceased being what they were, in all their diversity, and were transmogrified into an inverted mirror of other's reality: a mirror that belittles them and sends them off to the end of the queue, a mirror that defines their identity, which is really that of a heterogeneous and diverse majority, simply in the terms of a homogenizing and narrow minority.'" Petters-Melo, "Cultural Heritage Preservation and Socio-Environmental Sustainability," 140.

17. Rahnema, *Quand la misère chasse la pauvreté*, 176–77.

18. Tchamo, *Justice distributive ou solidarite à l'échelle globale?*, 168.

19. Ibid., 218.

20. Sen, indicates, "A 'poverty line' that ignores individual characteristics altogether cannot do justice to our real concerns underlying poverty, viz. capability failure because of inadequate economic means." Sen, *Repenser l'inégalité*, 185.

Chapter I: The Concept of "Globality"

It seems that this new concept of global poverty has left at least two kinds of traces—psychological and scientific.

On the psychological level, it is conceivable to suppose that the members of communities categorized as "underdeveloped countries" might have felt a vague sense of shame, placing them at the lowest end of the human scale with no way to improve their lot except through the protective hand of the strongest.[21]

On the scientific level, the new concept of "global poverty" has been the object of much conjecture. I will take a look at two points of view, those of German philosopher Thomas Pogge[22] and legal expert Samuel Moyn.[23]

For Pogge, there is no question that global poverty is a violation of human rights[24] and that there are concrete reasons to find a solution to it. For Moyn this belief, on which he passes no judgment, could have arisen only during an obvious conceptual shift in the vision originating from human rights as imagined in the 1940s. As he sees it, the human rights corpus has evolved dramatically from a transcendental utopia into a real political program.

> But the history of what have been known as "social rights" is perhaps even more revealing than the move to transitional justice of how human rights, born in moral transcendence of politics, had to become political agenda.[25]

Personally, I share Professor Moyn's doubts as to the relevance of placing poverty (now considered as global)—which of course is of the utmost importance politically—in the conceptual field of human rights. Indeed, I think we must not lose sight of the fact that as history testifies, human rights were born with the goal of fighting for freedom and against authoritarianism and totalitarianism as oppressive systems of government:

> Intellectually, the theoretical and doctrinal energy harnessed to the project of finding a vision of human rights adequate to global immiseration graphically illustrates the sheer distance from the landmark of their antitotalitarian invention that human rights have had to travel. The jury is clearly still out on whether a rights framework for global poverty is the right framework. But the verdict is debated only because human rights were forced to face—and it seemed believable that they might be able to face—problems that had been addressed by other schemes, and contending utopias, before.[26]

---

21. Petters-Melo, Milena, "Cultural Heritage Preservation and Socio-Environmental Sustainability," 142.

22. A professor of philosophy and international affairs at Yale University.

23. Formerly a professor of international public law at Columbia University of New York, later a professor of law and history at Harvard University.

24. Pogge, *Freedom from poverty,* cited by Moyn, *The Last Utopia,* 309 n26.

25. Moyn, *The Last Utopia.*

26. Ibid., 224–25.

Globality Has Dictated the Fusion of Human Rights and Humanitarianism

It is also interesting to read Samuel Moyn's opinion about the International Red Cross movement and other humanitarian institutions. For me the question of poverty, like that of coming to the aid of someone who is thirsty, falls under philanthropy, which brought about the golden age of Red Cross humanitarian action. Here is what Moyn has to say on this subject:

> [. . .] Red Cross, Oxfam, and others, inheriting the philanthropic impulse of the nineteenth century, provided succor for the horrors of war and campaigned against famine and hunger all along. But it is simply mistaken to conceive of these as human rights organizations, as they were almost never understood in that way by their participants.[27]
>
> Yet today human rights and humanitarianism are fused enterprises, with the former incorporating the latter and the latter justified in terms of the former.[28]

I believe it was the neoliberalism already mentioned above that caused humanitarianism to merge with human rights at the end of the twentieth century. Most likely the utilitarian goal of greater efficiency was the purpose and goal of this initiative.

Is this fusion irreversible? Only time will tell.

As far as the issue of potable water is concerned, did not it too "fuse" with human rights—reluctantly?

Answering this question now would be premature. First, we will look for criteria that might explain why potable water is a high-priority challenge for everyone today.

---

27. Ibid., 220.
28. Ibid.

Chapter II

"Thinking" Water in Terms of Its Vulnerability, through Case Studies

Introduction

What Is the "Water Problem"?

WATER IS RELATED TO life, since it makes up nearly 70 percent of our body on average; and also to death, when it is not available in the required quantity and quality.[1]

That is why it so strongly impresses the psyche, which Jung defined as "the totality of all psychic processes, conscious as well as unconscious."[2]

Water is plentiful on Earth, but only 2.5 percent of it is fresh water.[3] Of this, a mere 1 percent is suitable for supporting life; the rest is locked away in Arctic and Antarctic ice and glaciers.[4]

Is this why, today, we talk about water's "scarcity"?

No. The main reason for the great fear being expressed all over the planet with regard to fresh water is that its availability to humans and the ecosystem is decreasing. Over the past several decades, scientists have brought to light several contributing factors, namely global warming, an increase in the world's population, and pollution of surface water and even aquifers.

Following up on the warnings given by scientists and some representatives of civil society, the international community tackled the problem and called on its members to consider that ecological challenges had become a top priority. For example, the 1972 Stockholm conference laid the first foundations for a legal edifice meant to enlist countries to consider environmental protection efforts, and commit to them. These first steps led to significant research on protecting the ecosystem, especially water.

---

1. Survival requirements are estimated at 7.5 liters per person per day. (See case Xákmok Kásek and WHO guidelines. I note that other guidelines offered by this international organization suggest that the amount be increased to 25 or even 50 liters per person per day.)

2. Cuviller, *Nouveau dictionnaire philosophique*, 151.

3. A distinction must be made between fresh water and potable water. Only potable water is safe to drink without health risks.

4. Diop and Recacewicz, *Atlas mondial de l'eau*, 8.

This first stage was probably behind the UN General Assembly's 1993 decision to declare March 22 World Water Day. This annual event aims to make politicians and the general public aware of the current critical situation with regard to fresh water.

The United Nations also proclaimed 2005-2015 the International Water for Life Decade in support of point 7c of the Millennium Development Goals (MDGs)[5] announced in 2000, which aimed to halve the number of people without access to potable water and/or sanitation.

Case Studies: Middle East, North Africa, and China

One important example demonstrates the need for a radical change in how people perceive water in general, and potable water in particular. It comes from MENA (the Middle East/North Africa region), to which we will return in Part VI for an interview with Prince Hassan of Jordan. For thousands of years, people had managed to keep the problem of shortages in this area in check by sharing water as a common good. In the twenty-first century, this method of management is turning out to be ineffective.[6]

A group of experts convened by Asit K. Biswas[7] has reported some alarming numbers.

> Nowhere else in the world is the competition for water so strong as it is in MENA. Average annual supply of water for the region as a whole is well under 1500 m^3 per capita, and many nations fall below 500 m^3 (UNESCO 2003).[8] [. . .] Water scarcity has of course always been part of MENA's history but as a chronic rather than a critical problem. [. . .] the Millennium Ecosystem Assessment reports that MENA nations are using 115 percent of total renewable runoff, and that one-third of withdrawals come from non-renewable sources.[9]

In theory, there are many possible ways to react to this problem, which at first glance seems insurmountable. This is attested, for example, by the work of the MENA specialists mentioned above. High on the list of responses is a water ethic based on justice and good governance, which will be discussed in great depth later on.

The example of China is worth citing here as well.

Franck Galland, an expert on the geopolitics of water, gives an idea of the growing concern about this vital resource in China. He takes note of the severe pollution of this Asian country's rivers, with

---

5. MDG, Goal 7, Target 7.

6. Brooks, "Human Rights to Water in North Africa and the Middle East," 20.

7. A Distinguished Visiting Professor at the Lee Kuan Yew School of Public Policy in Singapore and the Indian Institute of Technology, Bhubaneswar, India; also the founder of the Third World Centre for Water Management.

8. Brooks, "Human Rights to Water in North Africa and the Middle East," 9.

9. Ibid., 20.

43 percent of the water resources in China's seven main rivers being unsuitable for human consumption (in 2009).[10]

These few figures and statistics are obviously inadequate to illustrate the cruel reality of the water stress experienced by too many people on Earth.

As my research proceeds, I will repeatedly underscore the importance of raising awareness of the facts in a world that is changing before our eyes at an ever-faster rate. China, which to Westerners seems bogged down in its (very real) pollution problems, is actually in the process not only of trying to solve them, but also of turning the world order upside down—at least on the evidence of its efforts to create its own institutions with standards for good governance. Just one example: a new banking institution known as the "Asian Infrastructure Investment Bank" was formally established on October 24, 2014.

Disparate Cases, Shared Challenges: India and Paraguay

The following are two brief examples that I believe should illustrate the real ramifications of this issue.

First, take the Indian city of New Delhi. Over twenty million people live there on the banks of the great Yamuna River, which flows down from the Himalayas. We recall that this river, which is sacred to the Hindus, runs through Uttar Pradesh and fills the Taj Mahal's reflecting pool, mirroring an image of the famous mausoleum's unmatched beauty.

At the other extreme, we can mention a rural community in Paraguay, called Xákmok Kásek, where 268 residents belong to 66 families. It was the subject of an important study by Laurence Boisson de Chazournes on the topic of fresh water in international law,[11] which attempted to analyze international jurisprudence concerning access to health and water. It covered the decision handed down in Paraguay on August 24, 2010 in the case of "Xákmok Kásek. Indigenous Community v. Paraguay."[12]

In the first case, the Yamuna's water serves as an unofficial dump site for households, industries, and agriculture. Very few water treatment systems are operating effectively, despite the considerable sums of money made available for this purpose by the political authorities.

In the second, the indigenous Kásek Paraguayans live in extreme poverty with no infrastructure at all (no schools, no health-care centers, and certainly no water supply systems whatsoever). They are the victims of a forced displacement due to drought.

A striking commonality between these two communities is the difficulty of gaining access to enough potable water of sufficient quality. Another point they have in

---

10. Galland, *Le Grand Jeu*, 37.
11. Boisson de Chazournes, *Fresh Water in International Law*, 158.
12. Xákmok Kásek.

common is the threat of increasing populations, which make any kind of sustainable development effort challenging.

In New Delhi's case, Indian authorities had made a plan to clean up the Yamuna River in 2002.[13] In a decision dated October 10, 2012, India's Supreme Court noted that pollution mitigation efforts had been completely fruitless:

> [. . .] the Supreme Court of India expressed its intense disappointment with water infrastructure expenditures which did not appear to have any impact. It said on 10 October 2012: "It is unfortunate that huge public funds were spent" to clean up the Yamuna River, yet "the pollution of Yamuna has increased by the day."[14]

In the second example, the Kásek community brought a lawsuit against Paraguay's government under the following circumstances. The community complained that it had been displaced during a drought in May and June of 2009 to a location known as the "25 de Febrero [February 25th] settlement," where there was no reservoir or lake, only forests. It asked for damages, basing its argument on the fact that in order to survive, residents had to travel to a reservoir located seven kilometers from their temporary home; and that this gave them access to only 2.17 liters of water per day, far less than the international standard of at least 7.5 liters per person per day.

> In this regard, according to international standards, most people need a minimum of 7.5 liters per day per person in order to meet all their basic needs, which included food and hygiene, including under extreme conditions. Also according to international standards, the quality of the water must be above a tolerable level of risk.[15]

In both cases, what is needed is an attack on the root of the evil. In India, according to two water management specialists, this would mean fighting corruption:

> Lack of political will, institutional incompetence, public apathy, absence of serious media scrutiny and pervasive corruption in the capital-intensive water sector have all contributed to water unsustainability.[16]

In Paraguay, the lack of access to water must be attributed to extreme poverty, and the Inter-American Court of Human Rights attempted to solve this issue by sentencing Paraguay to pay damages to the plaintiffs.

However, noting that the amounts awarded by the Court would in no way get to the root of this community's extreme poverty, Judge Augusto Fogel Pedrozo wrote

---

13. Monirul Qader et al., *Interlinking of Rivers in India*, 6.

14. Biswas and Tortajada, *Editorial*, 6.

15. Boisson de Chazournes, *Fresh Water in International Law*, 158, citing an excerpt of "Xákmok Kásek."

16. Biswas and Tortajada, *Editorial*.

a dissenting opinion bringing up the need to refer the issue not only to the accused South American government, but also to the international community.

> The State's duty to take positive measures to protect the right to life, even when it includes providing for vulnerable populations affected by extreme poverty, cannot be limited to them, given that assistance, by not attacking the root causes of poverty in general, and extreme poverty in particular, cannot create those conditions for a dignified life" and no. 25: "In this context, the capacity of State intervention in developing countries, including Paraguay, and the application of international standards relating to extreme poverty, is not a legal issue that involves only the State, which is often conditioned both by the limited financial resources available and the structural factors linked to the "process of adjustment," which transcend the domain of the State of Paraguay, considered in isolation. International responsibility is not limited to the right to international assistance in the event that a State Party is unable to achieve, on its own, the model established by the Covenant, enshrined in the International Covenant on Economic, Social, and Cultural Rights.[17]

Private-Sector Threats to Fresh Water Sources Lead to the 2005 Ecumenical Declaration by Swiss and Brazilian Churches[18]

When I interviewed theologian Otto Schäfer of the Federation of Swiss Protestant Churches (FEPS) and pastor Albert Rieger of Bern-Jura-Solothurn[19] in September 2010, they expressed the motives and reasons for the Swiss and Brazilian churches' commitment to potable water's cause.

This was in the context of two confrontations over the use of freshwater springs, pitting multinational corporation Nestlé[20] against movements originating in civil society. The incidents occurred almost simultaneously in Latin America and Switzerland at the dawn of the third millennium.

The battlegrounds were Brazil's Minas Gerais region[21] and Bevaix, in Neuchâtel canton (Switzerland). In both countries, bottled water production uncorked a flood of protests.

In Brazil, the São Lourenço Water Park boasts no fewer than nine hot springs, traditionally used by the local population for therapeutic purposes. Their very existence was being threatened. In the 1930s, private owners had sold them to the state of Minas Gerais, except for the São Lourenço spring, which had remained in private hands and was bought by Perrier-Vitel in 1950. Bottled water from this spring was

17. Xákmok Kásek, 92, dissenting opinion by Judge Augusto Fogel Pedrozo, nos. 23 and 25.
18. Ecumenical declaration on Water as a Human Right and a Public Good.
19. Ibid.
20. Headquartered in Vevey, Switzerland.
21. One of Brazil's 26 states, slightly larger than France.

sold all over Brazil. Then, when Nestlé took over the Perrier-Vitel company, it began systematically using the springs to sell bottled water under the name "Pure Life." So much water was pumped that two of the springs dried up.

In Switzerland, the multinational company was the target of public activism aimed at convincing it to stop using the Treytel spring in Bevaix.

In the first case, the multinational was forced to cease and desist; in the second, the request for a water concession was denied.

We can say that after these events, the Bern-Jura-Solothurn church had a real awareness of what is at stake with fresh water. It found FEPS and the bishops of Brazil and Switzerland ready to listen and make a strong commitment.

Conclusion

These examples[22] seem to me to show that water challenges are extremely topical and critically important to humanity's future. To be more specific, they are turning out to be ethical issues, since human beings themselves are at their center.

Can we understand this human being in his vulnerability, which is particularly striking in cases of extreme poverty? And do we realize that if he lacks water, his dignity is threatened?

These three topics—human vulnerability, poverty, and dignity—deserve special attention, and the following chapters are dedicated to them.

---

22. For other examples, see Part VI.

Chapter III

"Thinking" the Human Relationship to Water: the Phenomenology of Vulnerability

Introduction

THOUGH THERE IS A science called "phenomenology," generally associated with Edmund Husserl,[1] that is not what will be discussed here.

What "thinking water phenomenologically" means to me is that we consider it, in its twenty-first century guise, as a new value to defend, and in its relationship to humankind and more particularly to vulnerable persons. Or, to say it very simply, that we concern ourselves with the "phenomenon" of water insofar as it involves mankind to the highest degree, and in the new context of globalization.

Here I am drawing on a contemporary philosopher, a professor at the University of Saint-Gallen who has done in-depth studies on the appearance of phenomena and how they were perceived in Athens in the fifth and fourth centuries BC. Among his definitions of phenomenology I have selected the following, which Emmanuel Alloa calls "the most minimal there is":

> [. . .] the elucidation of the ways a thing appears when (and each time that) the thing appears to us [. . .].[2]

Below I will focus on water as it affects vulnerable Man, since the phenomenon of water is indissociably linked to that which is human.

> The phenomenon would inexorably always be *human*, would be directed toward and measured by the side; conversely, humanity would be not solely that for which phenomena were destined; its very destiny is to be *conditioned by phenomena*.[3]

---

1. Le petit Larousse illustré indicates, "German philosopher who originated phenomenology, which he wished to make into a rigorous science and a theory of knowledge that would serve the other sciences [. . .]," Le petit Larousse illustré, "Husserl," 1443.

2. Alloa, "La phénoménologie comme science de l'homme sans l'homme," 81.

3. Ibid.

Part I: Water Inequality

So just as it always has, water appears to us, to every human being, as a resource necessary for covering a vital need. Yet, people today see it differently from those of the past, because it is rare or too plentiful, sacred or an object of trade, clean or polluted, natural or changed by technology (in particular desalination and reverse osmosis), managed by the government or businesses, treasured or wasted.

I would like to note that the philosopher from Saint-Gallen was in turn drawing on his German colleague Hannah Arendt, for whom

> [t]he world men are born into contains many things [. . .] all of which have in common that they *appear* and hence are meant to be seen, heard, touched, tasted, and smelled [. . .] by sentient creatures endowed with the appropriate sense organs.[4]

Since she also supports the argument that

> [. . .] there are a great many things which cannot withstand the implacable, bright light of the constant presence of others on the public scene [. . .],[5]

and among these things she counts pain, which

> [. . .] is so subjective and removed from the world of things and men that it cannot assume an appearance at all[,][6]

I think she makes a useful contribution to our consideration of the vulnerability related to a shortage or surplus of water.

Of course, Hannah Arendt made a name for herself by studying Kant's concept of "radical evil" in the specific context of the Eichmann trial.

However, in *The Human Condition,* she also discussed physical suffering in a different, extraordinarily humane way. She showed that not only do we object to attributing importance to pain: we also do everything possible to hide it, to remove it from the public view:

> [. . .] there, only what is considered to be relevant, worthy of being seen or heard, can be tolerated, so that the irrelevant becomes automatically a private matter.[7]

She continues her argument by stressing that pain is "perhaps the only experience which we are unable to transform into a shape fit for public appearance [. . .]."[8]

Well then, since potable water has now been elevated to the status of a human right, are we not clearly casting a new light on suffering, namely by associating it with

---

4. Arendt, *La vie de l'esprit*, 2, cited by Alloa, "La phénoménologie comme science de l'homme sans l'homme," 85.
5. Arendt, *Condition de l'homme moderne*, 91.
6. Ibid.
7. Ibid.
8. Ibid., 90.

"global poverty"? Is this not precisely a new phenomenon, a new phenomenology that presents the human/water pairing in a context of suffering and vulnerability? At the very least, that is what I am postulating.

Human Vulnerability and Finiteness

In the Sermon on the Mount[9] physical poverty, hunger, and thirst are mentioned only metaphorically in the Beatitudes, to lend weight to Christ's theological argument and strengthen it.

In contrast, the book of Acts reveals them in plain sight. For example, a severe physical handicap affecting motor function provides an opportunity for Jesus' disciples to demonstrate God's power: the command "stand up and walk"[10] frees the lifelong cripple from his association with the congenital malformation.

Many other passages in the Gospels show how Christ and his disciples took care to tie physical and mental well-being together. Among the most striking examples are the stories of Jairus's daughter,[11] Lazarus being restored to life,[12] and the woman healed of her chronic hemorrhaging.[13]

So it is surprising to see the extent to which Christianity has minimized the importance of bodily ills over the centuries. To its credit, however, it has not swept the Old Testament book of Job under the rug.

In my opinion, Stoicism's enormous influence on Christian thought can be counted among the decisive factors underlying this sort of disregard for the body. One is reminded of Calvin's famous *adiaphora*,[14] meaning matters of indifference in relation to the concept of moral goodness as characterized by the four cardinal virtues: prudence, courage, temperance, and justice.[15]

It is true that at the instigation of the Apostle Paul, Christianity did add, to the Stoics' moral virtues, the three theological virtues of faith, hope, and love.[16]

In practice, however these wonderful speeches, these seven kinds of balm for the soul (Stoic and Pauline virtues), all too infrequently come to the aid of the unfortunate to console them when their body is subjected to harsh reality, as Job himself experienced so intensely.

---

9. Matt 5:3–12.
10. Acts 3:6.
11. Mark 5:22–23 and 35–43.
12. John 11:1–46.
13. Mark 5:25–34.
14. Calvin, indicates, "The third part of Christian liberty teaches us, that we are bound by no obligation before God respecting external things, which in themselves are indifferent; but that we may indifferently sometimes use, and at other times omit them." Calvin, *Inst.*, III, XIX, 7.
15. Smith, *Théorie des sentiments moraux*, 370–71.
16. 1 Cor 13:13.

I believe that in discussing today's potable water challenge, it is imperative that we phenomenologically "think" the physical pain associated with a shortage or surplus of water, both of which lead to death.

Two different philosophers, each in his own way, have prepared a conceptual approach to give us a better grasp of vulnerability. One is Paul Ricœur, who developed an in-depth analysis of "fallible man"[17] and "capable man."[18] The other is Emmanuel Lévinas, who is famous for introducing the "face of the Other"[19] into his philosophy.

Vulnerability: Emmanuel Lévinas and Paul Ricœur as Heralds of "Care" Philosophy

Taking on the task of making such complex philosophers as Paul Ricœur and Emmanuel Lévinas more accessible—the risk of tackling their work to tease out their main points—is a challenge very ably faced by Swiss philosopher Nathalie Maillard.[20] She has also tried to reconcile them in order to express the many sides of human frailty, especially its phenomenological and philosophical aspects.

I felt that a brief mention of her analysis was of interest because potable water is vital to the survival of every person, tying each to his or her human brothers and sisters. This means that water must necessarily lead each person to encounter the Other, not only as a fragile, vulnerable, suffering human being, but also as one capable of overcoming his ill-being, thanks to an agent-patient dynamic that is reaffirmed and facilitated by giving and concern.

Nathalie Maillard begins by recalling that contemporary philosophers of care express their regret that the aforementioned two authors did not recognize the true importance of human vulnerability. These philosophers of care feel that Lévinas kept his thinking on a level that eclipsed the body's concrete realities, and Ricœur merely scratched the surface of the real issue, the human condition.

She insists, however, that Lévinas did give a new meaning to anthropological reality by stressing the value of intersubjective proximity, and that Ricœur's thought made a real epistemological leap forward from Kant. Indeed, she believes that the French philosopher accepted a departure from the level of transcendental philosophy to take an interest in human beings as potential actors, capable of responsibility toward the Other whose power to act has been affected.

Yet she thinks that the moral patient should not be left a prisoner of his condition as a victim; rather it must be recognized that in many cases, depending on the circumstances, the moral agent and the moral patient can switch roles. Indeed, the agent—who is assumed to be morally afflicted by the patient's pitiful physical state,

---

17. Fiasse, *Paul Ricœur, de l'homme faillible à l'homme capable*.
18. Maillard, *La vulnérabilité*, 233.
19. Ibid., 297.
20. Ibid.

can himself undergo a physical change, while the patient can benefit from a restoration of his capabilities.

Though below I will sketch only a few fragments of the philosophy of care, which is distinguished by its concern for human frailty, I plan to devote some space elsewhere in this text to the new idea of "capabilities," an intellectual intuition formulated by Amartya Sen.[21] I find that he brings a perspective to agent/patient relationships that is just as relevant as the "care" philosophers' position.

Now we will turn our attention to the reality of water vulnerability.

Water Vulnerability in the Twenty-First Century

The philosophical enthusiasm that Paul Ricœur and Emmanuel Lévinas show for the Other, each in his own way, has most likely played a major part in understanding "vulnerability." It is interesting to note that instead of presenting passive moral agents and patients, the "care" philosophers who succeeded Ricœur and Lévinas in this conceptual effort preferred to bring out their active role.

Below, based on facts and the twenty-first century's context of "globalization," I will attempt to show that the moral patient's position will undoubtedly add a new dimension to that of the moral agent.

The "Patients" Are Subject to the Risks of Unsafe Water

There are hundreds, thousands, or even more news stories about potable water's precarious situation and the associated poverty. An inexhaustible supply of material on this topic can also be found on the Internet. It is not my goal to summarize them or to encourage the trivialization of water issues by repeating facts that are already known all too well.

However, this does not stop me from wondering whether sufficient effort has been devoted to "thinking" these realities and to trying, if not to "feel" them, at least to imagine them.

The real challenge of potable water in the twenty-first century actually hinges on five specific and very different vulnerabilities: those of men, women, youth, children, and persons who are "full of years."[22]

If I insist on such specifics, which each of these representatives of the human race experiences in a completely different way, it is because no egalitarian doctrine could ever eliminate them.

As it is, every person—male or female, here or elsewhere—is confronted with the potable water issue. Do we remember the medical community's radio and television

---

21. See Part IV, Chapter III, Amartya Sen's capabilities.
22. Gen 25:8.

appeals encouraging "at risk" populations to get enough to drink when very dry summers were threatening?

Unlike in the West, such "at-risk populations" in some developing countries are not limited to the elderly and infants. In a word, all of the people are "at risk." The following comments apply only to these very vulnerable persons.

What specific risks do they face?

Unfortunately, those that stand out and are picked up by the media represent only the tip of the iceberg. Aside from aspects touching on climatology and other sciences, which are more or less related to water's natural phenomena, humanity's share in our own water vulnerability is not insignificant.

I am referring here to risks related to health and hygiene, incomplete education, and economics.

A slight digression is needed here before we continue . . .

It is patently obvious that the scope of this study cannot do justice to the complexity of the three areas of risk I have just identified. They are in fact being investigated by researchers and leaders in the fields of medicine, education (in the broadest sense, and therefore including local education authorities and providers of artistic training), and economics (including industry and agriculture), not to mention specialists in the political and social sciences. Without recommending blind trust in such experts, I do wish to pay tribute to them, if only to encourage the next generation to follow in their footsteps, because I see their task as a noble one and worthy of respect.

Now, without further delay, I will get back to my inquiry on the risks that every human being potentially has the power to reduce in order to increase well-being.

Risks Related to Poor Health and Hygiene

There are still far too many examples reported by those whom we will henceforth call "water reporters" showing that many populations lack awareness about basic hygiene. This lack of knowledge about good hygiene's benefits is one contributing factor that is keeping mortality rates very high among parturients in Asian countries such as Bhutan and Indonesia, as Professor Jean-Luc Maurer reported in an August 2013 lecture[23] at National University of Singapore.

Added to the lack of basic hygiene is an absence of adequate sanitary systems, a concern which has justified ever-increasing mobilization in the name of sanitation. The UN General Assembly's July 17, 2013 decision[24] to set aside November 19 (World Toilet Day) as an annual reminder to consider this issue was a landmark in this regard.

Older and younger women and girls will benefit the most from this sanitary improvement if it is ever actually implemented. They are the ones most affected by a lack

---

23. Maurer, "Indonesia's Economic, Social and Political Development Process."
24. UN Resolution, Sanitation For All.

of toilets, because they often avoid drinking—to the detriment of their health—in order to put off the need to relieve themselves as long as possible.

An awareness of the need for good hygiene implies sufficient education, especially for those who work with infants (which would help reduce the infant mortality rate due to polluted water) and the elderly—who in some African traditions, it is true, are given priority for access to drinking water if there is a shortage.

Risks Related to Incomplete Education

The development of information technologies has allowed a great leap forward in terms of better access to education, and therefore to hygiene.

Here again, though, the hopes it brings are too high, if only because the use of such technologies already requires appropriate basic training. Moreover, nothing can replace family support or thoughtful support of a student by a teacher or professor, because motivation to learn is a decisive factor and is often emotionally based.

Driven by high unemployment among young people, calls for politicians to make education a higher priority are becoming increasingly strident throughout the world. These voices are worth listening to.

Personally, I am astounded—which is not too strong a word—at the considerable resources that Singapore devotes to this social cause. This view of a good education as a sine qua non is not exclusive to Singaporeans. I have seen a real trend in this direction throughout Asia in general, on the evidence of the economically disadvantaged people I met in Indonesia and the news I saw on Channel News Asia. Not a day passes without a news report about education, for example, the one aired on September 13, 2013, focusing on Cambodian children's efforts to learn English, which according to this important media outlet is the only escape route from poverty.

Why not endorse this view? Why not boost the enthusiasm of young people, in Europe as well, for the important profession of teaching? I cannot help but lament Europe's lack of recognition for teachers, whereas in Asia awarding something like an "Oscar" to the most deserving educators seems to be an established tradition.

It would perhaps not be out of place to clarify that these few paragraphs on education should not be considered a digression. In fact, though it may seem paradoxical at first sight, a correlation between water and education does exist. I mentioned this earlier, but it seems wise to repeat it here in this chapter on vulnerability: often parents in poor rural regions of Asia do not discover the health benefits of water until school infrastructure is set up in their towns.

PART I: WATER INEQUALITY

Economic Risks

Since the 2008 financial crisis, unemployment—especially of young people—has risen to dizzying heights, as noted especially by the International Labour Organization,[25] the Organisation for Economic Cooperation and Development,[26] and OXFAM.[27]

The fact that this worrisome job insecurity is growing, whether in industrialized or "emerging" countries,[28] should be of concern.

This scourge affects us all to varying degrees and no one, absolutely no one, has an interest in allowing it to progress. The ripple effects of this evil lead to serious vulnerability, with all its attendant miseries, up to and including a loss of interest in life itself. So efforts to save water and to know whether it is drinkable or not are at the same time likely to reduce the terrible feeling of "what's the point?" that slyly keeps rising to the surface.

Which means that here too, a relationship between the economy and water can be discerned. I note again that herein lies the paradox, in that serious economic problems go hand in hand with a phenomenal and disturbing increase in large—I would even say colossal—fortunes. This is seen especially in China.

Regulatory steps must be taken, and in fact are absolutely necessary. I will come back to this later, specifically in reference to a recent work by Mireille Delmas-Marty entitled *Résister, Responsabiliser, Anticiper* [Fight back, hold accountable, second-guess].[29]

However, something else is even more important, namely helping people rediscover their zest for life and kindling hopes likely to have real effects.

Finally, in order to act, we must find collaborative methods based on a mutual trust that must be built and rebuilt unceasingly, both among countries themselves (and since World War II no effort has been spared) and also among countries, local and transnational businesses (the famous PPP), and actual individuals. This important issue will also be revisited later[30] during the discussion on the concept of corporate social responsibility.

The Role of "Multistakeholders" in Water Vulnerability[31]

If this type of collaboration really were able to arise, and theoretically it appears quite possible, the issue of potable water would have everything to gain by it; because it

---

25. www.ilo.org.
26. http://www.oecd.org.
27. OXFAM is the acronym for Oxford Committee for Famine Relief.
28. It should be noted that China is a special case that falls between the two.
29. Delmas-Marty, *Résister*.
30. See Part IV, Chapter III, Multinationals and Tensions.
31. Delmas-Marty indicates, "[...] *stakeholders* or partners of the enterprise, such as its employees,

should be able to solve itself, I would tend to say, if we accept the premise of a connection between improved hygiene, better education, and a stronger economy, as I have tried to show.

Such collaboration would need to be rebuilt based on new paradigms due to a post-2008-crisis context that the world will have to accept in the end so as to be better able to find solutions. At least, that is what I understood from the remarks by an ILO leader[32] at the World Economic Forum held in Dalian,[33] China, from September 11-13, 2013. Other panelists considered that responsibility for the economic situation and the well-being associated with it lies not with governments and businesses alone, although they do have a heavy responsibility in this regard,[34] but also and especially with those seeking employment. This refers to the well-known concept of "empowerment" which, given the constraints of the economic crisis, is attracting more and more notice these days. I will come back to this later as well.[35]

Without minimizing in any way the importance of the State's social role as it has developed in the West, particularly with the welfare state, it is critical to provide an expanded conceptual space for the social responsibility of businesses and individual responsibility. According to the speakers in Dalian, in order to combat unemployment, governments can legitimately be called upon to provide educational resources, whereas we would need to be able to assign to businesses the role of helping create places for job-seekers and employers to meet, especially on Internet platforms.

A role for civil society was undoubtedly implied in Dalian since the "management of world affairs," as the Fondation pour Genève so aptly problematized it in four reviews *(cahiers)* issued between 2007 and 2010,[36] is too complicated to allow for efforts focused solely on individuals, even "empowered" ones. The individual must also be able to count on members of civil society that are likely to understand his vulnerability and help bring relief.

Water Vulnerability and Resilience: A Case Study

When Singapore, a small city-state in Southeast Asia, gained independence in 1965, its population was mostly illiterate and its economic, political, and social system seemed to foretell a bleak future. Citizens' safety was threatened by frequent and extremely

---

clients, and suppliers or civil society organizations." Delmas-Marty, *Resister*, 153.

32. ILO is the acronym for the International Labour Organization.

33. A port city of more than six million people, which has six large Protestant churches and one Catholic church, http://fr.wikipedia.org/wiki/Dalian.

34. Obviously I am thinking of the government's responsibility in many non-industrialized countries riddled with corruption, and that of companies that have not adopted the CSR or "corporate social responsibility" paradigm.

35. See Part VI, Interview with a Reprentative of a Swiss Protestant Diaconal Ministry.

36. Fondation pour Genève, "'Soft' gouvernance," "Multi-Stakeholders," "Responsabilité sociétale," "'Soft' Institutions."

violent conflicts, not to mention hegemonic forays by Indonesia, which aimed to take over the small territory nestled in its bosom through its "konfrontasi" policy. The outlook seemed even blacker because Singapore's dependence on Malaysia for its water supply made it yet more vulnerable.

So how is it that now, as I write these lines, I see before me a State that has risen from Third World status to become one of the world's most advanced industrial countries in less than fifty years?

In *The Singapore Water Story*,[37] published in April 2013, a group of international experts summarizes the stages of this spectacular development, which to a significant extent was due to the need for the public authorities to take on the challenge of reducing water vulnerability as quickly as possible.

Potable Water As a Lever for Development

Psychologists would use the word "resilience" to describe Singapore and its success story. Economists would say it was a question of well-understood innovation. German philosopher Immanuel Kant would have spoken of a condition of possibility, a radical mode of change in the interest of greater well-being.

The authors of the history of water in Singapore did not gloss over the fact that the keys to transforming Singaporeans' living environment were a strong political will and a long-term vision:

> It is thus appropriate to stress that one of the most important lessons Singapore can teach developed and developing countries alike is the exemplary political will of its leadership.[38]

Another key to development was the role played by the people, who were invited to participate in the changes beginning on day one of independence. Many campaigns to raise awareness about water issues were conducted, and specific school curricula were created. The media also helped broadcast news reports that got taxpayers to open their wallets. It was a question of finding economic incentives to encourage the population to reduce consumption of the precious liquid. A statistical table[39] presented by experts proves the considerable impact of water pricing regulations and the effect on individual behavior:

> As it has been proved that economic instruments can reshape consumption patterns and human behaviour, they should be given priority consideration in the future to further bring down water consumption.[40]

---

37. Tortajada et al., *The Singapore Water Story*.
38. Ibid., 3.
39. Ibid., 95.
40. Ibid., 102.

CHAPTER III: "THINKING" THE HUMAN RELATIONSHIP TO WATER

I would like to emphasize that the work I am citing in no way seeks to give an idyllic picture of development in this small Asian country, which has been forced by its geopolitical situation to work very hard—just to survive, initially, and later to maintain its current status. Indeed, while Singapore recognizes that its current circumstances are very favorable, its leaders are well aware that if the country were to drop its guard, its vulnerability would again be exposed. That is why the younger generation is singled out and taught about the water problem. Young people are made thoroughly aware of the fact that the potable water to which they have such easy access today was meted out drop by drop in the 1960s. It has even been reported that on the morning of August 19, 1961, no potable water whatsoever was available.[41]

In my opinion, the example I have just given perfectly illustrates Ambassador Benoît Girardin's clear and succinct paper in the proceedings of the 2011 W4W colloquium. His contribution is entitled "Does water have a cost, and if so, what? Ethical considerations," and the following is an excerpt from it:

> The ethical requirement [has to do with] [. . .] responsible consumption that promotes the sustainability of resources and their renewal, as well as efficient distribution and minimization of leaks [. . .].[42]

This involves not only individuals, but also and especially businesses asked to choose wastewater (NEWater system[43]) rather than potable water for their purposes.

Having looked into the matter, we can see that Singapore is among the most advanced countries on the planet in terms of water-related innovation. That is why it attracts investors from all over the world to make water desalination methods compatible with sustainable development. One example of innovation is the concrete industrial application represented by the invention of a membrane for water filtration (reverse osmosis technique). It was developed by Hyflux,[44] a company founded about thirty years ago.

---

41. Ibid.,85.

42. Girardin, *"L'eau a-t-elle un coût ? [Does Water have a cost?]."*

43. Tortajada et al. indicate, "[. . .] industries have been encouraged to become more efficient and substitute potable water with NEWater." Tortajada et al., *The Singapore Water Story*, 95.

44. "Hyflux is a leading provider of integrated water management and environmental solutions with operations and projects in Singapore, Southeast Asia, China, India, Algeria, the Middle East and North Africa." Wikipedia provides the following information: "Hyflux has become one of the world's leading water filter companies. It was founded by Olivia Lum, a chemist with an amazing story. She arrived in Singapore as a poor orphan at the age of fifteen, after the woman who was her guardian had apparently despoiled her of her inheritance. She doggedly pursued studies in chemistry then, after working for a large pharmaceutical company for three years, began what today would be called a start-up to develop an innovation in water filtration." www.hyflux.com.

Mini-Conclusion

Vulnerability seems to go hand in hand with the necessity to act. So the bringing of new life and hope centered on universal access to potable water does not seem to be an impossible dream, on one condition: that we agree to a change in direction, or paradigm shift—a secular expression for what in theology is called repentance. This will be discussed in Part V.

Chapter IV

"Thinking" the Human in Need

Introduction

Calvin, Marx, and Brundtland on the Needs of the Poorest as a Criterion for Justice

How can I legitimately make a connection between such disparate personalities from such different times and places? The answer is that they all assigned poverty, or further yet destitution, a high priority as a social concern.

The first two, who lived about three hundred years apart, helped give humanity the great economic systems that are still making their mark on the world today. They were John Calvin, a reformer, and Karl Marx, a denigrator of received wisdom.

The third, Gro Harlem Brundtland, is a very high-profile Norwegian politician. She presided over the eponymous commission in the context of preparations for the 1992 Rio conference on sustainable development.

John Calvin's Reaction to Poverty

A number of concepts at the root of capitalism—a term which, incidentally, did not exist in the sixteenth century—are often attributed to Calvin. To a certain extent, one of the decisive factors in the spread of this assumption is probably his approach to the concept of money, the ultimate medium of exchange, which was very novel in the early 1500s. At that time no one would have taken the liberty of questioning the sacrosanct rule laid down by Scholastic Thomas Aquinas, who subscribed to Aristotle's metaphorical catch-phrase "money is sterile." In other words, for Aristotle and medieval thinkers, money could not bear interest. Even German reformer Martin Luther remained in the Catholic camp on this point:

> Luther again perfectly illustrates the medieval tradition of mistrust of money and reveals himself to be clearly reluctant to embrace the economic boom taking place before his very eyes. He condemns lending at interest and feels that

the seller's freedom to set his own prices is a flagrant injustice, as is the rapid accumulation of wealth by the new merchant class.[1]

For his part, Calvin was struck by the penury in which some of his contemporaries were living and began searching for ways to solve the problem. He considered it important to accord dignity to all people and not to reduce the poorest people to begging, which he found degrading. We recall that he pleaded for begging to be prohibited in Geneva.

He especially could not subscribe to a common doctrine of the day holding that the poor were a blessing for the rich, because by giving alms the rich could ensure they would receive God's salvation.

Giving alms was actually merely charity, not justice, as Christoph Stückelberger, an ethics professor at the University of Basel, astutely notes in a contemporary essay on the right to food and water.[2] This means that the poor had the status of objects. Calvin wanted to help them become subjects and give them the resources to leave their abject poverty behind. So the concept of charity was replaced by that of justice.

> He mobilizes the affected persons and takes them seriously as subjects and not merely objects of commerce. Rights produce a strengthening that creates an identity and sense of dignity, especially in people whose liberation from poverty is associated with liberation from oppression.[3]

To encourage economic development, Calvin also considered elevating the concept of "work" to the rank of the desirable virtues, not only for people who needed it to survive, but also for the well-to-do who, being privileged, were in the best position to share the benefits of their well-being with the most needy. In this respect he was refuting the Scholastic tradition, which held that

> [t]hose who despise all for God's sake are bound to work with their hands, when they have no other means of livelihood [. . .] but not otherwise (Summa Theologica, IIa-IIae, Paris, Cerf, 1985, Q. 187, art. 3).[4]
>
> In contrast, the Puritans would stress that the rich, who have enough to live on without working, should work more than others, inasmuch as God has given them more and will ask for an accounting of their "talents" [. . .] (Matthew 25:14-30). [. . .] Calvin's exegesis of this text enables us to understand the Reformation's innovations in relation to commercial exchange.[5]
>
> Money also requires the rich man to "help his neighbors and provide for them" by giving them work if they are capable of working, or if not, alms.[6]

1. Dermange, "Argent," 43.
2. Stückelberger, *Das Menschenrecht auf Nahrung und Wasser*.
3. Ibid., 14.
4. Miegge, "Capitalisme," 188.
5. Ibid., 189.
6. Dermange, "Argent."

Such a sense of solidarity was completely revolutionary for the time, and it was to gain ground.

In a way, Calvin was supporting the transition from the exchange of services and the barter system to monetary transactions, a form of trade that came from Italy and which had enabled the fairs in Geneva and Lyons to contribute to real economic development since the fourteenth century.

So what did Calvin suggest? He believed that it was absolutely necessary to rethink mankind's relationship to money. If Man must work, money must also, thus becoming productive and likely to improve the material condition of the poorest of the poor. That is, contrary to popular opinion, Calvin did not idealize asceticism. Rather, he saw a society of abundance as a blessing from God. But—careful!—not to be indulged in with wild abandon. He considered all excess to be the work of usurers.

> So the rich man has nothing to be ashamed of provided that he shows by his austerity that he is not idolatrous.[7]

Later I will expand on the notion that Calvin's ideas were based on the Old Testament laws, that is, those written by Moses on the Tables of the Law.[8] The Ten Commandments undeniably allowed the reformer to construct his own sense of social justice.

At that point we will take a look at his broad and original interpretation of the Tables of the Law. At this juncture it is important and not too early to note that by going deeper into the meaning and content of the last three commandments (the eighth, ninth, and tenth forbidding stealing, bearing false witness, and coveting), one can postulate the social views—before such a term was ever coined—of solidarity held by this Geneva-based French reformer. Respect for the other and alterity, as French philosopher Paul Ricœur likes to say, can be read between the lines of these biblical precepts.

So Calvin was taking aim at two aspects of justice.

First, he insisted that accumulating wealth could be honest and legitimate provided that it was not done "by cruelty and at the expense of the blood of others."[9] Second, he held protection of one's reputation to be "more precious than any treasures whatever."[10] In other words, what stood out to Calvin was the importance to humankind of both respecting others and refraining from acting contrary to justice.

---

7. Ibid.
8. Exod 20:1–17.
9. Calvin, *Inst.*, II, VIII, 46, with regard to the eighth commandment.
10. Ibid., II, VIII, 47, with regard to the ninth commandment.

He felt that we must above all avoid thinking in terms that might "strike our hearts, and inflame them with cupidity"[11] or that would have mere personal profit "prejudicial to your neighbor"[12] as their aim.

Karl Marx's Reaction to Poverty

This German philosopher and economist has been (belatedly) credited with the advent of an economic system, usually called communist, that might work against poverty. He wanted to supplant a system which he criticized for its perverse effects and which, according to him, legitimized Man's exploitation of Man. He suspected every employer (whether agricultural, industrial, or commercial) of making its workers into some sort of slaves to be exploited at will. For him, with only a few exceptions, the labor of which Calvin spoke so highly became "alienation," a term which has, as Paul Ricœur elegantly phrases it, undergone a language distortion:

> [. . .] the concept of alienation suffers from semantic overload.[13]

Must one then choose between a sort of Calvinist veneration of labor—as revisited by the Puritans of America—which was mentioned above and was the source of the New World's prosperity; and Marx's hatred, not only of labor, but also of money[14] and of any kind of god[15] as well?

Or can we find a middle ground, to return to Aristotle's cherished idea of the "mean"?

History, which more often than not has been tragic, provides the answer.

The middle ground, the reflective equilibrium that John Rawls gives the place of honor in his book *A Theory of Justice*,[16] is to be sought anew each day. The pendulum is set in motion by politics, which tries to impose a direction on this capricious economy to avoid chaos.

> The market economy necessarily has rules and they cannot exist outside of a legal context that ensures, for example, that contracts are respected.[17]

Imparting this direction is the task of "political economy," a concept that turns out to be an oxymoron, at least from the Ancient Greeks' point of view:

---

11. Ibid., II, VIII, 50, with regard to the tenth commandment.
12. Ibid.
13. Combemale, *Introduction à Marx*, 28.
14. Combemale indicates, "This hatred of money permeates his work. Marx frequently cited Shakespeare's depiction of gold as the 'common whore of mankind.'" Ibid., 36
15. Ibid., 6.
16. Rawls, *Théorie de la justice*.
17. Miegge, "Capitalisme," 198.

Chapter IV: "Thinking" the Human in Need

The Greek term *oikonomia* [. . .] referred to the organization of the household. Not only was the *oikos* the center of family life; it was also the center for the production of goods. Yet above this sphere, which is essential to life and which they considered to be shared by humans and animals, the Greek philosophers (especially Aristotle) placed the higher and specifically human sphere of political life (the *polis*), where actions and relationships between free and equal actors occur. So for the Greeks, the very notion of political economy would have been nonsense.[18]

Can political economy claim an allegiance to ethics?

This is the issue tackled by Gro Harlem Brundtland, whom we will introduce here, and Adam Smith, whose answer we will hear a bit later.

Gro Harlem Brundtland's[19] Reaction to Poverty

The issue of water and other natural resources, and their unequal distribution, was looming so large by the end of the twentieth century that it had to be given a prominent place on the international political agenda.

Consequently, it was impossible to discuss environmental issues without addressing the problem of poverty, especially in developing countries.

The Brundtland Commission did considerable work in this area in the context of preparing for the June 1992 Earth Summit in Rio de Janeiro.[20]

In 1987, this Commission made some highly unusual recommendations in a report entitled "Our Common Future."[21] Though these suggestions were undoubtedly not as far-reaching as their originators would have wished, they were innovative and did profoundly mark the collective consciousness.

The Preferential Option for the Poor, a Criterion for Distributive Justice in the Twentieth Century

The experts convened by Gro Harlem Brundtland selected the concept of a "preferential option for the poor" and attempted to show its relevance to a world increasingly polarized between rich and poor. They demonstrated that pauperization must be recognized as having a structural cause.

---

18. Ibid., 185.

19. Le petit Larousse illustré indicates, "Brundtland (Harlem Gro) *Oslo 1939*, Norwegian politician. Chairwoman of the Labor Party (1981-1992) and Prime Minister in 1981, from 1986 to 1989, and from 1990 to 1996. After leading the World Commission on Environment and Development (Brundtland Commission) at the UN in the 1980s, she served as the director-general of the World Health Organization from 1990 to 2003." Le petit Larousse illustré, "Brundtland," 1236.

20. Dermange, "Course on sustainable development".

21. For the complete text of "Our Common Future," see www.un-documents.net/our-common-future.pdf.

Part I: Water Inequality

The development of the industrial society reveals poverty as a phenomenon with structural causes (employment, housing, education, etc.).[22]

This concept has had its ups and downs and has sometimes even been manipulated for various purposes. However, what should be remembered is that it was at the heart of reflections on a better kind of social justice, with the overriding goal of ensuring that the essential needs of the poor are met.[23] A corollary of this goal was a principle of equity that is both intragenerational and intergenerational. That is the definition of the "sustainable development" concept devised by the Brundtland Commission, which is significant in this regard.

> Sustainable development is development that meets the needs of the present without compromising the ability of future generations to meet their own needs. It contains within it two key concepts: the concept of 'needs', in particular the essential needs of the world's poor, to which overriding priority should be given; and the idea of limitations imposed by the state of technology and social organization on the environment's ability to meet present and future needs.[24]

It is important to stress the evocative power of this definition, which has a deliberate and revealing tautology at its center:

> [...] in particular the essential needs of the world's poor, to which overriding priority should be given [...]

We note that conceptually, this priority reveals the choice to appeal to distributive justice, a kind of justice that Aristotle distinguished from corrective justice.

Since human beings' essential needs differ depending on the contexts in which they live, a form of corrective justice that would apply a strictly egalitarian principle would make no sense. In contrast, a form of justice that takes inequalities into account, and therefore favors the poorest of the poor, is the most appropriate kind.

What became of this very broad and generous definition of sustainable development in the final version of the text adopted by the countries at the Rio conference in June 1992?

We note that the States agreed to twenty-seven principles in their Rio Declaration on Environment and Development[25] and confirmed the interdependence of the three now-classic areas of focus: environmental, economic, and social concerns.

---

22. Bovay, "Pauvreté," 1054.
23. www.un-documents.net/our-common-future.pdf, 41–42.
24. www.un-documents.net/our-common-future.pdf, 41.
25. Rio Declaration on Environment and Development.

Chapter IV: "Thinking" the Human in Need

After restating their sovereign rights to exploit their own resources,[26] they acknowledge that cooperation is necessary in order to eradicate poverty.[27]

A close reading and comparison of the Brundtland report and the Rio Declaration leaves no room for doubt: the States did revise the Brundtland Commission's recommendation in a nearly imperceptible way.[28] Having been unable to decide to give "overriding priority" to the essential needs of the world's poor, they chose a less restrictive option. Not only do they mention "peoples" and "countries" instead of the poor, they also give them only "special priority." Furthermore, by introducing a utilitarian criterion,[29] they aim to meet the needs of as many people as possible:

> All States and all people shall cooperate in the essential task of eradicating poverty as an indispensable requirement for sustainable development, in order to decrease the disparities in standards of living and better meet the needs of the majority of the people of the world.[30]

Nevertheless, the Brundtland Commission's work was not in vain. As proof: the Millennium Development Goals issued in 2000 revisited this priority. Some would say that the progress reported at the Johannesburg summit in 2002 and Rio+20 in 2012, which were held to evaluate the advancement of sustainable development, has come too slowly. Impatience is no doubt a bad adviser.

After all, is it not unjust and irresponsible to leave the States to bear the entire burden of worrying about the fate of the poor? There are other stakeholders—and not the least important ones—who are being called before the court of humanity: individuals themselves, namely those whom history has given dignity.

What is meant by human dignity? This will be the subject of the next chapter.

---

26. Ibid., principle 2.
27. Ibid., principle 5.
28. Dermange, "Développement durable."
29. The economic doctrine of utilitarianism will be brought up later.
30. Rio Declaration on Environment and Development, principle 5.

Chapter V

"Thinking" Human Beings in Terms of Their Dignity

The Origin and Formulation of "Human Dignity"

I WOULD LIKE TO refute Edelmann's position[1] right away. He considers this concept to be new.

Legal experts Alfred Verdross[2] and Xavier Bioy[3] theorize that it has been forged by thinkers dating back to ancient times. This actually seems more plausible to me. But let us take a look.

"Human Dignity" in World History, from Biblical Times to the Enlightenment

It is through the interpretation of biblical texts, more specifically Genesis, that we discover that a human is not simply a living being like any other, but instead an entity of higher value, since God created Man in his image and gave him dominion over all the earth. The concept of humanity was born.

In ancient times, the Stoics paved the way for individualization of the human being by incorporating the city *(polis)* into the idea of a Universal City, or "Cosmopolis."

Later, in the Middle Ages, Thomas Aquinas contributed to its development by explicitly stating

> [. . .] that the State is not an organism made up of cells, but a community of men having their own substance and dignity who have come together in pursuit of common goals.[4]

---

1. Edelman, "La dignité de la personne humaine," 185, cited by Aksoy, "La notion de dignité humaine," 49 n30.
2. Verdross, "La dignité de la personne humaine comme base des droits de l'homme," 415–21.
3. Bioy, "La dignité," 47–86.
4. Verdross, "La dignité de la personne humaine comme base des droits de l'homme," 419.

CHAPTER V: "THINKING" HUMAN BEINGS IN TERMS OF THEIR DIGNITY

Yet is was not until the Renaissance that the concept of "human dignity" itself was actually expressed and clarified for the first time in Pico della Mirandola's *De dignitate hominis oratio*[5] [Oration on the dignity of man]. At great personal risk, the Florentine dared to confront the Roman Curia, maintaining that Man could shape his own nature as he pleased. This radically new contention was the harbinger of humanism.

German philosopher Immanuel Kant was the thinker who was especially instrumental in developing this concept in all its glory, through his in-depth research on human autonomy, as we will see in a moment after a brief historical digression.

The Eclipse of "Human Dignity"

History with a capital H has played more than one trick on Humanity, also with a capital H.

It must be noted that between the Enlightenment and 1945, defenders of the concept of human dignity could be counted on the fingers of one hand!

At least, that is what emerges from some authors' theories. One such is Olivier de Frouville, for whom it was the tragic World War II era that gave new luster to concepts forgotten for over a hundred years.[6]

"Human Dignity" from 1945 to the Present

Four iconic dates mark the rise of the concept of "human dignity," namely 1945 and 1948, 1989, and 2010.

First, these historic milestones can remind us that the entire world's deep sense of outrage in the face of two traumatic World Wars was what brought about worldwide awareness in 1945. The Universal Declaration of Human Rights of December 10, 1948 was intended to create a new world order founded on new values that would keep humanity, torn apart by immeasurable atrocities, from ever having to live through such horrors again, and enable it as well to remember that human beings have intrinsic value.

Second, with the fall of the Berlin Wall and communism on November 9, 1989, more democracies were born, and they enshrined protection for human rights in their respective constitutions by introducing the concept of "human dignity."[7]

---

5. Pico della Mirandola, *De hominis dignitate*, cited by Bioy, "La dignité," 59 n39.

6. De Frouville indicates, "Une conception démocratique du droit international," 14: "The Nazi horror conclusively discredited any theory of law that professes to rule out in principle any reflection on the values on which it is formed. Beyond all doubt, the statement acknowledging human rights in the Preamble to the United Nations Charter is one of the most obvious signs of this trend. This return to a theme from Enlightenment philosophy after nearly a century of total oblivion on the international scene probably constitutes a turning point in the theory of law, while at the same time inviting new reflection." De Frouville, "Une conception démocratique du droit international," 14.

7. This concept first appeared in the Swiss federal Constitution in 1999, in article 7 of the chapter

Finally, the concept was reaffirmed in the UN resolution of July 28, 2010, in which water was given its status as a human right.

Figures such as René Cassin[8]—a Frenchman who won the Nobel Peace Prize—, Eleanor Roosevelt, and Stéphane Hessel relentlessly defended the inclusion of this concept in the UDHR's preamble[9] and article 1,[10] which gave it universal significance.

Despite the importance of "human dignity" to internationalists, the concept's boundaries are indistinct and defined only poorly or not at all. Some attribute it to religious origins,[11] while others even take a radical stance. These latter, such as Anne-Marie Le Pourhiet, a professor of public law at the University of Rennes 1, consider it a concept to be rejected as pointless or even dangerous[12] and likely to cause unacceptable abuses.

Such extreme positions attest to the notion's ambiguity, showing us that it is important not to adopt the concept without further examination.

The Meaning and Mechanism of "Human Dignity"

An Ambiguous Concept at the Heart of Modern Research

If one takes a look back at the beginnings of the concept of "human dignity," as we have just done, it is not surprising that today it is a very popular research topic, given its current success on the world stage.

"Human dignity" can be understood on many different levels, as Xavier Bioy was fond of saying in a lecture delivered in 2004.[13]

For him, the international legal corpus on human rights gives the human person a value that was denied during totalitarian regimes. The human person then leaves the realm of concrete reality to become a

> [. . .] value, a more valued and idealized form of the human being [. . .] as a founding and final value of the State, which thus declares that the State

---

on basic rights, but it is significant that since 1989, it has appeared with increasing frequency in the national constitutions of European countries and even outside of Europe, for example in South Africa.

8. Cassin, *Les guerres de 1914–1918 et de 1939–1945*.

9. Preamble of UDHR indicates, "Whereas recognition of the inherent dignity [. . .] of all members of the human family is the foundation of freedom, justice and peace in the world."

10. Article 1 of UDHR indicates "All human beings are born free and equal in dignity and rights."

11. Council of Europe's European comission for Democracy through law, "Le principe du respect de la dignité de la personne humaine," 26–44.

12. Le Pourhiet indicates, "Today, dignity is the most direct threat to Enlightenment philosophy and the republican ideal, a deadly weapon against our freedoms. Elevating this eminently subjective and relative philosophical and moral idea to a legal standard is madness. [. . .] It is also in the name of human dignity that "very active" euthanasia is being demanded, and it is furthermore not by chance that the most intellectually destitute and far-fetched recent jurisdictional decisions have been rendered on the basis of this overused catch-all notion." Le Pourhiet, "Touche pas à mon préambule."

13. Bioy, "La dignité," 47–86.

CHAPTER V: "THINKING" HUMAN BEINGS IN TERMS OF THEIR DIGNITY

must—insofar as what is at stake is its very existence—provide objective treatment and absolute protection. Alongside the infinite number of ways freedom can be expressed through each individual, it is the human being's unique dignity that enables the State to keep up the myth of an "anthropological function of the law."[14]

It is interesting to read yet again in this author's work that dignity, in contrast to freedom, is an abstract concept that can become established in "existential concrete reality." This postulate is clarified, for him, by the following chiasmus:

> [. . .] it is from freedom that I acquire my dignity and not from my dignity that I acquire my freedom.[15]

Shades of Kant? Perhaps. A self-examination in light of this German philosopher would seem unavoidable in any case, since some see him as the father of the concept of "human dignity."

A Hermeneutic "Dissection" of Kant's Imperative

We now know that the very concept of "human dignity" is paradoxical and polysemous.

Then we have philosopher Immanuel Kant coming along to put in his oar—and he certainly pulls more strongly than some others.

With Kant, we must proceed in stages to finally arrive at the point where we understand what "human dignity" means.

His extremely subtle approach leads to the emergence of a "categorical imperative" developed in three stages.[16]

The first, dealing with the objective aspect, brings out the objective concepts of the laws of nature[17] and universalization. The second, dealing with the subjective aspect, brings out the person—strangely, the rational being—as a subject of all ends-in-themselves, these last being "[. . .] the supreme limiting condition of every man's freedom of action [. . .]."[18] The third, through the intermediary of pure reason, allows a universally legislative will exercised by every rational being to break through.

Every rational being in a union with other rational beings in a kingdom of ends ("which is admittedly only an Ideal"[19]) will be a maker of universal laws ("he is also

---

14. Ibid., 76.
15. Ibid., 59, citing Mourgeron.
16. Kant, *Fondements*, 146.
17. Kant indicates, "[. . .] *nature* in its most general sense (nature as regards its form)—that is, the existence of things so far as determined by universal laws [. . .]." Kant, *Fondements*, 129.
18. Kant, *Fondements*, 145.
19. Ibid., 150.

himself subject to those laws"[20]) that will determine a value "infinitely above all price,"[21] namely dignity:

> For nothing can have a value other than that determined for it by the law. But the law-making which determines all value must for this reason have a dignity—that is, an unconditioned and incomparable worth—for the appreciation of which, as necessarily given by a rational being, the word *'reverence'* is the only becoming expression. *Autonomy* is therefore the ground of the dignity of human nature and of every rational nature.[22]

I note that Kant speaks of the "dignity of human *nature*," not of "human dignity." So he is not defining "human dignity" per se to create his concept of autonomy, which is autonomy of the will.

It is not my place to dive any deeper into this dialectic, and besides, my hermeneutic tools would not be equal to the task.

In my opinion, however, such Kantian "respect," such "dignity," becomes "human" if we begin a sort of hermeneutic dissection of the categorical imperative's second stage, of which the subjective aspect has become a famous leitmotiv, if not one of universal import.

Paradoxically, the principle of acting

> " [. . .] in relation to every rational being (both to yourself and to others) that he may at the same time count in your maxim as an end in himself [. . .] never *merely* as a means [. . .],[23]

has found a place for itself both in Marxist thought and at the top of the Roman Catholic hierarchy.[24]

Without expressly stating it, Kant thus developed a principle of justice that had equality as its criterion. Some authors theorize that, "solely because they belong to the human race, all individuals must be treated equally."[25]

---

20. Ibid., 154.
21. Ibid., 153.
22. Ibid., 154.
23. Ibid.
24. Ibid., n1 indicates, "This formulation of the categorical imperative is one of Kant's most elevated ideas. [. . .] Marxist thought is not unaware of the profundity of this formulation of the imperative, and its views in this regard can be summed up as follows: the worker is always a man. He cannot be used like a machine which, in contrast, is strictly a means." John Paul II wrote the following transcription of this formulation: "Whenever a person is the object of your activity, remember that you may not treat that person as only the means to an end, as an instrument, but must allow for the fact that he or she, too, has, or at least should have, distinct personal ends. [. . .]." Philonenko comments "Such agreement between thoughts coming from such different backgrounds should be mentioned. It testifies to the universal power of Kantian thought." Kant, *Fondements de la métaphysique des mœurs*, 142–43 n1 by A. Philonenko, commentator on Kant.
25. Noël and Paquet, "Un Québec zénonien," 16.

CHAPTER V: "THINKING" HUMAN BEINGS IN TERMS OF THEIR DIGNITY

This egalitarian spark in the human heart must be "human dignity," an ideal of our time, that is, that "something due to a human being simply because he is human,"[26] as Paul Ricœur grandiloquently summarizes it.

Can the Import of "Human Dignity" Be a Tool for Our Times in the Context of Potable Water's Ethical Stakes?

Many people feel that the "right to potable water" and the principle of "human dignity" are givens.

This stance tends to obscure the fact that the two concepts are still the objects of some disagreement. In the first case, this has especially been true since potable water has officially become part of the human rights corpus, which currently is experiencing a loss of momentum that attests to its fragility. In the second, it is due to the principle's paradoxical nature, as has been shown above.

Nevertheless, this concept of "human dignity" remains very important even to those who see its true pitfalls and dangers, such as Paul Martens, a professor and judge who says:

> We can—this is the professor speaking—continue to express doubts about the invasion of an enlightening standard that increases the power of judges and blurs the boundaries of a secularized law [. . .]. But [. . .]—and now you are hearing from the judge—[. . .] if we take this last bastion against new barbarisms away from constitutional judges, we are asking them to do their jobs without being properly equipped.[27]

Consideration of this concept is equally unavoidable outside of the judicial arena and the political sphere, where philosophers such as Karl Jaspers, for example, apply it to the real concrete individual and not to the abstract human being dealt with by human rights as indicated above. Jaspers states,

> [i]f I see Man exclusively as a natural being that we can know through objective methods, it is because I renounce all humanism for a kind of "hominism" (Windelband). I see him only as the representative of a natural species. All the individuals are nothing more than examples of this species, in endless numbers, without value in and of themselves. On the other hand, if I see Man in his freedom, his dignity is established intact. Every individual, including me, is irreplaceable—all of us, and much is asked of all of us.[28]

---

26. Ricœur, "Dignité humaine," 236–37. (This quotation is making the rounds of the Internet uncredited, for example on the French version of Wikipedia under the heading *"Dignité"* [Dignity].)

27. Martens, "La dignité humaine," 158.

28. Jaspers, "Conditions et possibilités d'un nouvel humanisme," 211.

It seems to me personally that this concept of "human dignity" must be handled with extreme care and circumspection, notwithstanding this great German philosopher's flight of lyricism.

Why?

The research I conducted on the concept of "human dignity" led me to conclude—and Professor Paul Martens's quotation is a clue that leaves little room for doubt[29]—that this concept falls under a different order of justice, that is, justice-in-itself and not contingent justice. Indeed the contemporary reading of it deals with the human being only in his idealized form and is unaware of the reality in the field, that is, the human person locked in the struggle with his earthly human condition—the man and woman who must, one day, die.

Conclusion

During the nearly fifty years since the first warnings about the challenges of fresh water, the world has rolled up its sleeves. Some people are working on finding new technologies, some on laws, and others on raising awareness among the world's inhabitants about their vulnerability and needs, in order to ensure their survival and well-being.

At the same time, industrialized countries have been working specifically on remedies for water pollution through appropriate treatment infrastructure. In developing countries, on the other hand, despite the accelerating construction of water conveyance infrastructure, most wastewater is discharged into seas, lakes, and rivers. The ecological disaster is real, as indicated above in the Yamuna River example and as I saw with my own eyes in Burma and Indonesia. Unfortunately these cases are not exceptions, far from it.

So is despondency our only choice? I would say no, for two main reasons—one technical, the other political.

From a technical standpoint, not only can surface water pollution be avoided thanks, once again, to water treatment infrastructure; today water scarcity per se is no longer a problem.

In fact, according to the experts who met in Singapore in June 2014 for Singapore International Water Week (SIWW), a truly dizzying array of potential—and materially feasible—options for producing potable water is available. I will come back to this point.

Moreover, if the political will to do so existed, it would be possible for mature economies to modernize infrastructure[30] that is not always adequately maintained,

---

29. Martens indicates, "[. . .] edifying standard that [. . .] blurs the boundaries of a secularized law." Martens, "La dignité humaine."

30. There is a need for sophisticated infrastructure to convey potable water from the aquifer or from surface water to the faucet; it must handle complex treatment in four stages: pumping, filtration

and for emerging economies to equip themselves with efficient infrastructure to supply high-quality fresh water to everyone and ensure that everyone benefits from sanitation related to the healthful use of water.

So the good news is that potable water is not scarce, as was thought in the late twentieth century. On the contrary: all of the water needed for household use, industry, and agriculture is recyclable through the use of technologies such as reverse osmosis[31] and ceramic membranes.

There is additional good news from Cambodia, a poor country that lived through the atrocities of repression and famine under the Khmer Rouge between 1974 and 1979. This country has shown truly astounding resilience, creating a water supply system that supplies high-quality water to taps throughout Phnom Penh at reasonable prices, with a financial exemption for the poor. Good governance was what enabled a people's dream to become reality in less than ten years. The study I consulted on this topic, entitled "Water Supply of Phnom Penh: An Example of Good Governance" was published under the auspices of Mexico's Third World Centre for Water Management and Singapore's Institute of Water Policy at the Lee Kuan Yew School of Public Policy.[32]

Things like these are more easily said than done. The two examples given above, encouraging as they are, remain exceptional cases in today's world. Yet they are sufficiently thought-provoking, and reflection is the first and necessary step for action.

Let us now continue down the path we are taking to move closer to the human being—the one wrestling with what is generally called water stress or water inequality—, and seek some normative solutions to this problem.

---

to make the water clear, ozonization to make it drinkable, and distribution (see Ramseier, "L'eau potable à Genève").

31. www.hyflux.com (two desalination plants in Algeria, one in China, and two in Singapore).
32. Biswas and Tortajada, "Water Supply of Phnom Penh."

Part II

Normative Solutions to Water Inequality

Many Rational Units for Water

Introduction

WE HAVE JUST LOOKED at a number of themes we can use in "thinking" potable water ethically—for example, globality, vulnerability, poverty, and human dignity.

We need to add some others that can approach this vital natural resource of potable water in a rational way. Such concepts, which are actors in the world's public sphere affected by the potable water challenge, deserve special attention.

In my opinion, they were devised with the goal of raising water to the top of the values hierarchy.

Two Areas of Focus

I have selected two areas of which we need to be aware: first, the asymmetry between rich and poor countries, and second, the fear of conflicts that might break out in cases of water stress.

I feel that illustrating these two areas of focus as follows is justified.

First of all, industrialized societies feel called upon to address the daily challenges faced by a continually growing fraction of the world's population that must grapple with unbearable insecurity, especially with regard to water. These societies cannot be unaware of the fact that the economic divide between the so-called democratic countries and the so-called failed states is widening.

To express this rather schematically, the former meet the criteria for the rule of law, while the latter still find themselves—to borrow an idea developed by Hobbes and revisited by Locke, Pufendorf, Kant, and Rousseau—in "the natural state of mankind."

The former have constitutions, laws, and regulations that are supposed to ensure access to potable water for those they govern, while the second do not have adequate systems of governance that could thwart attempts to corrupt local officials. It is important to note that, empirically speaking, this is one of the main causes of the lack of financial resources for building the infrastructure needed to achieve universal access to potable water.

The second area of focus is generated by worries that conflict will break out over water, a fear that is recognized and acknowledged in the expression "water wars."

Though some studies on this topic appeared as early as the 1980s, an event in Cochabamba, Bolivia in 2000 was widely reported and catapulted the issue of water and its privatization onto the world stage. Residents of this city rebelled against a water price increase imposed by an American multinational corporation. The higher rates benefited a licensed water service provider that had not been able to make the service profitable without excessively penalizing the affected residents. The World Bank had to intervene and the transnational company had to leave the country to bring the conflict to an end.

It must be noted that this is far from being the only such occurrence in "failed" states. It is tied in particular to the fact that governments ask companies to take over a public utility that has allowed the infrastructure to deteriorate. Even companies that keep their profit margins reasonable for ethical reasons have to raise water prices. However, it is clear that such an increase must be done transparently, after consulting the local population, and with actual costs being taken into account.

The Cochabamba incident made a lasting impression, with the challenge of potable water receiving considerable media attention. We will come back to this critical issue of water privatization later,[33] and attempt to better understand the stakes involved.

A New Role for Civil Society

What is striking about the formulation of the two areas of focus—disparities between the rich and poor and the fear of water wars—is the ever-increasing role that civil society[34] means to play where water is concerned, even though such issues are of global import. It is true that such involvement by citizens from around the world is not new, if we remember their success in pushing for the 1997 signing of the Ottawa Treaty

33. See Part IV, Chapter III.

34. Leclerc-Olive, *"Les notions de société civile."* In her pitch for the colloquium, Michèle Leclerc-Olive uses two meanings of this polysemous idea from the political vocabulary. I have chosen the most restrictive here: "Some contemporary authors see it as, if not a synonym, at least a concept that is related to or complements that of the public sphere. Others use it more restrictively to mean associations or groups that do not fall within the political and economic realms, are 'neither prince nor merchant.' Attempts to bring some order to these meanings and multiple usages are themselves a subject of debate."

banning antipersonnel mines. As the coalition's crowning moment of success, Judy Williams and the ICBL were even awarded the Nobel Peace Prize in September 1997.

It is also apparent that, like NGOs, individuals are being encouraged by the United Nations to mobilize for the cause of water. The UN started a water campaign called the International Decade for Action Water for Life 2005-2015—a call that was heard by the churches that signed the Ecumenical Declaration on *Water As a Human Right and a Public Good* in 2005[35] and by the World Council of Churches in 2006 in its *Statement on Water for Life*.[36]

One of the tasks that civil society has tackled is to seek or even invent new predicates for water. To clarify, I am taking the meaning of "predicate" here in its etymological sense of "that which is said" or "that which is declared."

---

35. See internet reference in the bibliography.
36. See internet reference in the bibliography.

Chapter I

Is The Human Right to Water An Ethical Normativity or a Legal One?

A Global Potable Water Ethic

I HAVE A FEELING that with the human right to water, people are dreaming of good and of a kind of universal justice, with the goal being that everyone can have equal access to enough potable water of sufficient quality to meet their essential needs and provide for their well-being.

These words hide so many concepts of philosophy and moral philosophy! Even merely attempting to cover them all would be a huge challenge. Nevertheless, as I stated in the general introduction, I propose to give a sort of summary with the help of the concept of a *global potable water ethic,* which I will use here and there, and then put into a table at the very end of our journey.[1]

As a preliminary, I feel it necessary to call to mind the distinction between ethics and morality. The literature on this topic is quite extensive, but most of it goes back to Aristotle's *Nichomachean Ethics* and Immanuel Kant's *Metaphysics of Morals.*[2]

To cite Aristotle on moral virtue (êthos, "character"):

> [. . .] while moral virtue comes about as a result of habit, whence also its name *(ethike)* is one that is formed by a slight variation from the word *ethos* (habit).[3]

Kant rationalizes morality to the extreme, as summarized by Denis Müller.

> [. . .] Kant's plan [is] to construct a metaphysics of morals, that is, a moral theory independent of any descriptive anthropology, dogmatic theology, or physics. Kant's rationalism also drives him to seize upon freedom of will and the moral law within the strict framework of reason's possibilities. The ethical

---

1. See Part VI, last interview.
2. Kant, *Fondements,* and Kant, *Métaphysique des mœurs II.*
3. Aristote, *Métaphysique,* book 2, section 1.

subject is established as unconditional freedom confronted with the universal requirements of the categorical imperative.[4]

In my opinion it is difficult to thoroughly grasp the subtleties of this distinction between ethics and morality without philosopher Paul Ricœur's original contribution. He simply puts it into context to bring out what is of practical interest.

Here is his demonstration.

First, in *Oneself as Another*,[5] he refers to the two sources mentioned above, the Aristotelian legacy for the good at which an action aims ("a *teleological* perspective"[6]) and the Kantian legacy "where morality is defined by the norm's nature of obligation, and thus by a *deontological* point of view."[7]

Then, in his lecture at the Centre Pompidou in 2000,[8] entitled "De la morale à l'éthique et aux éthiques" [From morality to the ethical and ethics], he further postulated that morality is the crux of the matter. According to him, it has a double function: from an objective or external point of view, it indicates the principles of what is allowed and forbidden; and, from a subjective or internal point of view, it places Man, as an autonomous subject, in relation to the norm that is set. Man would then be designated as "capable of recognizing in the norms a legitimate aim of regulating behaviors."[9]

This is what I myself, as a legal expert, call "the law," which I as the subject must obey otherwise the authority or government power can punish me by handing down civil, criminal, or administrative penalties. Now a philosopher or moralist understands morality as being "obligatory" for the subject, so for him it is a question, as an autonomous being, of submitting to duty in the Kantian sense.

At the above-mentioned conference in Paris, Ricœur continued his development of the distinction between morality and an ethic by noting that we use ethic to designate both a "metamorality," a sort of "second-degree reflection on norms, and also practical mechanisms that invite us to make the word 'ethic' plural in meaning and add a complement to the term, as when we speak of medical ethics, legal ethics, business ethics, etc."

In my opinion, Ricœur's argument legitimizes the adoption of the concept of a *global water ethic*, which could be created as one ethical sphere among others.[10] After all, he does say that we "need such a divided, fragmented, scattered concept of the ethic," an ethic that could "split in two" to bring to light two new ethics, described

---

4. Müller, "Morale," 951.
5. Ricœur, *Soi-même comme un autre*.
6. Ibid.
7. Ibid.
8. Ricœur, "De la morale à l'éthique et aux éthiques."
9. Ibid., 3.
10. My suggestion of this metaphor of the spheres for ethics follows the example of the spheres of justice described in: Walzer, *Spheres of Justice*.

as anterior or posterior—or, more metaphorically, as ethics that are upstream and downstream of a "realm of norms."[11]

While we must all, again according to Ricœur, "still turn to Aristotle's Nicomachean ethics, and those of Spinoza, Hume, Kant and Bonhoeffer"—with reference to the anterior ethic—, which are "pointing to the embeddedness of the norms in life and in desire," we also need a "posterior ethic that aims to insert norms into concrete situations," the content of which falls "on the level of practical wisdom."[12] Obviously, I would consider a *global water ethic* to be a posterior ethic according to Ricœur's definition.

As things stand, the debate about potable water, which is also called a foodstuff,[13] was opened nearly four decades ago on multiple fronts at the international, regional, and local levels. That is why legal experts and economists have already suggested norms in the form of treaties, laws, and ordinances, which have been implemented with good results in some countries but ignored by others; institutional divisions can be considered one of the major factors in unequal access to potable waters.

A prudential path opens before us, that of seeking to learn what practical wisdom can guide mankind in the context of the challenges of potable water, today, so that we know not only *how we can do things right*[14] with respect to this unpredictable vital resource, but also and especially how to anticipate potential conflicts through appropriate norms that have yet to be reformulated.

A Potable Water Ethic Crystallizes in the Human Rights Corpus

The concept of a human right to water was born on July 28, 2010, at a session of the UN General Assembly. I am duly noting that here, and in the course of this text I will not fail to come back to the circumstances that led up to this resolution, which was passed by a majority vote of 122 to 41.[15]

As the language of "the rights of Man" increasingly slips into the "vernacular,"[16] it is disturbing to hear one "of our greatest legal philosophers,"[17] Professor Michel Villey, explain the reasons for his skepticism about the concept of "rights of Man" in general which, in this work, we will more often see in its guise of *human rights*.

11. Ricœur, "De la morale à l'éthique et aux éthiques," 1.
12. Ibid., 2.
13. See Ordonnance du 23 novembre 2005 du Département fédéral [suisse] de l'Intérieur sur l'eau potable, art. 1, which indicadtes, "This ordinance specifies the following foodstuffs and sets requirements for how they are labeled and advertised: a. potable water; b. spring water; c. natural mineral water; d. artificial mineral water; e. carbonated water."
14. Fuchs, *Comment faire pour bien faire?*
15. Resolution A/RES/64/292.
16. Moyn, *The Last Utopia, Human Rights in History*.
17. Tribute on the cover page of Villey, *Le droit et les droits de l'homme*.

Part II: Normative Solutions to Water Inequality

Four quotations from his book entitled *Droit et les droits de l'homme* [Law and the rights of Man][18] force our thoughts so far out of the linguistic comfort zone in which we are used to nestling that they should leave us with something to think about. In reality, we must face the facts: this is an astonishing indictment against the very concept of human rights.

These excerpts from the work in question put forward three increasingly blunt hints: first, that of ignorance of the scope of language's values and of its structure; next, the frequency of unkept promises; and finally, a break with justice.

Let us take a look at these four disturbing passages:

1. It is not certain that there is any reason for the current semantic shift of the word ["]right["] other than our ignorance [. . .]. Is it possible to mix these two ideas of *man* in the singular, the generic nature of Man, and the notion of *right*, without contradiction?[19]

2. Their harm (that of the rights of Man) lies in that they *promise* too much: equal life, culture, health for all . . . a heart transplant for every cardiac patient? Every French citizen's right to "Health" alone would be sufficient to drain the French government's entire budget, a hundred thousand times over![20]

3. [. . .] another poor excuse for legal literature is the Universal Declaration of Human Rights.[21] [. . .] Generally a solution for the inhumanity of a right that has cut its ties to justice.[22]

4. Each of Man's supposed rights is the negation of other rights of Man, and when applied separately, generates injustices.[23]

Villey gives many examples of the contradictions in human rights programs,

[. . .] such as the "right to security" [which] will never be more than empty words if appropriate measures are not taken [. . .] to give the police more options for action and limit the protections guaranteed to persons answerable to the law.[24]

Are these last two quotations, which really must be described as pugnacious, powerful enough to cause the whole well-constructed edifice of the human rights corpus to totter?

---

18. Villey, *Le droit et les droits de l'homme*.
19. Ibid., 21–22.
20. Ibid., 11.
21. Ibid., 9.
22. Ibid.
23. Ibid., 13.
24. Ibid.

At the very least, they could and we cannot be indifferent to them, because what is at stake is one of the most fundamental values of all societies: justice.

Must we follow Michel Villey's lead in considering the rights of Man to be ambiguous, with some being a solution for injustice while others create it? Must we conclude from this that the new human right to water is not necessarily a solution to injustice, but can be suspected of being a sham?

Throughout this dissertation, I will be attempting to counter this premise, which seems to me to be . . . too unjust. My goal will be to gain a clearer understanding by analyzing the words and concepts surrounding the problem of potable water—namely, their meanings and import.

The Question Is Left Open for the Moment

It seems to me that at this stage, answering the question in the title of this chapter as to whether the normativity of the "human right to water" is ethical or legal would be premature.

As it stands, what we can remember is that the human right to water is a norm that ought to have justice rather than utility as its end. To once again quote the words of Michel Villey, which hold more than a hint of cynicism,

> We are not forgetting the rights of Man are "operational"; that they are useful to the champions of excellent causes [and] act as protection from abuses by the government and from the arbitrariness of "positive law." If, against all odds, this term were eliminated from our vocabulary, it would have to be replaced by another less inadequate term, we know not which. That is our problem.[25]

---

25. Ibid., 14.

Chapter II

Scientific Normativity for Water

The Water Footprint[1]

IN HIS PRESENTATION AT the first W4W colloquium, François Münger, the Swiss representative of the Department of Development and Cooperation (DDC), sketched out the potential of this new indicator that could help avoid wasting water.[2]

He noted that the Swiss Federal Department of Foreign Affairs, of which the DDC is a part, has begun using the "water footprint" (or virtual water) principle developed by Arjen Hoekstra of the Netherlands.

In cooperation with the WWF,[3] the DDC did an extensive study on the issue in which the water footprint is defined as follows.

> The water footprint is a measure of water consumption that can be calculated for an individual, a company, a city, or a country. It covers direct consumption (water used for drinking or cleaning) and indirect consumption (production of goods and services). This second category is called "virtual water."[4]

An article published by the DDC on its website on March 12, 2012, entitled "L'empreinte sur l'eau de la Suisse pour la première fois mesurée" [Switzerland's water footprint measured for the first time], gave the following examples. It takes

> 1,300 liters of water to produce one kilo of wheat, 5,000 liters for a kilo of cheese, and 15,400 liters for a kilo of beef.[5]

There is no doubt that this new concept was inspired by the "ecological footprint" invented by Mathis Wackernagel of Basel, which covers the idea of human pressure on natural resources and took the world by storm with its especially vivid image of

---

1. Hoekstra, *Water Footprint*.
2. Münger, *"Les défis de l'eau [Do Water's Challenges Require Mobilization?]."*
3. WWF is the acronym for the World Wildlife Fund.
4. Department of Development and Cooperation (DDC Switzerland) and WWF *"Etude de l'empreinte hydrique Suisse,"* 6.
5. Swiss Agency for Development and Cooperation (SDC) and WWF. *"L'empreinte sur l'eau de la Suisse pour la première fois mesurée."*

consumption measured in terms of planets. The metaphor of our footprint on the planet is used to

> [. . .] express the number of planets needed to support a given population, if its lifestyle and consumption were applied to the world's entire population.[6]

The goal of the in-depth study that Wackernagel and Rees[7] devoted to this new concept was to help the public, and consequently politicians, to understand that the myth of a separation between humanity and nature could be fatal. The authors do not deny that the updated instrument aims to educate everyone so people will accept that we are only a "subsystem of the ecosphere":

> [. . .] human beings are embedded in nature. This premise is so simple that it is usually forgotten or set aside as being too obvious to be relevant. Yet taking this obvious statement seriously leads to some fearsome conclusions. [. . .] If humanity is part of the fabric of nature, then the "environment" is no longer just a backdrop, but itself becomes the subject of the play. The ecosphere is the place where we live; humanity depends on nature and not the other way around. Sustainability requires that we shift our focus from managing resources to managing *ourselves*, that is, learning to live as a part of nature. Finally, the economy becomes human ecology.[8]

Like any concept, the water footprint has its ardent supporters and its detractors, which I will not go into here. Concerning the abovementioned article published on the DDC's website in March 2012, I will simply observe that it gave special attention to the importation of products from countries suffering from water stress.

> The DDC and WWF, in cooperation with the interdepartmental group IDANE Wasser, have issued the first report on Switzerland's water footprint. Finding: Eighty-two percent of the water needed to produce all the goods and services consumed in our country comes from abroad. The report stresses Switzerland's co-responsibility for sustainable management of water at the global level and establishes a series of recommendations.
>
> According to the researchers who participated in the study, taking steps to limit the importation of goods and services from water-stressed areas would be a mistake. Indeed, the populations of these regions often are poorer than those in water-rich countries. Boycotting their products would make their living conditions worse without providing a sustainable solution to their water problem.
>
> On the other hand, local stakeholders must move toward sustainable management of their water resources, and Switzerland can support them, especially through its cooperative programs. [. . .] The DDC feels that

---

6. Wikipedia, "Empreinte écologique."
7. Wackernagel and Rees, *Notre empreinte écologique*.
8. Ibid., 25.

Switzerland should also continue to be involved, whether on the level of international political dialogue or by looking for innovative solutions to help manage our planet's most precious asset sustainably.[9]

IWRM,[10] or "Thinking" Water in Governance Terms

Switzerland is very heavily involved in the Global Water Partnership and has helped develop another concept, IWRM, which aims to ensure that water is used in the most appropriate and sustainable way possible, whether in households or in nature, agriculture or industries, or for power or transport.[11]

In its "Water 2015" report, the DDC defined this concept as follows.

> Integrated Water Resources Management (IWRM) is a process that promotes the coordinated development and management of water, land and related resources in order to maximise economic and social welfare in an equitable manner without compromising the sustainability of vital ecosystems. (Source: TAC Background Papers no. 4 GWP) IWRM has to be applied through a complete rethinking of water management—putting human at the center.[12]

This statement of the concept deserves two comments, in my opinion.

First, it makes human beings a priority, a development that should not only be mentioned but applauded, because without this axiological priority there would still be a risk that industry and agriculture would rise to the top of the political agenda, as François Münger states.[13]

So IWRM adds a truly ethical dimension to the challenges associated with water. At the same time, it takes into account human vulnerability, which we mentioned previously.

I think we could even consider making a radical change in our priorities, as IWRM suggests. I will bring this topic up later in the theological section under the label of "a change in direction," which Calvin called "repentance."[14]

My second comment is that IWRM is an avatar of the governance concept, which is very much in vogue at the moment and also includes CSR,[15] which itself was taken up in ISO[16] standard 2600 in 2010.

---

9. Swiss Agency for Development and Cooperation (SDC) and WWF, ibid.

10. IWRM is the acronym for Integrated Water Resources Management.

11. Münger, ibid.

12. Department of Development and Cooperation (DDC Switzerland). *"Water 2015, Policy Principles and strategic guidelines for integrated water,"* 9.

13. Münger, ibid.

14. See Part V, Chapter II, Repentance and Works.

15. CSR is the acronym for Corporate Social Responsibility.

16. ISO is the acronym for the International Standardization Organization, which has its

This concern for better governance in general, and better governance of water in particular, is shared by many other entities besides those mentioned above, on an undeniably global scale. More specifically, I am thinking of the OECD[17] and the Global Compact, an initiative of former UN Secretary-General Kofi Annan.

To a significantly increasing degree it is also—and this must be stressed—civil society's prerogative.

Indeed, I note with great interest that in both the West and the East, there are some very vocal defenders of the argument that the twenty-first century may see the emergence of a better-governed and therefore more sustainable society, especially in the post-2008 world, which has survived a serious economic and financial upheaval that some have compared to the crisis in the 1930s.

These words breathe such optimism, in contrast to the prevailing pessimistic mood, that they might almost be called prophetic. They describe a world that would have a chance to tie theory to reality and see to it that the sustainable development principles developed in the late twentieth century at major international gatherings, for example in Rio in 1992, become effective.

That is why authors such as Patrick d'Humières, in *Le développement durable va-t-il tuer le capitalisme?*[18] [Will sustainable development kill capitalism?], and Pankaj Ghemawat in *World 3.0*[19] are ready to wager that better governance is achievable, within both companies and governments.

Patrick d'Humières, a French sustainable-development expert, supports the concept of "eco-capitalism." Pankaj Ghemawat, a professor of economics who formerly taught at Harvard Business School and is now in Barcelona, suggested the idea of a "World 3.0," which has yet to be invented but is possible. He dreams of the day when the previous Worlds 0.0, 1.0, and 2.0 will be supplanted by this new world.

What a strange way to carve up human history! What does it mean? What does the economics professor say about it?

Ghemawat explains in a long overview of human history. World 0.0 is that of Thomas Hobbes's "state of nature," in which all of humanity found itself from about two hundred thousand years ago until 1648. World 1.0, which Ghemawat calls "walled," is the one that arose from the Treaty of Westphalia along with the concept of nations-states. Finally, World 2.0 is the current globalized world,[20] which economist Ghemawat says was in its infancy around the 1950s.

I do not intend to expand upon these two authors' ideas, which really would be a topic for an economics dissertation. However, their respective approaches, which encourage a paradigm shift, are worth mentioning. Their tone invites the reader to

---

headquarters in Geneva, Switzerland.

17. OECD is the acronym for Organisation for Economic Cooperation and Development.
18. D'Humières, *Le développement durable va-t-il tuer le capitalisme?*, 71.
19. Ghemawat, *World 3.0*.
20. Ghemawat, *World 3.0.*, 20.

contemplate the future with joy rather than fear. So their writings can be a source of inspiration and lead to some constructive thinking, in more ways than one.

Patrick d'Humières feels we must leave behind an old world that is too closed in on itself and enter a new era in which a revamped version of capitalism would see businesses adopting action criteria other than those ensuring that their stockholders' material interests are met.

For Pankaj Ghemawat, the issue is to revive a world in which globalization would not be seen as the cause of all the problems we are currently experiencing. While he acknowledges encountering frequent resentment toward this phenomenon, he hypothesizes that it is still mysterious and misunderstood. He believes it to be a myth, since the world is nowhere near as "flat" as Thomas Friedman[21] suggested in an international best-seller published in 2005. On the contrary, the Indian economist finds that the world is still not interconnected *enough*, and is even threatened by unwholesome protectionism.

Therefore, in his opinion, globalization needs to be built up further, because too many countries are focused inward on their own problems.

He does not fail to note with a touch of irony that Friedman's prose is unaccompanied by a single reference to scientific fact, but today's minds have found the lyricism that permeates the book's four hundred and fifty pages much too captivating and flattering. He goes so far as to quote La Fontaine's fable "The Wolf and the Fox" and its moral, a reminder of human weakness.

> We need not mock this simpleton
> For we ourselves such deeds have done
> Our faith is prone to lend its ear
> To aught which we desire or fear.[22]

I find it interesting to hear from Patrick d'Humières again. He says that indicators are favorable for businesses ranging from the smallest companies to multinationals to commit to seeing themselves more and more as agents of societal and political change.

> Demands for fairness are becoming increasingly insistent; [...] A responsible business must ask itself whether its direct or indirect activity in areas with "weak governance" or "outside the law" improves, maintains, or aggravates the situation of the people there. The corruption issue is of the same order. [...] The principle [...] is that a business that produces and sells everywhere in the world cannot remain indifferent to the development situation in which it is immersed and from which it benefits. [...] That is why the tools developed by international law, such as the OECD Code imposed on multinational companies and WTO agreements, and also voluntary sector-specific frameworks [...] are means of collective regulation where local government is weak.

---

21. Friedman, *The World is Flat*.
22. La Fontaine, *Le Loup et le Renard*.

These supranational mechanisms influence local practices. Even though they are not yet setting the rules that would be desirable for fair worldwide competition, businesses cannot completely ignore them. Ignoring them also leads to legal risks.[23]

I find that these two visionary and practical approaches are the product of a highly developed moral sense, an undeniable generosity that Pankaj Ghemawat's conclusion and quotation of Adam Smith's *Theory of Moral Sentiments* only confirms:

> [. . .] that to feel much for others, and little for ourselves, that to restrain our selfish, and to indulge our benevolent, affection, constitutes the perfection of human nature [. . .].[24]

The Subsidiarity Principle: A Chance for Better Governance?

As we have seen, a multitude of normative solutions for better local and global governance of renewable and non-renewable resources has been proposed by a number of international institutions.

What must be done so they can actually be implemented in the real world? Must higher authorities be responsible for everything?

Merely by asking this question, we answer it in the negative, and so turn the spotlight on civil society's role.[25]

In the sixteenth century, things were not so obvious. The very idea of something that would counterbalance the authorities, such as civil society, was in its embryonic stages, as shown by the whole history of the development of democracy.

It is to a sixteenth-century German Calvinist legal scholar that we owe the discovery of an innovative principle called "subsidiarity"—the repercussions of which have been felt all the way down to the Maastricht Treaty. This thinker was Johannes Althusius, who spent his whole life in an

> incessant struggle in support of municipal autonomy and against interference by the princely powers.[26]

His political fight also extended to promoting *consociatio*, that is, "mutual commitments" by small groups within human society.[27]

Why not try to reinforce this subsidiarity principle in twenty-first century society?

---

23. D'Humières, ibid., 70–71.
24. Smith, *Traité des sentiments moraux*, 50, cited by Ghemawat, ibid., 334.
25. I take it in the restrictive sense, "neither prince nor merchant."
26. Miegge, "Althusius, Johannes," 20.
27. Ibid.

Part II: Normative Solutions to Water Inequality

In fact, I note that "subsidiarity" is about to emerge on two levels: that of non-governmental organizations networking with each other, which I will call "institutionalized subsidiarity"; and on an individual level within the iPhone and Android-tablet society, which I will call "spontaneous subsidiarity."

For example, on the first level of "institutionalized subsidiarity" I would place a promising lead that I will merely mention here. It arose in the wake of the 1992 international conference in Rio, which was careful to promote the role of public participation in natural resources management. An important colloquium on this topic titled "La participation du public et la gestion des ressources en eau: où en est le droit international?"[28] [Public participation and water resources management: Where do we stand in international law?] was held in Geneva in December 2013. Its specific goal was to underscore the potential of the 1998 Aarhus Convention and the 1999 London Protocol on Water and Health to the 1992 Convention on the Protection and Use of Transboundary Watercourses and International Lakes.[29]

What I call the second level, "spontaneous subsidiarity," is that of the individual who is completely free to express himself or herself on social networks, and who is doing so with growing boldness. Through this kind of self-expression, such individuals are actually newly empowering themselves.

Such power, intelligently exercised, can be used for the common good.

As an example of "bottom up" power that can help build ties for the kind of globalized World 3.0 advanced by Pankaj Ghemawat, I would like to cite the work done by an online media organization known as "Aqueduc.info".[30]

Its editor, Bernard Weissbrodt, does not stop at publishing articles and studies of notably high quality.[31] The article he chose to post online on October 15, 2013, which I quote below in a footnote, testifies to his caring and sense of responsibility. He is working, not to send unnecessarily maudlin messages, but to find witnesses from the very places where the countless difficulties related to inadequate governance of water are experienced.

I find such online testimony, which states the facts plainly but strongly, to be of the greatest interest.

The quality of this October 2013 article by Bernard Capo-Chichi of Benin shows that there are some Africans who are not only ready and willing to denounce government negligence with regard to water management, but also careful to advocate a radical change in how the relationship to water is viewed, which involves developing and sustaining cooperation with the stakeholders from everywhere that people live, from the family to the labor marketplace.

---

28. www.unige.ch/droit/eau.

29. Convention on Access to Information (Aarhus Convention) and London Protocol on Water and Health.

30. http://www.aqueduc.info.

31. Weissbrodt, *La Suisse et le droit à l'eau*.

CHAPTER II: SCIENTIFIC NORMATIVITY FOR WATER

Not without a touch of despair, he first laments a water shutoff in Dakar, Senegal, that lasted more than eighteen days and was metaphorically christened the "pipe crisis" *(crise du tuyau)*. After attributing this "disastrous" situation to inadequate governance for water, due largely to negligence and corruption, he wonders why Africans continue to either improvise in this area or put up with the problem, instead of acquiring the expertise necessary to overcome it.

But he is not about to throw in the towel. With humility and a touch of cynicism, he persists in believing in a better future, and that water-related professions will become more highly valued on his ancestral continent. He remains confident that the African saying "when your neighbor's house is burning, you must help him fight the fire" will overcome the temptation to leave the field clear for France or China to step in and solve the endemic water crises.[32]

32. Weissbrodt indicates,

> "Even aside from those who face the problem daily, water and power shutoffs are so frequent in African cities that they seem almost to have lost their front-page news value and become merely incidental. Are we to meet such events with nothing but indifference, even though the effects they have on people are turning out to be disastrous?
>
> Very few African cities, even capitals and large economic centers, escape this phenomenon that is so widespread on the continent. From Lagos through Cotonou, Lomé, Conakry, Bamako, and many others to Brazzaville, potable water shortages and power outages are beating all records for length and giving rise to mockery rather than anger. Better just to laugh it off, they say.
>
> The proof of this is in the anecdotes that have made the rounds on the continent. They use absurdity to illustrate the unease felt by users weary of the inevitable. Nigeria's electrical distributor, the National Electric Power Authority, only rarely responds to consumer requests, which has led its acronym, NEPA, to be viewed with derision through a reinterpretation as "Never Expect Power Again"!
>
> In Conakry, people were already used to pointing out the Republic's three "generals": General Water Shutoff, General Power Outage, and General Lansana Conté, the head of state. The last is no longer with us, but the other two have survived him. Running water and electricity continue to be rare commodities there. But jokes aside, most of the time these technically-induced shortages are caused by negligence, disorganization, and corruption.
>
> The African States have certainly made laudable efforts to supply their large cities with potable water, with the help of international institutions and cooperative entities. Sadly, these initiatives are often quickly crushed by a piecemeal approach and a flagrant lack of professionalism.
>
> Unfortunately, the supposed improvements in potable water coverage rates mentioned in many reports are laughable. The authors usually neglect to mention the huge losses due to deficient equipment. No matter what anyone says, access to potable water on the African continent remains a vain hope.
>
> The eighteen-day "pipe crisis" and the water shortage that resulted, to the great displeasure of half of Dakar's residents, shows how weak and inadequate potable-water management is both in Senegal and on the entire continent.
>
> Though salutary, France's intervention (at the express request of President Macky Sall) with the Senegalese government, which seemed to be struggling alone in the midst of general indifference on the part of its neighboring countries and friends, raises its share of questions. Why did Senegal lack the expertise needed to solve the

Part II: Normative Solutions to Water Inequality

In my opinion, this article highlights how necessary it really is for civil society in industrialized countries to "think" the entire water problem in a completely new way, in the context of political regimes that are voluntarily or involuntarily ignorant of the principles of the rule of law and of governance—or, worse yet, in the context of countries that remain perennially under the thumb of guerilla regimes.

This privileged civil society must be able to understand its role in terms of aid for a period of time that is as yet undetermined but should not continue beyond a few decades, if the development of education—especially via the Internet—meets expectations and changes the parameters.

Capo-Chichi's article mentions this appeal for help several times.

How can we fail to be moved by his wish that the problem of endless water shut-offs in Africa, and more particularly in Senegal, should not meet with total indifference, either in Africa or elsewhere?

This seems an opportune time to analyze some economic/political normativities.

---

problem of a broken water pipe? Why were the other African countries—especially giants Nigeria and South Africa—conspicuous by their silence? Why was no appeal made to nearby countries known for their water expertise, such as Morocco?

So we Africans would do well to be concerned about the fragility and precarious position of our respective countries in the face of water and power challenges. Or will we just give up and leave it up to France or China to save us from the outages and shortages? What then of the African proverb recommending that when your neighbor's house is burning, you must help him fight the fire?

In any case, Dakar's water crisis—and the feelings of shame, disgust, and revolt it elicits in us—serve to remind us that this resource cannot and should not be managed like some cash crop such as cotton, cacao, peanuts, or any other. But dealing with water differently than we do now means rethinking our behavior, knowledge, and skills at home and in school, at the market and in the workplace. And it is especially important to train men and women in all water-related professions to say no to negligence, Band-Aid solutions, and resignation. Otherwise, the future may hold very unpleasant and perhaps deadly surprises for us." Weissbrodt, "Dakar sans eau."

Chapter III

Economic/Political and Legal Normativities for Water

Introduction

Predicates for Potable Water

IN THE 1970s[1] WATER began to be one of the major challenges of sustainable development, a new concept later defined at the 1992 United Nations summit in Rio de Janeiro, Brazil, that is broken down into three areas of concern: environmental, economic, and social.

Water happens to be implicated in each of these components of the sustainable development concept. For example: as a natural resource, water is part of the environmental realm; as an essential resource it comes under the social sector, and as a basic resource for agriculture, food production, industry, and leisure, it falls within the economic sphere.

Of course, in practice this assignment of water to three distinct and therefore theoretical conceptual spheres is not a perfect match. While it does not seem terribly difficult to place water used for industry and leisure in the economic sphere, water used for agriculture comes under both the social and economic spheres, and water used for food falls within all three—environmental, to ensure unpolluted potable water; social, to ensure that it is distributed at an affordable price; and economic, to ensure that waste is avoided and water is managed according to the principles of good governance.

So in the context of our relatively recent awareness of threats to the quality and quantity of potable water, it is not surprising that controversies have sprung up, pitting supporters of sustainable development who give priority to the environmental and social aspects of sustainability, against those who put the economic aspect first.

---

1. Reports of the United Nations Conferences on the Human Environment (Stockholm) and Water (Mar del Plata).

My role will be use Kantian logic[2, 3] to demonstrate that we can transcend these debates, at least potentially. I am actually postulating that not all of the predicates for water are necessarily mutually exclusive, as Aristotle's famous principle of non-contradiction would have it.[4]

Now, water can be anything and its opposite, as pre-Socratic philosopher Heraclitus of Ephesus noted about 500 BC.

> The sea is the purest and most polluted water: to fishes drinkable and bringing safety, to humans undrinkable and destructive.[5]

Its peculiar nature invites us to appreciate that the predicates for this natural resource can be taken as possibility (*problematical judgment*[6]) or as sufficient reason (*assertorial judgment*[7]), which allows me to hypothesize that all of the predicates for water proposed in the twenty-first century are therefore not necessarily true and exclusive of all the others (*apodictic judgment*[8]).

To illustrate this postulate, I have chosen to use two points of view developed between 1992 and 2005 by scientific and ecclesiastical authorities.

I am referring, respectively, to the Dublin Statement on Water and Sustainable Development issued in January 1992 in preparation for the Rio summit on sustainable development, and the Ecumenical Declaration on Water As a Human Right and a Public Good of 2005.[9]

Though at first sight the authors of these two statements seem to have opposite perspectives, since the former document introduced the new concept of water as an *economic good*,[10] both aim to raise awareness among all the world's people of the challenges they must take up in order to have a better life, or, to express it more powerfully,

---

2. Kant indicates, "We are able therefore to lay down three principles as the universal merely formal or logical criteria of truth, namely: 1. *The Principle of Contradiction and of Identity* [. . .] by which the intrinsic possibility of a cognition is determined for *problematical* judgments; 2. *The Principle of Sufficient Reason* [. . .] as material for *assertorial* judgments; 3. *The Principle of Excluded Middle* [. . .] [for] *apodictic* judgments." Kant, *Logique*, 58.

3. Ibid.: "Opinion is a *problematical*, Belief an *assertorial*, and Knowledge an *apodictic* judging. For what I hold merely as an opinion, this in judging I consciously regard as only *problematical*; what I believe, I regard as *assertorial*, not however as objectively, but as subjectively necessary (valid only for me); finally, what I *know*, I regard as *apodictically certain*, that is, as universally and objectively necessary (valid for all); supposing even that the object itself to which this certain assent relates were a mere empirical truth." Kant, *Logique*, 119.

4. Aristotle indicates, "This, then, is the most certain of all principles, since it answers to the definition given above. For it is impossible for any one to believe the same thing to be and not to be [. . .]." Aristote, *Métaphysique*, 153.

5. Heraclitus, *Fragments*, 95–96.

6. Kant, *Logique*.

7. Ibid.

8. Ibid.

9. Ecumenical Declaration.

10. Dublin Statement. See internet reference in the bibliography.

to take human dignity into account. That is the real challenge of a global water ethic, as Professor François Dermange noted with relevance at the first W4W colloquium on the ethics of water, held March 22, 2011. On that occasion, he exclaimed,

> The ethics of water is not a question of water, but one of human dignity.[11]

So the way to achieve this goal is better water management, with fairness and sustainability representing the problem's ethical criteria.

It is not for me to convince one side or the other of the relevance of its semantic choices or phrasing, but I do need to raise three points.

First, regardless of the predicates humans attach to water, it is and will remain an odorless, transparent liquid with many properties, such as the ability to freeze and become ice, to fall on the earth as rain, to spread and move in rivers and seas, or to be mysterious and invisible in aquifers.

Second, these many concepts attest to the variety of approaches, to inklings of the multiple possibilities offered by freedom of thought, and also to the real work being done in pursuit of the goal just mentioned: human dignity.

Third, and finally, the various intuitions each of the parties brings out through the intermediary of predicates are of vital importance if water's challenges are to be taken seriously in the twenty-first century by individuals and by political, social, and economic entities. These intuitions are also likely to reveal to everyone the complexity of the issue and the need to find a dynamic, constructive approach.

In my opinion, these are the ingredients needed for a potable water ethic, understood here in its axiological role.

I have looked to philosopher Immanuel Kant for the keys to understanding concept creation. If I have understood him correctly, one could say that the churches, the UN, and the WMO's[12] group of experts have sought—via the various formulas and concepts they have selected for water (human right, common good, public good, private good, economic good)—to find a rational unit that could make their intuition more readily understandable.

In other words, the conceptual predicates for water adopted by these various institutions help us to understand intuitions that otherwise would remain blind, as Kant's apothegm thunders:

> [t]houghts without contents are empty; intuitions without concepts are blind.[13]

Now I will ask the question. Very simply, are not these concepts all excellent vehicles for encouraging or even forcing us to "think" water—and, while we are at it, to set things in motion and therefore mobilize for better justice for water?

---

11. Dermange, "Le pôle justice sociale [The Social Justice Focus]."
12. WMO is the acronym for the World Meteorological Organization.
13. Kant, *Critique de la Raison pure*, 77.

Part II: Normative Solutions to Water Inequality

Why not suppose that the UN, with its International Decade for Action Water for Life 2005-2015 was crying out a warning, even a resounding appeal, *"urbi et orbi"*—as an imperative to take up this huge challenge of potable water for everyone? For my part, I suggest that this appeal be formulated as follows.

> Start thinking water! Follow Pascal, for whom thinking well is the very principle of morality.[14]
>
> Before your very eyes, large numbers of human beings struggle daily to survive because of too much or not enough water. Scientists are working to provide you with the sensitive data and communicate them to you on the Internet. So start thinking water, not just within the confined setting of your own territory, but for the whole planet, because we live in a globalized world.
>
> The ball is now in your court, that of the thinkers, then of the doers. Who will pick it up?

Why should we fail to make use of such a tool? Why should we hesitate to reach out our hand and take it? Why not explore the complexities of an intellect affected and moved by the many representations of water in a globalized world? According to Kant it is understanding, as an *a priori* form of the mind, that can enable us to think the object of the intuition:

> What enables us to *think* the objects of our sensuous intuition is the *understanding*[15] (emphasis added).

So let us take a look at how water, this object of intuition, has filled an intellectual space reshaped by globalization and rethought by way of a whole procession of diverse and sometimes antinomic concepts (as just mentioned), some classic and some new.

Of course, the choice of predicates is not a matter of chance. It is dictated by an intent or an ethical preference. So I will now turn my thoughts to a sort of hermeneutics of predicates as values, because, as Christophe Gérard notes in an in-depth study on the hermeneutics of value according to Louis Lavelle,

> [. . .] every value implies the existence of a *difference* [. . .]. More specifically, understanding the value implies the existence of two *poles* [. . .] it always necessarily involves some form of preconceived notion.[16]

However, Gérard adds, such a preconceived notion has an impact, because it

> [. . .] directs its object's future in the present of an interpretation.[17]

It is this possibility of turning toward the future that lends its power to the two statements we will now discuss.

---

14. Pascal, Thought no 347.
15. Kant, *Critique de la Raison pure*, 77.
16. Gérard, "Herméneutique de la valeur (1)," 121.
17. Ibid.

Chapter III: Economic/Political and Legal Normativities for Water

Water As a Human Right and As the 1992 Dublin Statement's *Economic Good*

When it was readily available without limitations, water for a long time could be described as a free good. Because of its abundance, it has also long been considered a good of low value, as Adam Smith found in *The Wealth of Nations* with his famous diamond metaphor: water is necessary but without value; diamonds are not necessary but have a high value in exchange.

So what factor led to the emergence of the new predicate attached to water in 1992, namely *economic good*?

It was unquestionably the phenomenon of scarcity as exposed in the case of the Aral Sea, which was on the verge of drying up. A new reality was emerging: water was no longer infinitely available like air and wind.

The moment that a good becomes difficult to acquire is the moment that economic theory enters the picture. As water becomes scarce, we have no choice but to call it an economic good, taking into account the three classic criteria in economics as revisited by Samuelson in 1954:[18] divisibility, rivalry, and excludability.

Water is in fact divisible, since it can be held within a container such as a bucket, tank or pool, and when it becomes scarce, it is the object of rivalry and disputes (for example, a fight over the use of a well in the desert). It is also excludable, in the sense that anyone who does not help obtain it will get none, except by asking for charity.

This is how water was viewed by the WMO representatives who met at the UN's International Conference on Water and the Environment in Dublin in January 1992 in preparation for the June 1992 Rio conference on sustainable development. They considered that the predicate "economic good" would help with efforts to keep water from being wasted, especially in agriculture.

These five hundred experts were appointed by over a hundred countries and eighty international organizations and NGOs. They sent a recommendation to the world leaders meeting in Rio de Janeiro in June 1992 for the United Nations Conference on Environment and Development, alerting them to water's challenges from a sustainable development standpoint.

Having duly taken note of the earth's alarming water situation, the conference adopted four principles, the fourth of which stated that water was to be recognized as being simultaneously a "human right" and an "economic good."

> Within this principle, it is vital to recognize first the basic right of all human beings to have access to clean water and sanitation at an affordable price. Past failure to recognize the economic value of water has led to wasteful and environmentally damaging uses of the resource. Managing water as an economic

---

18. Samuelson, "The Pure Theory of Public Expenditure."

good is an important way of achieving efficient and equitable use, and of encouraging conservation and protection of water resources.[19]

The concept appears to have been born of "the depletion and degradation [of copious supplies of cheap water] caused by past profligacy."[20]

This fourth principle is expected to change the mentality of water users and encourage them to assign a value to this natural resource. In the case of scarcity cited above, the hope would be that farmers would reconsider how they use river water, for example, from the Syr Darya and Amu Darya Rivers, which flow into the Aral Sea. Would they then have to be forced to stop growing cotton, a crop that is water-intensive but ensures their prosperity? This is a serious dilemma.

The adversarial principle is intended to allow the opposing party to speak, following the constitutional principle of the right to be heard. Now it is time to devote some space to the churches' viewpoint.

Water As a Human Right and Public Good, Especially as Expressed by the Churches' 2005 Ecumenical Declaration[21]

The 2005 Ecumenical Declaration on *Water As a Human Right and a Public Good*[22] is of interest on two counts. First, it presents the ethical problem of human relationships to water into a single document; second, it raises the question of what methods can be used to meet water needs. By taking a position in support of public management of water, it chose one model among several, as we will see below.

To summarize briefly, the churches' statement initially conceptualizes potable water through the eyes of law and justice, then later risks a step toward economic and political issues associated with good governance and responsibility.

Part III will give the issue of "water as a human right" a prominent place. In it I will examine the churches' choice of "water as a public good."

In reality, I find that the church authorities did not make a real choice between water managed by the public sector and that managed by the private sector; rather, they simply confined themselves to the Swiss model of governance. Historian and economist Géraldine Pflieger, a Geneva professor and the author of a recent study on city water in Switzerland, sums up the prevailing attitude toward water policy in this European country. Here is what she has to say on the subject:

19. Dublin Statement.
20. Ibid., under the heading "Sustainable Urban Development."
21. We note that FEPS cosigned the Ecumenical Declaration on Water As a Human Right and a Public Good with its partners, the Swiss and Brazilian Conferences of Bishops, and Conselho Nacional de Igrejas Cristãs do Brasil, or CONIC (the National Council of Christian Churches of Brazil). See Ecumenical Declaration.
22. Not to be confused with the World Council of Churches "Statement on Water for Life of February 23, 2006."

Chapter III: Economic/Political and Legal Normativities for Water

[. . .] we are touching on the heart of the Swiss model: faith in the superiority of public management and fear of privatization.[23]

It is not up to me to approve or disapprove of the *public good* policy choice for water.

On the other hand, I do see the interest of doing a little study of this model: first, in order to better understand its goals; and second, to try to get a better grasp of why it was selected, particularly in Switzerland.

The Goals of a "Public Good" Predicate for Water

One of the obvious aims of a "public good" predicate for water is to ensure by means of government authority that people are supplied with potable water. So the criterion is public or state distribution of water, in contrast to distribution of the resource by private suppliers such as, for example, Veolia.

Does this predicate mean that water is free?

"Water as such has no price. The same is true of air and wind," stated Ambassador Benoît Girardin in an article published in the proceedings of the 2011 Workshop for Water Ethics colloquium.[24]

However neither the churches, nor Benoît Girardin for that matter, claims that water is free. The former recognize the need for governments to set a price for water, but it should be "affordable."[25] The latter gives reasons why water must cost something.

> (no. 2) What has a cost is harnessing and protecting the springs or any desalinization; conveying, distributing, and treating the water before it is used; and treating or recycling wastewater after use. This cost consists of infrastructures and their operation and maintenance, not forgetting research and development costs and insurance premiums for flood and erosion risks attributable to water's use and distribution [. . .].
>
> (no. 6) The ethical requirement for price consists in coming as close as possible to the true cost by revealing all components, even hidden ones, and avoiding the addition of exorbitant and unfairly selective profit margins. Any specifications developed by the local community would do well to limit this practice.[26]

---

23. Pflieger, *L'eau des villes*, 103.
24. Girardin, "L'eau a-t-elle un coût?"
25. Ecumenical Declaration, ibid.
26. Girardin, "L'eau a-t-elle un coût?"

Part II: Normative Solutions to Water Inequality
Historical Overview

In today's world, public authorities are called upon to offer their taxpayers high-quality, affordable water by means of increasingly sophisticated infrastructure, "as running water is becoming a status symbol."[27] Yet in the past, for a long time, even costly water supply systems did not hinder the public's free access to water, as the historical examples given below attest.

Take Bern, for example. Switzerland's capital boasts prestigious sites protected by UNESCO and flanked by magnificent, artistically sculpted fountains such as the Justice Fountain, the central column of which is topped by an eponymous allegorical figure wearing a blindfold, carrying scales, and brandishing a sword.

For its part Italy's capital, Rome, has been known for its famous aediculae since the Baroque period (sixteenth century), for example those at the Trevi Fountain, which is a major tourist attraction.

In the Eastern world, Byzantium was famous for its novel water-supply system. The gigantic underground Yerebetan cistern built by Emperor Justinian is still visible today.

These fountains and cisterns, while ensuring free access to water by all, were more than just utilitarian objects: they also rose to the status of artworks, for the greater benefit of city officials seeking more control and prestige. Hence the nobles of Bern prided themselves on hiring famous city planners, who enthusiastically strove to outdo each other in satisfying their masters. Pope Pius V managed to end the Eternal City's decay and ensure the Counter-reformation's success by having superb baroque fountains built, as art historian Katherine Wentworth Rinne[28] describes in a tone of realism tinged with humor in a fascinating reference work.

In contrast, modern facilities and infrastructure are not, strictly speaking, models of great art, thinking for example of the Geneva Prieuré building.[29] Still, it should be noted that before this building, in the same city, the monumental Bâtiment des Forces Motrices (BFM), or power plant building[30] was built on the Rhone river. Its main facade was decorated with sculptures representing Neptune, Ceres, and Mercury. This flamboyant edifice was eventually converted into a famous concert hall. An interesting side note is that to avoid dangerously high pressure in 1886, the water was diverted to create the original water jet fountain nearby. This idea was revisited some years later in the second Jet d'Eau, which today still rises to a height of 140 meters and lends an elegant touch to Geneva's harbor. It has even become the iconic symbol of this international city at Lake Geneva's end.

---

27. Pflieger, L'eau des villes, 16.
28. Wentworth Rinne, The Waters of Rome.
29. www.sig-ge.ch.
30. www.bfm.ch.

CHAPTER III: ECONOMIC/POLITICAL AND LEGAL NORMATIVITIES FOR WATER

Today's underground water distribution systems[31] are typically less noticeable, but the fact remains that their technological sophistication and scale are phenomenal. Even a modestly-sized building can hide incredible surprises, for example, the power plant in Frasnacht,[32] Switzerland, which supplies the city of St. Gallen with potable water from Lake Constance.[33]

Financing

It is interesting to note in this last example that water distribution systems can rely on both public and private investment. For example, the RWSG (Regional Wasserversorgung Sankt Gallen) company is responsible for distributing the water, while the city of St. Gallen holds 50 percent of the company's shares.

It is also relevant to clarify that although Switzerland has very widely adopted the public management system over more than a century, this type of management became established only after many political battles. Geneva is one of the last Swiss cantons to have finally opted for exclusively public service.[34]

---

31. Pflieger indicates, "Fluid and invisible, water has been flowing beneath our cities for nearly a hundred and fifty years." Pflieger, *L'eau des villes*, 11.

32. Frasnacht is near St. Gallen.

33. www.rwsg.ch (St. Gallen regional water supply company).

34. As a reminder, the people of Geneva decided in 1988 to entrust water management to the public sector (SIG). Previously, it had been handled by a private company, Société des Eaux de l'Arve. At that time, the price of potable water was set at 0.48 francs per m3 and the water treatment tax was 0.34 francs, while in 2011, the prices were 1.26 francs per m3 for water and 1.39 francs for the treatment tax.

The Société des Eaux de l'Arve company (1866–1988) indicates,"This water supply company has an unusual history, having been the only private water distribution company to have survived the transfer of such services to municipal control in Switzerland's principal cities in the late nineteenth century. The firm was created in the mid-1860s; its pumping station was built in Vessy, southeast of Geneva. At that time the demand for water was skyrocketing both in cities and across the countryside. Water was needed for firefighting, sprinkling roads (as yet unpaved), irrigation of gardens and farms, fountains, and daily household tasks. Relatively complex technical solutions were needed, namely elevators operated by hydraulic turbines which distributed the water through an extensive network of pipes. Despite their location on the shores of Lake Geneva, and the presence of the Rhone and many tributaries, the main part of the city of Geneva and most of the surrounding countryside are on higher ground and have few springs. Those that do exist dry up in the summer. Another challenge in the country is that water is needed to work the land.

The company's subscribers were spread across the Geneva countryside on a plateau located between the Arve River and the shores of Lake Geneva. It was pure chance that the firm escaped the municipalization movement. Geneva's municipal city water department was buying up private companies with an eye to making its powerful pumping station, which was built on the Rhone River between 1883 and 1886, turn a profit. Just when the rural private company's board of directors had decided to sell at the most opportune moment, a typhus [*sic*, read "typhoid"] epidemic broke out and was blamed on the waters of the Rhone. Consequently, the customers wanted to continue to be supplied with water from the Arve. They took control and refused to give in. So the growth of the Société des Eaux de l'Arve continued, fueled by urban expansion into some parts of its distribution area. When its license ended in 1988, the private company could no longer escape a buyout by Geneva's public utilities company,

Part II: Normative Solutions to Water Inequality

Géraldine Pflieger's very well-documented study, mentioned above, brings to life the heated debates that led up to the selection of public management. She feels that this decision was not a given right from the start, because

> [. . .] local, cantonal or national authorities also could have imposed their standards and control on the private distributors.[35]

Is not this assertion intended to completely discredit the statement that water management is by "nature intrinsically public"?[36]

Without jumping into the debate, the author of *Eau des Villes* displays a certain realism, even a certain political pragmatism, as she gives three possible motivations for the cities to "firmly"[37] reject the privatization of water management.

She believes that, of course, the cities saw two political advantages in this choice. The public powers could show how democratic they were, by first guaranteeing equal treatment among the users, and then "strengthening ties within a given area." Yet they were equally interested in securing revenues, as Géraldine Pflieger sees with impartial eyes (since she is French):

> [. . .] municipalities' financial interest in operating services of a commercial nature; [. . .] We should add that synergies among various services of a technical nature should allow for economies of scale.[38]

I believe this historical overview of water policy helps us to see more clearly that the challenges of water are truly local in nature and that management methods for this precious liquid can vary over time and from place to place.

No model seems an obvious fit for the entire planet, unless we want to risk globalizing a local problem instead of localizing a global problem,[39] as former WTO Director-General Pascal Lamy noted in a speech on February 19, 2011 at the European University Institute in Florence.

All of this begs the question as to whether the churches are justified in excluding all models other than public management, based on Switzerland's substantial and generally positive experience.

Of course, as a general rule the public authorities are the appropriate agent to distribute resources. The problem, as American philosopher Michael Walzer notes, is that in the end

---

SIG." The Société des Eaux de l'Arve company'webste: home.

35. Pflieger, *L'eau des villes*, 26.

36. Pfliger indicates, "[. . .] common good managed by the community to serve its residents [. . .]."Pfliger, *L'eau des villes*, 26.

37. Ibid.

38. Ibid.

39. Lamy, speech given at the European University Institute in Florence.

[g]roups of men and women will seek to monopolize and then to use the state in order to consolidate their control of other social goods.[40]

Hence the pressing need, as Walzer clarifies, to set limits on this power. A state under the rule of law does so effectively, as in the case of Switzerland, which has accepted limitations on its powers in a constitution that guarantees personal freedoms.

What happens to people living in a country with a dictatorial government that tramples its own citizens' interests underfoot, as described in the October 15, 2013 article from Benin discussing governance, which appears above[41] as a timely reminder? I feel that we ought to be able to consider an alternative model of governance, controlled privatization, when the government is unstable—but under the conditions stated earlier by Ambassador Benoît Girardin.

We will take this issue up again later, in the context of global responsibility.[42]

A Brief Comparison of the 2005 Ecumenical Declaration by the Churches and the 1992 Dublin Statement

The Dublin Statement is known for having generated the concept of water as an economic good, but it must be read in full to see that although in principle its viewpoints differ from those of the churches, there are many points of convergence.

First I will note that it would be a shame to confine ourselves to a superficial reading of these two texts, each of which in its own way shows evidence of deep convictions, conveyed by the extreme care with which the words were chosen.

Even though the forums in which the discussions by the churches and by the WMO experts took place had absolutely nothing in common, an observer cannot help noticing some striking similarities in the way these statements are formulated.

For example, I note that all of the participants were prompted by a noticeable desire to truly "think" the issue of water, and they all worked very hard to better understand its challenges and to try to gain a clear insight about the choices to make.

It should be stressed that the ecclesiastical context of the ecumenical document made it possible to highlight water's spiritual meaning, and the religious authorities have given real evidence of this in a few eloquent words.

> *Water is a force of faith*. Water is not only an economic commodity it also has a social, cultural, medical, religious and mystical value. In the story of creation we read that "the Spirit of God moved upon the face of the waters." (Gen.1.2). Through Moses God provided his pilgrim people in the desert with water. For us as Christians the symbolic force of water is found in baptism, "The one who believes and is baptized will be saved" (Mk.16.16). For many peoples and

---

40. Walzer, *Spheres of Justice*, 15.
41. See Part II, Chapter II, no. 2.
42. See Part IV, Chapter III, no. 3.

cultures water has a sacred significance and has value linked to its capacity to forge community and its ritual and traditional properties. [43]

I would like to raise two more points.

The first is the extreme care taken by the churches in describing water's challenges and looking to temporal institutions for the tools needed for universal water access.

For example, I note that they made an effort to "think water" by observing the various attacks it has suffered and the obstacles to the adequate use of it. They clearly showed the dangers that threaten the living conditions of "many human beings" if "high individual consumption, demographic growth, inadequate management, waste, lifestyle, and the destruction of forests, soil, and water reserves [do not receive] special attention." Even though they did not explicitly assign an axiological qualifier to these attacks, they were most likely thinking of the "evil" done to water.

The second is the fact that they refer to international institutions.

For example, already in the statement's preamble we read an expression of the need to refer to the United Nations. The churches mention its International Decade for Action "Water for Life" from 2005 to 2015.

Later, they draw support from the 1948 Universal Declaration of Human Rights and one of the two covenants associated with it, the 1966 International Covenant on Economic, Social and Cultural Rights (ICESCR).

Finally, after subscribing to the work of the UN's Committee on Economic, Social and Cultural Rights, namely its "General Comment No. 15,"[44] and also to that of the FAO in 2004,[45] they plead for the UN to "develop an international convention on water."

The statement issued by the five hundred WMO experts at the International Conference on Water and the Environment (ICWE)[46] appears as a sort of road map for "thinking" the most effective possible strategies for floating the water issue to the top of political agendas. It has all the earmarks of a systematic, technical approach like that taken by Agenda 21, the action plan that resulted from the work done at the 1992 Rio conference on sustainable development.

It must be noted, then, that the authors who crafted these two statements fully concurred with the need for international cooperation.

---

43. Ecumenical Declaration.
44. General Comment No. 15, The right to water.
45. FAO: Voluntary Guidelines.
46. Dublin Statement.

Chapter III: Economic/Political and Legal Normativities for Water

They also all understood that such cooperation does not work without participation by local communities,[47] and are now aware of the need to give women a say. That is why Principle 3 of the Dublin Statement[48] agrees with the churches' statement that

> [. . .] the problems and specific needs of women must be considered: in many countries woman (and children, particularly girls) bear the responsibility for providing water with consequences for women's health, through carrying heavy burdens, and for young girls who are thus prevented from attending school.[49]

Moreover, when I read the fourth Dublin principle,[50] I see no contradiction whatsoever with the Ecumenical Declaration on *Water As a Human Right and a Public Good* of 2005. In fact, the "economic" and "price" element for water occurs twice in the churches' document. It is true, the church authorities say, that "water is not only an economic commodity,"[51] but the State is to set "an affordable price for water."[52]

If I have correctly understood the churches' position, they reject a "privatization" principle for water,[53] and consequently, disapprove of having water distributed by private companies. On the other hand, they do not object to the scarcity criterion for water, which makes it an economic good for which users should pay a reasonable amount.

This nuance that the churches bring to the concept of water as an *economic good* must be emphasized. It attests to the legitimate concern they are expressing, namely that the rules of the market do not by any stretch of the imagination take into account what water can impart, first, to all living beings from an environmental standpoint; and second, to every human being from a social, spiritual, and cultural standpoint. The churches are right to speak of an *economic good* and not a *marketable good*, since water does not obey the principle of supply and demand as does, for example, oil. The idea of an *economic good* is broader, and in my opinion takes into consideration the many values I have just mentioned, besides price.[54]

---

47. Dublin Statement Principle 2 indicates, "Water development and management should be based on a participatory approach, involving users, planners and policy-makers at all levels"; the Ecumenical Declaration on Water As a Human Right and a Public Good (no. 2, §2) reads, "The State must take over the commitment to guarantee access to drinking water to all of the population. [This means] involving local councils and communities in decisions relevant to them on the use of available water resources." See Dublin Statement, ibid. and Ecumenical Declaration, ibid.

48. Dublin Statement Principle 3 indicates, "Women play a central part in the provision, management and safeguarding of water." See Dublin Statement.

49. Ecumenical Declaration.

50. Dublin Statement Principle 4 indicates, "Water has an economic value in all its competing uses and should be recognized as an economic good." Dublin Statement.

51. Ecumenical Declaration.

52. Ibid., no. 2, §2.

53. Ibid., no. 1, §1 and no. 3, §2.

54. Encyclopédie Larousse indicates: "The idea of an economic good is fairly broad: any product

Part II: Normative Solutions to Water Inequality

Inspired by Christiana Peppard, a Catholic theologian who participated in the second W4W colloquium on March 20, 2012, I would add that ultimately, water can in no way be limited by any economic definition, because it is in a class by itself, *sui generis*.[55] In other words, no one solution proposed for it is likely to be suitable for all of the contexts that must be taken into account.

In a word, we can do no more than discover and accept in our capacity as finite human beings that water is indeed a "matter of life and death."[56]

Water as a Common Good

Another of the many concepts on which we need to focus to achieve better water management is that of a *common good*.

The leading light in this area is Elinor Ostrom, winner of the 2009 Nobel Prize in economics. In particular, her study on the ancient canals *(bisses)* in Switzerland's Valais canton has made an indelible impression.

In *Governing the Commons, The Evolution of Institutions for Collective Action*,[57] this American economist undertakes an in-depth analysis of shared management of natural resources such as aquifers, lakes, irrigation canals, and dams.

Tragedy of the Commons, or Flexibility?

This work soon made its presence felt. Indeed, it refuted a doctrine that argued strenuously against the effectiveness of managing common goods, as espoused by Garret Hardin in "The Tragedy of the Commons."[58]

It is interesting to note that at the heart of Hardin's theory is the principle that

> [. . .] "what belongs to everybody ends up belonging to nobody" and generates behaviors such as "first come, first served"[59]

whereas Ostrom's approach undeniably offers flexibility for cooperation on water matters.

Ostrom demonstrates such flexibility through concrete examples. She has made field studies in Switzerland, Japan, Spain, and the Philippines that show as clearly as

---

intended to fill a need is considered to be an economic good. So all economic goods have a production cost and a price," Encyclopédie Larousse, *"Bien,"* and Fiechter-Widemann, *Eau comme droit humain*.

55. Peppard, *"Eau, besoin vital [Water, vital need]."*
56. Habel and Trudinger, *Water: A Matter of Life and Death*.
57. Ostrom, *Governing the Commons*.
58. Hardin, "The Tragedy of the Commons."
59. Calvo-Mendieta et al., "Patrimonial Economics and Water Management: A French Case," chapter 2.

one could wish that even though the systems used in the various countries are quite different, they have one thing in common.

What is this commonality?

It is the real commitment by private owners to shared ownership in order to manage the natural resource as effectively as possible, with personal investment being supported by an ability to adapt to extremely difficult natural conditions. Ostrom notes with genuine admiration how well those responsible for the upkeep of common goods have been able for centuries to withstand avalanches, floods, and other natural catastrophes.

> Ecological sustainability in a fragile world of avalanches, unpredictable precipitation, and economic growth is quite an accomplishment for any group of appropriators working over many centuries. Keeping order and maintaining large-scale irrigation works in the difficult terrain of Spain or the Philippine Islands have been similarly remarkable achievements.[60]

She also notes with some surprise that the systems are very reliable in terms of shaping the commons owners' behavior. In fact, very few violations of the established rules were seen.

So CPR (common-pool resource) is seemingly a miraculous solution, but is it an anachronistic one?

It is neither.

In fact, if it were Elinor Ostrom's goal to shed some light on effective management of common goods through success stories, in order to be credible she would also have to compare such cases to examples of less effective shared management of resources. These she found in Turkey, California, and Sri Lanka.[61]

She dismisses the objection that the shared management system for natural resources is a thing of the past, underscoring that these systems have lasted for centuries, which shows their ability to adapt to change.

> Netting dismisses the notion that communal ownership is simply an anachronistic holdover from the past by showing that for at least five centuries these Swiss villagers have been intimately familiar with the advantages and disadvantages of both private and communal tenure systems and have carefully matched particular types of land tenure to particular types of land use.[62]

When questioned as to whether the various institutions she had studied were applicable to Third-World countries, she unhesitatingly responded in the affirmative:

---

60. Ostrom, *Governing the Commons*, 60.
61. Ibid., 143–81.
62. Ibid., 63.

Part II: Normative Solutions to Water Inequality

> [...] the same design principles are relevant for solving CPR[63] problems in Third World settings. [...] the [case of the] *zanjera* institutions of the Philippines [...] provides a strong affirmative answer to this question.[64]

Her answer was all the more convincing because she based it on an exhaustive study of the *zanjeras*[65] system in the Philippines. The work presented practices that are still used (though the study does date from 1982) to provide enough irrigation for satisfactory plant growth.

As Westerners, we can only look on these practices with stunned amazement. Dams built by brute force using primitive materials such as sand, pebbles, banana leaves, and bamboo sometimes have to be rebuilt four times a year due to unpredictable, destructive flooding from the Bacarra-Vintar River.

R. Siy, the economist in charge of this study on commons in the Philippines,[66] did in fact ask the question as to whether these mechanisms were effective, and though he came up with different answers, he did comment on the high level of involvement of the *zanjeras* members, who were ready to work for nothing for more than two months a year to meet the community's water needs. He especially notes the importance of the rules set by the members themselves; any intervention by outside experts was a factor in failure to follow the rules.

> When external experts, working without the participation of the irrigators, have designed systems with the primary aim of achieving technical efficiency, they frequently have failed to achieve either the hoped-for technical efficiency or the level of organized action required to allocate water in a regular fashion or to maintain the physical system itself.[67]

In my opinion, the work by Elinor Ostrom and the experts with whom she surrounded herself in various parts of the world merits a great deal of attention. In view of the foregoing, then, the concept of shared water management is one that should not be ignored.

The Positions of Natural Resource Economists

Consideration of this option is exactly what natural resource economists have in mind, though they are aware of the theoretical pitfalls. The complexity of this issue is discussed in an article published by three researchers from the Centre National de

---

63. Ostrom indicates, "The term "common-pool-resource" refers to a natural or man-made resource system that is sufficiently large as to make it costly (but not impossible) to exclude potential beneficiaries from obtaining benefits from its use." Ostrom, *Governing the Commons*, 30.

64. Ibid., 61.

65. Ibid., 82–88.

66. Siy, *Common Resource Management*, cited by Ostrom, *Governing the Commons*, 82–88.

67. Ostrom, *Governing the Commons*, 88.

Recherche Scientifique (CNRS)[68] at the beginning of the twenty-first century, entitled *Entre bien marchand et patrimoine commun, l'eau au cœur des débats de l'économie de l'environnement:*

> Managing all these things efficiently is a considerable challenge and compels us to construct a mixed system of rules—some market oriented, some not, all intertwined.[69]

The authors admit the difficulty of making a connection, on a theoretical level, between a market-based system of logic and one based on a resource pool. However, they do acknowledge that in the field, water users can move into a deliberative process that favors better water management.

Elinor Ostrom emphasizes that the means by which such a process is carried out vary greatly and reflect the cultural and social characteristics of the people using it. I cannot deny myself the pleasure of summing up a few passages from her study of the association's by-laws that the commons owners of the tiny Valais village of Törbel[70] signed all the way back in 1483, concerning the use of common goods such as alpine pasture, forest, and water rights.[71]

I myself believe in the virtues of encouraging individuals to take responsibility, which can be done by associations and other cooperative structures. My visit to a South African village convinced me of this; its highlights will be reported in this work's final Part.

We can see that in the case of potable water, we truly are dealing with shared local resources and with local management—a far cry from globalization!

Here I am pleased to cite Mireille Delmas-Marty, who is also very favorable to the "common goods" approach:

> [. . .] reference to the criterion of common good(s) [. . .] both in the singular and the plural, would make it possible to ensure protection that would not be limited to the safeguarding of present and future human generations.[72]

Conclusion

In the foregoing chapters I have introduced a number of concepts that developed in connection with the potable water issue. This should raise, if not doubt, at least discussion, about what political choices to make in order to gain truly universal access to potable water.

68. Calvo-Mendieta et al., "Patrimonial Economics."
69. Ibid., 64, citing Griffin, R. C., *Water Resource Economics,* 240.
70. A Swiss village.
71. Ostrom, *Governing the Commons,* 62.
72. Delmas-Marty, *Resister,* 136.

Part II: Normative Solutions to Water Inequality

Though the ecological footprint and water footprint concepts put the focus on the laws of nature—those laws which, according to Kant, "follow necessarily"—they fall within the province of a material philosophy that the German philosopher says relates to freedom. This philosophy is an ethic characterized by "the will of man so far as affected by nature [. . .]."[73]

Now, the laws of freedom are those "in accordance with which everything ought to happen,"[74] but very often does not. For example, for the churches, water ought to be managed publicly and it ought to be a human right. For the Dublin experts, water also ought to be considered an economic good. For supporters of the water footprint and IWRM concepts, human behavior ought to be modified to anticipate what will happen because of the laws of nature.

Guided by reason, the inventors of the many concepts suggested here are attempting to raise awareness, but it is impossible for them to be certain of the results, because the obstacle of the human will must imperatively be taken into account. Already it is possible to speculate that in the near or distant future, other management methods and other concepts will turn current scientific theories and ethics upside down.

What all of these efforts have in common is the goal of choosing between good and evil, between good and bad solutions, between what would be best for human well-being and what would be harmful to it.

Such thoughts could indicate a certain amount of pessimism; whereas on the contrary they really should serve as a springboard to other viewpoints and other possible criteria for a changing water ethic.

Actually, I feel it is important to supplement the several causes for action that I pointed out in Part II with still other causes and motives that can separate the just from the unjust and good from evil, as I will discuss below.

---

73. Kant, *Fondements*, no 387, 67.
74. Ibid.

Part III

A Changing Water Ethic

Moral Causes and Motives for the
New Human Right to Water

Introduction

Thinking and Conceptualizing Mobilization for Potable Water

WATER MOTIVATES OR "MOBILIZES" people for three main reasons.

The first is physical, as I saw personally during my travels for this research. I can still picture young women in sub-Saharan Africa—Zimbabwe, to be more exact—balancing enormous containers of the precious liquid on their heads; I remember Ethiopian donkeys, led by young herders, loaded down with leather flasks swollen with river water; I think of the Balinese riding motorcycles through the Indonesian island's crowded streets while awkwardly clutching huge water bottles, only just managing to keep hold of them.

Water also motivates morally, through just this kind of unretouched real-life snapshot. So it is important to understand and define this urge to act, which could be called a motive for achieving a goal.

Finally, it can act upon us through an intellectual movement toward action, a *cause,* as it is labeled by philosophers such as Immanuel Kant and Jean-Paul Sartre, those ardent advocates of reason.

So how are these two concepts, the cause and the motive, defined?

In one of his books, *Being and Nothingness,* French philosopher Jean-Paul Sartre ascribes the following characteristics to them.

> Generally, by cause we mean the reason for the act, that is, the ensemble of rational considerations which justify it [. . .].[1]

---

1. Sartre, *L'Être et le Néant,* 522.

Part III: A Changing Water Ethic

> We shall therefore use the term *cause* for the objective apprehension of a determined situation as this situation is revealed in the light of a certain end as being able to serve as the means for attaining this end.[2]
>
> The motive, on the contrary, is generally considered as a subjective fact. It is the ensemble of the desires, emotions, and passions which urge me to accomplish a certain act.[3]
>
> [. . .] the event becomes wholly contingent since another individual with other passions and other desires would have acted differently.[4]

Having stressed the difference between the cause, which is the objective basis for action, and the motive, which is the subjective basis, he concludes that since both the cause and the motive have an end, the three concepts are indissociable.

> But it follows obviously that the cause, the motive, and the end are the three indissoluble terms of the thrust of a free and living consciousness which projects itself toward its possibilities and makes itself defined by these possibilities.[5]

Sartre calls this "thrust" a *jaillissement*, that is, a "gushing" or "outpouring." What better metaphor for a consciousness that is open and free to act? It is marvelously suited for "thinking" water and its value and, in other words, for "thinking" an axiology of water or even a changing water ethic.

Indeed, to me, mobilizing for water is axiological in the sense that it aims to consider water as precious, or something that can be appreciated, as the Greek word *axios* conveys so well.[6] French philosopher Louis Lavelle, who developed the science of values in the twentieth century, gives a very clear definition of this concept of value:

> It can be said that the word value applies *wherever we are dealing with a break in the interchangeability or equality among things, wherever one of them must be placed before or above another, wherever one thing is judged superior to another and deserves preference over it.* [. . .] We find it in the natural contrast we establish between *what is important and what is incidental, the main thing and the secondary thing, the significant and the insignificant, the essential and the fortuitous, the justified and the unjustifiable.*[7]

So it appears defensible to assume that the concrete action of making a commitment to potable water and universal access to it, as an end, can be conceptualized as

---

2. Ibid.
3. Ibid., 522–23.
4. Ibid., 523.
5. Ibid., 525–26.
6. Cuvillier indicates, "The Greek word *axios* means something that is precious, worthy of esteem, and the verb *axioô* means *I appreciate*." Cuvillier, *Nouveau dictionnaire philosophique*, 27.
7. Lavelle, *Traité des valeurs*, 3, cited by Gérard, *Herméneutique de la valeur*, 120.

an axiology intended to focus on what is essential,[8] and which can be divided into causes and motives.

First I will bring up the *intellectual cause* that brought about the new human right to water. At first sight, this would seem to consist of the challenges indicated in Part I, such as water inequality, global poverty, vulnerability, and human dignity, which—to go back to Jean-Paul Sartre's definition of the cause—are likely to represent "the ensemble of rational considerations" that justify creating a new human right. If we take a second look, however, I think it is valid to wonder whether there is not something even more, a kind of mysterious presence, hidden away at the very heart of the concept of a human right to water. I postulate that this could be "natural law," and I will develop this hypothesis and attempt to justify it in this part's first section.

In the second section, I will discuss the act of making a commitment to water as a function of a *motive* that can be subjectively defined by such feelings as the sense of duty, benevolence or philanthropy, solidarity, or compassion; but also by less desirable feelings such as selfishness, resentment, or even anguish in the face of death. In my opinion, it will be important to see the legitimacy of adding to all of these motives the need to live in security, especially water and food security. These are motives for living well, or living better.

The goal of the following chapters is thus to ferret out some of the causes and motives pertinent to mobilizing for water.

To spice up this dialectic a bit, I have occasionally taken the liberty of opening up a platform for discourse along the way, in the form of previously unpublished real and virtual interviews.

---

8. Brooks, "Human Rights to Water."

Section I

Is Natural Law a Justifiable Cause or Basis for the New Human Right to Water?

Introduction

IF, AS JEANNE HERSCH so aptly pointed out, human rights in general ought to surprise us,[1] there is all the more reason for a *human right to water* to pique our curiosity.

In a previous chapter we asked about its normative nature, but we have not yet found an answer. Perhaps we can move forward in our quest by inquiring about the basis for this new *human right to water*.

Is it not true that human rights in general, as collected in the 1948 Universal Declaration of Human Rights, aim to take into account this result of human nature: Man's quest for, first, freedom, and then freedoms? Is not water, being a constant that is external to Man, of a different order partaking of the nature of things? It is true that human beings need water to live, but have they not lived with water as a given, rather than a right, since the dawn of time, in its forms as rain, watercourses, and lakes?

With this new prerogative, is the United Nations offering better protection than that afforded by the human rights that have already been stated and confirmed? And if so, does this new instrument in and of itself have sufficient moral force, or even legal force, not only to make an impression on decision-makers' consciences, but to truly ensure potable water and sanitation for all?

I would theorize that this question is metalegal in nature and that any attempt to find an answer relative to the *human right to water* will not be made within a single discipline, which in principle would be law, especially constitutional law and public international law.

So my research, which is intentionally interdisciplinary, will seek to answer the questions we have raised through still other social sciences such as theology, philosophy, and even history and economics. The goal is to open new lines of inquiry on the possible bases for this new *human right to water* by asking about the possible bases for human rights in general.

---

1. Hersch, "Quelques paradoxes des Droits de l'homme", 185.

Part III: A Changing Water Ethic

Possible Bases

Why should we talk about "possible bases"? Because it seems to me that recognizing that there are multiple answers and that the very idea of a basis has a double meaning, shows intellectual honesty. Theologians Eric Fuchs and Pierre-André Stucki remind us of this:

> We ought not to allow ourselves to be led astray by the ambiguities of the idea of a basis. In one sense, when I am looking for the basis for something I am seeking an element on which I can lean and rely, that I can use to go farther because I *know* it cannot be shaken. In this first sense, the basis is *the object of knowledge,* of theoretical *mastery* [. . .].
>
> *In a second sense,* when I am looking for a basis, I am seeking the origin of a system in which I find myself, a starting point that will enable me to better understand or to reorganize the system in which I find myself.[2]

To summarize, in the first sense the basis relies on a fact and can be proven, while in the second it rests on an intellectual construct and cannot be proven. Fuchs's illustrations make this even clearer.

For the first sense of the idea of a basis, he gives the example of Newton's law, on which we can base "calculations to determine a planet's path."[3] His second example concerns his deep beliefs as a Protestant Christian:

> [. . .] I can seek the basis of Christian faith and find it in the Gospel of Jesus Christ rather than in the Pope's authority; it will not follow from this that I claim to *know* that Jesus Christ is the son of God and that I am released from the responsibility of believing in Him. But it is not unimportant that henceforth I know that my belonging to the Christian faith is decided through my relationship to the Word in the Gospels; to have found the basis of faith, in this sense, enables me to gain clearer insight into my decision, but not to replace my decision by knowledge.[4]

Creating a Space for Dialogue about the Human Right to Water

Thus I will undertake to start with the new concept of a *human right to water* suggested by the United Nations in 2010 and look for what might justify and legitimize it. This does not involve proving a system, but rather, creating a space for dialogue.

The study from which I just quoted is an in-depth examination of the theological basis for human rights, which was written at the height of the Cold War by theologian

---

2. Fuchs and Stucki, *Au nom de l'Autre*, 123.
3. Ibid.
4. Ibid.

Eric Fuchs, with Pierre-André Stucki contributing. It is entitled *Au nom de l'Autre. Essai sur le fondement des droits de l'homme*.[5] The authors were inspired by Calvinistic theology to suggest the divine promise as the basis for these rights:

> If you want to obey all the commandments and rid yourself of your evil desires and your sins, as the commandments formally require, you must believe in Jesus Christ, in whom I promise you all grace, justice, peace, and freedom. If you believe, you shall receive; if you do not believe, you shall not receive.[6]

Other theologians have also tried to look for a theological basis for human rights. Here I will simply mention the viewpoints expressed in a recent collective work entitled *Christianisme et droits de l'homme*[7] and ably summarized by Marc Lienhard.

Though Norwegian Einar Molland uses Paul's Epistle to the Romans (2:14-15)[8] to assert that human rights rest on *"faith in an unwritten law[. . .] inscribed on each person's heart,"*[9] most of the theologians quoted, such as Trutz Rendtorff, or Jüngel and Tödt, tend rather to see an analogy between God's justice and the law that governs human relationships: "there are some analogies that can give action a direction."[10]

It is interesting to note that in the same article, Lienhard refers to a position that is clearly hostile to the desire to justify human rights through theology, namely that taken by German legal scholar and theologian Martin Honecker:

> [. . .] human rights express a universal natural ethic, not a Christian one. Trying to justify them theologically would mean calling into question their universal nature. At the very most, we can entertain a convergence in the reasoning of secular social sciences and that of theology [. . .].[11]

In his contribution, Lienhard also mentions the Vatican's position, which was officially confirmed in 2009[12] and which holds that human rights are based on the

---

5. Fuchs and Stucki, *Au nom de l'Autre*.

6. Ibid., 117.

7. Agi, *Christianisme et droits de l'Homme*.

8. Rom 2:14–5 reads, "When Gentiles, who do not possess the law, do instinctively what the law requires, these, though not having the law, are a law to themselves. They show that what the law requires is written on their hearts, to which their own conscience also bears witness; and their conflicting thoughts will accuse or perhaps excuse them [. . .]."

9. Lienhard, "Le Protestantisme et les droits de l'homme," citing Einar Molland (without exact source) indicates, "It is sufficient to believe in the value of Man and in a written law, which is valid for all Men and for all times, which is the law that thinkers in ancient times called natural law. This is not what the natural sciences understand by natural law, for the law that is called this raises us above nature. The law in question here is specific to Man and corresponds to human nature. All that is needed for the coexistence of Men is to believe that such a natural law exists and that we can all perceive it more or less clearly." Lienhard, "Le Protestantisme et les droits de l'homme," 116.

10. Fuchs and Stucki, *Au nom de l'Autre*, 118.

11. Ibid., 117.

12. The Vatican's position was confirmed in 2009 in: Bonino, *À la recherche d'une éthique universelle*.

concept of human dignity. Fuchs and Stucki are adamantly opposed to this stance, because they see in this faith in human dignity such a

> [p]ersonalism [which] thus offers itself as a substitute for the theism of the eighteenth century. Human dignity would then be the basis for human rights, instead of the sacred character of "natural law." Does human dignity have the nature of a "simple and indisputable" principle that was attributed to natural rights in the preamble of 1789?
>
> With respect to the intent of Nazism or fascism, this reliance on human dignity is simply begging the question. What Nazism wanted, for example, if we believe Bettelheim, was to reduce the person to the condition of a docile instrument for power; to reduce individuals to the undifferentiated state of interchangeable and eminently replaceable beings. So claiming to adhere to human dignity means referring to the idea most hotly disputed by the opponent.
>
> So recognizing human dignity as the basis for human rights would seem to us to be difficult. In our quest true conviction, we must continue our search in another direction.[13]

The "other direction" is to base human rights on the divine promise; and is the one taken by Fuchs and Stucki. In a statement punctuated by quintessentially Calvinistic humility, they courageously suppose a theological basis for human rights:

> We can neither know nor prove that the promise is true and not illusory; it is intended for us, and it is up to us to respond to it. We are in a dialogue, not in a position of spectacular control. But it is not immaterial to the strength of our conviction to note that the decision in favor of human rights is not motivated by the utopia of a future world in which everyone will be kind, any more than by a fierce idealistic determination not to face reality. The promise is close to us, at the heart of our daily existence, in the seat of our emotions, and behind our rational undertakings. It is because of the promise that we respond when we enter into the human rights system.[14]

They add:

> The promise does not have its true meaning unless it is *passed on* by human communication, that is, recognized as being of transcendental origin: it is not we humans who invented it, it is not we who determine it, and yet, it is essential to our existence. Which means, implicitly, that the promise comes from God, that it is the Word of God.[15]

So is *natural law* or *human dignity* the basis for human rights? This is what is at stake.

---

13. Fuchs and Stucki, *Au nom de l'Autre*, 113.
14. Ibid., 123–24.
15. Ibid., 124.

And the stakes are high. Two completely opposing world views lie behind these concepts. For the moment, they can be outlined as follows: *natural law* would relate to transcendence, *human dignity* would relate to Man.

As we have just seen, Fuchs and Stucki defend the position that human rights are based on natural law, while Honecker contends that they are based on a universal ethic.

These two points of view are the subject of the next two chapters.

Chapter I

A Theological Inquiry Into *Natural Law* from ABRAHAM Through the Apostle Paul and the Church Fathers to Calvin

Abraham, Moses, and the Apostle Paul: From Oral to Written Law

SINCE PAUL'S EPISTLE TO the Romans is one of the founding texts of Christian theology,[1] and reformers such as Martin Luther devoted special attention to it, it seemed to me that it should be the first source consulted in attempting to shed light on the concept of *natural law*.

In chapter 4 of Romans, the Apostle Paul recalls Abraham's central role in understanding the nature of faith. As the father of all, Abraham believed God's promise that he could still beget children despite his advanced age.

> Hoping against hope, he believed that he would become "the father of many nations," according to what was said, "So numerous shall your descendants be."[2]

In his study on Romans, Paul Bony[3] relays the words of Philo of Alexandria, a contemporary of Jesus, who said that Abraham, through his unshakable faith in God, behaved as a strict observer of *natural law* even before it was set down on Moses' Tables of the Law.

> For Philo, the Torah is the revelation of natural law to Moses, the "Law above Laws," observed by "all those [. . .] living a blameless and irreproachable life."[4]

---

1. Dumas, "Justification."
2. Rom 4:18.
3. Paul Bony is a professor of biblical exegesis at the Institut de Sciences et de Théologie des Religions, a department of the Institut Catholique de la Méditerranée. Pierre Bony is a priest who taught at the Institut de Sciences et Théologie des Religions in Marseilles.
4. Bony, "Une lecture de l'épître aux Romains," 19.

In the course of his research, Genevan theology professor Robert Martin-Achard, an Old-Testament specialist, also makes mention of this *natural law*—without, however, specifying its content, though he quotes authors[5] who say it was "written by God in the heart of every man."[6] In addition, he refers to Saint Augustine's commentary on John 11:17[7] and to the death of Lazarus. The Bishop of Hippo found that we must see a symbol in the fact that when Jesus came to Lazarus, the body had been in the tomb for four days.

> Saint Augustine explains the symbolism he sees in the fact that Lazarus had been dead for four days: the first day symbolizes natural law, the second the law of reason, the third the law of Moses, and the fourth the Gospel.[8]

We cannot rule out the possibility that Calvin, who held Saint Augustine in very high esteem and whose work is known to have been heavily influenced by him, might have been guided by this point of view in his own conception of *natural law*, which we will discuss later.

Romanists, Scholastics, and Nominalists Grapple with Natural Law

In this Chapter I will follow the lead of Michel Villey[9] and Peter Haggenmacher.[10] In their publications, they have succeeded in bringing out the most striking features of this mysterious *natural law*, sparing no effort in going back to the Greco-Roman sources and consulting them in the original languages.

Using a contemporary and scholarly yet accessible approach, they both remind us that it was from Aristotle that we inherited "natural law," which can also be called "natural justice" or "natural right" depending on how the Greek term *dikaion physikon* is translated. In *Nichomachean Ethics*, Aristotle explains that "– *dikaion physikon*— [. . .] is the just-in-itself, which can universally be recognized as such because it owes nothing to our conventions."[11]

So some things are just even without reference to a convention or standard; such things are the result of a certain situation.[12]

---

5. Martin-Achard, "Israël et les nations," 47, citing Feuillet, "Le sens du livre de Jonas," 343.

6. Ibid.

7. John 11:17 reads, "When Jesus arrived, he found that Lazarus had already been in the tomb four days."

8. Martin-Achard, et al., *La figure de Moïse*, 114.

9. Villey, *Le droit et les droits de l'homme*.

10. Haggenmacher, "III. La nouvelle physionomie du 'Ius.'"

11. Villey, *Le droit et les droits de l'homme*, 64.

12. For example, we can consider the attitude of a mountain guide who learns that the weather is bad and is going to cancel a trip with his clients. This decision is not made because of any rules for the guides, but because of the situation's inherent danger.

CHAPTER I: A THEOLOGICAL INQUIRY INTO NATURAL LAW

To be clear, I should state that what most interested the authors I have just quoted in regard to natural right was defining what exactly was meant by "justice" as expressed in the Latin word *jus*, or *ius* ("law, just treatment, right").

Capturing the Elusive Natural Law

It is not my intent to make the issue of *law/justice/right(s)* in the concept of "human rights" even more confusing. My reason for highlighting a few passages from Michel Villey's work on the subject,[13] written in his capacity as a Romanist, is to bring out the fierce determination with which intellectuals, along with political and religious leaders, have tried since ancient times to capture this elusive *natural law* using reason's most sophisticated tools. Yet Abraham understood its meaning with no need to refer to a written text.

Villey explored these learned sources with passion, and according to my information it took him no less than forty years to gain a clearer understanding.

His journey led him to try to discover what was embodied in the concept of *droit* ("law," "justice, "right(s)") in ancient Greece, so he could compare it to that in the expression *droits de l'homme* (literally, "rights of Man," or as we now say, "human rights").

Back to the Source of Roman Law

Villey began with the legal arts of Greece, the finesse and subtlety of which Cicero skillfully succeeded in bringing out in the Roman world in which he lived. This art was strengthened by Emperor Justinian, whose Codex underlay the doctrine of law for centuries not only in Europe (notably through the Napoleonic Code), but also in English-speaking countries through common law.

Every former law student of my generation will remember Celsus's axiom *"ius est ars boni et æqui,"*[14] which was part of the introduction to law course and which Villey elegantly invokes.

Yet is there a connection of any kind between this art of law and the notion of *droit* in the concept of *droits de l'homme*? Initially, an affirmative answer to this question would seem legitimate, because in the minds of many, *droits de l'homme* are supposed to confer what is *good and equitable* upon everyone.

Villey does not see it this way, however. He engages in a rigorous analysis to demonstrate the need to clarify the concepts and avoid confusing the usages of the words, since semantic disorder can lead to trivialization and even rejection of values that are important to humanity's future.

---

13. Villey, *Le droit et les droits de l'homme*.
14. Translation from Latin: "law is the art of the good and the equitable."

Part III: A Changing Water Ethic
Clarifying the Concepts to Save Human Rights

It is that very danger, trivialization, that threatens the expression *droits de l'homme* when it is used improperly. By way of example, Christian Tomuschat, a professor of public international law, exclaims,

> [...] a wishful thinking may be presented as the law in force. Such overzealous pressing ahead, however, may have devastating consequences in undermining human rights as a branch of the law that must be taken seriously. Not everything that may serve to improve the wellbeing of individuals can or should be accepted as a human right.[15]

Another expression related to the issue of human rights, and which is misunderstood, is *Etat de droit*[16] ("Rule of Law"), in which the word *law* appears without its full meaning being clear to everyone. In contemporary political discourse, "Rule of Law" is often defined as the government's respect for democracy and human rights.[17] As a matter of fact, not all nations agree on these two concepts, though they try to create for themselves the illusion of consensus. For example, Swiss constitutional law did not acquire a definition of *Etat de droit* until 1999, and it takes a publicist[18] to understand it. Here is the wording of article 5 of Switzerland's federal Constitution, which decides under the heading "Rule of Law" that

1. All activities of the state are based on and limited by law.

2. State activities must be conducted in the public interest and be proportionate to the end sought.

3. State institutions and private persons shall act in good faith.

4. The Confederation and the Cantons shall respect international law.

---

15. Tomuschat, *Human Rights, between Idealism and Realism*, 2.

16. Literally, a "State of Law."

17. Two examples: 1. The speech by 1991 Nobel Peace Prize laureate Aung San Suu Kyi on February 4, 2013. The subject was the "Rule of Law," which was also the topic of the National League for Democracy Party's convention in Myanmar. Kyi stressed the fact that Myanmar has no separation of powers between the executive, legislative, and judicial branches. 2. At a spring ASEAN conference on May 23, 2013, Japanese Prime Minister Shinzo Abe mentioned it as the highest value to be respected in Asian economic development. The *Straits Times* of May 24, 2013 reported his words: "[...] a revived Japan can and will be a force for good in the world. It will be better poised to contribute to Asia's economic dynamism and to ensure the rule of law in the international arena [...]."

18. *Le petit Larousse illustré* indicates, "A legal scholar specializing in public law." *Le petit Larousse illustré*, 87.

Subjective Rights and Human Rights

According to Villey, the root of the Roman term *ius* is *iusticia* (justice, fairness, equity),[19] whereas the *ius* embodied in human rights is *droit subjectif*—"subjective law" or "subjective right—, a notion dating back to the nineteenth century. It was German Pandectists such as de Savigny and Jhering—influenced by Kant[20]—who held forth "at great length"[21] on this new concept and made it, respectively, a *Willensmacht*[22] ("power to act") or a "legally protected interest."[23]

Villey's flash of irritation concerning *droits subjectifs* or "subjective rights" is definitely noticeable. Yet did not such thinkers as Hannah Arendt and Jeanne Hersch also mention their perplexity where human rights were concerned?[24]

Laws and Rights

In my estimation, Villey's heavily documented critical reflection provides some valuable keys to understanding the skepticism of many of my present-day colleagues, who feel that human rights are nothing but a utopia[25] destined to feed academic debate and serve the interests of governments rather than the people for whom they are responsible.

I see at least two key ideas.

First, Villey gives a useful reference when he cites Hohfeld. This American legal scholar finds that subjective law or "right" can have four meanings. It can be a "freedom," an "affirmative claim against another," a "power," or an "immunity."[26] Villey goes on to say that

> all of these cases [have to do with] "legal advantage." "*Droit subjectif*" dies hard; it still has a large place in general theories of law. Obviously, "*droits de l'homme*" fall within the category of "subjective rights."[27]

The kind of semantic division of the single word "right" that Hohfeld proposes shows the essential distinction that must be made in French between *droit* as the body of all laws and *droits* as rights, that is, as *prerogatives* or *benefits*.

---

19. Villey, *Le droit et les droits de l'homme*. "Others believe that the root is *iussum*, which is a different discussion altogether, since *iussum* means an 'order' or 'command.'"
20. Ibid., 70.
21. Ibid., 69.
22. Ibid.
23. Ibid.
24. Hersch, "Quelques paradoxes des Droits de l'homme," 185.
25. Moyn, *The Last Utopia, Human Rights in History*.
26. Villey, *Le droit et les droits de l'homme*, 24.
27. Ibid., 69.

Second, Villey demonstrates that this subjective right, when broken down into four forms, cannot coexist with any kind of obligation, in stark contrast to the Roman notion of *ius,* which necessarily implied an opposite to counterbalance the right.

This disturbs legal scholars, even those from the twenty-first century.[28]

Michel Villey supplies a number of very enlightening examples. For example, a right of ownership necessarily implies paying taxes, a right to inherit can mean the risk of having to, as he says, *tirer du passif,*[29] that is, acquire a loss.

To clarify, his opponents are the Romanists who support the idea that because it is "based on reason,"[30] subjective right must have existed in Roman law, even though there is no explicit formulation of it.

Villey retorts, however, that his colleagues did not read all the way through the texts.

> You simply have to read all the way to the end. When Gaius's text (reproduced in the *Digest,* VII, 2, 2) speaks of *'jus altius tollendi,'* [the *ius* or "right" to build one's house high] he continues in the same sentence ' . . . *aut non extollendi.'* [or to not build too high] Here is a *jus* that says *not to build one's house* too *high* (so as not to deprive one's neighbor of a view of the lovely landscape)! Granting me the benefit or freedom of "not building too high" would make no sense at all: in this case, a burden is placed on me, and a restriction of my freedom.[31]

The Subjective Right's Shadowy Counterpart: Obligation

The question then arises as to how the term *ius* could have undergone such a radical transformation since ancient times, and how the *right's* partner and alter ego—which ought to be *obligation*—surreptitiously gave ground and faded into the shadows.

As it turns out, posterity has inherited some true intellectual monuments on this point. They record in minute detail the lines of reasoning, which have given rise to bitter controversies, sometimes risking the lives of their authors—theologians, philosophers, and jurists alike.

Michel Villey and Peter Haggenmacher, both legal scholars and intimately familiar with Catholic and Protestant doctrines, helped me to convince myself of the importance of this precious legacy. The vital clues they give will, I hope, enable us to penetrate part of the mystery and remove several layers of the dust these erudite tomes have been allowed to collect.

---

28. Dumont et al., *La Responsabilité, face cachée des Droits de l'Homme.*
29. Villey, *Le droit et les droits de l'homme,* 78.
30. Ibid., 70.
31. Ibid., 77.

Chapter I: A Theological Inquiry Into Natural Law

The Controversies: Scholastics versus Nominalists

Having sung the praises of Thomas Aquinas and his *Summa Theologica*, which he finds to be a true temple to the intellect,[32] Michel Villey wonders about the impact of Duns Scotus's work and William of Ockham's.

He supports the view that William of Ockham's Nominalism created a break, a real turning point in Western thought. He says that Ockham's voluntarist doctrine—which made divine will the central focus and not reason as found at the heart of *natural law*—is the origin of the modern conception of natural law. We know that the main proponents of the latter were Francesco de Vitoria and Francisco Suarez of the Salamanca School,[33] who themselves inspired the modern natural-law school, the leading figure of which was Dutchman Hugo Grotius.

I will quote a significant passage from Villey's work that helps us understand this notion of "unalienable and sacred rights"[34] that was so highly prized during the French Revolution. He explains that there are *iura fori* [rights of the forum] and *iura poli* [rights of heaven]; the first can be demanded, because they are granted by the Prince, and the second are unalienable, because they are granted by Heaven, and cannot be demanded. According to Villey, among the latter group are some freedoms that:

> [. . .] are for everyone; for a Franciscan there is no question of relinquishing permission to eat, to get dressed, or to make "customary use" (*usus facti*) of things . . . These, too are called rights, or *iura poli* in William of Ockham's language, because we receive them from Heaven (*polus* [is] a term borrowed from Saint Augustine), but they cannot be claimed before the courts of the temporal prince, so they are not exactly rights in the true sense of the word [. . .].
>
> William of Ockham has the virtue of being aware that these "rights" cannot be *demanded*. Rather, God gave them to everyone and no one can abdicate them. Already, these were "human rights" before the term was ever thought of, and were inferred from divine moral law, which is universal.
>
> Scotism[35] and Nominalism spread through most faculties of theology in the late Middle Ages and this new language took hold there. Luther and Hobbes were Ockhamists [. . .]. The theme of freedom for the Christian, who has been emancipated from the Law, was very much cultivated up until the sixteenth century (Erasmus, Driedo, etc.).[36]

---

32. Ibid., 109.
33. Ibid., 126.
34. Preamble of the 1778 Declaration of the Rights of Man and of the Citizen, see Fuchs and Stucki, ibid., 227.
35. Referring to John Duns Scot.
36. Villey, *Le droit et les droits de l'homme*, 125.

This theory about Nominalism's role in the development of Protestantism and modern natural law is controversial[37] today, yet two other eminent Romanists, Peter Haggenmacher[38] and Alfred Dufour,[39] also accepted it.

The Science of Law in Ruins

In any case, Michel Villey's statements clearly convey his great bitterness toward Nominalism. He feels that this doctrine ruined Aristotle's philosophy and the science of law.

> Nominalism destroys Aristotle's ontology. Although Ockham probably did not personally intend it as his target, when he used Aristotle as an argument against extreme "realism," he ruined Aristotelian philosophy, politics, and law. If there is no longer order governing the relationships between individuals, if society itself is in no way a reality, then a science intended to study these social relationships directly has lost all reason to exist. The art of finding what is just in the midst of reality, which describes the Roman art of jurisprudence, becomes purposeless.[40]

He also says, not without a glint of humor tinged with cynicism,

> Shortly after Saint Thomas's death [. . .] a number of his theses were condemned [. . .]. And the primacy or monopoly of sacred literature was restored. Was this not natural for clerics? Would it be scandalous if their education were dominated by the Gospels, and dispensed with philosophy and law? To preserve what is essential, it is permissible to forego the splendor of cathedrals and polyphonic music for the poverty of the liturgy, spare architecture, and intellectual indigence.[41]

He goes even further in his diatribe against Saint Thomas's opponents:

> [. . .] theology will extend its imperialism at the very least to *morality*. Saint Thomas had made a distinction between "theological" virtues—faith, hope, and charity—and "moral" virtues in the narrow sense, the four cardinal virtues. With regard to morality itself, he had dared to recognize and respect secular philosophy's jurisdiction. Our Franciscans will again make[42] all of morality subject to the control of the Gospel; will construct a "Christian morality." This is one of the parts of their theology treatises that is likely to give rise to a new idea of law.

37. Piron, "*Congé à Villey*."
38. Haggenmacher, "La nouvelle physionomie du 'Ius.'"
39. Dufour, *Droits de l'homme*, 120.
40. Villey, *Le droit et les droits de l'homme*, 120.
41. Ibid., 117.
42. Ibid., 121.

Chapter I: A Theological Inquiry Into Natural Law

What could not fail to be present in their works is a theory of the *law*, a traditional topic of sacred doctrine, especially since Saint Augustine. With Nominalism's sudden emergence, and even earlier with Duns Scotus's voluntarism, the word took on a new value. It no longer evoked the world order, hidden within the world, that Greek lawmakers and philosophers had tried for better or worse to express in written formulations. The law became the fact of the intentional *commandment* of an authority.[43]

In history's fits and starts, we can read a frequent swing of the pendulum between the concepts of reason and will—God's will—at the heart of *natural law*. This can already be seen in Philip Melanchthon's efforts to balance these two concepts and therefore to distance himself from Martin Luther, who was quite a voluntarist. Indeed, Melanchthon's *Loci Communes Theologici*[44] showed his desire to be open to Aristotle's philosophy, and represented the Wittenberg theologian's movement back toward the Thomist intellectualism so highly praised by Villey.[45]

We can see the movement along the spectrum in the path chosen by the thinkers I will examine shortly, such as John Calvin and Hugo Grotius. I believe I can say that the former is closer to the voluntarist doctrine, whereas Hugo Grotius, a staunch Calvinist, followed his teacher in his youth but opened a new field of intellectual activity in his later years, as we shall see.

To better understand the oscillations in the history of thought, I will try to revive, in their historical context, some of the authors whose works played a considerable role in understanding *natural law*.

I was inspired to take this approach by Wilhelm Dilthey's method, mentioned above. I will begin with John Calvin.

John Calvin's New Hermeneutics of Natural Law

After recalling Calvin's pivotal role in the Reformation movement, I will look into his hermeneutics of *natural law* for clues both to any legacy with political import and to a basis for human rights.

Calvin's Place in History

John Calvin's five-hundredth birthday in 2009 marked a revival of interest in his work,[46] not only for Christians but also for those trying to more easily get their

---

43. Ibid., 122.
44. Melanchthon, *Loci communes theologici*, cited by Haggenmacher, 487 n229.
45. Haggenbacher indicates, "The doctrine of the *Præceptor Germaniæ* [Melanchthon], which is not incompatible with Thomism, in fact was to have greater practical influence on German legal scholars than did that of Luther himself." Haggenbacher, "La nouvelle physionomie du 'Ius,'" 487.
46. Abel, et al., *Jean Calvin et Thomas Hobbes*, 8.

bearings with respect to current events marked by a radicalization of political Islam.[47] After all, is it not high time for Europe to relearn the meaning of debate and dialectic, and to rediscover that politics "cannot do without a theology—or at least a connection to theology"?[48]

Incidentally, it was demonstrated at the 2009 colloquia that "Calvin unquestionably deserves to be considered Machiavelli's equal in the lineage of modern political thought, from Hobbes to Rousseau."[49]

Would not ascribing such a role to him be an exaggeration?

In trying to answer this question, I think a brief history lesson is in order, especially since it could help us to better understand this French theologian and legal expert.

In his 1929 work devoted to Calvin's *Institutes of the Christian Religion*, Albert Autin seems to me to have been something of a visionary in pleading over eighty years ago for renewed curiosity about Calvin's work. It is not exaggerating to say that he presented the *Institutes* as a work essential not only to theology, but to Western culture as well.

> [. . .] *Institutes of the Christian Religion* marks an important date. It revealed to France some more serious concerns than those from which our literature had drawn inspiration up until then. It opened up a new territory for French letters: that of religious feeling.[50]
>
> [. . .] *Institutes of the Christian Religion* is perhaps the first work of theology our national literature has produced. Up to then we lived, so to speak, on the shared heritage of the universal Church: the Bible's two testaments, the Church Fathers of the Greek and Latin church, and finally the commentaries, in which theologians endeavored to highlight Christian dogma and morality. [. . .] With *Institutes of the Christian Religion*, for the first time, our national genius has taken on the religious problem as set out in our Western world over fifteen centuries ago by the Judeo-Christian tradition spread by the Roman Empire.[51]

Autin goes so far as to say that without Calvin, authors such as Bossuet and Pascal could not have come along.

> It would not be irrelevant [. . .] to note [. . .] that *[Institutes]* cleared the way for a whole series of works, among which the names Pascal, Bossuet, [and] Fénelon [. . .] suffice to clearly show its place in our national legacy [. . .].[52]

47. Ibid.

48. Ibid., indicates, "[. . .] the issue of the sources through which we know the divine word is not a schoolboys' squabble: it is an inescapable problem of all theology and all politics [. . .]."

49. Ibid., back cover.

50. Autin, *L'Institution chrétienne de Calvin*, 9.

51. Ibid., 8.

52. Ibid., 9.

Chapter I: A Theological Inquiry Into Natural Law

Autin's very meticulous approach to Calvin's work also enables us to better understand the multidimensional impact this reformer's contribution had on Western civilization.

To this end, Autin insists on the need to place Calvin's work in its historical context. He says it appeared during the second of the Reformation's three phases in France, and gives approximate dates for the three stages.

> Today it is a well established fact of the Reformation's history in France that this movement of ideas and feelings first appeared as underlying and vague leanings in nearly all classes of society; that it then became a Church that grew increasingly fervent as it was persecuted; and that finally, from its original strictly spiritual nature, it transformed itself into a political party determined to use every means at its disposal, including violence, to impose what it considered, rightly or wrongly (that is not the issue here) to be the truth.
>
> If we had to give dates, we would say that the first period ended in 1534 with the persecution triggered by the Affair of the Placards Against the Mass; the second extended from 1534 to 1559, when the famous national synod of the reformed churches of France was held in Paris; and the third was between 1559 and 1598, when the Edict of Nantes was promulgated [...].[53]
>
> So the Reformation first developed within a circle of scholars, in the shadows and nearly completely protected from royal power. From there, it spread to the world of "mechanical" people, workers from the city and the countryside. At that time, it was more of a kind of passion than a schismatic trend, a political party even less so.
>
> But [...] Francis I allowed himself to be led into persecutions. He [...] created the Inquisition in 1540 [...]. From 1545 to 1548, there was the Chambre Ardente of infamous memory. The French Reformation was banished to Geneva with Calvin. [...] In France, faith was attested in the prisons and at the stake. [...] A schism became necessary. [...] From a Church, the Reformation became a political party. As such, it became involved in conflicts of interest and ambitions. [...] On the battlefield, it lost the best of its true glory, that of being a spiritual message.[54]

Our Calvin specialist is even more convincing when he highlights the truly subversive power of Calvin's work to shape political direction, and presents *Institutes of the Christian Religion* as a contribution that was critical to the Reformation's spread itself.

> *Institutes of the Christian Religion* [...] made no small contribution to guiding the reform movement onto the road toward schism, and then toward ecclesiastical organization, insofar as it offered the faithful—who up to that point had been reduced either to local preaching by "evangelicals," or to individual

---

53. Ibid., 10.
54. Ibid., 11.

Part III: A Changing Water Ethic

> inspiration drawn from reading the Bible—a kind of official *Summa*, a "catechism," a rigorous overview above and beyond which conversations about religion were not allowed, and which, in fact, Geneva-trained pastors were to spread—or, as was said at the time, "peddle"—from that city to all French-speaking countries as a revealed, authentic, and indisputable doctrine.
>
> In the absence of a book such as *Institutes*, it is difficult to see what would have become of the Reformation in the hands of those who—with Bishop Briçonnet in Meaux, with Marguerite d'Angoulême in Nérac, with Duchess Renée in Ferrara, with Farel in Geneva itself—settled for generous but vague aspirations. In contrast, it is easy to see how *Institutes* sounded assembly for the willing and achieved unanimity in the faith through a set method.
>
> In the same way, remove *Institutes* from the vast body of literature produced in the sixteenth century. Part of Montaigne,[55] [. . .] and Catholic apologetics of this period, [. . .] and the sermon as it was then understood, in churches, on public squares, and at the foot of the stake, all disappears.[56]

Are Albert Autin's statements so overblown as to verge on hagiography?

I think not, even though today we live in "a world where one can no longer refer to teleologies or harmonies that used to be taken as a given, where a universal God or divine basis cannot supply the framework for ethics [. . .]."[57]

Our secularized world suffers from an absence of reference points, as was so lucidly expressed by Jean Monod, the 1965 Nobel laureate in physiology and medicine, three-quarters of the way through the twentieth century.

> No society can survive without a moral code based on values that are understood, accepted, and respected by most of its members. We no longer will have anything to do with that. Can modern societies indefinitely control the incredible powers science has given them based on the criterion of a vague humanism tinged with a sort of optimistic and materialistic hedonism? Can they resolve their unbearable tensions on these bases? Or will they collapse?[58]

So today there is every incentive to reread texts that discuss moral law in such a structured and enlightening way—from an ethical, legal, and even political standpoint; and with the goal of discovering in them some normative hints that would be useful in our time.

---

55. Ibid., 12.
56. Ibid., 13.
57. Russ, *La pensée éthique contemporaine*, 13.
58. Monod, "La science et ses valeurs," cited by Russ, *La pensée éthique contemporaine*, 14.

Chapter I: A Theological Inquiry Into Natural Law

Natural Law, a Goad for the Conscience

How could we fail to be surprised at finding a lucid definition of *natural law* flowing from Calvin's quill? Have we not been warned that *natural law* was ambiguous and unclear? Though Eric Fuchs and Pierre-André Stucki shed some light in the following relevant statement.

> Historical experience has shown that no consensus can be found with regard to the content of natural law. We can only postulate that it is necessary. This was duly noted by Reformed theology.[59]

For Calvin, then, it is very simple: the Ten Commandments sum up natural law. He did not neglect to demonstrate, in a slightly disillusioned and especially scathing tone, that this is in fact a tautology.

> Moreover, the internal law, which has before been said to be inscribed and as it were engraven on the hearts of all men, suggests to us in some measure the same things which are to be learned from the two tables. For our conscience does not permit us to sleep in perpetual insensibility, but is an internal witness and monitor of the duties we owe to God, shows us the difference between good and evil, and so accuses us when we deviate from our duty. But man, involved as he is in a cloud of errors, scarcely obtains from this law of nature the smallest idea of what worship is accepted by God; but is certainly at an immense distance from a right understanding of it. Besides, he is so elated with arrogance and ambition, and so blinded with self-love, that he cannot yet take a view of himself, and, as it were retire within, that he may learn to submit and humble himself, and to confess his misery. Since it was necessary, therefore, both for our dulness [sic] and obstinacy, the Lord gave us a written law; to declare with greater certainty what in the law of nature was too obscure, and by arousing our indolence, to make a deeper impression on our understanding and memory.[60]

These Ten Commandments still must be interpreted if their content is to be understood. Therein lies the whole challenge and the difficulty.

We must acknowledge that this reformer met the challenge brilliantly.

Teleological Interpretation of the Ten Commandments

I note that John Calvin's interpretation of the Ten Commandments was far from being moralistic, laborious, or daunting. On the contrary, it is a breath of fresh air. He suggested what I will call a "modern" interpretation of the Ten Commandments from

---

59. Fuchs and Stucki, *Au nom de l'autre*, 129.
60. Calvin, *Inst.*, II, VIII, 1.

the two Tables of the Law that Moses brought down from Mount Sinai.[61] He not only noted the letter, but also looked for the spirit, proceeding with what can be called in legal terms a teleological interpretation.

For Calvin,

> It is plain, then, that a sober exposition of the law goes beyond the words of it; but how far, remains doubtful, unless some rule be laid down. The best rule, then, I conceive will be, that the exposition be directed to the design of the precept; that in regard to every precept it should be considered for what end it was given.[62]

After a reminder that the first five commandments, those from the first Table, were devoted to God's glory and Man's submission, he gave an interpretation of the other five from the second Table which, to my great surprise, addressed the very same issues as the writers of the UDHR in 1948.

The laws of Moses and the 1948 UDHR especially reflect concerns for protecting life and safeguarding well-being, which an appropriate government must achieve through respect for the law and the preservation of security.

The Universal Declaration of Human Rights and the "Do No Harm" Principle As Counterpoints to the Second Table of the Law

Who would not be struck by the parallelism between Calvin's interpretation of the Ten Commandments in Book 2, chapter 8 of *Institutes of the Christian Religion* and the content of several of the articles in the 1948 Universal Declaration of Human Rights?

Indeed, is not Moses' fourth commandment on keeping the sabbath[63] quite obviously related to article 24 of the UDHR, which decrees that

> Everyone has the right to rest and leisure, including reasonable limitation of working hours and periodic holidays with pay?[64]

At least, that is how I see it. What is more, I would say that for article 24 of the UDHR, an interpretation is not even necessary; the similarity speaks for itself.

---

61. Exod 19.

62. Calvin, *Inst.*, II, VIII, 8.

63. Exod 20:8–11 reads, "Remember the sabbath day, and keep it holy. Six days shall you labor and do all your work. But the seventh day is a sabbath day to the Lord your God: you shall not do any work—you, your son or your daughter, your male or female slave, your livestock, or the alien resident in your towns. For in six days the Lord made heaven and earth, the sea, and all that is in them, but rested the seventh day; therefore the Lord blessed the sabbath day and consecrated it."

64. Universal Declaration of Human Rights.

I will now look more closely into Calvin's interpretations of the sixth and eighth commandments, especially, which are "You shall not murder"[65] and "You shall not steal."[66]

Here is how the French Reformer (Genevan by adoption) interpreted the sixth commandment.

> Therefore, in this precept "Thou shalt not kill," the common sense of mankind will perceive nothing more than that we ought to abstain from all acts of injury to others, and from all desire to commit any such acts. I maintain that it also implies, that we should do every thing that we possibly can towards the preservation of the life of our neighbour.[67]

So why should we not consider the "right to life" established in article 3 of the 1948 UDHR as being a reflection of the sixth commandment, in light of Calvin's interpretation?

This position seems defensible to me.

However, let us move on to Calvin's interpretation of the eighth commandment, which I find to be of real interest. Is his interpretation not very broad? Listen to what he said.

> And this kind of injury relates not only to money, or to goods, or to lands, but to whatever each individual is justly entitled to; for we defraud our neighbours of their property, if we deny them those kind offices, which it is our duty to perform.[68]

Later, with regard to the authorities responsible for enforcing the laws, he said that it is incumbent upon the governing authorities to behave as men who are respectful before God, and indirectly, before men.[69]

> [. . .] [L]et governors take care of their people, preserve the public peace, protect the good, punish the wicked, and administer all things in such a manner, as becomes those who must render an account of their office to God the supreme Judge.[70]

Again, I am surprised. Is not, in a way, Calvin's point of view taken into account in the 1948 UDHR, the preamble of which sets forth general principles of justice and peace, on the one hand, and good governance on the other?

65. Exod 20:13.
66. Exod 20:15.
67. Calvin, *Inst.,* II, VIII, 9.
68. Calvin, *Inst.,* II, VIII, 45.
69. Dermange indicates, "By making the governing authorities *responsible* to the public, Calvin invites the subjects to verify the status of their "benefit." Dermange, "Calvin contre la puissance souveraine," 85.
70. Calvin, *Inst.,* II, VIII, 46.

Part III: A Changing Water Ethic

Justice and peace are mentioned in the preamble's first paragraph.

> Whereas recognition of the inherent dignity and of the equal and inalienable rights of all members of the human family is the foundation of freedom, justice and peace in the world [. . .].

Its third paragraph mentions the rule of law, which presupposes that the governing authorities respect the law:

> Whereas it is essential, if man is not to be compelled to have recourse, as a last resort, to rebellion against tyranny and oppression, that human rights should be protected by the rule of law [. . .].

Calvin did not stop there. We know by his encouragement of the development of the Hospice Général in Geneva how much he cared about eradicating poverty and providing work for everyone. So it was very logical for him to find that the eighth commandment, "you shall not steal,"[71] paid special attention to material and social issues.

Here, again, I see a connection between his words and specific articles of the 1948 UDHR, such as the right to own property in article 17 and the right to work in article 23.

Let us compare these two provisions to Calvin's assertions. Article 17 decrees that

(1) Everyone has the right to own property alone as well as in association with others.

(2) No one shall be arbitrarily deprived of his property.

Article 23 states the following.

(1) Everyone has the right to work, to free choice of employment, to just and favourable conditions of work and to protection against unemployment.

(2) Everyone, without any discrimination, has the right to equal pay for equal work.

(3) Everyone who works has the right to just and favourable remuneration ensuring for himself and his family an existence worthy of human dignity, and supplemented, if necessary, by other means of social protection [. . .].

Here are three excerpts from Calvin's *Institutes of the Christian Religion*, concerning protection of property and the right to work:

> The end of this precept is, that, as injustice is an abomination to God, every man may possess what belongs to him. The sum of it, then, is, that we are

---

71. Calvin, *Inst.*, II, VIII, 45.

forbidden to covet the property of others, and are therefore enjoined faithfully to use our endeavours to preserve to every man what justly belongs to him.[72]

We again note Calvin's vivid language, which makes the imperative of the eighth commandment more palatable than a straightforward legal text prohibiting theft:

> (God) sees the tedious manoeuvres with which the designing man begins to decoy his more simple neighbour, till at length he entangles him in his snares. He sees the cruel and inhuman laws, by which the more powerful man oppresses and ruins him that is weaker. He sees the baits with which the more crafty trepan the imprudent. All which things are concealed from the judgment of man, nor ever come to his knowledge.[73]

As far as the right to work is concerned, it was the masters' respect for those who serve them that Calvin wished to awaken. In other words, as we would express it today, Calvin's broad interpretation of the eighth commandment has to do with employer/employee relationships.

> Neither let masters behave morosely and perversely to their servants, harassing them with excessive asperity, or treating them with contempt; but rather acknowledge them as brethren and companions in the service of the heavenly Master, entitled to be regarded with mutual affection, and to receive kind treatment.[74]

With this brief comparative study, I wished to emphasize both Calvin's political and social role and the agreement between his vision and that of the authors of the 1948 UDHR over four centuries later.

So I feel justified in adding to what François Dermange asserted in 2009 at the colloquium on Calvin and Hobbes held in Paris.[75] He said,

> [. . .] the function he [Calvin] assigns to natural law as grasped by the conscience anticipates that ascribed to human rights two centuries later.[76]

I myself postulate that Calvin anticipated not only the American Declaration of Independence in 1776 and the French Declaration of the Rights of Man and of the Citizen in 1789, but also the Universal Declaration of Human Rights in 1948.

I would also add that Calvin subtly rounded out his analysis of the eighth commandment by injecting a critical element that was, if not forgotten, at least very understated in the 1948 UDHR, namely the factor of an obligation or responsibility that

---

72. Ibid.
73. Ibid.
74. Calvin, *Inst.*, II, VIII, 46.
75. Abel et al., *Jean Calvin et Thomas Hobbes*.
76. Dermange, "Calvin contre la puissance souveraine," 95.

is implied by a right. He saw this commandment as having both a material and a spiritual side:

> Moreover, our attention should always be directed to the Legislator; to remind us that this law is ordained for our hearts as much as for our hands, in order that men may study both to protect the property and to promote the interests of others.[77]

We will discover a similar standard in the Golden Rule, a saying that will be brought up later in Part V.

The Imperative of Natural Law

I said earlier that for Calvin, the content of *natural law* was clear, namely the Decalogue, that is, the Ten Commandments.

Yet this raises the central question of knowing which persons supposedly obeyed this *natural law*. Were the Jews, then later Christians, who adhered to this Decalogue through Christ's command (Romans 13:9), the only ones to whom this law applied and who were required to follow it?

The Apostle Paul replied categorically that *natural law* applies to all people.

> When the Gentiles, who do not possess the law, do instinctively what the law requires, these, though not having the law, are a law to themselves.[78] They show that what the law requires is written on their hearts, to which their own conscience also bears witness; and their conflicting thoughts will accuse or perhaps excuse them [. . .].[79]

Calvin echoed,

> Since then all nations, of themselves and without a monitor, are disposed to make laws for themselves, it is beyond all question evident that they have some notions of justice and rectitude [. . .] which are implanted by nature in the hearts of men. They have then a law, though they are without law: for though they have not a written law, they are yet by no means wholly destitute of the knowledge of what is right and just; as they could not otherwise distinguish between vice and virtue.[80]

What then remains is to interpret this law. Do the governing authorities interpret it in accordance with God's command, or independently of God? Is it a moral law, with or without God?

---

77. Calvin, *Inst.*, II, VIII, 46.
78. Rom 2:14.
79. Rom 2:15.
80. Calvin, *Commentaires sur le Nouveau Testament*, vol. 3, 40 (cited by Dermange, "Calvin contre la puissance souveraine,» 87).

Chapter I: A Theological Inquiry Into Natural Law

The Apostle Paul laconically answers this question in Romans 13:4: "[. . .] it [the governing authority] is God's servant for your good."

It is appropriate to note that this verse seems to give rise to varying interpretations.

We know how important Calvin considered governing authorities, and they are to judge equitably.

François Dermange and Irena Backus[81] feel that Calvin revisited the concept of equity espoused by philosophers in ancient times,[82] and it is this concept that would guide the authorities, whether Christian or not.

In contrast, others believe that a governing power in God's service could be nothing else but a governing power that placed itself under the Church's authority.[83]

François Dermange defends his position with a logical argument. He begins by stating that "the Reformer [Calvin] was well aware that most of the legal experts whose work he praises as so many gifts from God knew nothing at all about the Revelation of the Christian God."[84] From this he concludes that Calvin opted for two ethics, the "ethic of holiness" and the "political ethic."[85]

Those who feel that Calvin did not "give his blessing to [. . .] real political autonomy" have yet to be convinced."[86]

A Plausible Answer

My task is not to decide between these two viewpoints, but to remember that it is possible to find a plausible answer from Calvin to the question I am asking about the basis for human rights and consequently for the *human right to water*. This response consists of a supposition that there is a *natural law* shared by all people, whether or not they are Christians. This would be a "moral law with God" for Christians and a "moral law without God" for non-Christians.

I also remember, though, that from the moment it comes to meeting the demands of this *natural law*, all people run up against an aporia, or dead end.

> Therefore, if we direct our views exclusively to the law, the effects upon our minds will only be despondency, confusion, and despair, since it condemns and curses us all, and keeps us far from that blessedness which it proposes to them who observe it.[87]

---

81. Dermange, "Calvin contre la puissance souveraine," 89.

82. Ibid., 88, with the reference to the typology of the four meanings of equity according to Haas, "The concept of equity," 123.

83. Ibid., 88.

84. Ibid., 87.

85. Ibid.

86. Ibid.

87. Calvin, *Inst.*, II, VII, 4.

Part III: A Changing Water Ethic

In fact, it is this very difficulty, this daily noticing of violations of human rights, and consequently of the *human right to water*, that is striking.

Calvin believed that human beings' knowledge of their powerlessness to fulfill the Law's imperative should lead them to take the following position:

> [. . .] that leaving their foolish opinion of their own strength, they may know that they stand and are supported only by the power of God; that being naked and destitute, they may resort for assistance to his mercy, recline themselves wholly upon it, hide themselves entirely in it, and embrace it alone for righteousness and merits, since it is offered in Christ to all who with true faith implore it and expect it. For in the precepts of the law, God appears only, on the one hand, as the rewarder of perfect righteousness, of which we are all destitute; and on the other, as the severe judge of transgressions. But in Christ, his face shines with a plenitude of grace and lenity, even towards miserable and unworthy sinners.[88]

So equity, such as Men can share among themselves, is not the only criterion for *natural law*,[89] but is joined by divine mercy, which the Stoics also posited. Indeed, Cicero wrote as follows.

> True law is right reason in agreement with nature; it is of universal application, unchanging and everlasting; it summons to duty by its commands, and averts from wrongdoing by its prohibitions. And it does not lay its commands or prohibitions upon good men in vain, though neither have any effect on the wicked. It is a sin to try to alter this law, nor is it allowable to attempt to repeal any part of it, and it is impossible to abolish it entirely. We cannot be freed from its obligations by senate or people, and we need not look outside ourselves for an expounder or interpreter of it. And there will not be different laws at Rome and at Athens, or different laws now and in the future, but one eternal and unchangeable law will be valid for all nations and at all times, and there will be one master and ruler, that is, God, over us all, for he is the author of this law, its promulgator, and its enforcing judge. Whoever is disobedient is fleeing from himself and denying his human nature, and by reason of this very fact he will suffer the worst penalties, even if he escapes what is commonly considered punishment.[90]

Who will have listened to Calvin, who is going to listen to him? Therein lies the question of how Calvin is received, of whether or not his legacy is accepted.

---

88. Ibid., II, VII, 8.

89. Concerning whether or not there is a religious criterion for *natural law*, see Dermange, "Calvin contre la puissance souveraine," 90.

90. Cicero, *De republica libri*.

CHAPTER I: A THEOLOGICAL INQUIRY INTO NATURAL LAW

Calvin's Natural Law As a Political Legacy and Basis for the Human Right to Water

A Difficult Challenge

Making *natural law* fit in with the tragic twists and turns of history is a difficult challenge, as well as a way to exploit it for one's own purposes. Yet legal philosophers have been trying ever since the late sixteenth century.

Whether they heeded Calvin's warnings or not is a controversial point.

After a historical overview, I will conclude this chapter by alluding to these dialectics. This will be helpful to understanding, in the next chapter, what might have led to the transformations in the concept of *natural law* that occurred under the tutelage of the modern natural law school's founders.

Is twenty-first century humanity still feeling the repercussions of this reinterpretation of *natural law* in its "human rights corpus"? In an attempt to answer this question, I must continue with my inquiry.

Two Centuries of Violence and Confrontations

I believe it would be worthwhile at this point to recall that two centuries separated Calvin's death from the French Revolution, as François Dermange alluded to above, and they were filled with civil wars, the ferocity and cruelty of which rivaled those endured by some peoples today, in Syria, for example. Deadly violence of all kinds was the result primarily of religious wars, including the Saint Bartholomew's Day massacre in 1572, instigated by Catherine de Medici, which furnished Theodore Beza with the occasion for writing some of his finest pages on civil resistance.[91]

Political upheavals in the Netherlands during the fight for independence from the Spanish monarchy provided fertile ground for Hugo Grotius (1583-1645) to construct his concept of natural law; the same is true of the first English Civil War and Thomas Hobbes (1588-1679), who was led to write *Leviathan*. The war moved Hobbes to wonder about a system of government that could protect the people against tyranny. We can also cite events in the New World, namely the American Revolution, which brought independence for the thirteen English colonies (see the Declaration of Rights of Virginia, signed on June 12, 1776, which contains a list of rights inspired largely by John Locke (1632-1704), and the Declaration of Independence, signed July 4, 1776).

---

91. Beza, *Du droit des magistrats*, cited by Bouvignies-Bouchindhomme, *Hobbes sans Calvin?*, 116.

Part III: A Changing Water Ethic
Is Calvin's Natural Law Reflected in Political Treatises?

The next issue to tackle is learning whether figures such as those mentioned above—theologian and legal scholar Grotius, and philosophers Hobbes and Locke—who witnessed these severe conflicts, were led to refer to the *natural law* inherited from Calvin as a basis for their political writings.

The answer is not self-evident, but I will cite French philosopher Isabelle Bouvignies's theory. It is perhaps somewhat daring in this regard, but at least it has been put forward.

According to her, Calvin's thought could have been a resource on which Thomas Hobbes built when considering the bases for the Republic and developing the rudiments of the rule of law.[92]

She is doubtless taking the opposite tack from François Dermange, for whom the two subjects of the December 2009 colloquium, which virtually pitted Calvin against Hobbes,[93] have absolutely nothing in common. In particular, Dermange stresses that Calvin's concept of shared sovereignty is the very antithesis of Hobbes's support for the sovereign's absolute power.

These two contributions to the 2009 colloquium, which was held at the Institut Protestant de Théologie-Faculté de Paris, brought a great deal to the debate. I fear that untangling the threads of their rigorous lines of reasoning would be beyond me as I have no magic wand to wave to accomplish this feat.

However, I would like to paint in a few strokes what I see as the crucial challenge of Calvin's political legacy as postulated by Bouvignies: Can we, yes or no, find Calvinist traces in the modern doctrine of natural law?

The abovementioned authors position their contributions on two different levels, in that François Dermange gives a scholarly description of the sensitive issues on which Calvin and Hobbes differ,[94] while Isabelle Bouvignies builds a bridge between the reformer and the English proponent of natural law.

They no doubt would be able to agree on two essential traits of Calvin's work that prepared the way for the advent of modern democracy—or at the very least, it is possible to catch glimpses of how they might have done so.

On the one hand, there is Calvin's new interpretation of *natural law*, discussed above, which come hell or high water upheld the notion that the secular and the spiritual had to be kept separate. His contention was still being hotly contested by the supporters of Erastianism shortly after his death.[95]

---

92. Bouvignies-Bouchindhomme, "Hobbes sans Calvin?" 127.
93. Abel, et al., eds., *Jean Calvin et Thomas Hobbes*.
94. Dermange, "Calvin contre la puissance souveraine," 92–95.
95. Ibid., 91.

On the other, both Dermange and Bouvignies insist on Calvin's essential contribution in the political sphere, through his idea of creating a collective of governing authorities responsible for keeping the higher authority in check.

Let us examine Isabelle Bouvignies's working hypotheses.

She believes that Calvin's late changes to his *Institutes of the Christian Religion* with regard to civil government would—unknown to him—have had two consequences: first, that of legitimizing political (but not individual) tyrannicide, and then that of giving rise to a "contract language"[96] between society and the sovereign, of which Hobbes made use a number of decades later.

Her reasoning is as follows.

With regard to the first point, Calvin is said to have changed his mind about tyrannicide shortly before his death, when he proposed the creation of minor authorities such as those mentioned above. Bouvignies believes that there were historical reasons for this about-face. Our reformer is said to have altered some passages in *Institutes of the Christian Religion* when the persecutions suffered by Protestants in the Kingdom of France were made public, with the horrible death inflicted on a well-known Huguenot, Anne de Bourg, in 1559, being one of the most serious examples.[97]

Bouvignies hypothesizes that in connection with these events and the subsequent Saint Bartholomew's Day massacre, John Calvin's successors—especially Theodore Beza and Stephanus Junius Brutus—would have been faced with a serious dilemma. Did they find any passages in Calvin's work that they could use to legitimize a right to oppose the arbitrariness of royal power?

After a long chain of reasoning, Bouvignies answers "yes."[98]

In her view, it is indeed Calvin's proposal to establish elected authorities (magistrates) that were to act as checks and balances on each other, and to whom a higher authority would have to answer, which would constitute "an undeniable advance justifying resistance."[99] She quotes a passage from *Institutes of the Christian Religion* that she feels leaves no room for doubt:

> [...] magistrates appointed for the protection of the people [...] and the moderation of the power of kings [...].[100]

She continues,

> So, given all of the magistrates' equal responsibility to their duty (sovereignty), the subjects were protected against the fallibility of the monarch or higher

---

96. Ibid., 126.
97. Bouvignies-Bouchindhomme, "Hobbes sans Calvin?," 123.
98. Ibid.
99. Ibid., 122.
100. Ibid., 123–24, quoting Calvin, *Inst.*, IV, XX, 31 (OO, vol. 2. p. 1116).

authority. This was Calvin's final word, which his French followers were about to be obliged to appropriate.[101]

Concerning the second point, the "contract language," she says that Theodore Beza and Stephanus Junius Brutus discovered a new meaning for sovereignty, based on this very right to resist a sovereign who was bound by an *oath*.

> The sovereign is bound by an *oath* which obligates him toward the "sovereign government" and is not weakened by his death. The government outlasts the life of its highest authority, which consequently must reinforce that which preceded it.[102]

Consequently, Calvin and those who came after him drew upon the register of mutual commitment, promise, and consent or contract, not to mention the oath and the dual covenant, to form a response to the arbitrary exercise of royal power and cope with completely unexpected and very deadly events.[103]

For example, Thomas Hobbes used contract language in his two main works (*De Cive* and *Leviathan*) in which, less than a century later and in the context of the English civil wars, he reflected on how a civil society could provide itself with a legitimate instrument to protect each of its members.[104]

Preliminary Conclusions

Was Isabelle Bouvignies right in seeing a double influence of Calvin's reform on Hobbes, in terms of both the right to resist and the "contract language"?

Can we therefore postulate, if I follow her reasoning correctly, that the roots of Hobbes's theory of the "social contract" lie with Calvin?

I would answer, first, that interpreting history, particularly the history of ideas, remains an aporetic undertaking.

Next, I would say that in his contribution, not only did François Dermange underscore the differences between Calvin and Hobbes—already mentioned above—with regard to the concept of sovereignty, that is, *shared sovereignty* for the former and *absolute sovereignty* for the latter; he also insisted that they were diametrically opposed as far as "to the need to impose a transcendent authority in politics."[105]

> It is precisely because he was convinced of God's living and present action in the world, through his Providence and his Spirit, that Calvin was so firmly opposed to omnipotence.[106]

101. Ibid., 124.
102. Ibid., 125–26.
103. Ibid., 126.
104. Ibid., 126–27.
105. Dermange, "Calvin contre la puissance souveraine," 95.
106. Ibid., 93.

He becomes even more incisive in defending society against absolute power, adding:

> Between Calvin and Hobbes, Calvin is perhaps, in the final analysis, the most modern, and not solely because he makes it possible to envision society as a conjunction of a number of autonomous spheres, with the mission of the liberal State being to protect each of these from domination by the others; [...] After all, and at the risk of an anachronism, does not Calvin provide better protection than Hobbes from the totalitarianism that is the most fearsome temptation in politics?[107]

Finally, I salute Isabelle Bouvignies as a talented historian who has raised a very interesting point about the right to resist. However, the question of the connection between "contract language" and the doctrine of the "social contract" I will leave open.

For my part, in the context of my inquiry into the basis for the *human right to water*, I think that Calvin's interpretation of the Ten Commandments was both original and rational, thus opening up favorable prospects for the appearance of human rights.

In conclusion, I will state positively that Calvin did leave a legacy on which to base the human rights of the twentieth and twenty-first centuries.

I do agree with Isabelle Bouvignies about the impact that the Reformation and the events associated with it had on a "rationalization of the old world" that led to "the end of traditional society."[108]

For better or for worse, Hobbes and Grotius contributed heavily to this new, rationalized vision of the world, especially by starting a new intellectual movement that philosophers of law and history have named the modern school of natural law.

I will now take up the question of the connection between *natural law* and the modern school of natural law, with the person that posterity calls the "father of international law," Hugo Grotius.

---

107. Ibid., 95.
108. Bouvignies-Bouchindhomme, "Hobbes sans Calvin?," 118.

Chapter II

A Philosophical Inquiry Concerning *Natural Law* From Grotius to the *Human Right to Water* via Kant and Bonhoeffer

Jusnaturalism:[1] Toward a Subtle Transformation of *Natural Law*

AS WE HAVE SEEN above, publications by Michel Villey[2] and Alfred Dufour[3] state their objections to the ways in which law changed after the death of Thomas Aquinas. They see him, particularly through his monumental *Summa Theologica,* as the defender of a legal system inspired mainly by Roman law, which made law an independent discipline all its own, and they find it regrettable that law has lost this quality, especially through two schools of thought that dominated European culture from the Middle Ages to the Enlightenment.

This refers, on the one hand, to the influence of the nominalist and voluntarist theologians who were discussed in the previous chapter; and on the other, to the second or "modern" natural law school, which will be discussed here.

Villey and Dufour find nothing more harmful to the purity of the legal discipline than law drawn from the Holy Scriptures to establish a theological morality, as advocated by Franciscans such as William of Ockham. How could law remain an *art of the good and the equitable*[4] if all of jurisprudence were to be colored with scientific and technical principles that paradoxically led to confused and contradictory formulations, and which therefore were a danger to the peace and safety of society? Michel Villey, especially, cannot find words harsh enough for philosophers whose reputation has nevertheless survived the centuries, à la Hobbes and Locke (not to mention names), neither of whom was a legal scholar,[5] as he emphatically points out.

---

1. In this text, I am using "jusnaturalisme" as a synonym for "modern natural law."
2. Villey, *Le droit et les droits de l'homme.*
3. Dufour, *Droits de l'homme, droit, droit naturel et Histoire.*
4. Villey, *Le droit et les droits de l'homme,* see *"Jus est ars boni et æqui,"* 62.
5. Ibid., 136–37.

CHAPTER II: A PHILOSOPHICAL INQUIRY CONCERNING NATURAL LAW

Alfred Dufour, who probably felt the same way, is more diplomatic with respect to these same names:

> Regardless of one's opinion of the jusnaturalist tradition—as a degenerate legacy of the High Scholastic period or a catalyst for reform in Western legal thought—, it still must be noted that the modern Natural Law School marks a very special moment in the history of European legal thought and science.[6]
>
> [. . .] nowhere [. . .] is the connection between the blossoming of Western philosophy and scientific thought and the concomitant development of jurisprudence more obvious than in the *modern Natural Law School.*

It is this moment in time, which some call very special and others view less favorably, that we will now explore.

Definition of Natural Law from the Perspective of the Modern Natural Law School

As we have seen, Calvin's definition of moral law or *natural law* seems elementary in its simplicity:

> Moreover, the internal law [. . .] suggests to us in some measure the same things which are to be learned from the two tables [. . .].[7]

Since understanding it is almost a foregone conclusion, one might wonder why Calvin's statement of *natural law* left center stage in the seventeenth century.

In addition to the historical circumstances discussed earlier, one plausible explanation can be found in the radical change in world view that followed Copernicus's discoveries, which led him to reject geocentrism and the Ptolemaic system. While it is true that Calvin was his contemporary, the reformer seems to have been unaware of this Polish astronomer's work.

First the Copernican revolution, then Galileo's discoveries, were the focus of attention for learned scholars at a time when the sciences were undergoing phenomenal development. So the temptation for them to build a new legal and political system, by adding the new data about heliocentrism to Euclid's principles and other scientific knowledge, was just too strong.

Three among them are especially worth mentioning, namely Dutchman Hugo Grotius, Englishman Thomas Hobbes and German Samuel von Pufendorf, who allowed these new discoveries to shape their thoughts and demonstrated insatiable curiosity about them. Alfred Dufour clearly shows this "frightening allegiance"[8] of thought to scientific methods and gives three causes for it.

---

6. Dufour, *Droits de l'homme, droit naturel et histoire*, 111.
7. Calvin, *Inst.*, II, VIII, 1.
8. Dufour, *Droits de l'homme, droit naturel et histoire*, 113.

[...] the reasons for this ascendancy of the physical and mathematical sciences over the representatives of the Jusnaturalist School, [...] ha[ve] to do either with Grotius's and Hobbes's personal and epistolary relationships with Galileo, Descartes, and Harvey, and likewise Wolff's with Leibnitz [...] or with the fascination exercised by Galileo's and Harvey's discoveries in astronomy, physics, and physiology, and by the methodological and mathematical principles of Descartes and Leibnitz [...].[9]

Of course, treatises by the authors of the jusnaturalist school had different objectives, as Jean-Marc Tétaz describes very well in *L'Encyclopédie du protestantisme*.

> The principle of self-preservation, a manifestation of Man's sovereign will, becomes the genetic principle of modern natural law: modern natural law becomes law of reason and the basis for the theory of government (Hobbes, Locke, Rousseau), the systematics of civil law (Pufendorf, Thomasius), and international law and the law of war (Grotius).[10]

In contrast, except for Grotius, whose position is ambivalent as we will see shortly, they all agree in stating that modern natural law had been stripped of "any theonomy or biblical basis"[11] and clothed in new raiment.

It is not my purpose here to delve into the deepest arcana in the works of these giants in the history of Western thought. Not that I am indifferent to questions of government sovereignty or civil law, but it seemed to me that Hugo Grotius's approach, which is both internationalist and theological, would be more in keeping with the issue of the ethical challenges of water in general and my research on the basis for the *human right to potable water* in particular.

However, before I let Grotius speak, it is appropriate to give some of the definitions of *natural law*, in its incarnation as the modern natural law formulated by Thomas Hobbes and Samuel von Pufendorf, if only to show how different they were.

Michel Villey and Alfred Dufour found in *Leviathan* and *De Cive [The citizen]*, respectively, the Hobbesian options for *natural law(s)*.

> The right of nature which writers commonly call Jus naturale, is the Liberty each man hath to use of his own power, as he will himself, for the preservation of his own Nature, that is to say of his own Life, and consequently of doing anything which in his own Judgment and Reason he shall conceive to be the aptest means thereunto.[12]
>
> [...] [T]hey are nothing else but certain conclusions understood by Reason, of things to be done, and omitted [...].[13]

9. Ibid.
10. De Tétaz, "Droit naturel," 376.
11. Ibid.
12. Hobbes, *Leviathan*, chapter XIV, cited by Villey, *Le droit et les droits de l'homme*, 10.
13. Hobbes, *Elementorum philosophiæ sectio tertia de Cive*, cited by Dufour, *Droits de l'homme*,

Chapter II: A Philosophical Inquiry Concerning Natural Law

Michel Villey gives the following commentary on the first definition:

> This text [. . .] is the first I know of in which "human right" is defined. We will not maintain that Hobbes was the term's inventor, but that in his work its sources, content, and original function are brought strikingly to light.[14]

I myself find that the second definition ought also to speak to us. Does it not agree with Calvin's moral law, as an internal law, that is, a law of the conscience?

Pufendorf's definition seems to me to cast the possible content of *natural law* in a different light. We note that Alfred Dufour describes it as terminologically ambiguous,[15] because the German philosopher sometimes bases natural law on sociability *(socialitas)*, and sometimes he makes this sociability the very norm of modern natural law, or

> [. . .] the most common rule for human actions, which every person, as a reasoning animal, is bound to obey.[16]

For the purposes of our topic—that is, the impact of the "modern natural law" version of *natural law* on the human rights corpus and the *human right to water*—I felt that the most appropriate of these figures to interrogate was Grotius, as the "father" of the law of nations or public international law, especially as a nod[17] to the fact that he was one of the first Western legal scholars to have discussed the law of the sea.[18]

Paradoxically, Hugo de Grotius's work seems to have influenced the history of human rights less than that of the English and German philosophers mentioned above. Peter Haggenmacher reports that

> [. . .] by its structure, it [his general theory of subjective rights] also heralds the modern doctrine of human rights, though Grotius is rarely associated with this because of his authoritarian conception of government power.[19]

Haggenmacher's observation is rather surprising, since Hobbes is usually the one seen as the great defender of the monarch's power, especially absolute monarchy.

Regardless, history has remembered that this Dutch legal expert and theologian employed his talents as a jurist and fiscal expert in a world that was open to international exchanges, especially with Asia. He was especially known for a legal opinion he wrote for the Dutch East India Company. This powerful private company, a sort

---

droit naturel et histoire, 116 n27 and 122 n71.

14. Villey, *Le droit et les droits de l'homme*, 136.
15. Dufour, *Droits de l'homme, droit naturel et histoire*, 124.
16. Ibid., p. 123.
17. In the context of our study on the ethical challenges of potable water.
18. De Grotius, *Mare liberum*, cited by Forthomme, 24.
19. Haggenmacher, "Grotius, Hugo (1583-1645)," 556.

of multinational corporation before such a thing was invented, had retained him in the matter of a Portuguese vessel that the Dutch had seized in the Strait of Malacca.[20]

As we will now see, Grotius employed these same talents to serve his Calvinist faith, which heavily influenced his doctrine of modern natural law.

Hugo de Grotius: Caught in Midstream

Grotius's work consists of a number of legal and theological treatises, including an early contribution from his youth, *De Jure Prædæ* (1605)[21] [Commentary on the law of prize and booty] and another from his mature years, *De Jure Belli ac Pacis* (1625)[22] [On the law of war and peace] that are still widely consulted today.[23] Although historians have classified him among the members of the modern natural law school, Hugo Grotius really was "caught in midstream." That is, he found himself in the paradoxical position of supporting the rationalism that typified his era while remaining a Protestant firmly committed to his Calvinist faith.

I would now like to do something a little unusual to try to add some dimension to the work of the great Dutch legal expert and theologian.

I have chosen to proceed by means of a virtual dialogue with Hugo de Grotius, an interview transposed into the twenty-first century, with the goal of clarifying his vision of the many-faceted concept of modern natural law.

A Virtual Dialogue across Time between Evelyne Fiechter-Widemann and Hugo de Grotius

Evelyne Fiechter-Widemann

First I would like to thank you for taking part in a particularly difficult exercise, since I am asking you to step across nearly four centuries from beyond the grave. I hope this experience, which will bring up some of your political, legal, and theological battles, will not be too painful for you.

Hugo de Grotius

Not at all. You are honoring my Manes and I am quite willing to answer your questions.

---

20. Alexandrowicz, "Le droit des nations aux Indes orientales."

21. De Grotius, *De Jure Prædæ* (cited by Dufour, Alfred, *Droits de l'homme,* droit naturel et histoire 50 n24).

22. De Grotius, *Le Droit de la guerre et de la paix.*

23. Haggenmacher, "III. La nouvelle physionomie du 'Ius' et le remaniement du droit naturel."

CHAPTER II: A PHILOSOPHICAL INQUIRY CONCERNING NATURAL LAW

EFW

Could you define the concept of modern natural law for my contemporaries?

Hugo de Grotius

It was the Salamanca School, especially Francisco Suarez, that inspired my formulation of the concept of "modern natural law." You will see that my definition differs from the Stoic concept, which postulates a *cosmos* governed by the *logos* or divine laws.[24]

I would like to begin by stating the following. The seventeenth century, in which I had the privilege of living, was an extremely productive period for Western thought. Alfred Dufour has understood very well that there were two revolutions, one methodological and the other philosophical. What you are interested in here is obviously the philosophical revolution, "in the sense that it began the process of substituting science for theology as the primary food for human thought and its regulating principle."[25]

What does this mean? What is this substitution of science for theology?

While my colleagues of the modern natural law school, for example Thomas Hobbes and Samuel von Pufendorf, constructed a legal system based on human nature alone, independent of any divine revelation, I myself devised a mixed system. I thought up this dual system based on my experiences as a lawyer in the real world, and readers will doubtless see noticeable differences in my works of 1605 and 1625.[26]

In *De juris Prædæ* of 1605 you will find my defense of God as the source of the law, for it "ensues from the very order of the Creation."[27]

> Therefore, since God fashioned creation and willed its existence, every individual part thereof has received from him certain natural properties whereby that existence may be preserved and each part may be guided for its own good, in conformity, one might say, with the fundamental law inherent in its origin.[28]

On the other hand, in my *Jus Bellum ac Pacis* of 1625 I was less categorical.

---

24. De Tétaz indicates, "Stoicism resolved the issue of a normative ethical authority by referring to natural law, the rational and divine principle (*logos*) governing the cosmos (ontological theorem)." De Thétaz, *Droit naturel*," 376.

25. Dufour, *Droits de l'homme, droit naturel et histoire*, 49.

26. Haggenmacher, "Grotius, Hugo," 556.

27. Dufour, *Droits de l'homme, droit naturel et histoire*, 118.

28. Ibid., 118, with Latin quotation in n45 taken from De Grotius, Hugo, *De Jure Praedae,* chap. II, p. 9: *Cum igitur res conditas Deus esse fecerit et esse voluerit, proprietates quasdam naturales singulis indidit, quibus ipsum illud esse conservaretur et quibus ad bonum suum unumquodque, velut ex prima originis lege, duceretur.*

Part III: A Changing Water Ethic

And indeed, all we [the science of natural law] have now said would take place, though we should even grant, what without the greatest Wickedness cannot be granted, that there is no God, or that he takes no Care of human Affairs.[29]

To summarize, I thought it judicious to distinguish between an *absolute natural law* or *divine law*, and a *relative or secondary natural law*.[30]

To clarify this distinction of mine, I will give you some examples. *Absolute natural law* or *divine law* is that which consists of "offering worship to God and [. . .] loving one's parents."[31] On the other hand, *relative or secondary natural law*[32] is "civil liberty, inheritance by related persons, and the establishment of the Synods."[33]

Perhaps it would interest you that I prove *natural law* not only "through *a priori* knowledge," *but* "also [. . .] *a posteriori*."[34]

> The former [way of reasoning that a thing belongs to natural law], which is more "subtle and abstracted," consists of "shewing the necessary Fitness or Unfitness of any Thing, with a reasonable and sociable Nature. But the Proof by the latter is, when we cannot with absolute Certainty, yet with very great Probability, conclude that to be by the Law of Nature, which is generally believed to be so by all, or at least, the most civilized, Nations. For an universal Effect requires an universal Cause. And there cannot well be any other Cause assigned for this general Opinion, than what is called Common Sense."[35]

EFW

So would "common sense," as we still say in the twenty-first century, be the key to universal recognition of *natural law*?

Or rather do you think, as Elisabeth Dufourcq says in her recent seven-hundred-page treatise on the invention of natural law,[36] that we ought to be more conversant with the abundance of controversies natural law has caused? Would such knowledge allow us to move beyond "ancient archetypes of such rigidity that they have long impeded the progress of knowledge"[37]?

---

29. De Grotius, *Le Droit de la guerre et de la paix* (1625).
30. Dufour, *Droits de l'homme, droit naturel et histoire*, 139.
31. Ibid.
32. Ibid.
33. Ibid.
34. Ibid., 137.
35. Ibid., 137–38.
36. Dufourcq, *L'invention de la loi naturelle*, 10.
37. Ibid., 9.

Chapter II: A Philosophical Inquiry Concerning Natural Law

Hugo de Grotius

This ethicist and former politician is probably right when she says,

> In this day and age of the global village, and perhaps global danger, the search seems more urgent than ever. Yet it is ancient.[38]

She demonstrates a laudable concern for the future and, like you, wants to reopen the drawers of history to search for any clues that would be useful in the twenty-first century.

But let's get back to my century, the seventeenth.

May I take a turn and ask you a question? You are a legal scholar, but are trying to learn more about theology and philosophy, and have also lived in Asia. Are you aware that I debated modern natural law in a highly explosive context, against Seraphin de Freitas, Portugal's defender in a dispute between the Dutch and the Portuguese in Asia?[39]

EFW

Yes, I believe the issue was the *natural freedom* of trade as a "natural limitation of a country's sovereignty."[40]

But I admit to some surprise at finding modern natural law associated with commercial law . . .

Hugo de Grotius

I myself am very surprised by your reaction. After all, Max Weber[41] dates capitalism back to the beginnings of Calvinism, which I strongly support.

EFW

I think it would be perilous to continue this discussion here.

I have indeed been told that you were influenced by the doctrines of Thomas Erastus, also known as Lieber. This doctor and theologian from Aargau was implicated in a controversy in the Palatinate shortly after Calvin's death, the stakes of which were discussed by François Dermange at the 2009 colloquium I have already mentioned.[42]

---

38. Ibid., 15.
39. Alexandrowicz, "Le droit des nations aux Indes orientales," 1066 n1.
40. Ibid., 1067.
41. Weber, *l'Ethique protestante*.
42. Dermange, "Argent," 91.

Part III: A Changing Water Ethic

This issue had to do with what limits should be placed on State sovereignty. Should matters of religion be independent from matters of politics, as Calvin felt, or should Erastus's point of view that the secular arm or Prince should have authority over both civil and religious matters be defended? I believe you were of the second opinion?

Hugo de Grotius

Thanks be to God that I am no longer of this world. I have gotten out of the habit of crossing swords with anyone—which I would never have done with a lady in any case! Of course, like Thomas Hobbes, I share Erastus's opinion on sovereignty.

But I was involved in other battles that were even more important to me.

You seem to be completely unaware that I took a rather moderate position in the debate that pitted strict Calvinists such as Franciscus Gomarus against Arminius at the famous Synod of Dordrecht, which was held from the autumn of 1618 to the spring of 1619.

I defended Arminius's conception of predestination, for which I was sentenced to life in prison, a fate I barely escaped. My legs were still young—I was forty-four years old in 1621—and I was able to flee . . . and to put the finishing touches on my work by publishing my best-known treatise concerning just warfare[43] in 1625.

I would add that fortunately, later on and thanks mainly to Moses Amyraut, Arminius's propositions met a better fate and my stance made possible a transition to modern times, which pleases me. All of these details were reported by theologian Pierre Bühler of Zurich in a very lengthy article on predestination and providence, which you can read in *Encyclopédie du protestantisme*.[44]

EFW

I can see that not only are you a gentlemen, your courage against all odds has "moved mountains."

As this virtual interview, which I thank you for granting me, draws to a close, I note two things, especially.

First, with regard to the subject at hand, I see that you made a lasting impression in the sense that your theories on international law continue to influence the international law corpus today, for example, through the "do no harm" principle that was incorporated into the Convention on the Law of the Non-navigational Uses of International Watercourses of May 21, 1997.[45]

---

43. De Grotius, *Le Droit de la guerre et de la paix*.
44. Bühler, Pierre, "Prédestination et Providence," 1101.
45. Convention on the Law of the Non-navigational Uses of International Watercourses.

Second, your role as a theologian, which was not insignificant, needs to be rediscovered.

As Alfred Dufour found, you rejected both the Scholastics and the theoreticians of natural theology as defended by, for example, Jean Domat[46] in France.

You established a unique kind of natural law that took into account both elements of traditional dogmatics, that is, Christian orthodoxy, which continued to "be based on the revealed datum"[47]; and the elements of the new, "modern" conception of a thought free of Church authority, a kind of thought based on "rational evidence and [. . .] experience."[48]

I conclude from this that you did not make the task any easier for us, Earth's inhabitants in the twenty-first century, because you allowed us to continue to play on both angles—the metaphysical (or "theological voluntarism"[49]) and the materialistic or contingent.

Perhaps it is this ambiguity that we find reflected in the 1948 Universal Declaration of Human Rights (UDHR),[50] which has two very distinct parts. In fact, I see traces of metaphysics in the first part of the UDHR, which contains the freedoms in articles 1 through 21, and of the International Covenant on Civil and Political Rights (known as Covenant II).[51] In contrast, I see aspects that could be called materialistic in the second part of the UDHR, articles 22 through 27, and of the International Covenant on Economic, Social and Cultural Rights (known as Covenant I).[52]

This is the ambiguity we find in the *human right to water* proclaimed by the United Nations in 2010. Some publicists classify it within the metaphysical concept of the "right to life" in article 3 of the UDHR, while others infer the *human right to water* from the materialistic concept of the right to food in article 25 of the UDHR.

In any case, I congratulate you on the power of your thought, which has survived the centuries and continues to speak to us today.

Hugo de Grotius

Your tribute is chipping away at my modesty somewhat, but I will accept it.

May your century find the peace for which I always hoped, from the bottom of my heart, when I created the foundations of public international law.[53]

---

46. Renoux-Zagamé, *Du droit de Dieu au droit de l'homme*, 78–116.
47. Dufour, *Droits de l'homme, droit naturel et histoire*, 55.
48. Ibid., 49.
49. Ibid., 58.
50. Universal Declaration of Human Rights.
51. International Covenant on Civil and Political Rights.
52. International Covenant on Economic, Social and Cultural Rights.
53. Dufour, *Droits de l'homme, droit naturel et histoire*, 65–66.

I respect Alfred Dufour's perspective about me: I was indeed a solitary man, a man of order and a man of peace "in a century of partisan enrollments, revolts and sedition, controversies and inexpiable wars, but [. . .] one must often know how to swim against the tide."54

In conclusion, I would like to clarify that my work sprang mainly from the extraordinary open-mindedness and entrepreneurial freedom demonstrated by the Asian peoples when the Europeans arrived in the Orient in the sixteenth century.

> European merchants arriving in the East Indies would have found it impossible to build their businesses without [. . .] the Asian custom of allowing the creation of legally autonomous enclaves of foreigners. It was thanks to this ancient institution, which reflected an attitude of tolerance, that the East India Companies were able to obtain from territorial sovereigns the licenses they later transformed into extensive administrative, political, and military organizations.55

The Europeans quite frequently acted unfairly and behaved as conquerors toward what were, after all, sovereign nations. This state of affairs led me to develop the concept of freedom of trade, that is, modern natural law, especially on the seas. This was the *mare liberum* [free sea] as opposed to the Europeans' *mare clausum* [closed sea].

Though the Europeans severely weakened Asia's economic rise by a system of discriminatory treaties imposed upon their Asian partners, current events in the twenty-first century seem to indicate that revenge—a peaceful one, I hope—is in the offing . . . Will Europe rouse itself soon enough to keep up with the new economic reality in the East?

EFW

Naturally I, too, have the same hope.

We would be honored if you would stay with us for a few moments. We are going to move on to the Enlightenment to see how *natural law* was defined in that century, specifically by Immanuel Kant.

Immanuel Kant Completes the Break

At the crossroads of humanity's future, German Enlightenment philosopher Immanuel Kant forded the stream in the middle of which Grotius had remained caught. His *natural law* no longer made any reference whatsoever to transcendence, to God. The break with the past was complete.

54. Ibid., 68.
55. Alexandrowicz, "Le droit des nations aux Indes orientales," 1076.

CHAPTER II: A PHILOSOPHICAL INQUIRY CONCERNING NATURAL LAW

Another break seems to be coming in our time, this time unknown to the Konigsberg thinker.

Indeed, in a world that has suffered the agonies of World War II, many voices have been heard saying that deontological ethics in general, and Kant's in particular, have lost their audience, as Martin Leiner sums up.

> The deep crisis that today is rending the classic traditions of ethics—the Kantian tradition and the Platonic ethics of values (M. Scheler, N. Hartmann)—is tied [especially to the fact that] [. . .] rational arguments in favor of universal obligations are in reality based on a fictitious construct: the kingdom of ends for the Kantian imperative, an ideal communication community without domination for Habermas's discourse ethics, K. O. Apel's *a priori* of the communication community, Rawls's original position and veil of ignorance.[56]

So all indications are that, in keeping with the theories of a man named Michel Foucault,[57] our contemporaries see the search for happiness as the only true virtue. In a nutshell: probably without realizing it, they mean to base their behavior and way of life on an Aristotelian (teleological) or utilitarian ethic.

Yet Kant and his different way of "thinking" modern natural law by suggesting a *universal law of nature*[58] can illuminate the debate about the bases for human rights and the *human right to water*, for two reasons.

First, his unconditional defense of reason explains how, little by little, modern natural law has had to give way to positivism and legal positivism.[59] French philosopher Simone Goyard-Fabre goes so far as to say, "in order to [']think['] modern natural law, reason threw off the yoke [. . .] of a cosmo-theological metaphysics" marked by "dogmatic assurance."[60]

Second, it will be interesting to see whether the German philosopher's repeated encouragements to set thought free, together with his desire, "through education," to "enlighten an *age*,"[61] succeeded in furthering the emergence of a civil society like the one we know today.

Before coming back to this point in more detail, we will allow Immanuel Kant, first, to offer a defense of reason in the face of a natural law that is comparable to common sense, and then to explain his vision of the moral law that he expects to see obeyed by both individuals and nations.

These "four moments" argue that Kantian thought made no small contribution to providing a moral foundation for human rights.

56. Leiner, "Droit, Ethique et Justice," 183.
57. Ibid., 185.
58. Kant indicates, "I ought never to act except in such a way *that I can also will that my maxim should become a universal law.*" Kant, *Fondements*, 12.
59. Goyard-Fabre, "Les rapports du droit et de la morale aujourd'hui."
60. Goyard-Fabre, *Les embarras philosophiques du droit naturel*, 116.
61. Kant, *Que signifie s'orienter dans la pensée?*, 72n.

Part III: A Changing Water Ethic

Kant Attacks Natural Law through Reason

For Kant, reason is "the final touchstone of truth."[62]

To accommodate a controversy in which reason finds itself tangling with "common sense," Kant chose in a text entitled "What Does it Mean to Orient Oneself in Thinking"[63] to set the scene as a fictitious trial.

He offers his powerful plea for reason before the Court of Humanity, which he addresses in these ceremonious terms: "Friends of the human race and of what is holiest to it!"[64]

With a stunning sense of rhetoric, Kant attempts to overturn the argument of the defender of "common sense," also called "healthy reason." He dissects his opponent's reasoning to demonstrate that if reason will not give itself laws, it will be subject to laws given by another,[65]

> [. . .] for without any law, nothing—not even nonsense—can play its game for long.[66]
>
> So he unleashes a devastating attack on those who hide behind freedom and stop trying to give themselves a law, then turn to external laws—one of which may be *superstition*, which "at least has the *form of law* and so allows tranquility to be restored."[67]

The Enlightenment thinker also has nothing more than a condescending smile for someone who justifies himself through

> [. . .] any transcendent intuition under the name of faith, on which tradition and revelation can be grafted without reason's consent [. . .].[68]

So Kant does not dispose of transcendence, which is mentioned here, but in fact revisits it in light of reason.

> The *concept* of God and even the conviction of his *existence* can be met with only in reason, and it cannot first come to us either through inspiration or through tidings communicated to us, however great the authority behind them.[69]
>
> Thus if it is disputed that reason deserves the right to speak first in matters concerning supersensible objects such as the existence of God and the

---

62. Ibid., 71n.
63. Ibid., 55–72.
64. Ibid., 71.
65. Ibid., 69.
66. Ibid.
67. Ibid., 70.
68. Ibid., 56–57.
69. Ibid., 66.

future world, then a wide gate is opened to all enthusiasm, superstition and even to atheism.[70]

Yet did our Konigsberg philosopher fear that he would fail to obtain a conviction from the fictitious court he convened? That is what he seems to hint at the end of his pleading, in which a prosopopoeia shows us reason personified as a victim to be rescued.

It was just this "innocent party [. . .] well disposed and [which] would have used [its] freedom lawfully, and hence in a way which is conducive to what is best for the world!"[71] that he defended throughout his life with the construction of his famous categorical imperative.

His goal was not a modest one:

> Purifying the common concept of reason of its contradictions and defending [. . .] the maxims of healthy reason.[72]

So must we follow Kant in coming to the rescue of reason, prompted by a feeling of empathy—to its defender's great displeasure, since his stance is that where matters of morality are concerned, any "inclination" is to be banished?

We should make no mistake. Even though history describes Kant as a cold-hearted philosopher, not all of his work expresses disdain for the realm of the senses. On the contrary, in "What Does It Mean to Orient Oneself in Thinking?" he offers a number of arguments to convince us that we are necessarily prompted by the principle of "a *subjective* ground of differentiation,"[73] whether it be to orient ourselves geographically in relation to the stars, or to find our way in the evening in an unlit neighborhood.

So, by analogy, he applies an instrument of the sensuous world to thought. When transposed into the world of abstraction, the concept of a "*subjective* ground of differentiation" then becomes the concept of "maxim":[74]

> And since this guiding thread is not an objective principle of reason, a principle of insight, but merely a subjective one (i.e.[,] a maxim) [. . .].[75]

We find this maxim in the famous categorical imperative, which is stated in three ways, as we shall see again several times in other chapters. Here, what interests me is the fact that this formulation is associated with *nature*:

---

70. Ibid., 67.
71. Ibid., 72.
72. Ibid., 57.
73. Ibid.
74. Ibid., 63.
75. Ibid.

Act as if the maxim of your action were to become through your will *a universal law of nature*.[76]

Kant clarifies what *nature* is for him:

> [...] the universality of the law governing the production of effects constitutes what is properly called *nature* in its most general sense (nature as regards its form)—that is, the existence of things so far as determined by universal laws [...].[77]

Do those of Kant's concepts set out here untangle the knot of complexity that surrounds the "law/nature" pair as already described by Michel Villey? I note the latter's perplexity when 255 different formulations are identified for this oxymoron.

> It must also be noted that the marriage of the two terms *droit* ["law"] and *nature* ["nature"] is extremely obscure. For example, Michel Villey, citing legal historian E. Wolf, who had classified and commented "with Germanic rigor" on the multiple meanings of these two words, wrote, "the word *nature* can have 17 meanings, while the word *droit* has 15, which yields 255 possible combinations. [...] these possibilities [...] indicate [...] the fluidity of this concept. The task of expanding and comprehending it is easy to bungle thoroughly, even in its most orthodox formulations."[78]

A. Philonenko, a commentator on the French translation of *Groundwork of the Metaphysic of Morals,* suggests that Kant meant to be reassuring.

> When Kant refines the wording of the imperative by specifying that the maxim of the action should "become ... a universal law of nature," he does not intend to confuse ethics and knowledge of nature. He also does not want to introduce a natural morality in the bad sense of the term. He intends only to convey the idea of law which, coming from nature or freedom, always serves as an example of lawfulness, since a law is universal. [...] Nature, in its lawfulness, is the *model* (type) of moral lawfulness. [...] In fact, the point is to make the categorical imperative more *sensuous* (understandable in a more precise way).[79]

The categorical imperative's criterion of universality already gives a first clue about the German philosopher's contribution to building human rights in the twentieth century. In my opinion, he also lent a certain welcome authority to *natural law* (in the sense of moral law), notwithstanding the lack of clarity surrounding this concept, as exposed by Michel Villey.

It is this power conferred upon moral law that will be our next topic.

76. Kant, *Fondements,* 129 (The typography reflects Kant's emphasis).
77. Ibid.
78. Goyard-Fabre, *Les embarras philosophiques du droit naturel,* 17.
79. Kant, ibid., 129 n1.

CHAPTER II: A PHILOSOPHICAL INQUIRY CONCERNING NATURAL LAW

Kant's Moral Law for the Individual: Incentives of the Heart in Free Thought

Kant is dreaded because of the rigor of his thought, derived from a noticeable rigidity in the morality he advocates, namely one of a duty to be fulfilled, that is, of a moral rule that the individual must set for himself and to which he must submit.

If we take a closer look, we find that this much-disparaged raising of the moral standard, this "deontological" ethic, may have some virtues.

I was led to this remark by the fictitious debate I just summarized and the text on which it is based, namely "What Does It Mean to Orient Oneself in Thinking?"

In a way, Kant uses this text to lay all his cards on the table by shedding some light on the subtle mechanisms that led him to formulate the categorical imperative.

His main intent is to demonstrate that in order for the members of a society to enjoy freedom of thought that is not repressed by the State or any other outside authority, each member would be wise to use that freedom to make his own reason reasonable, that is, by curbing it through a law *"which it gives itself."*[80]

However, he immediately clarifies that reason ought not to submit to just any law, but to one that gives "force" and "authority" to "the incentives of the heart"; such force and authority cannot arise except through *duty*.

To Kant, any other way of governing reason would be a "precarious state of the human mind," which he calls "unbelief of reason."[81] He intones the following warning: the individual who has adopted "the way of thinking one calls libertinism"[82] thereby "has cast off the thread by which reason used to steer [him]."[83] His reason will indeed have been freed, but as it is unaccustomed to freedom, this release will necessarily "degenerate into a misuse and a presumptuous trust in the independence of its faculties from all limitations [. . .]."[84]

This disastrous release could then lead the authorities to

> [. . .] get mixed up in the game, so that even civil arrangements may not fall into the greatest disorder; and since they regard the most efficient and emphatic means as the best, this does away with even the freedom to think, and subjects thinking, like other trades, to the country's rules and regulations. And so freedom in thinking finally destroys itself if it tries to proceed in independence of the laws of reason.[85]

---

80. Kant, *Que signifie s'orienter dans la pensée?*, 69.
81. Ibid., 71.
82. Ibid.
83. Ibid., 70.
84. Ibid.
85. Ibid., 71. My comment: Do we not have an illustration of state control of freedom in the case of Edward Snowdon, which was making headlines in June 2013? It concerned an American citizen who was condemning invasion of privacy in the United States.

To avoid this inopportune intrusion from outside, the German philosopher suggests some principles of reason, including the categorical imperatives mentioned above.

So we can infer from the foregoing that for Kant, the concept of a categorical imperative is a bulwark against arbitrariness. Can we not see this as a way of protecting Man against all sorts of abuse?

"Universality" and "a bulwark against arbitrariness": now we have in hand two of the criteria that will enable us to theorize about Kant's role in building human rights in the twentieth century. What about the other two?

Kant's View on Moral Law for Nations: From an Individual Categorical Imperative to One for States

This path, which must be explored again and again for individual ethics, must also be traveled by all of humanity. Kant felt that the categorical imperative alone could ensure coordinated order among nations and favor peace.

Will not the expansion of individual moral law to all States give us a third clue in support of the premise mentioned above, stating that the categorical imperative and human rights are connected?

One might think so.

In contrast to Hugo de Grotius, our Baltic-based philosopher—even comfortably ensconced in his office and therefore distanced from the world about which he theorized—showed remarkable clairvoyance in the late eighteenth-century international context in which he lived. Naturally the Copernican revolution played a role, but I also note Kant's astonishing curiosity about the world's future. In the texts he left us, readers will also detect anxiety, even a profound bitterness, about the attitude of Europeans who conquered distant lands and showed the greatest disregard for their inhabitants:

> [. . .] the inhospitable conduct of the "civilised" countries of Europe, especially the ones driven by commerce. Their wrong treatment of the lands and peoples they visit (here "visit" = "conquer"!) is terrifying in its extremes. [. . .] they counted the inhabitants as nothing. In India, under the pretence of intending to establish trading posts, they brought in foreign soldiers to oppress the natives, started up widespread wars among the various Indian states, and spread famine, rebellion, treachery, and the whole litany of evils that afflict mankind.[86]

Kant again stresses that he was extremely shocked that Christians would shamelessly attack other human beings in this way, under cover of religion:

---

86. Kant, *Vers la paix perpétuelle, esquisse philosophique*, 94–95.

> [. . .] and these atrocities are the work of powers that make a great show of their piety and—drinking injustice like water—regard themselves as being, in the matter of correct religious belief, the chosen people![87]

Prompted by his sense of duty, he began to dream of world peace safeguarded by an international association of rational nations, and to seek ways of achieving it.

In other words, using a remarkable kind of logic, Kant proceeded to transpose a maxim developed for an individual ethic to make it fit all of the countries in the world. According to Kant, if these nations—which had long been considered to be living in a state of nature—wanted to get beyond their differences to arrive at universal peace, they must agree as equals to set rules for cooperation based on the model of the categorical imperative.

It is of course true that his intellectual construct takes as a point of reference a subtle legal argument that many thinkers had already been refining for quite some time. This was the idea of the "legal person," a construct that today has been fully assimilated into all of the "rule of law" nations worthy of the name.

Kant was careful to make clear that what he was proposing was far from utopian but absolutely necessary for peace, because

> [t]he peoples of the earth have now gone a good distance in forming themselves into smaller or larger communities; this has gone so far that a violation of rights in one place is now felt throughout the world. So the idea of a law of world citizenship is not a legal flight of fancy; rather, it is necessary to complete the unwritten code of civil and international law and also mankind's written laws; and so it is needed for perpetual peace. Until we can establish a law of world citizenship, we mustn't congratulate ourselves on how close we are coming to that.[88]

While the first two hints of Kant's postulated contribution to the basis for human rights in the twentieth century fell under a topology of thought, this third piece of evidence is anchored in a global world and is a wonderful addition to our case file.

Civil Society's Emergence: Thought Set Free by the Enlightenment

It must be noted that active participation in the overall challenges of the contemporary world we know as "civil society" has increased considerably since the end of the twentieth century.

For a long time, civil society was inefficient, as Swedish Ambassador Jan Eliasson reminded us in May 2013, at a conference organized by the National University

---

87. Ibid., 96.
88. Ibid., 96–97.

of Singapore[89] and held in that Asian city-state. Now it can openly contribute to the addition of new content to human rights.

It caused a great deal of commotion by demonstrating in Seattle[90] and, which is of interest given our topic, in Cochabamba,[91] a place that will be remembered for its iconic "water war" that played a key role in the 2010 Resolution by the UN General Assembly concerning the human right to water.

It also made itself heard among some churches in a flood of ecumenical support for water in 2005[92] and 2006.[93] I discussed the first of these declarations in Part II. While the WCC (World Council of Churches) as a whole subscribed to it, I do not want to gloss over these two statements' unique points, which were brought up in a relevant discussion written by theologian, biologist, and FEPS ethicist Otto Schäfer. I refer my readers to this article.[94]

So civil society seems to have appropriated, instinctively in a way, that which governments had intentionally agreed to grant it after World War II, namely, the status of responsible "peoples," as the United Nations Charter of 1945 expressly stated in its preamble: "We the peoples [. . .]."[95]

However, these highly promising beginnings cannot hide some pitfalls that are already apparent. In fact, civil society is merely a rather variable entity that is difficult to pin down, consisting of many actors or "stakeholders," and described by Joseph Nye as a "soft power" society.[96] So, in the globalized world of the twenty-first century, we will have to be careful to avoid any deviance or fundamentalism[97] that might lead the world into new dead ends. And the churches will have a role to play in this regard.

Having been warned of these dangers, this civil society that has emerged from its minority[98] into maturity is showing its independence and free will, to repeat a key Kantian expression.

Civil society's "freedom of will," as it exists in the twenty-first century, seems to me to be the very thing that constitutes the fourth clue to the connection between Kant's thought and the emancipation of peoples.

So we have been able to find affirmative answers to my four postulates.

---

89. Often known by its acronym, NUS.

90. De Frouville, "Une conception démocratique du droit international."

91. Postel and Wolf, "Dehydrating Conflict. 60–67, cited by Tignino, "L'eau et son rôle pour la paix et la sécurité internationales" 6. See also Mélançon, *La guerre de l'eau de Cochabamba, Bolivie.*

92. Ecumenical Declaration.

93. Statement on Water for Life.

94. Schäfer, "Brasilianisch-schweizerische 'Oekumenische Erklärung zum Wasser als Menschenrecht.'"

95. www.un.org.

96. Nye, *Soft Power*, 122–23.

97. Bourguinat, *Les intégrismes économiques.*

98. Kant, *Qu'est-ce que les Lumières?*

CHAPTER II: A PHILOSOPHICAL INQUIRY CONCERNING NATURAL LAW

I remain cautious, though, and while I think that Kant certainly helped to justify the legitimacy of the human rights proclaimed in the twentieth century, I will not go as far as some authors who see Kant as "the" originator of the UN's 1948 declaration.

Preliminary Conclusion

Like Calvin, Kant is known for his strict views on moral law.

While Calvin referred to the Decalogue and the law of loving one's neighbor, in accordance with the Scriptures, to guide his thought and behavior, Kant created his own maxims to direct his life as well as that of the members of society and that of nations.

A theologically-based maxim for one, rationally-based maxims for the other, and both aspired to a universal moral law.

What remains of this today?

As the antithesis of the Kantian ethic, but closer to Calvinistic theology, Bonhoeffer's *Ethics*—written in the midst of the Hitlerian Nazi crisis—contains a new variation for our already monumental file on *natural law*. Will it surprise us? I think it will. Let us see.

Dietrich Bonhoeffer and the Eclipse of Natural Law

As the editors of Dietrich Bonhoeffer's *Ethique* [Ethics] indicate in a note inserted at the end of the last paragraph of the chapter entitled "le naturel"[99] [The natural], the German theologian's thoughts on *natural law* remained unfinished.

However, he did say enough about it to sweep away all conformism and comfort, as Swiss theologian and ethicist Denis Müller testifies.

> The *lex naturæ* is [. . .] an element of the natural life and a tool of human reason, no more and no less. Humanized, it is also deconsecrated, deabsolutized. So in Bonhoeffer, the destabilization of natural law subtly appears.[100]

For Bonhoeffer, the Gospel is at the heart of a consideration of *natural law*, with the Decalogue being the "ultimate criterion."

> This formulation does not envisage the possibility of a *lex naturæ* which deviates from the decalogue and gives rise to a conflict; the decalogue in any case always remains the sole criterion. It is, therefore, the will of God and not the will of man which takes effect in the *primus usus* or the *lex naturæ*. "God demands and requires such an outwardly seemly life, and for the sake of God's commandment one must do these same good works which are commanded in the Ten Commandments" (A.C. IV, 22). The organ through which the *lex*

---

99. Bonhoeffer, *Ethique*, 149 n1.
100. Müller, "La loi 'naturelle' au risque de l'instabilité évangélique," 11–30.

naturæ takes effect is reason. Reason is opposed by the demonic forces ("evil lust and devils"), and these are more powerful than reason, so that despite its "violent efforts" reason seldom achieves its purpose (A.C. XVIII, 71f.). This makes it clear that not every human impulse can pretend to be a natural law. The ultimate criterion is always the decalogue.[101]

He even goes so far as to state that "the place of the decalogue is both in the church and in the government building."[102]

Did Dietrich Bonhoeffer break a taboo? Does his exclusion of *natural law* in favor of the Gospels mean that a bothersome concept has been sent off into oblivion?

Regardless, his position is completely in line with that of the reformers. Theologians Eric Fuchs and Pierre-André Stucki stress that

> [the reformers] excluded a recourse to natural law only because it seemed infinitely less interesting to them than recourse to the Holy Scriptures, in which they would discover a teaching on the Law that they found to be of incomparable power and effectiveness.[103]

Denis Müller opened Pandora's box with regard to Bonhoeffer's position, according to which "natural law is only an instrument, a means, which acquires value through *ratio* [the reasoning faculty],"[104] on the one hand, but on the other "may all of this happen *coram deo* [in the presence of God] and in the service of God's will."[105]

In this Swiss theologian's view, the assertion is not insignificant, even well into the twenty-first century.

So the thinker from Breslau might unknowingly be called upon to referee a latent quarrel that it would be better to defuse than to allow to explode.

What is this mystery, this secret to which only Denis Müller has the key? The answer can be written in four letters: Rome!

An Unexpected Revival

As my studies on the basis for the *human right to water* drew to a close, I was quite astonished to learn that the Roman Curia had undertaken significant work on *natural law* in recent years. This was published in 2009 in an official document entitled *À la recherche d'une éthique universelle*.[106]

---

101. Bonhoeffer, *Ethique*, 257–58.
102. Ibid., 260.
103. Fuchs and Stucki, *Au nom de l'Autre*, 132.
104. Müller, "La loi 'naturelle' au risque de l'instabilité évangélique."
105. Ibid.
106. Bonino, *À la recherche d'une éthique universelle*.

Chapter II: A Philosophical Inquiry Concerning Natural Law

This revived interest in *lex naturæ* piqued the curiosity of both Protestant and Catholic theologians, who met in Tours in September 2009 for an ATEM[107] colloquium at which they asked why this concept was returning to center stage.

To stir up interest in this ancient topic, the academic conclave's organizers did not hesitate to choose a somewhat iconoclastic title for their seminar: "Natural law: the return of a concept in tatters?"[108]

The Tours colloquium left us with a lucid, assured, and slightly controversial article by Protestant theologian Denis Müller. In his attempt to understand, the author suggests several hypotheses,[109] among which he does not rule out a universalist maneuver that might exacerbate interdenominational tensions.

> As Jean Porter clearly saw, aside from the fact that the correlation between reason and nature is not philosophically self-evident, depending on the kinds of definitions used, it is weakened by the multifaceted upsurge of shifting Scriptures and wandering subjects. We are no longer in an arrangement of peaceful triangularity, but in a Bermuda triangle that looks more like a whirlpool than a firm foundation. Now this freeing up of new energies ought to be done outside of "revisionist" strategies that settle for shaping natural law to the tastes of the day. Behind Porter's reconstruction it is all too easy to read Ratzinger's restoration and Benedict XVI's taking in hand, already largely put in place under John Paul II by his prefect himself. The return to the theme of natural law is not at all innocent: its universal aim can hardly be dissociated from the ties between theological discourse and authoritative power, on the one hand, and the precariousness of faith on the other. The case of natural law is decided at this crossroads between the oppressive power of an authoritarian mode and the destabilizing "authority" of a Gospel that alone is capable of instituting a humanizing universality while introducing some active listening at the heart of our will to power.[110]

Even though Denis Müller insists on a second hypothesis that is "much more plausible"[111] because it is "scientific" rather than "strategic," would this not risk the resurgence of the medieval tension between Scholastics and Nominalists that I discussed earlier? The former gave *ratio*, or reason, preeminence over God's will, whereas the second believed that God should be the one to direct Man.

Should we not therefore worry that we will see the controversies of the Middle Ages back in the news, at risk of casting a pall over relationships between Christians, who really should have every reason to unite, especially given the rise of fundamentalism? Should we not pay heed to Denis Müller's warning?

---

107. ATEM is the French acronym for the Theologians' Association for the Study of Morality.
108. Gaziaux and Lemoine, "La loi naturelle—Le retour d'un concept en miettes?."
109. Müller, "La loi 'naturelle' au risque de l'instabilité évangélique," 13.
110. Ibid., 28–29.
111. Ibid., 14.

The question is all the more worth asking because, as I have said, some Catholic and Protestant churches have become involved in human rights and the *human right to water*, and the issue of the bases for these rights is closely related to this question of *natural law*, as I have attempted to explain.

So is this a bothersome concept, one in tatters, or one that should be revived?

I would say, along with Denis Müller, that "it should be handled with kid gloves,"[112] and that if *law* and *nature* must be mixed, let the combination be beneficial to all, to lay out

> universality to conquer, a field of meaning [for escaping] perhaps the alienating power of those who would make it a rallying cause.[113]

Conclusion

In Chapter I of Part II, I left open the question of the legal or ethical normativity of the human right to water.

The authors I surveyed did not directly answer the question. Worse yet, it became clear from the "virtual interview" with Hugo de Grotius that the sources and origins of human rights remain completely ambiguous. In any case, he showed that while he had indeed moved away from natural law, he had not made a complete break with things theological.

I learned that the authors I consulted, whose viewpoints I have outlined, had nothing to say against my hypothesis that a moral law is the principle or basis for human rights in general, and consequently for the new human right to water. So I feel that I have confirmed my viewpoint that the new *human right to water* has no foundation in law, but a basis that is, if not theological, at least ethical. What emerges from this is that it does not by its own nature compel, and that it is not a legal rule that can be applied as is by the courts. For this to happen, it would have to become part of a nation's legal corpus, first via a constitution, then by way of legal and regulatory paths. At the very most, the new human right to water can serve as a point of reference when a judge makes a fair decision.

As I undertook this exercise, I believe I was able to discern that this moral law could draw its strength not only from theology or philosophy, but also from a science that makes Man the sole criterion because he is endowed with reason or common sense.

In other words, theology offered me *natural law;* philosophy, *modern natural law;* and rationalism, the *categorical imperative.*

At the end of the journey that led me from Abraham to the Apostle Paul and John Calvin, during which *natural law* moved from an oral precept to a written

---

112. Ibid., 29.
113. Ibid., 15.

commandment, we found that a revisited *natural law* appeared with Hugo de Grotius, who transformed it and shaped it into a unique kind of modern natural law.

What historians call modernity, that is, the period that brought about a break with theological metaphysics, is rationalism, with its conception that Man is to be acclaimed. It is to Immanuel Kant that we owe the universal law of nature in the form of a categorical imperative.

For his part, Dietrich Bonhoeffer returned to the wellspring, the Gospel, and had little use for *natural law*.

We now see doubt slyly creeping in.

Is it necessary to examine history and strive to penetrate the mystery of the basis for the *human right to water*?

Optimists answer in the affirmative, because for them, the models of the past are likely to lend moral force to the new *human right to water*—provided, that is, that we take the trouble to consult them.

Pessimists, on the other hand, will answer in the negative. They stress that in the third millennium, Man no longer needs to rely on the archetypes of his predecessors, which they say are obsolete.

Ignorance is a poor adviser, as Kant reminds us, and reason alone is the "touchstone" for finding the truth. Ancient writings likewise counsel prudence and vigilance, as we find in the book of Proverbs in the Old Testament:

Buy truth, [. . .] wisdom, instruction, and understanding.[114]

Where can such instruction be had, so that thought will unfold, not in the direction of "the" truth, but in such a way as to get beyond the limits that unpracticed thought will not fail to set for itself? How can we avoid the exaltation and superstition so roundly criticized by Calvin, long before Kant appeared on the scene? What must we do to prevent human rights, and therefore the *human right to water*, from becoming the object of such exaltation and being transformed into a dogma or even a religion?

Here we have the question of where thought can be fed, practiced, and structured to blossom in the interest of the common good—in a word, to awaken a desire, a moral force for action.

Intuitively, this should be in the context of schools and universities, on the one hand, and virtual spaces such as the Internet and cybercafés on the other, taking note that the first two are also increasingly present on the web. Thanks to these new technologies and social networks, freedom of thought as an instrument of civil society can contribute to the harmonious development of human rights. This is a complicated and dangerous exercise, however, because as Kant says, thought that sets no duty for itself will end up bringing about its own destruction.

---

114. Prov 23:23.

Part III: A Changing Water Ethic

I would add, and this point is important, that initiatives such as those undertaken by some churches in 2005 show that they, too, can be a place to learn about human rights and the *human right to water*. The Roman Curia also pulled *natural law* back out of the catacombs to which it had been relegated by modernity, the Copernican revolution in thought.

So the twenty-first century offers multiple religious and secular spaces for thought to use as its home port. It must take care to find the right one, especially one that is tolerant and open to constructive dialogue. Such is the challenge.

That is why I feel that an attempt to "think" an ethic of water, to be shaped in space and time, is legitimate.

Inherent in the bases for human rights and the *human right to water* that have just been suggested are many criteria that must be taken into account for a fair and responsible water ethic.

Two unavoidable aspects of such an ethic, namely Justice and Responsibility, will be the central focus of the discussion that follows.

Before we come to them, however, we will inquire into what led the United Nations to start, in 2010, this new adventure of extending the already long list of intentions that are so difficult to implement.

Indeed, what members of a UN organization or NGO have not, at one time or another, wondered why it was so necessary to concern themselves with people lacking access to water and sanitation? What are the motives for such worry, such solicitude? Could they be kindness, empathy, solidarity, pity, or perhaps shame in the face of a horrible injustice?

Here, again, there are no ready answers. So, once again, I will take up my pilgrim's staff and continue the journey.

Section II

Motives for Actions that Are in Conformity with Duty, Good, and Useful for Universal Access to Potable Water

Introduction

WE HAVE NOW SEEN the efforts that religious, political, economic, and scientific entities are making to "think" water.

What all of these attempts have in common is the objective of choosing between good and evil, between good and bad solutions, between what would be better for humanity's well-being and what would be detrimental to it.

Now, finding the right solution means introducing ethics into politics and economics, finding intersection points between these three spheres of human activity, as Paul Ricœur conceptualized it so well in one of his major works, *Du texte à l'action*.[1] I will comment on the connections he makes at the end of this section.

But for now, let us ask why Man can be led to concern himself about the fate of the billion individuals who lack access to water and the two-and-a-half billion without sanitation. Against such motives as benevolence, pity, or even shame, we can also set duty, which can imply an obligation to act on behalf of those who suffer.

I will group some of the motives listed above, along with still others, within the three "classic" ethics—deontological, eudaemonistic, and utilitarian—and will ask what they can bring to the potable water issue in today's globalized world.

---

1. Ricœur, *Du texte à l'action*, 433–48.

Chapter I

Deontological Motives for Action, or "Thinking" Water Philosophically with Immanuel Kant

IMMANUEL KANT IS PROBABLY one of the philosophers who best knew how to look deeply into the human soul. Desiring to construct a rational metaphysics distinct from anthropology, which he called empirical metaphysics, he systematically compared and contrasted the intelligible world, that is, that of reason; and the sensuous or sensible world, which is that of inclinations.

When it comes to inclinations, Kant displays the deepest skepticism. For example, in *Groundwork of the Metaphysic of Morals* he says,

> [. . .] man, affected as he is by so many inclinations, is capable of the Idea of a pure practical reason, but he has not so easily the power to realize the Idea *in concreto* in his conduct of life.[1]

But why? Did the great philosopher have an answer for this fundamental question?

Writing makes it possible to overcome the vagaries of space and time. That is why, for the second time in this study, I have chosen to create a virtual platform to which I can invite this philosopher, one of the greatest scholars of modern times. Although my approach might be called daring or perhaps even foolhardy, I believe it is well adapted for providing some parts of the answer to such serious and important problems as those relating to Man's duty to his fellows, in general, and also those pertaining to the dialectic of good and evil.

So I have tried to suppose that philosopher Immanuel Kant would have accepted my invitation. Since he dedicated his life to seeking "the common Idea of duty [. . .] and the laws of morality,"[2] it seemed wise to offer him a virtual space created by imaginative reason.

---

1. Kant, *Fondements*, 72.
2. Ibid., no. 389, 70.

Part III: A Changing Water Ethic

Virtual Interview with Immanuel Kant

General Duties of Man toward His Fellows

Evelyne Fiechter-Widemann

Sehr geehrter Herr Doktor, herzlichen Dank für Ihre heutige Präsenz auf meinem virtuellen Podium. Es ist eine Ehre, Sie hier begrüssen zu dürfen. [Doctor, I would like to offer you my warmest thanks for joining me today at my virtual podium. It is an honor to have you here.]

I am turning to you for some insight into the twenty-first century's moral disquiet, as so well interpreted and laid before us by philosopher Monique Canto-Sperber.[3] I was hoping that as the father of modern philosophy, and as someone from a Pietist background, you would be able to help me in my attempt to find a moral benchmark for my contemporaries that might be useful in a context of globalization, in which challenges seem ever greater and more complex, and therefore more difficult to address.

In fact, in the third millennium humankind is weighed down by contradictions, conflicts, and tensions, and people are struggling to find their place and come to a consensus about values. We have indeed tried to suggest a catalogue of reference principles, such as human rights, to which the human right to water was added in 2010, but despite these efforts humanity seems no less troubled than before.

Would you be willing to answer a few questions to get the discussion about the ethical challenges of potable water off to a good start?

Immanuel Kant

Of course. You may be interested to know that while you see me primarily as a philosopher and ethicist, I have always been fascinated by physical geography, which I taught for a long time. I looked at maps with hundreds of students, and together we located the seas and traced our planet's great rivers.

To avoid any misunderstanding, I will warn you that while I am quite willing to answer your questions about "Man's duties to himself and others,"[4] I cannot give an opinion about concerns that were still unknown in my century. So as far as the issue of the vital resource of water is concerned, you will have to undertake the necessary ethical explorations yourself to see whether my work can be of some help to you.

I will also remind you that *a priori* cognition, rather than *a posteriori* cognition, was at the heart of my work. The former seeks understanding in an abstract way, while the latter has to do with experience and the sensible world, that is, the world of the

---

3. Canto-Sperber, *L'inquiétude morale et la vie humaine*.
4. Kant, *Métaphysique des mœurs II*, 373.

Chapter I: "Thinking" Water Philosophically with Immanuel Kant

concrete problems that part of the global population experiences in the field you are studying.

EFW

I'm well aware that at first sight, we are working on very different levels. Yet your concern for a more peaceful world and your dream of laying the foundations for better understanding among nations, strike me as attempts to build a bridge between these two levels.

That being the case, allow me to carry on with the interview, starting with some historical data concerning your work's reception in Western thought. There is no doubt it has provoked mixed reactions, both long ago and now in our day. It even seems to have dropped into obscurity in the second half of the twentieth century.[5] Notwithstanding, despite your detractors—such as Schleiermacher and Nietzsche in the nineteenth century, then Husserl and his phenomenology in the early twentieth, in particular—it is once again finding favor in the twenty-first.

While not very accessible to those not conversant with it, your metaphysic has left traces that I find useful to bring up again for the purposes of my study. I would like to talk about your three fundamental questions addressing the human condition: *What can I know? What should I do? What may I hope?*

The first and last of these questions frame the existential question of action, which is especially relevant to the present-day dilemma of water, implicit in the *human right to water* proclaimed in 2010—namely knowing what must be done to make it accessible to everyone. This was the very topic selected for the Workshop for Water Ethics (W4W) colloquium held on March 22, 2011, entitled "Too Much Water or Not Enough: How Can We Wisely Use This Unpredictable Vital Resource?"[6]

Immanuel Kant

In this case, you have indeed tried to proceed with a moral consideration, namely of duty. Among the examples I provide in *Groundwork of the Metaphysic of Morals* and *The Metaphysics of Morals*, you have probably noticed that we must distinguish between actions taken in conformity with duty and those taken from the motive of duty. For example, I consider that if a merchant sells his products to all buyers at the same price, regardless of the customer's wealth, he is acting in his own interest and to ensure his own good reputation. So he is not acting from the motive of duty, but only in conformity with it. To be even more specific, I will take the liberty of citing my example:

---

5. See Part III, Section I, Chapter II, Immanuel Kant Completes the Break.
6. W4W colloquia. http://www.fiechter.name.

[. . .] it certainly accords with duty that a grocer should not overcharge his inexperienced customer; and where there is much competition a sensible shopkeeper refrains from so doing and keeps to a fixed and general price for everyone so that a child can buy from him just as well as anyone else. Thus people are served *honestly*; but this is not nearly enough to justify us in believing that the shopkeeper has acted this way from duty or from principles of fair dealing; his interests required him to do so. We cannot assume him to have in addition an immediate inclination towards his customers, leading him, as it were out of love, to give no man preference over another in the matter of price. Thus, the action was done neither from duty nor from immediate inclination, but solely from purposes of self-interest.[7]

EFW

So if I've understood you correctly, if I were to call an ambulance to help an elderly person who had been knocked down, robbed, and left injured and helpless by a group of thugs, then I would be acting from the motive of duty and not merely in conformity with it?

Immanuel Kant

That is correct, but only if you were not acting out of self interest and were not trying to get your name in the local newspaper or, to bring myself up to date, to see your charitable act "liked" on Facebook.

EFW

So as I see it, if I respond to an appeal by EPER or Swiss Solidarity for gifts after a tsunami or heavy flooding by announcing a gift of 1,000 francs, then according to your criterion for duty my act could be called moral, since the motive would be the good work and not self-interest.

Immanuel Kant

Good heavens no! The will must be good "without qualification"[8] or "absolutely good."[9] I fear I will disappoint you in terms of your own ability truly to perform a good action. Try to understand my reasoning.

---

7. Kant, *Fondements*, 88.
8. Ibid., 79.
9. Ibid., 161.

Chapter I: "Thinking" Water Philosophically with Immanuel Kant

This good will must exclude motives such as inclination, the desire to do good, and benevolence. What determines whether an action is moral is this:

> [. . .] solely reverence for the law, is the motive which can give an action moral worth. Our own will, provided it were to act only under the condition of being able to make universal law by means of its maxims—this ideal will which can be ours is the proper object of reverence; and the dignity of man consists precisely in his capacity to make universal law, although only on condition of being himself also subject to the law he makes.[10]

In other words, if there is inclination, we are in the presence of a hypothetical imperative; if there is not, then we have a categorical imperative.

I will explain my thought in another way, so that you can clearly understand what, to me, constitutes true moral law.

> [. . .] practical reason (the will) may not merely administer an alien interest, but may simply manifest its own sovereign authority as the supreme maker of the law. Thus, for example, the reason why I ought to promote the happiness of others is not because the realization of their happiness is of consequence to myself (whether on account of immediate inclination or on account of some satisfaction gained indirectly through reason), but solely because a maxim which excludes this cannot also be present in one and the same volition as a universal law.[11]

I see you are hesitating. You are not yet convinced. I would like to put your mind at ease. It seems that the rational being capable of this ideal will does not exist on this earth. We are on a metaphysical level, and I will let you name this creature for yourself.

EFW

Thank you for having asked me to read one of your commentators. In fact, it was in reading a footnote by A. Philonenko in the French edition of *Groundwork of the Metaphysic of Morals* that I realized that only God can claim

> [to be] a fully independent being, without needs, and with a power that is, without restriction, adequate for his will.[12]

So I confess to being perplexed. Should I throw up my hands, forget benevolence, and forego all acts of charity, since according to your metaphysic of morals it's impossible for me to perform a good deed?

---

10. Ibid., 161–62.
11. Ibid., 163–64.
12. Kant, and footnote by Alexis Philonenko who indicates, "So *in principle,* the finished rational being, following the path of autonomy, is God's equal. *In fact,* [. . .] only God fulfills all the conditions for autonomy." Kant, ibid., 151.

Part III: A Changing Water Ethic

Immanuel Kant

Now, now, don't get up on your high horse! As far as charity is concerned, you will find a passage of mine that might reconcile you to the problem of giving.

> To be beneficent, that is, to promote according to one's means the happiness of others in need, without hoping for something in return, is everyone's duty.[13]
>
> [. . .] [T]he maxim of common interest, of beneficence toward those in need, is a universal duty of human beings, just because they are able to be considered fellowmen, that is, rational beings with needs, united by nature in one dwelling place so that they can help one another.[14]

EFW

I see Christ's commandment to love one's neighbor.

Immanuel Kant

You say so. You realize that we are now on a different level, no longer in the sensible world, but in the intelligible world. If you delve into the details of my work, you will understand that I tried to base my entire moral system on the idea of freedom, which though it is impossible to demonstrate, is not impossible to conceive, even if it can "never admit of full comprehension, or indeed of insight."[15]

This point is important for you, because in *Groundwork of the Metaphysic of Morals* I add that if freedom of will is impossible to *explain* we run into another impossibility, namely that

> [. . .] of finding out and making comprehensible what *interest* man can take in moral laws; and yet he does take such an interest. The basis of this in ourselves we call 'moral feeling.' Some people have mistakenly given out this feeling to be the gauge of our moral judgements: it should be regarded rather as the *subjective* effect exercised on our will by the law and having its objective ground in reason alone.[16]

To avoid any misunderstanding, I should clarify: this does not mean an interest as "sensibility" on which "practical reason" would depend and which would belong to the sensible world as "mere appearance"; rather,

---

13. Kant, *Métaphysique des mœurs II*, 319.
14. Ibid., 320.
15. Kant, *Fondements*, 193.
16. Ibid, 195.

CHAPTER I: "THINKING" WATER PHILOSOPHICALLY WITH IMMANUEL KANT

> [t]he [moral] law interests us because it is valid for us as men in virtue of having sprung from our will as intelligence and so from our proper self.[17]

Even if the interest for moral law is impossible to explain, that does not compromise the integrity of your firm belief that we must

> [. . .] [be] scrupulous to live in accordance with maxims of freedom as if they were laws of nature,

for

> [the Idea of a purely intelligible world] serves to produce in us a lively interest in the moral law.[18]

However, I am reaching

> [. . .] the extreme limit of all moral enquiry. To determine this limit is, however, of great importance in this respect: by so doing reason may be kept, on the one hand, from searching around in the sensible world—greatly to the detriment of morality—for the supreme motive and for some interest, comprehensible indeed, but empirical; and it may be kept, on the other hand, from flapping its wings impotently, without leaving the spot, in a space that for it is empty—the space of transcendent concepts known as 'the intelligible world'—and so from getting lost among mere phantoms of the brain. [. . .] all knowledge ends at its boundary [. . .].[19]

EFW

What a great lesson, Dr. Kant!

The Dialectic of Good and Evil

EFW

Dr. Kant, I am pleased to tell you that I will now give you a little break so I can explain why I want to ask you some questions about the dialectic of good and evil.

"Thinking" water means not only being concerned about its quality, but also and especially asking why, since there are many scientific solutions for protecting water,[20] some political and commercial authorities, and even nations and the affected populations themselves, resist implementing them.

---

17. Ibid., 196.
18. Ibid., 199.
19. Ibid., 198–99.
20. For example, the NEWater concept in Singapore.

Part III: A Changing Water Ethic

This finding was made by a group of experts with established credentials in "water governance," namely SIWI (the Stockholm International Water Institute), in "The Problem with Water is Not Water But Lack of Societal Stewardship."[21]

The resistance phenomena include a lack of governance in some countries, corrupt political authorities, and a lack of awareness among the affected populations. They result in what daily statistics cannot help but emphasize: poverty, disease, and death. These endlessly recurring issues, raised mainly by bodies of the UN and many NGOs,[22] end up leading to indifference, a "what's the use" attitude, especially since the large number and wide variety of efforts to solve the problems being criticized are turning out to be completely inadequate.

Given this reality, the ethical inquiry should in my opinion dig even deeper to uncover the origin of this intolerable situation and see whether there is some hope of finding a solution. In a word, despite the obsolescence of the term "evil" in today's world,[23] we need to unmask it and try to find its root.

Before I go on with my interview, I would still like to focus on what I feel is a critically important point in the context of water's challenges for human beings, namely physical evil or, more simply put, physical suffering.

Suffering arises not solely from the human condition, as we like to say, but rather—as Jean-Paul Sartre solemnly and dramatically put it—from a "universal human condition" manifested as that which the human being experiences in his body.

> By "condition" they [today's thinkers] refer, more or less clearly, to all limitations that à priori define man's fundamental situation in the universe. Historical situations vary: a man may be born a slave in a pagan society or a feudal lord or a member of the proletariat. What never varies is the necessity for him to be in the world, to work in it, to live out his life in it among others, and, eventually, to die in it. These limitations are neither subjective nor objective; rather they have an objective as well as a subjective dimension: objective, because they affect everyone and are evident everywhere; subjective because they are *experienced* and are meaningless if man does not experience them [. . .].[24]

Since physical suffering associated with water is the topic of this study, I would also like to hear from Saint-Exupéry, who experienced thirst in the desert after an airplane accident:

> Farewell, eyes that I loved! Do not blame me if the human body cannot go three days without water. I should never have believed that man was so truly the prisoner of the springs and freshets. I had no notion that our

---

21. Falkenmark, *No Freshwater Security Without Major Shift in Thinking*.
22. Bourguinat, *Les intégrismes économiques*, 81.
23. Dupuy, *Avions-nous oublié le mal?*
24. Sartre, *L'existentialisme est un humanisme*, 60.

self-sufficiency was so circumscribed. We take it for granted that a man is able to stride straight out into the world. We believe that man is free. We never see the cord that binds him to wells and fountains, that umbilical cord by which he is tied to the womb of the world. Let man take but one step too many ... and the cord snaps.[25]

These words ring so true, such a feeling of empathy suddenly runs through me like an electric shock, that I find it almost unseemly to go on.

But Calvin comes along at just the right moment to remind me that we are neither to tremble in the face of death nor to despise life, for "it is a post at which the Lord has placed us, to be retained by us till he call us away."[26]

Still, the author of *Institutes of the Christian Religion* gives no quarter in exposing both natural physical evil and that inflicted by Man.

> For all whom the Lord has chosen and honoured with admission into the society of his saints, ought to prepare themselves for a life, hard, laborious, unquiet, and replete with numerous and various calamities[27] [...] poverty, or loss of relatives, or disease, or other calamities; to the bearing of which being in ourselves unequal, we ere long sink under them.[28]

and

> I call it *persecution for righteousness' sake,* not only when we suffer in defence of the gospel, but also when we are molested in the vindication of any just cause.[29]

Calvin says to defend a just cause, and suffer for it? I see it is time to get back to my interview...

Dr. Kant, you should know that my contemporaries worry about leaving future generations a planet that is still livable and viable. In the introduction to this chapter, I indicated the presence of opposing forces that some people perhaps too simplistically describe as good or evil. Water is also beset by antagonistic forces as illustrated, for example, by the conflicts that arise when dams are built.

So a discussion of the problem of evil seems to me to be unavoidable in the context of water.

As the philosopher who came up with "radical evil," could you enlighten us on this concept which, for you, is clearly separate from that of "original sin"?

---

25. Saint-Exupéry, *Terre des hommes*, 149.
26. Calvin, *Inst.*, III, IX, 4.
27. Ibid., III, VIII, 1.
28. Ibid., III, VIII, 2.
29. Ibid., III, VIII, 7.

Part III: A Changing Water Ethic
Immanuel Kant

You have probably read some passages from the book I wrote when I was already well advanced in years,[30] and which I thought would be able to bring consistency to my philosophy. In *Religion Within the Boundaries of Mere Reason*,[31] I wanted to answer the question "What may I hope?," which followed up on my first two questions, "What can I know?" and "What should I do?"

I think that my thoughts about evil are original. I believe that "evil" cannot find a place in either time or space, the two *a priori* principles of the mind.[32] So I reject the idea of original sin as conceived by Saint Augustine, taken up by the Church Fathers, and then perpetuated in Christian doctrines. Here is what I said.

> Whatever the nature, however, of the origin of moral evil in the human being, of all the ways of representing its spread and propagation through the members of our species and in all generations the most inappropriate is surely to imagine it as having come to us by way of *inheritance* from our first parents; for then we could say of moral evil exactly what the poet says of the good [...].[33]

Though this may have put me in an awkward position with the Church, I did take the time to reflect and wonder, like Paul in Romans, why "I do not do the good I want, but the evil I do not want is what I do."[34]

Even exploring my deepest, innermost thoughts unfortunately did not allow me to discover the root of evil. I simply had to acknowledge that its origin is "unfathomable"[35] and "shrouded in darkness."[36]

EFW

Excuse me for interrupting. You might be gratified to hear that your "radical evil" doctrine played a particularly important role in the twentieth century after the genocide against the Jews, when the divine commandments from the Tables of the Law were turned completely upside down.[37] That is how philosophers such as Karl Jaspers and Hannah Arendt came to develop your concept when faced with the reality of an atrocity that was unthinkable in your day.

---

30. Kant speaks of "the difficulties that old age poses especially in the way of working with abstract ideas." Kant, *La religion dans les limites de la simple raison*, 79.
31. Ibid.
32. Kant, *Critique de la raison pure*, 92.
33. Kant, *La religion dans les limites de la simple raison*, 109.
34. Rom 7:19.
35. Kant, *La religion dans les limites de la simple raison*, 113.
36. Ibid.
37. Manon, "Le mal radical. Kant. Arendt, 3.

CHAPTER I: "THINKING" WATER PHILOSOPHICALLY WITH IMMANUEL KANT

Immanuel Kant

It is not up to me to judge whether my reasoning was clearly understood in this dramatic historic context.

I should clarify, however, that although Man is of course evil *by nature,* he is not necessarily evil but rather contingently so, and makes use of his freedom to do evil acts:

> [. . .] the statement, "The human being is *evil,*" cannot mean anything else than that he is conscious of the moral law and yet has incorporated into his maxim the (occasional) deviation from it.[38]

To summarize . . .

For me, Man is "inclined towards evil," but not likely to want "evil for evil's sake," otherwise he would be a diabolical being.[39] Of course I do say that evil "[. . .] is found in the human being by nature,"[40] which is why I talk about "*radical* innate *evil* in human nature."[41] But I stress the fact that Man has chosen this evil and it is "brought upon us by ourselves."[42] I also add that we ought to be able to conquer it.

> This evil is *radical,* since it corrupts the grounds of all maxims; as natural propensity, it is also not to be *extirpated* through human forces, for this could only happen through good maxims—something that cannot take place if the subjective supreme ground of all maxims is presupposed to be corrupted. Yet it must equally be possible to *overcome* this evil, for it is found in the human being as acting freely.[43]

EFW

I see that thanks to Man's moral freedom, you credit him with a propensity for good. That allows you to believe in humanity's progress, its fitness for self-improvement. You are a philosopher of hope, not of despair.

Immanuel Kant

That is indeed how I see it.

---

38. Kant, *La religion dans les limites de la simple raison,* 99.
39. Ibid., 103.
40. Ibid.
41. Ibid., 100.
42. Ibid.
43. Ibid., 105.

Part III: A Changing Water Ethic

However evil a human being has been right up to the moment of an impending free action (evil even habitually, as second nature), his duty to better himself was not just in the past: it is still his duty *now* [. . .][44]

EFW

I understand your insistence on Man's duty to better himself very well. But what pushes him to fulfill this duty?

Immanuel Kant

For me what matters is, first, to clearly understand the difference between the causes and motives that drive people to act in either good or evil ways.

To clarify, only human beings, not animals, can determine a maxim for action for, I repeat, they are endowed with the faculty of freedom of thought. Animals are driven by a deterministic natural law; human beings, on the other hand, are not subject to this causality, and so are able to choose between the best and the worst, as I tried to express in this adage:

> The history of *nature* thus begins from good, for that is the *work of God;* the history of *freedom* from evil, for it is the *work of the human being.*[45]

EFW

Does that amount to saying that animals are innocents and human beings are guilty?

Immanuel Kant

Your reaction is a little too simplistic for what I was trying to say. We need a more nuanced interpretation.

In fact, disguised in the qualifier "guilty" is the "sin word," with its religious connotation. Now, I am not a theologian.

What I see as a philosopher is Man being pulled in one direction by his intellect, which tells him what he should and can do—acts of charity, for example—, which I describe as "intellectual incentive." But he is pulled in the other direction by his desire to do the exact opposite, that is, to follow his propensities, which I call "sensuous incentive." In other words, Man is the one who gives in to laziness, or the temptation to satisfy his own needs without considering those of others.

---

44. Ibid., 110.
45. Kant, *Conjectures sur le commencement de l'histoire humaine*, 17.

CHAPTER I: "THINKING" WATER PHILOSOPHICALLY WITH IMMANUEL KANT

You yourself have noticed how difficult, even impossible, it is for Man to subordinate sensuous incentives to intellectual ones.

EFW

If I understand you correctly, then when I choose to go to a concert instead of visiting my sick aunt, I am giving in to my sensuous incentives. Would I be doing the same if I were to decide to use part of my salary to take a vacation at the beach instead of sending that amount to EPER[46] to help finance a water supply system in Zimbabwe?

Immanuel Kant

Those are nice examples, but I would like to go further.

You seem to want to show that your natural inclinations are solely responsible for any bad decisions that are made. Now I say that "*sensuous nature* [...] contains too little"[47] to express evil.

EFW

What do you mean by that?

Immanuel Kant

I mean that Man is neither "animal" nor "diabolical" as I said a little while ago. I will explain.

> Sensuous nature therefore contains too little to provide a ground of moral evil in the human being, for, to the extent that it eliminates the incentives originating in freedom, it makes of the human a purely animal being; a reason exonerated from the moral law, an evil reason, as it were (an absolutely evil will), would on the contrary contain too much, because resistance to the law would itself be thereby elevated to incentive (for without any incentive the power of choice cannot be determined), and so the subject would be made a diabolical being. —Neither of these two is however applicable to the human being.[48]

To clarify,

> [t]he depravity of human nature is therefore not to be named *malice* [...] but should rather be named *perversity of the heart* [...]. Its origin is the frailty of

---

46. Swiss Church Aid, www.eper.ch.
47. Kant, *La religion dans les limites de la simple raison*, 103.
48. Ibid.

human nature, in not being strong enough to comply with its adopted principles, coupled with its dishonesty in not screening incentives (even those of well-intentioned actions) in accordance with the moral guide, and hence at the end, if it comes to this, in seeing only to the conformity of these incentives to the law, not to whether they have been derived from the latter itself, i.e., from it as the sole incentive.[49]

EFW

I understand that you are assigning three degrees to the propensity for evil, as French philosopher Simone Manon has summarized—and very well, I think. They are, first, human frailty as mentioned by the Apostle Paul; second, impurity; and third, depravity.

> Impurity [consists] of incorporating sensuous incentives for obeying the law into the maxims that determine one's volition. A merchant who is honest in order not to compromise his interests, or a person who is benevolent out of pity or out of fear of the consequences of malevolence does not act in order to comply with the moral law, but for other incentives. His behavior has an aspect of legality and has no morality even if the action as viewed externally obeys the law.
>
> Depravity [is] the tendency to subordinate incentives derived from moral law to those that are not moral.[50]

Still according to Simone Manon, evil exists in Man because he "reverses axiological priorities." Did she understand you correctly when she wrote the following?

> Whereas [Man] ought to make morality his supreme end and the thing that would make him worthy of being happy, instead he tends to behave as if his search for happiness and the satisfaction of his desires were more important than obedience to moral law, and as if the latter were dependent on the former. More simply put, Man is inclined to place a higher priority on something that would make him happy than on something that would make him moral. Therefore, when there is a conflict between the two aspirations, the one as natural as the other, he is prone to sacrificing the moral law to the fulfillment of his desire. He reverses the rightful hierarchy between enjoyment of life and morality, between its sensuous dimension and its intelligible dimension—or, to use the language of Saint Paul, he gives victory to Man who lives according to the flesh and acknowledges the defeat of the man who lives in the Spirit, or freedom.[51]

---

49. Ibid., 105.
50. Manon, *Le mal radical*, 9.
51. Ibid., 11.

CHAPTER I: "THINKING" WATER PHILOSOPHICALLY WITH IMMANUEL KANT

Immanuel Kant

Clearly this is an interpretation, and nothing compares to reading me in the original, in German if possible!

EFW

I will hazard one more question about this "reversal of incentives."[52] Is there a risk that the considerable efforts of those who have suggested predicates to encourage a better allocation of the resource "water" will be fruitless in the end? To make the question more specific, do you think that these predicates, these causes which in a way are equivalent to maxims may never take priority over mankind's "sensuous incentives"?

Immanuel Kant

I cannot answer you. What I can imagine, on the other hand, is that these concepts' supporters will have their hands full trying to persuade their contemporaries to apply them, and that they will have to face the fact that if even the very idea of "evil" seems to have become obsolete, it is difficult to believe in the "natural goodliness of human nature."[53]

Without meaning to be cynical, I think it very likely that they will not even ask themselves about the "innate evil" that I tried so hard to explain, and which I also called the "natural propensity to evil."[54]

EFW

You seem to have read that in the stars. In fact, philosopher Jean-Pierre Dupuy is of the same opinion. In *Avions-nous oublié le mal?* he says

> [e]vil exists in the world, it affects it, but neither the rationalist model nor its critical demystification can recognize it. Their naive ingenuousness is reproachable because by obscuring evil, it helps it to gain ascendency over the world and the beings that live there.[55]

Thank you very much for your kindness in answering my many questions. I will continue my consideration of "intellectual incentives," or causes, and "sensuous incentives," or motives, and more specifically will investigate them further by enlisting the aid of philosophers who favored empiricism.

---

52. Kant, *La religion dans les limites de la simple raison*, 105.
53. Ibid.
54. Ibid., 100.
55. Dupuy, *Avions-nous oublié le mal?*, 30.

Chapter II

Eudaemonist and Anti-Eudaemonist Motives for Action, Or How to "Think" Water Emotionally

Introduction

IN AN EPIGRAPH TO Part III, I indicated the extent to which water motivates or "mobilizes" both the mind and the heart. In particular, the heart can be affected by compassion, resentment, or selfishness.

These human feelings make it necessary to "think" water emotionally. I will call them the "motives" for action, in contrast to the "causes" discussed earlier.

As we shall see in Part V, at the heart of ethics in general lies the Golden Rule, the two sides of which can be pithily summed up by the negative formula "do no harm" and its positive counterpart "do good." The more usual extended expressions are the negative and positive imperatives, respectively *whatever is hurtful to you do not do to any other person* and *do unto others as you would have them do unto you.*

One of the defining characteristics of water and its challenges in the context of globalization is that they invite humanity to think about a new way of living together in global harmony.

The result is that we "think" the Golden Rule more broadly, from a cosmopolitan perspective—or, to borrow Vladimir Jankélévitch's terminology,[1] that we reflect on an unlimited human brotherhood.

Now whoever brings up brotherhood will also have to mention rivalry. As a case in point, consider brothers Cain and Abel in Genesis.[2]

This single example typifying the dialectic of good and evil allows us to postulate that the Golden Rule, which assumes compassion, giving and selflessness, will be faced with the opposing forces of hate, resentment, and selfishness. Or, to speak plainly and directly, perhaps even bluntly, we are talking about peace and war.

An ethical reflection is the appropriate forum for bringing this dialectic out into the open.

---

1. Jankélévitch, *Le paradoxe de la morale.*
2. Gen 4:1–8.

To continue along these lines, below I will try to bring out such surprising paradoxes as compassionate giving and human brotherhood set against resentment and selfishness.

The goal is to emphasize that individual psychological mechanisms may also operate at the global level. Accordingly, in order to make my reasoning easier to follow, I will talk about a *global potable water ethic*. We will see, for example, that such an ethic can truly begin to take shape if it not only dares to encourage individual and global compassion, but also aims to discourage the development of such strong negative emotions as resentment and selfishness, especially when they set about inflaming whole communities.

In other words, a global water ethic is not restricted to the single goal of questioning the relevance of a new human right to water. It also imperatively includes an investigation of how to prevent hotbeds of revolt from forming around the issue of access to water, as well as a search for modes of conflict resolution.

This ethic will have the triple assignment of encouraging the education of boys and girls, improving governance through training, and achieving peace by promoting it.

In a word, the global water ethic has to do with the positive formulation of the Golden Rule.

Compassion and Philanthropy as Factors in Peace

Compassionate Giving, Christian Works, and Philanthropic Deeds

At issue here will be compassionate giving, in which the act of giving is motivated by sympathy or "suffering with," as indicated by the etymologies *cum patere* (Latin) (for "compassion") and *syn pathein* (Greek) (for "sympathy").

Let me say right away that the following discussion excludes "self-interested giving," the kind practiced by arrogant and powerful patrons drunk with expanding their power and influence and having no qualms about doing so. Still, I am not unaware that the line between these two types of giving is not always so easy to draw in practice.

The concept of giving has caught people's attention since time immemorial, mainly because of its paradoxical quality.

The New Testament reminds Christians that "it is more blessed to give than to receive."[3]

In their teachings, reformers such as Martin Luther and John Calvin chose the word "works" for the act of giving. The topic of works is a fundamental element of their doctrine. Luther considered that charitable works were not the means to salvation, but a consequence of it. Calvin found the requirement to act for the good of others more meaningful. At the least, Calvin's thought served as the basis for a very strict

---

3. Acts 20:35 (last sentence).

morality, perhaps even too strict. According to some observers, his followers were truly weighed down under the yoke of the duty to give to their neighbors in need.[4]

So what has become of this morality today, in particular now that the time to "think" a global water ethic has come? As far as the "neighbor" who is to receive our works, that is, the person subject to water insecurity, are we to consider anyone in the whole wide world as our "neighbor"? Or, in other words, what should be the scope for the charitable works of Christians and world citizens?

Some Christian churches do not seem to flinch at considering the entire world as a field for their missions, for example through EPER among Protestant churches and Caritas for Catholic churches. However, the fact remains that conceptually, the expanse of space in which giving can occur is not self-evident: cosmopolitanism in the broad sense contradicts cosmopolitanism in the narrow sense.

I will cite two sources to justify this statement, the first theological and the second philosophical.

Did John Calvin Subscribe to "Narrow" Cosmopolitanism before the Term Existed?

Christ's words as reported in Matthew 28:19, "Go therefore and make disciples of all nations," provided an opportunity for John Calvin to express his views of what today we call cosmopolitanism. It is true that this Bible verse refers to evangelizing and not to gifts or works. Yet Calvin's reasoning about evangelism as the spiritual gift of the Word seems to me to apply, *mutatis mutandis,* to the expression of love for one's neighbor when it takes the form of a material gift.

The biblical command may very well seem to the twenty-first century reader to apply to the entire planet, especially if he considers that as of 2014, the United Nations Charter associates 193 of the world's countries. Calvin, however, thought the opposite—that this imperative was addressed solely to Christ's Apostles. After their deaths, the mission to the many peoples around the globe was ended. This long-prevailing idea explains why Protestant missions did not have the same influence as those of the Catholics, such as those proposed by Calvin's contemporary Ignatius of Loyola,[5] at least until the nineteenth century.[6]

At the risk of an anachronism, I find it possible to theorize that Calvin understood cosmopolitanism in the narrow sense, and Ignatius of Loyola took it in the broad sense.

Would they also have been at odds about the legitimate field for charitable action based on the Gospels, with Calvin limiting it to Protestants, for example, and Loyola ruling out any limit?

4. Dermange, *L'éthique de Calvin.*
5. Dermange, *La diffusion du calvinisme.*
6. Ibid.

Of course this question is impossible to answer. However, it is important to note that the geographic area, and therefore the scope, of aid is an issue of what we call *global justice,* the complexity of which many contemporary philosophers have noted and for which multiple answers are possible.[7]

I hasten to add that EPER has declined to set any exclusion criteria for recipients of its gifts, no doubt in application of the following Bible verse from Acts.

> Then Peter began to speak to them: "I truly understand that God shows no partiality, but in every nation anyone who fears him and does what is right is acceptable to him.[8]

Philosopher Vladimir Jankélévitch terms this a refusal of prosopolepsy (partiality):

> In the Gospels, the refusal of prosopolepsy[9] expresses a fundamental indifference to all social, professional, and ethnic distinctions [. . .].[10]

Does Vladimir Jankélévitch's Unlimited Brotherhood Correspond to "Broad" Cosmopolitanism?

Vladimir Jankélévitch, a French philosopher originally from Russia, writes about philanthropy and human brotherhood in his small book *Le paradoxe de la morale.*[11]

After recalling that etymologically, "philanthropy" means *to love man,* he adds a global dimension by talking about "Man to be loved *in general."*

> The principle of an infinite open-mindedness has already been foreseen. It will not appear in the full light of day except through universalism and the "totalitarianism" of Stoicism's *philanthropia.*[12]

Jankélévitch then notes the fundamentally paradoxical nature of philanthropy, because he finds it difficult to explain how one person can love another "simply because the other is a person."

> It most often happens that a man loves his neighbor when that neighbor is of the same religion, a resident of the same town, or a fellow countryman [. . .]. It most often happens that a man loves other men provided that they—he and the others—belong to the same flock [religious community]; or provided

---

7. Miller, *National Responsibility and Global Justice,* 23-50 (chapter 2 on "Cosmopolitanism").

8. Acts 10:34–35.

9. Jankélévitch, indicates, "[. . .] prosopolepsy is the dishonesty that consists of turning the mask into meaning [. . .] of considering features and skin color, or in other words the persona. In short, *prosopon* is a superficial appearance." Jankélévitch, *Le paradoxe de la morale,* 42.

10. Ibid.

11. Ibid.

12. Ibid., 41.

that they are part of the same clan, tribe, or caste. The person who loves his neighbor because this neighbor is a parishioner in the same parish does not love men [. . .].[13]

He wants to go even further, though, and discover the human essence.

In the end, it is by tying together the "philanthropic paradox" and the "cosmopolitan paradox"[14] that Jankélévitch is led to concede "the unthinkable immoderation of human brotherhood,"[15] which is excessive "to the limits of the absurd and the ridiculous."[16]

This reading makes me think that Jankélévitch would probably have described an NGO as philanthropic, for example, the Swiss foundation Helvetas, known for its development aid strategy focusing on water challenges. He also would have qualified it as cosmopolitan, referring to the Stoic wisdom that held a "cosmopolitan" person to be a citizen of the world. As I mentioned above, for this French philosopher,

[. . .] both paradoxes [philanthropic and cosmopolitan] are related to each other through the same paradoxy, and Stoic wisdom asserted both of them.[17]

Examples of Philanthropic Acts As Compassionate Gestures

To do justice to an aspect of contemporary humanitarian work's attraction for many young people that too often is kept in the background, I am duty-bound to point out the relevance of Kant's analysis of benevolence that I mentioned above[18] by giving an example.

At a conference in Singapore in August 2013, the still-youthful founders of the Child's Dream[19] NGO explained how they had wanted give up banking careers that brought them little satisfaction. Ten years before, at the cost of significant monetary sacrifices, they had focused all their energy on promoting education for underprivileged children in Laos, Vietnam, Cambodia, and Myanmar. The joy they expressed about the new lifestyle they had chosen is worth emphasizing.

German philosopher Hans Jonas also addressed the issue of the duty to do good, and denied that it is absolutely one-sided in nature. He felt that even though there is not necessarily any reciprocity on the part of the gift's recipient, the philanthropist does not lose by the transaction. Indeed, even though the giver is not necessarily

13. Ibid.
14. Ibid., 42.
15. Ibid.
16. Ibid.
17. Ibid.
18. See Part III, Section II, Chapter I.
19. Child's Dream, www.childsdream.org.

rewarded for the undertaking—since its success is not assured—paradoxically, he still profits by it.

> However, just as little as we are willing to part with the distinction between desire and obligation will our feeling let go of the certainty that doing good for its own sake also in some sense benefits the agent, and this regardless of the success of his action. Whether he is allowed to enjoy the achieved good himself, or not; whether he lives to see it achieved, or not, even should he see his action fail—his moral being has gained with the obedient acceptance of the call of duty. [...] The secret or paradox of morality is that the self forgets itself over the pursuit of the object, so that a higher self [...] might come into being. To be sure, I am allowed to say "I wish to be able to look myself in the eye (or: pass God's scrutiny), [...]."[20]

Were the founders of Child's Dream motivated primarily by "being able to look themselves in the eye," and was the joy merely an unexpected reward?

Be that as it may, it is interesting to further note that Hans Jonas's focus on the "coming of a higher self" and the "forgetting of self" as duty is performed is more theological in flavor than philosophical. To support this I can refer both to Calvin's morality and to that of Saint Francis of Assisi. For Calvin, as Eric Fuchs notes, ethical intent comes down to a paradox:

> [...] one must act as if everything depended on oneself, while knowing all the time that everything depends on God's gracious providence.[21]

The prayer of St. Francis as given at the end of section 3.1 below specifically mentions this "forgetting of self," the effacement of the personality.

"Good Actions": Western Modesty versus Asian Display

The corollary of Western modesty, which could even be called Calvinistic self-restraint, is that Westerners use euphemisms when speaking of benevolent acts. Even the expressions "benevolence" and "benefactor" seem rather quaint.

There will always be benefactors. I would even say that this is cause for rejoicing, given the radio and television announcements about donations to Swiss Solidarity during major natural disasters—such as the tsunami in 2004, the Fukushima nuclear catastrophe in 2011, and Typhoon Haiyan (Yolanda) in the Philippines in November 2013—and deadly wars, such as the one in Syria, that awaken our compassion.

The trendier term "sponsor" is often preferred to "benefactor." This is something of a paradox when we consider that etymologically, the use of "sponsor" goes back to Roman law and its meaning is "guarantor" rather than "benefactor," as François

---

20. Jonas, *Le principe responsabilité*, 167–68.
21. Fuchs, Eric, *La morale selon Calvin*, 32.

Part III: A Changing Water Ethic

Dermange noted on March 19, 2013, at the end of the third Workshop for Water Ethics (W4W).

> The Latin *sponsio* [. . .] is an exchange of consent between two people, with an outside person—the *responsor*—acting as the guarantor of the exchange [. . .].[22]

It must be noted that the Western media are parsimonious in reporting on individual or institutional commitments to a humanitarian cause. The role of benefactor is generally left up to the Red Cross movement and major NGOs such as Oxfam. One might say—but this would be evidence of a kind of cynicism akin to Max Weber's[23]—that these entities ease our consciences in the face of anguish and human misery.

Perhaps I am exaggerating a bit, but only the better to show how much more readily the Asian media—especially in Singapore—will recount some philanthropists' unusual life stories, which are intended not only to stir up emotion but also to stimulate new acts of solidarity.

For example, as a Westerner I cannot help being surprised by an account that appeared in the *Straits Times* on Monday, September 2, 2013. This kind of incidental news story would never have been taken seriously in Europe, and the Western media would never have stressed the motive with such simplicity and authenticity.

Let us take a look.

In 2000 a pilot for Singapore Airlines, who is still flying today, was disturbed by televised reports about troubles in East Timor. Broadcast images of children wandering the streets, abandoned to their sad fate, made him angry. Up in arms, the Christian pulled himself together and decided to publicly demonstrate his faith in divine Providence[24] and take action. Having found an ideal partner in his wife, he decided to build an orphanage in one of the driest parts of East Timor. This was accomplished during his vacations and spare time.

But that was not all. On one of the properties, the couple spent three days digging with the sarcastic remarks of derisive neighbors ringing in their ears. And on the fourth day, they found an unexpected reward: water burst forth![25]

---

22. Stahl Gretsch, "*Notes*."

23. Weber indicates, "argent de la conscience" [*Gewissensgeld*, "conscience money"]. Weber, *L'éthique protestante*, 76.

24. *The Straits Times* indicates, "Though the finances are tight, the staunch Christian said he trusts in God to provide." *The Straits Times*, B7.

25. *The Straits Times* indicates, "[. . .] on the fourth day, they struck 'gold'. Natural spring water burst forth and they used it to irrigate the fields. Today the older [. . .] children help out in the fields. As well as rice, they grow papaya, mangoes and dragonfruit, some of which are exported." *The Straits Times*, B7.

Chapter II: How to "Think" Water Emotionally

Singapore, Philanthropy, and the International Cause of Sanitation

To some people, the very rapid economic rise of this small Southeast Asian area looks like a caricature of a capitalist society. We must remember that Lee Kuan Yew, the famous Prime Minister who was the most important driving force behind the development, was a socialist.

While we must of course continue to think critically, in my opinion we ought not to minimize this community's efforts to bring a breath of fresh air not only to the business world, but also to the sciences, green technologies, art, and international solidarity.

Again, it is strange to a Westerner to read daily recommendations about morality in the papers. It is a little as if Calvin had been resurrected and were dictating messages to the journalists. Every day the public is invited to get involved in solidarity projects, whether for the elderly or populations affected by cataclysms.

I quite understand that we should not stray into angelism. Human tensions there are the same as everywhere else, but they are held in check remarkably well. In fact, memories of the dark times of violence in the years following independence are still fresh.

Nevertheless, this state of mind does motivate the public to surpass itself. I cite as evidence an example that directly concerns the topic of a water ethic.

I am referring to Singaporean Jack Sim who, like the founders of Child's Dream mentioned above, left his job as a banker at the age of forty and founded a non-profit in 2001. The name of his undertaking, World Toilet Organization (WTO), leaves no room for doubt about its goal: promoting sanitation internationally.

Sim wanted to devote himself to serving the poor who have no voice, and his project succeeded so well that in July 2013, the UN General Assembly decided to set aside November 19 as a day to commemorate the cause of sanitation. The first World Toilet Day, dedicated to the two billion individuals without access to toilets, was November 19, 2013.

Geneva and Singapore: Banks, Philanthropy, and Peace

A study on the comparisons that could be made between Geneva (a Swiss city) and Singapore (a city-state), each of which is host to major international financial centers, would be a task for a sociologist.

A discussion of the pertinent facts explaining the prosperity of these two communities would be up to a historian.

Additionally, the historian could recall the exploits of renowned figures known for their philanthropy, such as Count Jean-Jacques de Seillon, who fervently and unceasingly fought against the death penalty in Geneva in the early nineteenth century. Such a scholar would certainly mention in his work that Henry Dunant, winner of the first Nobel Prize in 1901 along with Frédéric Passy, was one of the five founders of the International Committee of the Red Cross in 1863, along with General Guillaume-Henri Dufour. Additionally, he would make a point of noting that in 1859, Geneva residents Countess Valérie de Gasparin and her husband started "La Source,"[26] the world's first secular school for independent nurses—though it was located in Lausanne.

The sociologist could also note that in our day and age, the two cities' banks and bankers are involved in major philanthropic projects.

I myself will be content simply to encourage such sociological and historical studies. They would provide evidence of the ties between good governance, education, prosperity, and peace, on the one hand, and philanthropy on the other.

Such studies would also show that as far as the ethical challenges of potable water are concerned, these banks in fact play a not insignificant role, both by financing small projects such as Child's Dream, discussed above, in whole or in part; and by making every effort to promote education in philanthropy. As proof of this I can cite the very recent work done by the National University of Singapore and its Asia Centre for Social Entrepreneurship and Philanthropy (ACSEP).[27]

For that matter, I find a study done by the Swiss bank UBS in 2010[28] to be not uninteresting. It presents the rather unusual story of the Lien Foundation's creator, Lien Ying Chow. [29] Today, this organization is not only active in the education of underprivileged children and in elderly care, but also on the issue of water.

Philanthropy and Reciprocity

While I felt it was important to spend some time mentioning the acts of benefactors and philanthropists, I think some space should also be devoted to the question of reciprocity. Must the act necessarily be completely altruistic, or is the philanthropist legitimately entitled to expect some kind of reward for it?

The following answers that philosophers Immanuel Kant and Hans Jonas gave for this question, albeit nearly two centuries apart, caught my attention.

It is striking to note the extent to which Hans Jonas was influenced by the "Master of Konigsberg" in his understanding of mankind's duty to accomplish ends that the latter calls "meritorious" and the former describes as "worthy" or "truly worth the effort."

Kant considers that it is indeed legitimate for a benefactor to expect a certain amount of gratitude for his act, which therefore is in the nature of a reward. He calls

26. http://www.notrehistoire.ch/periods/1.

27. http://bschool.nus.edu/ascep.

28. Mahboob, and Santos, *The UBS-INSEAD Study on Family Philanthropy in Asia*, 100–01.

29. Lien Ying Chow founded the Overseas Union Bank, which in 2001 became the United Overseas Bank. http://eresources.nlb.gov.sg/infopedia/articles/SIP_1787_2011-02-24.html?s=OUB foundation.

this both "ethical *reward*"[30] and "moral pleasure."[31] Not only can the benefactor say that he is content to have acted as a good person; he will also feel true joy along with his satisfaction. To stress the nature of the reciprocity between the agent and the recipient, Kant even speaks of

> [. . .] *sweet merit;* for consciousness of it produces a moral enjoyment in which human beings are inclined by sympathy to *revel* [. . .].[32]

In contrast, Kant makes no secret of the fact that someone who sees no reaction to the act he had considered good can be overcome by a kind of bitterness:

> But *bitter merit,* which comes from promoting the true well-being of others even when they fail to recognize it as such (when they are unappreciative and ungrateful), usually yields no such return. All that it produces is contentment with oneself [. . .].[33]

Could the bitterness described here even turn into resentment, as philanthropy's down side?

I believe that a discussion of this unflattering human characteristic will be useful here, especially to bring out the fragile nature of compassionate giving. Resentment is not the exclusive province of frustrated benefactors, however. Quite the contrary: this is a real human passion that seems to spare no one and is also likely to endanger "global harmony."

Resentment from Adam Smith to Our Times

Is Resentment a Motive for Action in the Context of Water?

While, as we have just seen, water can set people in motion on their own behalf or in order to help others who are vulnerable, it much more often sets them in motion against others, particularly in cases of injustice.

Tensions and conflicts have surrounded water since time immemorial. What has become a characteristic phenomenon of our time, however, is that it is not solely those most affected who react, sometimes with physical violence. On the contrary, their discontent is often transmitted by "world citizens," the paradoxical and contradictory nature of whom was mentioned by Vladimir Jankélévitch:

> The cosmopolite is a world citizen. [. . .] To be a citizen of one society and not of another makes sense. But how can someone be a citizen of the *universe?* A citizen of the planet, of this terrestrial globe—which is in no way a *society*—,

---

30. Kant, *Métaphysique des mœurs II*, 233.
31. Ibid.
32. Ibid.
33. Ibid.

these are simply a manner of speaking, and to a Greek ear, the expressions sound more like contradictions or absurdities. One might as well speak of galactic patriotism! Yet it is this infinite expansion, to the limits of the absurd and the laughable, that is the measure of the unthinkable immoderation of human brotherhood.[34]

Here we have verbal violence that acts—through social networks, for example—to awaken and encourage a worldwide awareness of water issues.

Popular reactions express disapproval of the exercise of political or commercial power, and can include, for example, action against power imbalances in water matters, called "hydro-hegemony," and action against the construction of dams, with China's Three Gorges Dam being a classic illustration.

Equally striking was the Cochabamba affair, which is well known in part because the facts of the case were pieced together to create the plot of a James Bond film in 2008.[35] The "incident" itself, which occurred in 2000, not only made the headlines but was also the subject of many articles in the press as well as books and documentary films. There were many repercussions, and unfortunately it seems that the current situation of Bolivia's poor has become even worse.

I might be tempted to discuss these conflicts, but instead will refer the reader to the explanations in some excellent studies presented on March 19, 2013, at the third W4W colloquium on the Global Ethics of Water. The hydro-hegemony presentation was led by Mark Zeitoun, and dam issues were discussed by Evelyne Lyons.[36]

The violence takes many forms, according to Jean-Pierre Dupuy in a book published after the events in New York City on September 11, 2001, entitled *Avions-nous oublié le mal?*[37]

It can especially come out as resentment.

Jean-Pierre Dupuy finds that not only is this human quirk despicable; it also has very far-reaching effects, because it prevails everywhere in the world.

It is precisely because resentment is a dishonorable feeling that it is usually hidden or disguised. Dupuy himself hunted it down in the form of *intérêt*, or *(self-)interest*, the ambiguity of which he works to reveal.

In a fine demonstration on the topic of self-interest, he contrasts the views of two thinkers, French sociologist Pierre Bourdieu and German philosopher Hannah Arendt. He observes that the former corrupts the meaning that should be attributed to the word *self-interest* by likening it to selfishness,[38] while the latter brings out its

---

34. Jankélévitch, *Le paradoxe de la morale*, 42.

35. Forster, "The Quantum of Solace."

36. Zeitoun, "Hydropolitique internationale," and Lyons, "Conséquences sociales de la construction des barrages."

37. Dupuy, *Avions-nous oublié le mal?*

38. Dupuy indicates, "Common sense has been so corrupted by the spirit of demystification that as a result the word *intérêt* [interest] has come to mean exclusively what the English call 'self-interest,'

positive side by going back to the word's etymology to find the "inter-esse" among human beings or their desire "to live together."[39]

Dupuy does not hesitate to warn us about this demystification game played by Bourdieu's critical sociology. He finds that not only is it not innocent, it is even likely to lead to "the most hopeless nihilism."[40]

He invites us not to sweep evil under the rug.

> Evil exists in the world, it affects it, but neither the rationalist model nor its critical demystification can recognize it.[41]
>
> [Evil] is also an explanatory principle. Evil has a causal power that cannot be reduced to the logic of self-interest. In the form of resentment, envy, jealousy, [or] destructive hate, evil can acquire considerable power, destroying as it passes everything that enables Men to live together by keeping them at a distance from each other.[42]

There is no doubt that if the nature of evil were more clearly defined, the search for a remedy would be easier.

As we saw in the previous chapter,[43] Kant noted that evil cannot be rooted out by human hands. Its hidden form, resentment, is no exception.

Now who would ever claim that this nagging feeling of resentment never rears its head when the question of justice related to water, and potable water in particular, comes up?

I have chosen to cite Adam Smith, who as the author of *The Theory of Moral Sentiments*[44] wrote about the mysterious and unsettling passion of resentment. It is important to note that he penned this key work in the mid-eighteenth century as a moralist and not as an economist, while the holder of the "chair of moral philosophy at the University of Glasgow, one of the centers of the Scottish Enlightenment."[45] It was only later that he became famous when he wrote *An Inquiry into the Nature and Causes of the Wealth of Nations*.[46]

Before attempting to summarize Adam Smith's thoughts on resentment, however, I would like to mention Saint Francis of Assisi's beautiful words intended to calm hearts inflamed by hatred, which is so akin to resentment, or by other human heartaches:

---

which is only imperfectly translated by *intérêt égoïste* [selfish interest]." Dupuy, *Avions-nous oublié le mal?*, 30.

39. Arendt, *Condition de l'homme moderne*, 92.
40. Dupuy, *Avions-nous oublié le mal?*, 29.
41. Ibid., 31.
42. Ibid.
43. See Part III, Section II, Chapter I.
44. Smith, *Théorie des sentiments moraux*.
45. Ibid., 1.
46. Smith, *Recherches sur la nature et les causes de la richesse des nations*.

Lord, make me an instrument of your peace.

Where there is hatred, let me sow love,
Where there is injury, pardon,
Where there is discord, union,
Where there is error, truth,
Where there is doubt, faith,
Where there is despair, hope,
Where there is darkness, light,
Where there is sadness, joy

O Lord, grant that I may not so much seek
To be consoled as to console,
To be understood as to understand,
To be loved as to love.
For it is in giving that we receive,
In forgetting self that we find ourselves,
In pardoning that we are pardoned,
In dying that we are born again to eternal life.
Amen.[47]

This resonant dialectic perfectly captures human wretchedness and its possible elevation in the interest of humanity.

Moral Evaluation of an Act by Merit and Demerit, Approval and Resentment

Very naturally, Adam Smith used the vocabulary of his day to analyze moral feelings. Some of his terms, such as "merit" and "demerit," sound obsolete to our modern ears. The term "indignation," on the other hand, which I think of as an avatar of the feeling of resentment, is quite familiar to us, especially since the moment when Stéphane Hessel, one of the authors of the Universal Declaration of Human Rights, called upon young people to express their disagreement, especially with political authorities, in his small book entitled *Indignez-vous*, published in 2010.[48]

I find the psychological mechanism of resentment as presented by Adam Smith to be one of the most interesting to explore in order to explicate global indignation phenomena, as in the Cochabamba incident mentioned above.

His reasoning is rather astute.

First, he compares the mechanisms of merit and demerit, showing that in both instances two feelings develop, one in the agent and one in the patient.

---

47. I have seen several versions of this prayer on the Internet with slight variations; this version is a composite of them.

48. Hessel, *Indignez-vous*.

Chapter II: How to "Think" Water Emotionally

In the case of merit, the agent carries out a benevolent act and the patient (in this case a recipient) will express his acknowledgement or gratitude to the agent.

In the case of demerit, the agent does the patient (in this case a victim) wrong, and the patient expresses his suffering.

Now an "impartial spectator" (an original concept chosen by the moralist to make the phenomenon of the conscience understandable), for his part, will in the first case approve of and praise the agent, and in the second case express his resentment to the agent, putting himself as best he can in the suffering victim's shoes.

It is at this point that Smith introduces the strange mechanism of resentment, in what I find to be a completely original way.

First, he discovers that this emotion has two sides. It is made up of both hatred and empathy.

> As we cannot indeed enter into the resentment of the sufferer, unless our heart beforehand disapproves the motives of the agent, and renounces all fellow-feeling with them; so upon this account the sense of demerit, as well as that of merit, seems to be a compounded sentiment, and to be made of up two distinct emotions; a direct antipathy to the sentiments of the agent, and an indirect sympathy with the resentment of the sufferer.[49]

In the context of the Cochabamba example, his observation seems very plausible to me. We can see an indirect sympathy expressed by NGOs and the media toward Cochabamba's farmers, and a direct antipathy (resentment) toward the decision-makers of the multinational corporation that had increased the price of water. This resentment was not expressed by verbal means alone, since on-site violence had to be quelled by the police.

Second, Smith sees resentment as fertile ground for excesses:

> Our sympathy with the unavoidable distress of the innocent sufferers is not more real nor more lively, than our fellow-feeling with their just and natural resentment. The former sentiment only heightens the latter, and the idea of their distress serves only to inflame and blow up our animosity against those who occasioned it. When we think of the anguish of the sufferers, we take part with them more earnestly against their oppressors [...].[50]

Third, he insists that this resentment is kept within certain limits, though he concedes that it is one of the most difficult human passions to master.

> And as experience teaches us how much the greater part of mankind are incapable of this moderation, and great an effort must be made in order to bring down the rude and undisciplined impulse of resentment to this suitable temper, we cannot avoid conceiving a considerable degree of esteem and

---

49. Smith, *Théorie des sentiments moraux*, 124.
50. Ibid., 125.

admiration for one who appears capable of exerting so much self-command over one of the most ungovernable passions of his nature.[51]

Finally, he clarifies that, legitimate though this sentiment that "boils up in the breast of the spectator" may be, it is to be condemned. He even sees any expression of resentment as a degradation of mankind.

> To ascribe in this manner our natural sense of the ill desert of human actions to a sympathy with the resentment of the sufferer, may seem, to the greater part of people, to be a degradation of that sentiment. Resentment is commonly regarded as so odious a passion, that they will be apt to think it impossible that so laudable a principle, as the sense of the ill desert of vice, should in any respect be founded upon it. They will be more willing, perhaps, to admit that our sense of the merit of good actions is founded upon a sympathy with the gratitude of the persons who receive the benefit of them; because gratitude, as well as all the other benevolent passions, is regarded as an amiable principle, which can take nothing from the worth of whatever is founded upon it. Gratitude and resentment, however, are, in every respect, it is evident, counterparts to one another; and if our sense of merit arises from a sympathy with the one, our sense of demerit can scarce miss to proceed from a fellow-feeling with the other.[52]

I could wish that, after giving his negative evaluation of resentment, Adam Smith would have found some solutions for it. Yet I can well imagine that during the time period in which he lived, nothing prompted him to do so.

In contrast, in our time, it is imperative to forestall or neutralize resentment, especially when it is expressed in the context of real needs for potable water and sanitation. That is what I will briefly endeavor to do now.

"Thinking" Solutions for Present-Day Water-Related Resentment

Here I am referring to two occurrences that are highly symptomatic of the conflicts surrounding water. They were expanded upon at the third W4W colloquium in March 2013 by Evelyne Lyons,[53] with regard to the issue of dam building, and by Benoît Girardin[54] on the topic of transboundary aquifers.

The first issue is more familiar to the general public due to significant media coverage over the past few decades; the second no doubt will attract more attention in the near future, especially following UNESCO's work in 2008[55] and as a result of it.

---

51. Ibid., 126 n1.
52. Ibid., 125 n1.
53. Lyons, "*Conséquences sociales de la construction des barrages.*"
54. Girardin, "*Gestion juste des aquifères transfrontaliers.*"
55. Ibid.

At this 2013 gathering, Lyons noted the enormous gains that have been achieved since the 1990s in terms of putting normative texts in place. She specifically cited the establishment of "international ombudsmen to which victims can turn."[56] She made a point of mentioning the considerable institutional obstacles that had to be overcome in order for this to happen.

She also diplomatically stressed the ambiguity of civil society's systematic resistance—which in my opinion is a form of resentment—to building structures that are necessary for both regional economic development and access to water. So she offered a plea for the creation of mechanisms for "dialogue [. . .] including information, empowerment, and monitoring."[57]

Girardin in turn emphasized the potential for conflict among countries that share an aquifer, and saw intervention by neutral third parties as beneficial to both sides:

> [. . .] in many parts of the world, countries that share an aquifer do not have equal institutional capabilities or technical expertise. The risk that the stronger country will take advantage is far from zero. Recourse to an independent multilateral or regional third party, which would be involved beginning with a joint evaluation of steps taken and their risks, might turn out to be wise.[58]

I note that appealing to ombudsmen or neutral third parties is a use of conflict resolution mode, also called mediation or "alternative dispute resolution" (ADR). This is a promising method of which the full potential has not yet been adequately recognized, especially in Switzerland.[59] The use of mediation at the international level—notably at work in the South African Truth and Reconciliation Commission, where it facilitated the transition from apartheid to a new democracy—is to be welcomed.[60]

The road to mechanisms that will allow stakeholders to be both informed and heard seems very long indeed. Yet it is the path that will turn out to be the wisest to follow, because it is likely to predict feelings of resentment and the violence usually associated with them.

Concerning Selfishness, with Emmanuel Lévinas

With our study of resentment, we have just seen that another task of ethics is to take into account the dark side of human nature.

---

56. Ibid.
57. Lyons, "*Conséquences sociales de la construction des barrages.*"
58. Girardin, "*Gestion juste des aquifères transfrontaliers.*"
59. Fiechter and Zbinden, "La médiation en Suisse: les raisons d'un manque d'impact."
60. Fiechter-Widemann, *Pardon, catharsis de la violence extrême.*

Part III: A Changing Water Ethic

In this respect, Emmanuel Lévinas has made an important contribution off the beaten path, as Nathalie Maillard showed in her work *La vulnérabilité, une nouvelle catégorie morale?*[61] already cited above.

Lévinas's beginning in ethics was notable in that it made a clean break with Enlightenment philosophies, which were centered around reason and freedom; it focused on human weakness rather than human power and knowledge.

Man's weakness is typified especially by his selfishness or "egoism." The French philosopher is not hesitant about finding this human trait, vile though it may be, to be the essence of mankind:

> Evil shows itself as sin, that is, responsibility in spite of itself for refusing responsibilities. Neither beside nor facing Good, but in second place, under, lower than Good. Being persevering in being, egoism or Evil, designates the very dimension of lowliness and the birth of hierarchy.[62]

There are mainly two reasons for which I find it useful to bring up Lévinas's stature and philosophy—which some call subversive—within the context of considering our ethics of potable water "under construction."

First, his new perspective on human vulnerability, which was brought up at the beginning of this study,[63] highlights, not Man and his humanism, but Man and his human condition. So, at issue here is Man with his sensitivity and his vital needs, Man who depends on potable water to live and survive. Nathalie Maillard summarizes Lévinas's telos as follows.

> For him [Man], plagued by need, the world is first—before being the object of theoretical knowledge—a place of fulfillment and satisfaction. Man delights in the elements of the world. In this dialectic of need and satisfaction, we rediscover the very movement of selfishness, which is a return from the transcendent to the Self; in the act of satisfying oneself, the things of the world are considered only as a function of the subject's needs; the subject takes ownership of them to enjoy them. So, in order to get rid of selfishness, leaving the level of intentional consciousness is not enough: the living subject itself is preoccupied with its own happiness, tending towards pleasure. And this desire to enjoy is the basis for understanding the will to know, which therefore is merely a higher form of avatar.[64]

Second, Lévinas's philosophy can provide a key for considering the perception, at the national level, of selfishness that might arise in the pursuit of a self-centered kind of sovereignty.

---

61. Maillard, *La vulnérabilité*.
62. Lévinas, *Humanisme de l'autre homme*, 89.
63. See Part I, Chapter III, Vulnerability: Emmanuel Lévinas and Paul Ricoeur.
64. Maillard, *La vulnérabilité*, 299.

Chapter II: How to "Think" Water Emotionally

Without a doubt, the topic of water is tied to both national and global politics. Some people talk about political ecology, others about public international law. Consequently, water's challenges are associated with questions of sovereignty, hegemony, and power, as Mark Zeitoun noted at the March 2013 W4W colloquium.[65]

So we are not far from the concept of selfishness in the case of nations which, when faced with the need to come up with rules for general sharing of the water resource, issue guidelines that look after their own interests first. According to researchers Lasserre and Boutet, there are a number of doctrines:

> [. . .] in reality there are three main trends: one protecting downstream regions or countries, one protecting upstream regions or countries, and one that looks at the watercourse as a whole. The first two are the result of the dominant Westphalian concept of the State and aim only to protect the sovereignty to which it gives rise. The third seeks to overcome this obstacle, which leads only to half-results.[66]

It is interesting to note that the doctrine that has caused the most controversy is the one adopted by the United States during a late nineteenth-century conflict with Mexico over the use of the Colorado River. Following Westphalian principles, Judge Judson Harmon upheld the principle of absolute territorial sovereignty against Mexico's contention that the principle of prior appropriation applied. This amounted to saying that

> [t]he nation is therefore free to use the water in its territory as it sees fit: the resource is not seen as shared at all.[67]

Though today the United States has generally abandoned this doctrine of absolute territorial sovereignty, some other countries, such as Turkey,[68] still cite it.

So I find it relevant to say that the lens through which Lévinas views human selfishness can also be used to take a look at nations' selfishness when it comes to water issues.

An example will illustrate this viewpoint more clearly.

In his previously mentioned book *Avions-nous oublié le mal?* Jean-Pierre Dupuy says that economics has become the primary virtue and that we "are currently experiencing an invasion of political philosophy by the economic paradigm [. . .]."[69]

The facts seem to prove him right. I would even say that this is a kind of truism, for in this second decade of the twenty-first century, everything can be bought and

---

65. Zeitoun, *"International Hydro-politics."*

66. Laserre and Boutet, "Le droit international réglera-t-il les litiges du partage de l'eau ?, 497–514.

67. Ibid., 501, citing Lazerwitz, "The Flow of International Water Law," 15.

68. Ibid., 501, citing Mubiala, *L'évolution du droit des cours d'eau internationaux à la lumière de l'expérience africaine*, 19.

69. Dupuy, *Avions-nous oublié le mal?*, 75.

sold. Disciples of political ecology or political conviviality—inspired by Ivan Illich, for example—will not contradict me.

I will take as an example the economy's importance in European and Asian institutions. Europe and Asia have tried to unite their countries, the former by means of very familiar institutions such as the European Union and the Council of Europe, and Asia through ASEAN,[70] which consists of an economic institution called the AEC[71] and a social and cultural institution, the ASCC.[72]

In both cases, the economy is the dominant force, with non-commercial values such as human rights and culture having been given secondary roles.

I must stress that through its leading light, the European Human Rights Court, the Council of Europe has attained a stature that is the envy of the rest of the world. Nevertheless, it is the economic institution of the European Union that is foremost in everyone's mind.

In Asia, we must note that human rights and non-commercial values are not such a great success in ASEAN either. This is probably due to the desire to play economic catch-up with Europe. At the least, an accelerated or even frantic pace, maintained to make up for lost time, is increasingly noticeable every day.

This is what struck me when I read an article in the September 25, 2013 edition of the Singaporean newspaper *The Straits Times*, which laid heavy money that ASEAN's social and cultural goals for 2015 would not be met. Thai author Kavi Chongkittavorn[73] noted that in reality, backing values such as peace and reconciliation requires a much greater effort from the ASEAN countries than does settling economic questions.

> Many ASEAN countries are not comfortable broaching issues concerning social justice and human rights, let alone provide details of their implementation. This helps explain why human rights promotion and protection, as well as media development, still continues at a snail's pace.[74]

In ASEAN's defense, the journalist added that it had taken "an important step in the right direction by deciding in November 2011 to create the Institute for Peace and Reconciliation."[75]

---

70. ASEAN is the acronym for the Association of Southeast Asian Nations.

71. AEC is the acronym for the Asian Economic Community.

72. ASCC is the acronym for the Asian Social and Cultural Community.

73. Before returning to journalism, Kavi Chongkittavorn was a Reuters Fellow at Oxford University and a Nieman Fellow at Harvard University in 2001. He was named the Human Rights Journalist of 1998 to commemorate the 50th Anniversary of UNDHR by Amnesty International, Thailand, http://aseanidpp.org/chongkittavorn.

74. Chongkittavorn, "Is the ASEAN Community withering?," A 21.

75. Ibid.

Protagoras said that man is the measure of all things.[76] In today's globalized world, it certainly seems as if money has become the measure of all things.

Now as we saw earlier, in the eyes of the Greeks, money and wealth had no moral value. They are *adiaphora*, that is, *morally neutral*, whereas the values conveyed by human rights are not.

It is actually this normative neutrality that enables economic operators to understand each other and negotiate on the basis of the same codes. Probably this is just an illusion, since economic dogmas such as positive growth for some people and negative growth for others, are also values—but to clarify, they are economic values, not moral or humanist ones.

Mini-Conclusion

Let us try to understand, like Lévinas, that Man—including nations—is *ontologically* driven by the desire to monopolize and dominate the Other. In my opinion, this helps explain why countries are so reticent in committing to improved governance of water on a global scale. I cite as evidence the fact that the May 21, 1997 Convention on the Law of the Non-navigational Uses of International Watercourses,[77] which contains real solutions to water problems, only entered into effect on August 17, 2014. I would even say that the States took their time ratifying this pivotal international treaty.

Is it impossible to "think" a potable water ethic that takes into account collective well-being? I say it is not. Indeed, many philosophers have wondered about the possible connection between politics, ethics, and economics, as we shall see in the next chapter.

---

76. Protagoras, cited by Alloa, *La phénoménologie comme science de l'homme sans l'homme,* 82.
77. Convention on the Law of the Non-navigational Uses of International Watercourses.

Chapter III

Empirical and Utilitarian Motives for Action, or How to "Think" Water for the Well-Being of All

Introduction

EVER SINCE INDUSTRIAL DEVELOPMENT began, Western thinkers have had to grapple with deteriorating living conditions for the poorest people, and they have been facing a deep crisis in Christianity, which had already begun during the Reformation and subsequent tragic religious wars.

The moral rules promoted in the Judeo-Christian tradition, such as the Ten Commandments and the second part of the Greatest Commandment, "You shall love your neighbor as yourself" came to seem obsolete. So new doctrines—each more seductive and varied than the last—sprang up and were disseminated by talented authors who built their ideas up into whole systems, usually classified as moral and political philosophy. Industrialization dictated the rise of two new branches of "Ethics": economic ethics and social ethics.[1]

Since water does not meet mankind's many needs equally everywhere on our planet, the obvious question arises as to its economic distribution. In a moment we will see in an illuminating way, with reference to pivotal theological and philosophical arguments, that economics and ethics make strange bedfellows.

After this quick overview, we will have to concede that three centuries after the Enlightenment,[2] economics versus justice and ethics still remains a highly topical subject. As proof of this we can adduce the many criticisms directed against private water markets, especially multinational corporations, since the end of the twentieth century, not to mention the resentment—that human trait we have just discussed—expressed toward them.

---

1. Arnsperger and Van Parijs indicate, "[. . .] social ethics [. . .] is none other than the part of ethics that deals with social institutions rather than individual behavior [. . .]. [It] is simply political philosophy understood as a part of moral philosophy or ethics." Arnsperger and Van Parijs, *Ethique économique et sociale*, 6.

2. Authors such as Montesquieu, in *De l'Esprit des lois*, and Rousseau in his discourse on political economy in *d'Alembert's Encyclopedia*, wrote on this subject, which is still of interest today.

CHAPTER III: HOW TO "THINK" WATER FOR THE WELL-BEING OF ALL

With the theory that meeting essential needs cannot be the sole objective of a potable water ethic, which must also incorporate a broader concern for collective well-being, we will now address such an ethic's connection to several economic theories.

Where Economics and Ethics Meet

Adam Smith on the Connection between Economics and Ethics

Is it possible to conceive of a harmonious balance between economics and ethics? That is what François Dermange implied in a thorough and systematic study of Adam Smith's work.[3] He cautioned, however, that the condition for such a highly desirable balance is that the rules of justice must be respected:

> Harmony between ethics and economics depends on one essential thing: the stakeholders' obligation to follow the rules of justice.[4]

While Smith placed the search for a balance between economics and ethics at the heart of his work, the English-speaking moralist unfortunately did not find a satisfactory solution,[5] leaving the never-ending task of trying again up to his successors.

So it is not news to say that the search must go on, for better or worse.

We have mentioned Hugo de Grotius's early seventeenth-century attempts to preserve Christian teachings to the best of his ability, and take them as his inspiration. As discussed above (Part III, Section I, Chapter II), this meant revisiting the concept of "natural law" in the sociopolitical context of his day.

A century later, Adam Smith constructed a work that aimed to decode the bases for the development of prosperity in his country and the world while—unlike his contemporary colleague David Hume—maintaining ties to Christianity.

A Scottish Theologian Like No Other

This effort to go against the tide of a certain anticlericalism (which was to help fuel the late eighteenth century's social revolutions in the United States and France) is at least implicitly manifest on every page of Smith's two major works, *An Inquiry into the Nature and Causes of the Wealth of Nations*[6] and the previously mentioned *Theory of Moral Sentiments*,[7] which this Scottish theologian, ethicist and economist left as his legacy.

---

3. Dermange, *Le Dieu du marché*.

4. Ibid., 105.

5. Dermange indicates, "[. . .] in my eyes, the failure of Smith's project leads to a three-fold challenge: economic, ethical, and theological." Dermange, *Le Dieu du marché*, 216.

6. Smith, *La richesse des nations*.

7. Smith, *Théorie des sentiments moraux*.

Part III: A Changing Water Ethic

All of Smith's work emanates an irresistible desire to act for good and justice. For him, this means attempting to bring the discipline of economics into harmony with ethics.

The Morality of Good

Smith's example of the philosopher and the porter,[8] contrasting a man who is well off with one of more humble station, illustrates his humanistic attitude, since he places the two on an equal footing regardless of their social status. We can see that the "father of economics" pays attention to human social relationships, and the original goal of his "division of labor"—a reworking of one of Plato's concepts[9]—was to ensure

> that development would spread to all classes of people.[10]

I note that, like Calvin, Smith did not voice any objections to the acquisition of wealth by an individual,[11] always provided that said individual took care not to harm others in the process.

> One individual must never prefer himself so much even to any other individual as to hurt or injure that other in order to benefit himself [. . .].[12]
>
> Every man, so long as he does not violate the laws of justice, is left perfectly free to pursue his own interest his own way, and to bring both his industry and his capital into competition with those of any man or order of men.[13]

So he simply felt that a wealthy individual must confront the dilemma of "maximizing his wealth without losing the identity he receives from others."[14]

On the other hand, it is appropriate to note that Smith did warn against the dominant positions of merchants and manufacturers, who must be supervised by a political authority.[15]

---

8. Dermange, *Le Dieu du marché*, 71 n103, citing Smith, *Jurisprudence* (A) vi, 48–49.
9. Ibid., 70 n96.
10. Ibid., 71.
11. It is interesting to note that Calvin and Rousseau, those two great thinkers who lived in Geneva two centuries apart, had diametrically opposed views of Man. This was critical to their philosophy, especially where economic ethics were concerned. Calvin, for example, felt that Man is corrupt *by nature* and therefore wealth cannot corrupt him merely *by its nature*. In contrast, for Rousseau, Man is good *by nature* and both society and wealth can corrupt him *by their nature*.
12. Dermange, *Le Dieu du marché*, 78 n140, citing Smith, *Moral Sentiments* III, 3, 4–6, 200–01.
13. Ibid., 78 n143, citing Smith, Adam, *Wealth of Nations* IV, ix, 51.
14. Ibid., 79.
15. Ibid., 115.

Chapter III: How to "Think" Water for the Well-Being of All

The Morality of Righteousness

Law, in particular the respect owed to negotiated agreements, is a condition for the peaceful coexistence of ethics and economics.[16]

As a reminder, to promote this respect and encourage everyone to offer it, Smith chose feeling—more precisely, sympathy[17]—as a criterion for righteousness. At the center of his original moral theory is an "impartial spectator," who is there not only to observe Man's behavior without judging it, but also to "suffer with him" in the etymological sense of the Greek term for "sympathy," or to "be glad with him."

The Scandalous "Fable of the Bees"

One cannot understand Smith and his morality without considering the real aggravation he felt when he read "The Fable of the Bees," an apologia that created a scandal in 1714, shortly before his birth.

Its author, physician Bernard Mandeville, was a Dutch Huguenot who had chosen to emigrate to England. He had dared denunciation by the wealthy by expressing the very novel idea that the economy had both a negative and a positive effect. He felt that while the economy allowed people to acquire wealth and spend, that is, to engage in actions which he did not hesitate to label "private vices," these acts also advanced the public good.[18] In a word, the polemist theorized that of course the economy was an evil, but one that was necessary to everyone, because everyone could benefit from it.

Economics and Morality: An Oxymoron?

François Dermange reports a close relationship between Mandeville's Huguenot background and his astonishing profession of faith. He obviously must have seen ascetic Protestant morality as a

> theological condemnation of self esteem and the rational acknowledgement of its usefulness.[19]

Galvanized by Mandeville, Smith felt himself called to dedicate his life to an attempt to reconcile the economic and moral spheres, which his adversary had "paradoxically helped to dissociate."[20]

---

16. Ibid., 104.
17. See Part III, Section II, Chapter II, Compassionate Giving, and Moral Evaluation.
18. Smith indicates, "[. . .] private vices were public benefits, since without them no society could prosper or flourish." Smith, *Théorie des sentiments moraux*, 416.
19. Dermange, "Bernard Mandeville," 865.
20. Ibid.

His project was an ambitious one and he made no secret of it. He dreamed of being the Isaac Newton of morality.[21]

Perhaps he succeeded, for he did leave posterity a masterly double portrait, an extraordinarily detailed description not only of economic mechanisms, but also of the moral mechanisms that govern human relationships.

I think it useful to note that in general, only one face of Smith's literary diptych, namely *The Wealth of Nations,* as it is often called for short, appears today on syllabi throughout the world. His *Theory of Moral Sentiments* would be worth adding to supplement the training of young economists with the goal of facilitating more in-depth reflection about the development of the national and international economy in the twenty-first century.

In the context of the new ethic we are seeking in the context of potable water's challenges, I feel it is relevant to lend an ear to certain of Smith's observations, especially those concerning the most powerful economic actors—in his day, the great landowners and manufacturers. This might help us find some keys to understanding the reasons behind the controversy surrounding multinationals and their position as an alternative for managing potable water. This will come up again later (Part IV, Chapter III, Multinationals and Tensions Related to Global Responsibility).

The "Invisible Hand," a Jusnaturalist Concept

Smith was well aware of human weaknesses and the fact that the market provides an excellent opportunity for a "knave"[22] to fill his purse at others' expense. So he began searching for a concept that could reconcile economics and ethics.

First, he wanted to understand why Mandeville's hypothesis in his controversial *Fable of the Bees* paradoxically seemed to embody a certain degree of truth.[23]

So he began to observe the behavior of economic actors and to ask why the owners of large agricultural estates produced vital commodities for a large number of people, thereby serving society, notwithstanding their "rapacity."[24] He was also curious to know why investors, who after all were motivated by the self-centered concern of making the most of their capital, allowed the labor market to develop *ipso facto.*

---

21. Dermange indicates, "By transposing his method to all human and social phenomena, Smith hoped to build moral philosophy into a true science." Dermange, *Dieu du marché,* 20 and 21.

22. Ibid., 104 n1, citing Smith, who indicates, "The natural course of things decides it in favour of the knave: the natural sentiments of mankind in favour of the man of virtue [. . .]. Man is by nature directed to correct, in some measure, that distribution of things which she herself would otherwise have made." Smith, *Moral Sentiments III,* 5, 9, trans. 236.

23. Smith indicates, "But how destructive soever this system may appear, it could never have imposed upon so great a number of persons, nor have occasioned so general an alarm among those who are the friends of better principles, had it not in some respects bordered upon the truth." Smith, *Théorie des sentiments moraux,* 416.

24. Ibid., 163.

Neither of these, Smith had to conclude, is concerned with serving anyone's interests other than their own. Yet if the capital mobilized serves a useful purpose,[25] the large landowners and manufacturers are indeed working for the public good. Yet, and herein lies the paradox, the public good is served by both types of economic actors, completely without their knowledge.

Since no rational argument could explain this astonishing phenomenon, Smith had no other recourse but to turn to natural law and Providence. So he created the concept of the "invisible hand," interpreted as a "metaphor for Providence, believed to commute evil and good, unknown to Men."[26]

The Creature's Humility before Nature and God

If society is able to grow and develop despite the injustice of its most powerful members, it is because nature and a higher order are involved. That is the conclusion reached by our Glaswegian moralist:

> [. . .] the care of the universal happiness of all rational and sensible beings, is the business of God, and not of man. To man is allotted a much humbler department, but one much more suitable to the weakness of his powers, and to the narrowness of his comprehension—the care of his own happiness, of that of his family, his friends, his country [. . .].[27]

Jeremy Bentham and Utility as a Criterion for Collective Well-Being

Specialists generally agree that Jeremy Bentham defined utilitarianism very simply.

> The goal of morality is the greatest good for the greatest number, understood as maximization of the arithmetic sum of individual utilities.[28]

What does this mean?

Belgian philosopher Philippe Van Parijs explains the procedure as follows.

> Each time a decision must be made, utilitarianism requires that we establish the consequences associated with the various possible options, evaluate these consequences from the standpoint of the affected individuals' utility, and finally, choose one of the possible options for which the consequences are such

---

25. Ibid.,164.
26. Dermange, "Adam Smith," 1343 and Dermange, *Dieu du marché*, 167.
27. Ibid.,166 n80, citing Smith, *Moral Sentiments* VI, ii, 3, 6, trans., 329.
28. Dermange and Müller, "Utilitarisme", 1457.

Part III: A Changing Water Ethic

that the sum of its individual utilities is at least as great as the sum associated with every other possible option.[29]

How did Christians understand utilitarianism? According to Swiss theologians François Dermange and Denis Müller, John Mill raised a serious objection to this doctrine, which

> by focusing only on the sum total of utility and not on its distribution, [...] justified [...] that some would be seriously hindered if others benefitted from it.[30]

This potentially sacrificial character of utilitarianism unquestionably poses a problem for Christian ethics.

> The Christian theological ethic is hostile both to the way in which utilitarian thought subjects and sacrifices the human being to the ends of economics and profitability alone; and to the way in which, as a result, it elevates suffering (human and animal) and makes it the ethic's sole criterion (see utilitarian philosopher Peter Singer's controversial theories).[31]

At the end of the twentieth century, Van Parijs noted that utilitarian doctrine had marked the normative economy for over a hundred years.

> [...] the normative economy [...] [having] as its philosophical basis this distinctive doctrine of utilitarianism [...] must deal with an all-out attack on its own bastion, the political philosophy of English culture and its offshoots, over which it has held nearly unchallenged sway for more than a century.[32]

He emphasizes, and this is a very interesting point in the context of current ecological debates (including the water issue), that the extremes to which utilitarian doctrines can lead are what have made the concern for "intragenerational" and "intergenerational" collective well-being a focus of attention.

> [They] have devoted many lively discussions to the topic of future generations.[33]

In fact, utilitarians do not all speak with one voice and considerable differences can surface between classic[34] and moderate[35] utilitarianism. Van Parijs and his col-

---

29. Van Parijs, *Qu'est-ce qu'une société juste?*, 32.
30. Dermange and Müller, "Utilitarisme."
31. Ibid.
32. Van Parijs, *Qu'est-ce qu'une société juste?*, 31.
33. Arnsperger and Van Parijs, *Ethique économique et sociale*, 21.
34. Van Parijs indicates, "[...] classic utilitarianism (from Bentham to Sidgwick) [understands] the 'sum' of the utilities in its narrow sense and [requires] maximization of the aggregate utility [...]." Van Parijs, *Qu'est-ce qu'une société juste?*, 34.
35. Van Parijs indicates, "[...] moderate utilitarianism (that of Mill or Harsanyi) [divides] the

league Christian Arnsperger give a particularly edifying example concerning the positions put forward with regard to global demographics, a subject related to the water issue.

> The disparity between the policies recommended by these two versions of utilitarianism can be considerable. Let us suppose, for example,[36] that we have a choice between, on the one hand, family and socioeconomic policies that keep both the world population and its average level of well-being constant; and on the other, policies that triple the world population while reducing the average well-being by half. The classic utilitarian will of course choose the second option, while the moderate utilitarian will select the first. Neither of these positions is terribly comfortable. The classic utilitarian can in fact be led to recommend that humanity become more impoverished from one generation to the next. But the moderate utilitarian can conclude that reducing the population through the extinction of its less well-off members is justified.[37]

So Van Parijs could only applaud the emergence of doctrines that could serve as alternatives to utilitarianism beginning in the 1970s, which reintroduced the concepts of equality and liberty in the English-speaking world. These were advanced mainly by American philosophers such as John Rawls, whose *Theory of Justice* has the concept of equality at its heart, and libertarian Robert Nozick. I will decipher some aspects of Nozick's work below, because I am convinced that these references are of more than passing interest as far as the ethical challenges of potable water are concerned.[38]

Robert Nozick and Freedom as a Criterion for Collective Well-Being

Libertarians have fiercely opposed doctrines based on utilitarianism. In the 1970s, it became necessary to restore freedom's respectability:

> [...] it was only beginning in the 1970s [...] [that the libertarian approach] became a real alternative to utilitarianism, under the impetus of North American philosophers and economists such as [...] Robert Nozick [...].[39]
>
> The starting point for libertarian thought is the fundamental dignity of each human being, which cannot be flouted in the name of any collective imperative. This dignity lies in the sovereign exercise of freedom of choice in the context of a coherent system of rights.[40]

---

sum by the number of individuals and therefore (requires) maximization of average utility [...]." Van Parijs, ibid.

36. Arnsperger and Van Parijs, *Ethique économique et sociale*, 19.
37. Ibid., 20.
38. See Part IV, Chapter III, John Rawls: Toward Policical Liberalism.
39. Arnsperger and Van Parijs, *Ethique économique et sociale*, 29.
40. Ibid.

Van Parijs found the libertarians to be on the wrong track. Having himself chosen to expand upon Karl Marx's work as part the "September Group"[41]—a focus group that ended up restructuring the thought of the German philosopher and economist into "analytical Marxism"—he did not hide his reservations concerning Robert Nozick's libertarianism. He criticized it for being "theoretically" compatible "with colossal inequalities of income and wealth,"[42] and for being "a right with no real scope, a purely formal freedom," completely wanting in the "means essential for *effectively* exercising this freedom." So libertarianism distorts the very concept of freedom, because it is a

> [. . .] peculiar notion that is in no way justified in terms of freedom or the historical genesis of legitimate rights. In this light, libertarianism probably appears less as the coherent and plausible formulation of an ideal of a free society than as the fetishizing of "natural rights."[43]

Since the water issue is inextricably tied to that of land-grabbing, which is a very sensitive topic these days, I felt it would be useful to put forward two contemporary ideas about this subject, the "narrow Lockean proviso" and the "revisited Lockean proviso."

According to Van Parijs, Nozick's libertarian theories need not all be refuted. He acknowledged that Nozick had softened Locke's "first come, first served" principle[44] as far as first possession was concerned:

> Appropriation of a natural resource (and, more generally, of an asset that has never before belonged to anyone) is illegitimate if and only if those deprived of the opportunity to take ownership of it find themselves worse off than they would be in a "state of nature" in which no property rights existed, with everything accessible to everyone. In that case, *compensation* of the non-appropriators can make appropriation legitimate even if it would not be in the absence of compensation.[45]

This is the "narrow Lockean proviso."

As to the "revisited Lockean proviso," libertarian Thomas Paine, in particular, is acknowledged to have provided a correction for Nozick's "Lockean" proviso by adding a distributive justice element taken from the market.

> In their [libertarians'] eyes, appropriation can be legitimate only if the owner pays a tax in an amount reflecting the value of the natural resources of which he is taking ownership. This value can be determined by estimating the price

---

41. Ibid., 46.
42. Ibid., 41.
43. Ibid., 42.
44. Ibid., 34.
45. Ibid., 35.

that a fully competitive market would assign to it, and the revenue from the corresponding tax must be equally redistributed among everyone.[46]

The Connection between Economics, Ethics, and Politics according to Ricœur

A Word of Caution

A space for discussion and dialogue can help us to better "live in harmony."

Now if it is scarcely humanly conceivable that such a dialogue will lead to a consensus, then why should we not offer those involved in the debate a word of caution as did Paul Ricœur who, in one of his works, endeavors to "think" the points of convergence among ethics, politics, and economics? I am referring to a chapter in *From Text to Action*[47] that the French philosopher devotes to this question.

In this chapter, entitled "Ethics and Politics,"[48] Ricœur brings his own perspective to the economic history of the industrial era and provides some solutions for reasonable actions by a citizen of a globalized world.

The Dramatic History of the Industrial Age

Having drawn three overlapping circles representing ethics, politics, and the economy, Ricœur comes up with a striking theory about the possible intersections among these three disciplines.[49] In his explanation of this diagram, he recalls the characteristics of democracy and the State of Law[50] in order to bring out the drama of the industrial age's history, which he considers to have favored tyranny. The following is his demonstration.

---

46. Ibid., 36.
47. Ricœur, *Du texte à l'action*.
48. Ibid., 433–48.
49. Ibid., 433.

50. Ricoeur indicates, "it is not violence that defines the State but its finality, namely, helping the historical community to *make* its history. [. . .] Rationalist philosophies, such as all those of the eighteenth century as well as those of Arendt and Weil, tend to place their main emphasis on *form* rather than on force, while Marxists and thinkers who focus on totalitarianism stress force. Let us state straightaway that a reflection on force leads directly to the enigma constituted by the phenomenon of power, whereas a reflection on form, better suited to the concrete rational function of the State, leads to an emphasis on the constitutional aspect characteristic of a State of Law. Let us understand by State of Law a State that posits real conditions and guarantees of equality for all before the law. [. . .] Consequently, the emphasis will be placed on the independence of the public function, on service to the State of an honest bureaucracy, on the independence of judges, on parliamentary control, and especially on the education of all in the use of freedom through discussion. All of these criteria constitute the reasonable side of the *State*: it is a State of law in which the government observes certain legal rules limiting its arbitrariness." Ricœur, *Du texte à l'action,* 440–41.

Part III: A Changing Water Ethic

By starting from the premise that economic liberalism was characterized by "private appropriation of the means of production" taken as the sole criterion for modern "alienations,"[51] Marxists sacrificed freedoms that had been won—not without a cost—in Italy, Flanders, and Germany.

> It has become a terrifying drama for Europe and for the rest of the world that Marx and, even more so, Marxists saw in the popular struggles that led to political liberalism, such as it was observed in the nineteenth century in Anglo-Saxon countries, no more than a mere hypocritical screen for economic liberalism. There resulted from this identification between economic liberalism and political liberalism the dramatic erroneous belief that the elimination of economic liberalism had to be paid for by the loss of properly political benefits stemming from historical struggles as ancient as those of the urban communities in Italy, Flanders, and Germany for self-determination.[52]

In a context of technical and economic competition, everything possible must be done to ensure that this competition does not dissolve the "ethico-political core,"[53] and thus that it does not allow itself to be stifled solely by the rationality of what is reasonable.

This, says Ricœur, is the task of the political philosopher: to pay more attention to "what, in political life, is the bearer of meaningful action in history."[54] By asking about meaningful action, one is posing the ethical question of responsibility.

Paul Ricœur opens this field for discussion by ending his demonstration with Max Weber's famous distinction between an ethic of *conviction* and an ethic of *responsibility*.

> Addressing young pacifists just after World War I, he [Max Weber] admitted to them that politics necessarily splits ethics into two parts: on the one hand, there is a morality of *conviction*, which could be defined by the excellence of what is preferable; and, on the other hand, a morality of *responsibility*, defined by what can be realized within a given historical context and, Weber added, by moderation in the use of violence. It is because the morality of conviction and the morality of responsibility cannot completely merge that ethics and politics constitute two separate spheres, even if they do intersect.[55]

I note that Ricœur does not hold back in lamenting that

> [. . .] the modern State, in our ultrapluralistic societies, suffers from a weakness of ethical conviction just when politics readily calls upon morality; we

---

51. Ibid., 437.
52. Ibid., 436.
53. Ricoeur indicates, "[. . .] the dissolving action exerted by technology, now ruling supreme over the ethico-political core of these societies." Ricœur, *Du texte à l'action*, 438.
54. Ibid., 447.
55. Ibid.

then see fragile constructions erected on a soil that has been mined of its cultural contents.[56]

And, he adds, this weakness is due mainly to the fact that we think social peace is possible only if it is based on abstract values. Such values are "like cut flowers in a vase."[57]

I think it would be wise to take Ricœur's advice and focus more on what brings the two spheres together rather than what separates them. The citizen, then—and in the context of considering a global potable water ethic, I would say the global citizen—can find meaning in his commitment.

> It seems to me that there is a much greater danger today of failing to recognize the intersection of ethics and politics than of confusing the two spheres. Cynicism feeds on the apparently innocent acknowledgment of the abyss separating moral idealism from political realism. It is, on the contrary, the concern with providing a sense for the involvement of citizens, who are at once reasonable and responsible, that requires our being as attentive to the intersection of ethics and politics as to their unavoidable difference.[58]

In the next chapter, I will take up the issue of responsible action. First, though, I still need to examine how the Protestant ethic fits in with the connection between economics and politics.

The Connection between Economics, Politics, and Ethics according to the Protestant Ethic

Without wanting to display unwholesome skepticism, I feel we must follow Adam Smith's lead and note that in the twenty-first century, too, economics and ethics have their own independent spheres and it is very difficult to see where they intersect.

The boldness of Swiss Protestant churches in publicizing their Ecumenical Declaration on *Water As a Human Right and a Public Good* in 2005 caught my attention, and I thought it would be judicious to put forward the question of the Protestant ethic in relation to capitalism and politics.[59]

Swiss theologian Denis Müller gave an interesting answer. For him, the Protestant ethic

---

56. Ibid.
57. Ibid., 446.
58. Ibid., 448.
59. Mehl and Müller indicate, "The [French] term *'politique'* is polysemous. In the feminine, it designates activity in the service of society. In the masculine, it designates, first, the essence or nature of the aim of this activity; and second, the citizen who engages in it or even devotes himself to it [. . .]." Mehl and Müller, "Politique," 1074.

never stops testing the economy for its conformity to the requirement of justice; without this, neither the individual nor society can find any acceptable meaning for their existence or any chance of survival.[60]

As to the connection between economy and politics, Müller lucidly—it is appropriate to point out—invites his contemporaries to "show [. . .] vigilance and imagination."[61] He finds it completely incongruous to impute any ideological position whatsoever to the Protestant ethic. So he strongly refutes both those who "want to see in Max Weber's theses a non-problematical continuity between the Protestant ethic and the spirit of capitalism" and others who, in contrast, try "to identify the content of the Christian social ethic with Marxist or socialist values."[62]

This statement could probably be qualified, but in my opinion the tone has been set: the usual political divides have no place in the Protestant ethic. At the least it would be completely inappropriate to try to exploit that ethic one way or the other, or to try to curb its freedom of thought, because this fundamental value, freedom, is its distinguishing feature.

So, getting back to the subject of water, it is important to think with "vigilance and imagination"[63] about the formulation of a potable water ethic, which is at the heart of

> [. . .] social and global challenges [. . .] [and which is] suited to the realities of poverty, exploitation, and famine (here the Catholic attitude toward demographic and birth-rate issues seems thoughtless and irresponsible).[64]

So the Protestant ethic has complete freedom to try to distinguish

> [. . .] functional issues from the problem of values.[65]

It will find that economics must enjoy a certain degree of autonomy which, however, can be only relative, since there are some choices that necessarily have to be made.

> A socioeconomic system can turn out to be effective; it always will ask about the personal and social values on which it is based.[66]

---

60. Müller, "Morale," 957.
61. Ibid.
62. Ibid.
63. Ibid.
64. Ibid., 960.
65. Ibid., 959.
66. Ibid.

CHAPTER III: HOW TO "THINK" WATER FOR THE WELL-BEING OF ALL

Conclusion

Water conflicts are inevitable, because human passions such as resentment and selfishness play a pivotal role in this regard.

Solutions do exist, however.

First, as Adam Smith so lucidly set forth, the imbalance in the forces present must be stated and understood.

Second, to create an opportunity to better "live in harmony," one possible solution is to accept this reality with the goal of foreseeing conflict, as Hannah Arendt said, combining lyricism with a certain realism.

> To live together in the world means essentially that a world of things is between those who have it in common, as a table is located between those who sit around it; the world, like every in-between, relates and separates men at the same time.[67]

Coming down on the side of the relationship among human beings rather than the separation between them means making the choice for worldwide human brotherhood, compassion, and peace, a choice that has been made by the persons I was privileged to interview, which will be discussed in Part VI. It also means caring about justice and responsibility, to which I will now turn my attention.

---

67. Arendt, *Condition de l'homme moderne*, 92.

Part IV

Justice and Responsibility

From a Logic of Normativity to One of Implementation

Introduction

Justice for the "Other" Human Being, the One Who Thirsts

POVERTY LIES AT THE heart of the problem of universal access to potable water. So if we are to achieve justice in water matters, we must eradicate this scourge, a topic that was on the agenda for the Millennium Development Goals.[1]

Trying to pin down the concept of Justice is probably one of the most perilous undertakings there is. Each person has his or her own notion of it, which does not necessarily correspond to his or her neighbor's idea.[2]

In contrast, the sense of injustice that someone might feel, the inkling that another may have done him wrong, is much more common, even universal. It is often accompanied by a reprisal in the form of revenge, which has left its bloody mark on human history.

Added now to the wars and revolutions that have permeated the historical narrative is the growing worry that mankind no longer is capable of coping with disturbances of nature, such as climate change, and is even partly responsible for them.

In this respect Mario Miegge, an Italian philosopher from Ferrara, expresses himself as follows in an article about the economy, more specifically capitalism, which he was asked to write for the *Encyclopédie du protestantisme*.

> [...] it is obvious that the production and consumption model under which "strong" economies operate is changing the balances of the biosphere. At the peak of so-called economic development is the very place where "ecological debt" is created and grows. The uncontrollable acceleration of this debt is easy

---

1. United Nations Millennium Declaration, para. III/19.
2. Heraclitus indicates, "To God all things are fair and good and just, but men hold some things wrong and some right." Heraclite, *Fragments*, fragment no. 9, 96.

to foresee, at the moment when this same model is about to govern economies that currently are still "weak," which for two centuries have been subjected to the pillaging of their resources and which today encompass three-quarters of the global population.

A world polarized between a minority of ever-wealthier countries and a majority of poor ones; a planet devastated by the waste of resources, industrial waste, and the poisoning of the land, water, and air: is this result of a strange kind of "rationality" our legacy to future generations? Will we have the time and ability to rebuild the fabric of our public institutions, regulations and political constraints, our cultural and ethical practices, to try to control this economy before it has irreversibly undermined not only the foundations of civilization but also those of life on Earth?[3]

By acknowledging the existence of an ecological debt owed to poor nations by wealthy ones, especially where water is concerned, Miegge is not only reporting a feeling of injustice, but also emphasizing the challenge brought out by this ecological debt, that is, the need for good governance of the economy to ensure that future generations can continue to live on the earth. He believes that an economy that is unregulated, whether from a legal or moral standpoint, does not have good governance.

Does the Reality Affect Us and Make Us Responsible?

How do we react when we see documentaries on the topic of water scarcity in some parts of the world, or water that devastates by its superabundance? Are we shocked or indifferent when the precious resource is carried either in huge jars balanced on the head or in containers loaded on donkeys, as I have personally seen in Zimbabwe and Ethiopia?

As a citizen of a "developed" country as opposed to a "developing" country, I am selecting three possible answers to these questions, in accordance with the world's overly simplistic semantics, as formulated by U. S. President Harry Truman in 1949.[4]

First, I could consider that these populations live under primitive conditions and that as a fellow human being and responsible person, I ought to do everything possible to aid them, for example by helping them obtain financing for a well through a charitable association.

---

3. Miegge, "Capitalisme," 184–99.

4. Truman indicates, "Fourth, we must embark on a bold new program for making the benefits of our scientific advances and industrial progress available for the improvement and growth of underdeveloped areas. More than half the people of the world are living in conditions approaching misery. Their food is inadequate. They are victims of disease. Their economic life is primitive and stagnant. Their poverty is a handicap and a threat both to them and to more prosperous areas." Truman, Harry, "Inaugural address on January 20, 1949." http://www.herodote.net/20_janvier_1949-evenement-19490120.php.

Second, I could decide that the government of a disadvantaged country is solely responsible for that land's intolerable situation, and that it must modernize living conditions there because of the new human right to water, in particular by stimulating industrialization and building appropriate water supply infrastructure.

Finally, I could suppose that all "more advanced" countries have a responsibility to enable everyone in Third-World[5] countries to gain access not only to piped water in their homes, so as to compensate for negligence on the part of local officials, but also to high-quality wastewater treatment infrastructure.

Conceptually, we can speak of these three hypotheses as individual responsibility, national responsibility, and global responsibility.

Some may object that I am taking too short-sighted of an approach, and that thoughts about a potable water ethic must necessarily (because they relate to environmental issues) be able to open out from responsibilities that are limited in space to responsibility over time, to be broken down under the two qualifiers "intergenerational" and "intragenerational."

I accept the objection and will make it a point of honor to set to work studying this new ethic, the future ethic,[6] before coming back to the terrestrial globe.

However, I will not undertake this process until after I have attempted to gain a better understanding of the ambiguous concept of responsibility itself.

---

5. I note that a whole range of qualifiers emerged after President Truman's speech: "Third World," "less advanced" countries, "failed States," etc. I will employ them as necessary for my argument.

6. Birnbacher, *La responsabilité envers les générations futures*.

Chapter I

Responsibility: A Problematic Concept

Responsibility as Otherness

DISCUSSING RESPONSIBILITY AS PART of a study on the ethical issue of potable water means getting to the very heart of the human challenge, since this concept is a tool with complicated inner workings. Philosopher Marc Neuberg elegantly and metaphorically described it as one "of the threads in the knot of the enigmatic reality of the self."[1]

"Enigmatic reality" of the self, indeed, but also first and foremost the enigmatic reality of the Other. This unavoidable alterity, this Other to whom human beings cannot remain indifferent, especially when he or she suffers, does and should play a key role in the concept of human responsibility.

Is There a Conceptual Disconnect between the Industrialized and Non-Industrialized World with Regard to the Concept of Responsibility?

Here is an important question that lies on the practical end of the ethical consideration, as opposed to the theoretical end, according to the classification mentioned by German ethicist Dieter Birnbacher[2] for use in moral philosophy.

As a Westerner, entitled to the autonomy inherited from the Enlightenment, who am I to judge the status of men and women who for long ages have been accustomed to transport a vital resource without the help of modern technology? Do I have the right to impose my vision of the lifestyle of industrialized nations on them? Do I have the right to inculcate in them, by force, a concept of responsibility that according to the experts was shaped by the twists and turns of history under often tragic circumstances?[3]

---

1. Neuberg, *La responsabilité, questions philosophiques*, 1.
2. Birnbacher, *La responsabilité envers les générations futures*, vi and 13.
3. Genard, *Les métamorphoses de la responsabilité*, 133–34.

Part IV: Justice and Responsibility
From Ancient to Modern Times

In fact, "thinking" the human relationship to water also means "thinking" the status of human beings in society. For example, the Bible has many stories in which women are responsible for offering the precious liquid to any living creature that is thirsty.[4]

It is not at all my intent to idealize or uphold this vision for today. Quite the contrary, as I will explain in a moment.

Yet it is good to remember, like French philosopher Jean-Louis Genard, that at the turn of the eighteenth century the Western world felt the jolt of a previously unseen transformation of Man as an actor. It became possible for people to "make a commitment" in a totally new way, that is, autonomously, no longer locked into a status permanently carved in stone by society.

Genard believes that we must take into account diametrically opposed anthropological notions, namely those that in ancient times gave each person a permanent status in society, and those that correspond to the "modern idea" of social status, defined as "acquisition, construction or commitment,"[5] which seem to have appeared beginning in the eighteenth century,[6] the time of Enlightenment philosopher Jean-Jacques Rousseau.

According to Rousseau, we owe to Aristotle the idea that "[. . .] men are by no means equal naturally, but [. . .] some are born for slavery, and others for dominion."[7] He reacts strongly to this: "If then there are slaves by nature, it is because there have been slaves against nature. Force made the first slaves, and their cowardice perpetuated the condition."[8]

It is important to observe that emancipation was not accomplished in a day, nor in all parts of the world—far from it.

Considering the issue of an individual's status in society turns out to be critical to the topic of universal access to potable water. For Westerners, it means nothing less than remembering that the modern concept of responsibility has contributed to the wealth of industrialized countries, and also keeping in mind something that has long gone unrecognized: this prosperity is due in large part to the emancipation of women.

While the West ultimately improved the condition of women considerably, progress has been minimal to nonexistent in countries such as those cited by Cameroonian philosopher Daniel Tchamo. In a real defense of women's rights as a development

---

4. Gen 24:45-46 reads "[. . .] there was Rebekah coming out with her water jar on her shoulder; and she went down to the spring, and drew. I said to her, 'Please let me drink.' She quickly let down her jar from her shoulder, and said 'Drink, and I will also water your camels.' So I drank, and she also watered the camels." See also John 4 concerning Jesus and the Samaritan woman.

5. Genard, *Les métamorphoses de la responsabilité*, 136.

6. Genard indicates, "If we follow Cassirer's work on *Le Siècle des Lumières* [The Enlightenment century], we can in fact place this victory in the eighteenth century." Ibid., 138.

7. Rousseau, *Du contrat social*, 44.

8. Ibid.

factor, he classifies India, Pakistan, Bangladesh, China, Iran, and many African countries[9] as non-liberal societies, according to John Rawls's preferred terminology.

Changing mindsets turns out to be more difficult in the real world than in academia.

The hope that goes along with the new human right to water is just that: the hope of achieving a radical shift in mentality, especially with regard to the status of women, and empowering[10] "less advanced" societies and their industrialization.

However, I would like to stress that if this change comes about, it will have an important social cost, as the following example of Singapore proves.

In the 1970s, the government of this small Southeast Asian nation decided to make a potable water tap available to anyone. It clearly informed the public through all kinds of posters and radio announcements that this meant Singapore residents would have to leave their dwellings built on pilings—which, though precarious, were familiar—and accept the keys to an apartment in a skyscraper (HDB or "Housing Development Board").[11] As Singapore prepared to celebrate its fiftieth anniversary as a country in August 2015, there were any number of newspaper reports about this radical social change, which was imposed and in the end accepted. Former Prime Minister Lee Kuan Yew described the transformation of this tiny Asian country in a book entitled *From the Third World to the First: The Singapore Story—1965-2000*.[12]

Must we really hope for such transformations, and agree to the social cost with which they are inextricably linked? It is not up to twenty-first century Westerners to pass judgment, since they have not personally had to live through the upheavals of industrialization that their ancestors experienced.

We must note that Singapore's neighbors have taken it as a model, and a phenomenon of growing individuality, and therefore responsibility, has been perceptible to varying degrees for the past twenty years or so in the different Southeast Asian countries, such as Indonesia, the Philippines, Myanmar, and of course China.

The Classic Concept of Responsibility

I would be remiss if I did not take the precaution of clarifying that the three types of responsibility (intergenerational, intragenerational, and global) covered in the next two chapters are new concepts that have emerged from research and publications by contemporary thinkers since World War II.

---

9. Tchamo, *Justice distributive ou solidarité à l'échelle globale?*, 186.

10. Genard indicates, "Built on the word 'power' [. . .] which aims to acquire or possess expertise and capabilities for action that enable [stakeholders to] make choices and put forward acts that make a difference, and so to respond to situations with which [they] are faced." Genard, *Les métamorphoses de la responsabilité*, 150.

11. Tortajada, et al., *The Singapore Water Story*, 2013.

12. Lee Kuan Yew, *From the Third World to the First*.

Part IV: Justice and Responsibility

Since responsibility can be understood on many different levels, I find it unavoidable and necessary to specify which of its profiles can be used as a reference point to support what I have to say.

The origin of this concept goes far back in history, if we are to believe German philosopher Friedrich Nietzsche's analysis as set forth in a dissertation entitled *On the Genealogy of Morality*.[13] François Dermange's research on this notion, undertaken in an economic context and presented in *Dieu du Marché*,[14] is also highly suggestive.

I will have to be content with simply mentioning both of them, because for my purposes it seems sufficient to highlight a practical and ordinary distinction between a legal responsibility and an ethical one. As French philosopher Olivier Abel states,[15] the first sets limits on the chain of causality, while the second can open out to infinity, toward the future and future generations.

Olivier Abel's statement was probably inspired by the writings of Hans Jonas, for whom this responsibility, especially to future generations, was absolutely new and characteristic of our time, with the new Man having become a "Prometheus unbound."[16]

I will discuss this in a moment, once I have clearly delineated Abel's distinction.

As the opposite of this unlimited responsibility, we must consider "responsibility" in law, said to be a source of obligations. Swiss civil law, for example, recognizes three sources of obligations, namely contracts, (subjective or objective) responsibility for illicit acts, and unlawful enrichment.

The legal corpus concerning responsibility for illicit acts (also called civil responsibility) defines the obligation to make good any harm caused either directly (subjective responsibility) or indirectly (objective or causal responsibility) insofar as four cumulative conditions are met: the illicit act, the offense (intention or negligence), the harm, and the causal relationship between the offense and the harm.

I believe that the most important difference between legal and moral responsibility lies in the fact that the person who causes harm, the "agent," must answer for the harm he has caused and compensate society for that harm as prescribed by pre-established rules of law.[17]

In the case of moral responsibility, the agent is not required to accept this obligation, but has the ability or the freedom to respond or not to a situation, for example, one in which someone else is in danger, in which case he cannot be charged with a legal offense for his decision.

---

13. Nietzsche, *Eléments pour la généalogie de la morale*.
14. Dermange, *Dieu du Marché*, 216–66.
15. Abel, *La responsabilité incertaine*, 1.
16. Jonas, *Le principe responsabilité*, 15.
17. I hasten to add that "criminal responsibility" also exists, with its own sanctions.

Chapter I: Responsibility: A Problematic Concept

For example, this would be ability to actively react or to refrain from acting that philosopher Marc Neuberg called "*souffrance à distance*,"[18] or "distant suffering," which means the suffering of others throughout the world that is reported to us daily by the media, especially during severe droughts.

Once endowed with the aptitude for moral feeling, this moral agent has the ability to act as such.

This is what we can call openness to otherness, which "is actuated in intersubjective relationships."[19]

At the conceptual level, Guy Jobin postulates that there is an "explosive break" between the "reductionist" definition "of responsibility as imputability" and the expansion of "the responsibility to openness to alterity."[20]

I myself will refrain from making a peremptory value judgment between a legal responsibility that would be strictly reductionist in nature, and a moral responsibility that would be endowed with every virtue because it is potentially open to the Other's vulnerability.

Indeed, and this must be stressed, the four criteria for legal responsibility for illicit acts mentioned earlier do have the advantage of a certain amount of clarity, even though Swiss judges interpret them daily in their jurisprudence; and they can be subsumed.

Moral responsibility's criteria are another story altogether, and its openness, ideal though it may be, attests to its fragility, as is proven by the spread of the most varied and contradictory doctrines.

Of these, two may be of interest to us in the context of potable water, namely Jürgen Habermas's ethic of communication and Jonas's new ethic of responsibility.

These two German philosophers disagree in the purpose of their ethics, with the former basing his on Man's vulnerability and the latter on that of nature. The anthropocentrism of the one contradicts the naturalism of the other.

What brings them together, on the other hand, is the search for the responsible human being as a moral agent.

If another person is suffering and vulnerable, should my conscience move me to action? Should I *answer* the call of this suffering and be *answerable for* it?

Habermas formulated this feeling of moral responsibility in today's world very well. It aims to draw ever more attention to individual vulnerability.

> From this anthropological viewpoint, morality can be conceived as the protective institution that compensates for a constitutional precariousness implicit in the sociocultural form of life itself. Moral institutions tell us how we should behave toward one another to counteract the extreme vulnerability of the individual through protection and considerateness. Nobody can preserve

---

18. Neuberg, 254, using an expression that originated with Boltanski, *La souffrance à distance*.
19. Jobin, "Le paradigme de la responsabilité comme condition de l'éthique théologique," 134.
20. Ibid.

his integrity by himself alone. The integrity of individual persons requires the stabilization of a network of symmetrical relations of recognition in which nonreplaceable individuals can secure their fragile identities in a reciprocal fashion only as members of a community.[21]

Following these historical, political, social, philosophical, and legal reflections, I will now take up the problem of humanity's relationship to water in time and space.

---

21. Habermas, *De l'éthique de la discussion*, 19.

Chapter II

Intergenerational Ethics

Is Nature Living on Borrowed Time?

HUMANKIND'S WHOLE HISTORY TESTIFIES to the fact that up to the twenty-first century, Man has so far been able to make use of his abilities in order to succeed—even though his path has been littered with many failures—in ensuring the survival of living species in general and the human species in particular.

What is new since about the 1950s is that nature, which since mankind's beginnings had been considered a "given," has burst into the ethics debate and become a point of contention with regard to legitimate ways to encourage what is good for humanity, on the one hand, and nature, on the other. It has actually led to confrontations, because those who espouse the tenets of what has become ecology look upon industrial society with a very critical eye; they strongly dispute theories from the Enlightenment, which praised progress to the skies.

So we have seen, inspired by increasingly alarming and alarmist scientific reports about the state of the planet, the germination of new doctrines suggested by philosophers, sociologists, and ethicists, and new strategies offered by politicians, legal experts, and economists, with some Christian churches having let it be known that they too wished to be included in the debate, as already mentioned.

In my opinion, we are living through an extremely stimulating phase of history, though it most definitely is also marked by great uncertainty, sometimes fear, as set forth by both Albert Camus, in a famous speech,[1] and German philosopher Hans

---

1. Camus indicates, "Each generation doubtless feels called upon to reform the world. Mine knows that it will not reform it, but its task is perhaps even greater. It consists in preventing the world from destroying itself. Heir to a corrupt history, in which are mingled fallen revolutions, technology gone mad, dead gods, and worn-out ideologies, where mediocre powers can destroy all yet no longer know how to convince, where intelligence has debased itself to become the servant of hatred and oppression, this generation starting from its own negations has had to re-establish, both within and without, a little of that which constitutes the dignity of life and death," Camus, excerpt from his acceptance speech for the Nobel prize for literature.

Jonas, with his well-known "heuristics of fear" in a work we have already quoted that was devoted to *The Imperative of Responsibility*.[2]

That is where we will now turn our attention.

Hans Jonas's Ethic and Appeal on Behalf of Future Generations

Philosopher Hans Jonas's work first made an impression in 1979 with the publication of *In Search of an Ethics for a Technological Age*.[3]

Better known as *The Imperative of Responsibility*, it sold over a million copies.[4] It contains a section concerning "The Limits of Nature's Tolerance"[5] and brings up the topic of water[6] in relation to the issue of food.

So it seems apropos to plumb its depths.

Jonas's theory is a determinedly forward-looking reflection on the future and hope for the planet's survival and sustainability, with a concern for future generations as its keystone.

This having been said, the responsibility that Jonas invites us to consider is a very specific one, a concept to be revisited in the context of globalization.

The fact that his call for the creation of a new ethic suited to our postmodern era resonated with so many is due in part, I believe, to this German philosopher's rhetoric, his impressive method that was meant to convince.

I find that, building on the solid knowledge developed from his examination of Gnosticism, and having a premonition that humanity was at a crossroads because of its enormous technological abilities that were becoming increasingly difficult to control, he sought a method that could create new behavioral norms for humankind.

His process recalls the one employed by the founders of the modern natural law school, who were champions of a methodology inspired by the mathematical sciences. For example, in the preface to *De Cive*, Thomas Hobbes described how the method for acquiring new knowledge consisted of imagining himself taking apart the complex mechanism of a watch to reveal the various wheels and the shape and movement of the parts.[7]

Did not Jonas, like Hobbes' watchmaker and spurred on by what he considered a real emergency, set himself something of a Herculean task? Did he not begin to gather innumerable facts, mostly of a scientific nature, to try to understand them and examine them from a forward-looking perspective?

---

2. Jonas, *Le principe responsabilité*.
3. Ibid.
4. De Stexhe, Guillaume, "Devoir, pouvoir?"
5. Jonas, *Le principe responsabilité*, 364.
6. Ibid., 352.
7. Dufour, *Droits de l'homme, droit naturel et histoire*, 105.

Chapter II: Intergenerational Ethics

I believe that it was to establish the truth of his hypothesis, namely that unless a paradigm shift occurred the world would be rushing toward its doom, that he chose a very familiar concept, *responsibility,* as the starting point for his demonstration, with the well-defined goal of convincing as many people as possible.

So it is my theory that Hans Jonas chose to move his readers by placing an example from antiquity in the first chapter of *The Imperative of Responsibility* and introducing it in the form of a magnificent poem taken from Sophocles' tragedy *Antigone.* Was reading this poem, which I include here, what made him decide to set out on the road to a new ethic? I cannot rule it out.

Here is the poem.[8]

> Many wonders but nothing more wondrous than man.
> This thing crosses the sea in the winter's storm,
> making his path through the roaring waves.
> And she, the greatest of gods, the Earth—
> deathless she is, and unwearied—he wears her away
> as the ploughs go up and down from year to year
> and his mules turn up the soil.
>
> The tribes of the lighthearted birds he ensnares, and the races
> of all the wild beasts and the salty brood of the sea,
> with the twisted mesh of his nets, he leads captive, this clever man.
> He controls with craft the beasts of the open air,
> who roam the hills. The horse with his shaggy mane
> he holds and harnesses, yoked about the neck,
> and the strong bull of the mountain.
>
> Speech and thought like the wind
> and the feelings that make the town,
> he has taught himself, and shelter against the cold,
> refuge from rain. Ever resourceful is he.
> He faces no future helpless. Only against death
> shall he call for aid in vain. But from baffling maladies
> has he contrived escape.
>
> Clever beyond all dreams
> the inventive craft that he has
> which may drive him one time or another to well or ill.
> When he honors the laws of the land and the gods' sworn right
> high indeed is his city; but stateless the man
> who dares to do what is shameful.

---

8. Jonas, *Le principe responsabilité,* 22, referring to Sophocles, *Antigone,* 14–15.

Part IV: Justice and Responsibility

I think that Hans Jonas jolted many consciences when he ended his demonstration by suggesting that a new principle, "responsibility," be adopted as a new law to follow, a new imperative even, which in his eyes was more effective than Kant's categorical imperative.

In this way, he probably contributed to developing ecological doctrine, otherwise known as "political ecology." He very likely also contributed to the international movement that resulted, in 1989, in the installation of the "sustainable development" concept, which has been "maturing" since the 1992 Rio conference and continues to do so today.

How Jonas's Philosophy was Received

As Jonas was writing his article for *Esprit*[9] in 1974, ecology was a new science that he felt would have a bright future. It has obviously been invading our daily lives for about forty years now, but at a pace I would say has accelerated since the major international gathering in 1992 at which the principle of "sustainable development" was established in Rio de Janeiro, where its progress was assessed twenty years later at another meeting in June 2012.

Over forty years, with help from the media and especially thanks to the development of such technologies as the Internet and social networks, for example, Facebook, Twitter, and LinkedIn, the planet has shrunk to the size of a global village.

Villagers—in the literal sense of the word—out in the middle of nowhere can now use their cell phones to call a central service and ask about the best planting times. This type of "success story" can be immediately contrasted with the tyrannical power of multinational corporations, which have the ability to move in and log hundreds of hectares of tropical forest in a few hours.

So the temptation, already mentioned by Hans Jonas, is to control human activity through new imperatives on Kant's model, as applied not to Man's immediate space and proximate time, but to the whole planet and even future generations.

It is probably this attempt to extend such "responsibility," which I will call Jonasian, to infinity that gave rise to varying reactions.

It is true that some of Jonas's contemporaries, including well-known thinkers such as André Dumas, did hail his visionary mindset; but they also expressed a certain amount of skepticism even as early as 1974 when an article published in *Esprit*[10] offered a reminder that utopian ideas do not mix well with realities such as unemployment and the need for growth.[11] Marienstras upped the ante: "Man can control nothing . . ."[12]

9. Jonas and Favre, "Technologie et responsabilité.," 163–84.
10. Ibid.
11. Dumas, "Réponse à Hans Jonas."
12. Marienstras, "Réponse à Hans Jonas."

Wanting to control everything can lead to a dead end, or even totalitarianism:

> [...] through a curious reversal, the more we tried to strengthen controls by eliminating factors that seemed uncontrollable, the deeper into opaqueness, lies, or terror we went.[13]

For his part, Paul Ricœur devoted a significant portion of his article in *The Just*[14] to the Jonasian position on responsibility. It was this article that guided my exploration of the new ethic proposed for our technological civilization. In it, he mentioned his perplexity when confronted with a doctrine intended to justify

> [...] the double relation of responsibility on the one side toward those precautions and the prudence required by what he calls the "heuristic [sic] of fear," and on the other toward the potentially destructive effects of our action.[15]

Taking a Critical Look

In light of the definitions presented in the first chapter, I have an initial question. Was Jonas right to turn to the concept of "responsibility" as the basis for a doctrine aiming to take the part of future generations rather than those of the present, a doctrine that looks solely to the future with the deliberate intent of "birthing" a new dynamism to ensure humanity's survival?[16] My second question will be more pointed: was it legitimate for Jonas to appropriate the concept of "responsibility" to use as the basis for his ideology, as he himself says?[17]

I will attempt to answer these two questions in the following discussion.

In response to the first, I would say this: as a jurist, I cannot fail to be surprised that a philosopher should choose a concept that has so many legal connotations and is so morally sensitive, as I explained above. I must concede, though, that the approach won enormous success for its author—how many politicians, writers, philosophers, and even scientists are aligning themselves with the *Imperative of Responsibility*?

Replying to the second question is more difficult.

Those of us from democratic countries all enjoy freedom of expression. In the end, new concepts are born every day, and how many concepts throughout history have taken on different meanings?

Legal scholars fear that precedent will be overturned, because this threatens the security of law. Judges make such a serious decision only for justified and well-founded reasons.

---

13. Ibid.
14. Ricœur, "Le concept de responsabilité," 64.
15. Ibid.
16. Jonas indicates, "question [...] of survival." Jonas, *Le principe responsabilité*, 246.
17. Ibid.

Part IV: Justice and Responsibility

By giving a new interpretation of the concept of responsibility, Hans Jonas essentially "overturned precedent." So I will take the liberty of analyzing this reversal with a critical eye in a manner akin to a Swiss juridical method that has sometimes allowed the Federal Supreme Court of Switzerland to make bold judgments.

Hans Jonas said that Man is "Prometheus unbound."

This reference to a mythological figure allows the creator of *The Imperative of Responsibility*[18] to develop a systematic line of reasoning in support of his contention that when humanity left the state of submission to nature to enter a new era in which nature is tamed by science and technology, it crossed a critical threshold and there is absolutely no going back.

He emphasizes that this historic break has had increasingly noticeable consequences, and that humanity is on the verge of no longer controlling the progression, which is running away with us. These effects, beneficial though they may have been in lightening Man's workload, especially where agriculture is concerned, increasingly seem to be threatening our future.

> [. . .] The promise of modern technology has turned into a threat, or [. . .] the latter is inextricably linked to the former.[19]

This threat translates into

> [. . .] the irresistible exercise of this ability [. . .] which is unparalleled in past experience.[20]

With new abilities come new obligations, and therefore new responsibility, said Jonas. These new obligations summoned by the German philosopher are unlimited in time and space. Are they bound to befall us? Is this inevitable?

I myself am very tempted to find something to counterbalance to them.

And just in the nick of time, along comes another German philosopher to provide it. Robert Spaemann wrote a book about an act's *side effects*,[21] in which he gave a solemn warning about ascribing too much significance to human schemes. He feels that taking every last effect of an action into account

> [. . .] is to turn responsibility into a kind of fatalism in the tragic sense of the word, even into a terrorist denunciation: "You are responsible for everything and guilty of it all!"[22]

Unfazed, Paul Ricœur steps into a debate that could lead either to a dialogue in which neither side listens to the other, or to confrontation, which is far from being my

---

18. Jonas, *Le principe responsabilité*, 15.
19. Ibid.
20. Ibid.
21. Spaemann, "Nebenwirkungen als moralisches Problem," 66.
22. Ricoeur, *Le Juste 1*, 69.

purpose, by referring to Hegel in the second part of his *Elements of the Philosophy of Right*.[23]

For Ricœur, simply reviving the Kantian imperative in order to extend it to future generations, as Jonas does, would mean avoiding the Hegelian dilemma, which a moral vision of the world can make intelligible. Hegel studied the subjective will and found it to be finite, and he distinguished the voluntary act from the involuntary act. Thus, while he was able to state that a change caused by externalization of the act attached to "the abstract predicate 'mine'"[24] is clearly imputable to the agent, conversely, he also brought up the question of knowing whether a change brought about by externalizing the act, but not desired by its author, could also be imputable to him.

Hegel's answer to this is *Sittlichkeit*, that is,

> [. . .] concrete social morality that brings with it the wisdom of mores, customs, shared beliefs, institutions that bear the stamp of history.[25]

This Hegelian response led Ricœur to suggest—to frame the discussion I started between Jonas and Spaemann in what I would call an "operational" way—a happy medium between the agent's refusal to consider the consequences of his act and therefore to "answer" for them, and the taking of full responsibility—which is impossible—for all of his action's *side effects*, such as nuisances, pollution, and other harm to nature and the environment.[26]

The happy medium is practical wisdom, *Sittlichkeit*, and as Ricœur says again, it is one of "a detailed moral judgment," more specifically that of the Greek virtue of *phronesis* or *prudentia*, which is more than simple prudence, but a kind of caution directed at

> [. . .] recognizing among the innumerable consequences of action those for which we can legitimately be held responsible [. . .].[27]

Open Questions

In *The Imperative of Responsibility: In Search of an Ethics for the Technological Age*, Jonas himself intimated that he had hesitated to choose the "principle of fear" to counter Bloch's "principle of hope," because

> [. . .] fear itself becomes [. . .] the first preliminary obligation of an ethic of historical responsibility.[28]

23. Ibid., 67, referring to Hegel, Georg Willhelm Friedrich, "*Principes de la philosophie du droit*."
24. Ibid., citing Hegel §115.
25. Ibid., 68.
26. Those things that economists term "externalities."
27. Ricœur, *Le Juste 1*, 70.
28. Jonas, *Le principe responsabilité*, 422.

He concedes, however, that fear has a

> [. . .] less attractive face, and [. . .] among the narrow-minded, has something of a bad reputation, morally speaking [. . .].[29]

Though his *heuristics of fear* does indeed play a very important role in his work, we must conclude by the philosopher's own admission that in fact his intent was not to add a new facet to the concept of "responsibility," but rather to suggest a theory for an ethic of the future.

The goal of this was to reverse the earlier Platonic view of an ontology focused on eternity to make a temporal ontology.

> The Platonic eros, directed at eternity, at the nontemporal, is not responsible for its object [. . .] *Our* concern about the preservation of the species, to the contrary, is thirst for temporality in its ever-new, always unprecedented productions, which no knowledge of essence can predict. Such a thirst imposes its own novel duties: the striving for ultimate perfection [. . .] is not among them.[30]

Jonas called this temporality horizontal approximation,[31] in contrast to Platonic vertical approximation,[32] which could translate into sustainability, a word that today is a well-established part of the "sustainable development" concept established in Rio in 1992.

I believe I have shown that, when Jonas recommended setting limits on the immoderate development of technology, he was calling for sustainability and human survival; and, without rejecting progress, he hoped that it would be used cautiously in keeping with the virtue of "caution,"[33] since the "ethic of the future" aspect is the corollary of the goal of sustainability.

As a final argument demonstrating once and for all that the greatness of the concept of responsibility concerns humankind here and now, not abstract future generations, I will contrast "humanism" and "hominism," according to the formula by the great German humanist Karl Jaspers.

> If I see Man exclusively as a natural being that we can know through objective methods, it is because I renounce all humanism for a kind of "hominism" (Windelband). I see him only as the representative of a natural species. All the

---

29. Ibid., 420.

30. Ibid., 243.

31. Jonas indicates, "For the time being, the horizontal dynamics we have unleashed ourselves 'has' us by the scruffs of our necks. Even the suspicion that what I called the abolition of transcendence may have been the most colossal mistake in history, does not relieve us of the fact that, now and until further notice, responsibility for what has been set afoot and is kept moving by ourselves, takes precedence before everything else." Jonas, *Le principe responsabilité*, 247–48.

32. Ibid.

33. Ibid., 359.

individuals are nothing more than examples of this species, in endless numbers, without value in and of themselves.[34]

So Hans Jonas was not a humanist, but as a master with words he successfully proclaimed his *Imperative of Responsibility* to illustrate the fear of technology's out-of-control development, like Max Weber, who communicated his ethic of conviction and ethic of responsibility.[35]

Must we then resign ourselves to accepting Jonas's change to responsibility's meaning? Or consider it merely a form of the virtue of prudence that is in the interest of human life's sustainability? I will leave these questions open.

Conclusion

The World of 2014 Is not That of 1979

Now, over thirty-five years after the publication of Hans Jonas's *Imperative of Responsibility*,[36] a book that lit a fire under late twentieth-century consciences, do the environmental stakes and the threats hanging over humanity remain the same? Is the situation worse or better?

A book published in France in early 2014, entitled *L'eau entre réglementation et marché*,[37] stresses the fact that since the theories of 2009 Nobel laureate Elinor Ostrom were published in *Governing the Commons*,[38] the world has changed.

> G. Hardin's approach and that of E. Ostrom purported to be universal but are heavily marked by North American administrative culture, customs and traditions which today are difficult to transpose to other countries, whether rich or poor, that do not share this culture. The main characteristic of a trend is that it does not last. We are now in the decade of 2010-2020, not the 1970s.[39]

How, indeed, could we avoid seeing how much "green" awareness has invaded every continent, especially Asia?

It is true that a Taiwanese city such as Kaohsiung had no choice but to take drastic measures to help the environment. In the first decade of the new millennium, its air was so unbreathable from industrial carbon emissions, and its rivers were so polluted, that it was even considered "clinically dead." It was a life or death situation.

---

34. Jaspers, "Pour un nouvel humanisme," 215.

35. Weber, indicates, "One cannot prescribe to anyone whether he should follow an ethic of [conviction] or an ethic of responsibility, or when the one and when the other. [. . .] an ethic of [conviction] and an ethic of responsibility are not absolute contrasts but rather supplements [. . .]." Weber, "Le métier et la vocation d'homme politique," 217–18.

36. Jonas, *Le principe responsabilité*, 359.

37. Falque, *L'eau entre réglementation et marché*.

38. Ostrom, *Governing the Commons*.

39. Falque, *L'eau entre réglementation et* marché, 7.

Life has won out.[40]

Today, the mountains of garbage are processed to create electricity, the waters of the Love River delight tourists, new technologies convert coal with a considerably reduced environmental impact compared to ten years ago, and wastewater is treated for domestic and industrial use.[41]

So has Asia accepted its responsibilities in order to ensure its inhabitants a life worth living? Has it accepted them only for itself? It seems also to have taken the UN's "global responsibility" guidelines to heart. After all, since 2014 have we not been seeing young Chinese soldiers among UN peacekeeping forces, in Mali for example?[42]

We should not be naive. Strategic and political considerations underlie these spectacular changes reported by the media. However, in my opinion, the pessimism expressed in the 1990s by many philosophers, such as Frédéric Lenoir in his interviews on ethics collected in *Le temps de la responsabilité*,[43] should be tempered.

---

40. https://fr.wikipedia.org/wiki/Kaohsiung.
41. Ibid.
42. www.onu.org.
43. Lenoir, *Le temps de la responsabilité, Entretiens sur l'éthique.*

Chapter III

Intragenerational Ethics

Global Justice vs. Global Poverty: A New Dialectic for the Emergence of Global Collective Responsibility

RIGHTING WRONGS AND INJUSTICES: such is indeed the essence and the end of immanent justice.

The dream of a perfect society, a just society, has been haunting persons of culture since the dawn of time. Thomas Moore's *Utopia* is a good example.

Today's philosophers, concerned by so-called global poverty, are attempting to "think" methods for redistributing wealth, a matter which falls under distributive justice, so that everyone worldwide can enjoy an equal level of well-being.

That is the challenge of what we will henceforth term global justice, which serves as the basis for the action to be taken (and thus, for the responsibility to be assumed) by the citizens and governments of wealthy countries on behalf of poor countries with insufficient access to potable water.

Here I need to clarify that the concepts of global justice and global responsibility are not carved in stone and are a subject of research in universities around the world. Potable water is a key challenge where the issue of global poverty is concerned. So in order to provide food for discussion, I found it useful to mention—though without solving them—the dilemmas confronting both the researchers and the global citizen.

David Miller and Global Responsibility

"Global responsibility" is a new concept born of globalization, a fertile ground that has given rise to countless semantic innovations, perhaps in accordance with Antoine Garapon's insight. He found that globalization makes thought processes more fluid.

> Global reasoning has a *decompartmentalizing* effect on the thought process, as on the flows that are its object.[1]

---

1. Garapon, *Raison du moindre Etat*, 205.

Part IV: Justice and Responsibility

Then why not rather speak of "collective responsibility," like British philosopher David Miller? I would guess that we are dealing with synonyms, and his thought interests me here.

As Miller understands "collective responsibility," it calls into question the relationship of one group of individuals, companies, or countries to another such group when an injustice is present—poverty, for example. In short, this means "thinking" the possible subjects of "collective responsibility" as well as the complexity of such a responsibility.

He takes the vulnerability of the human condition as his starting point.

He has qualified this vulnerability by placing human beings in two very distinct categories: those who cannot meet their own needs without help from others, and those who—regardless of whether they themselves are rich or poor—are likely to help the needy (if rich), or those needier than themselves, (if poor).

He continues by acknowledging that

> [r]esponsibility has proved to be one of the most slippery and confusing terms in the lexicon of moral and political philosophy[2]

and can lead to a "slippery slope."

To simplify, he confines his discussion to the result of the action by an agent (A), which he calls "outcome responsibility," and the agent's obligation to remedy the damage suffered by the patient (P), which he calls "remedial responsibility." So he is stressing the obligation placed on A when A unjustly creates a situation.

> Identifying responsibility is a matter of looking to see who, if anybody, meets the relevant conditions for being responsible.[3]

He then uses examples to expose the ins and outs of collective responsibility.

In the case of rioting, he says, damage is caused by an indeterminate number of people during a violent demonstration. The specific responsibility of each group member (instigators or mere participants, even nonviolent ones) is too difficult to determine due to the general state of chaos, so each person must be held equally responsible. (I find that Swiss civil law has a clear answer for this type of responsibility with its concept of *shared responsibility* as found in articles 143 ff. of the Swiss Code of Obligations.[4])

---

2. Miller, *National Responsibility and Global Justice*, 82.

3. Ibid., 84. I would like to emphasize that Swiss law provides a specific article for rioting in its penal code, namely article 260, para. 1: "Any person who takes part in a riotous assembly in public in the course of which acts of violence are committed against persons and property by the use of united force is liable to a custodial sentence not exceeding three years or to a monetary penalty"; para. 2: "Participants who remove themselves when officially ordered to do so are not held to have committed an offence if they have not used violence or encouraged others to do so."

4. Two articles of the Swiss Code of Obligations clarify "external" and "internal" relationships. a) article 144, concerning the responsibility of joint creditors to the injured party, which indicates, "A creditor may at his discretion request partial performance of the obligation from each joint and

He also gives the example of a worker-owned factory managed by the employees, who have no scruples about polluting a river to improve production. If a minority of them is aware of the environmental issue and opposes continued activities by the company, then according to David Miller the members of the minority still share in the responsibility for the decision, unless they leave the company.

Having gotten through these preliminaries, the philosopher next wonders whether his reasoning applies to nations. He answers cautiously, noting that the issues of global justice are not yet clear[5] but that they bring up two questions, specifically those related to outcome responsibility and remedial responsibility. He sees that the issue must be raised of knowing whether a nation should be held responsible not only for the benefits and burdens it creates for its own members, but also for the impact of its actions on third-party countries.[6] This would mean not only taking global poverty into consideration, but also asking what its victims might be able to demand in the name of global justice, and from whom (individuals or collective bodies)—that is,

> [. . . what] responsibility we may have, as individuals and as members of collective bodies, to respond to human deprivation, including global poverty. So by accepting the idea of national responsibility, we have not foreclosed the question [of] what global justice demands of us.[7]

Next, Miller turns to Peter Singer and begins asking about Singer's theory,[8] according to which, by analogy, we can ascribe to nations the same responsibility that would apply to someone out walking who saw a child drowning in a shallow pond.[9] Singer considers this child, like the poor, to be an innocent victim of injustice, whom the rich—like the walker—ought to rescue. In contrast, Miller is not convinced by this example, in the first place because the saved child can grow up and live out its adult life, while a person in poverty, once rescued, might still die of hunger the next day, since poverty is a macroeconomic problem. In the second place, if the example is made more complicated by assuming that several children are in danger of drowning and several pedestrians are ready and willing to save them, the dilemma crops up of

---

several debtor or else full performance from any one of them"; and b) article 148 concerning the relationships among joint debtors, which indicates, "Unless the legal relationship between the joint and several debtors indicates otherwise, each of them assumes an equal share of the payment made to the creditor. A joint and several debtor who pays more than his fair share has recourse against the others for the excess. Amounts that cannot be recovered from one joint and several debtor must be borne in equal shares by the others."

5. Miller indicates, "[. . .] the bearing this has on questions of global justice is not yet clear. For one thing, nations can be held responsible not only for the benefits and burden they create for their own members, but also for the impact that their actions have on outsiders." Miller, *National Responsibility and Global Justice*, 134.

6. Ibid.

7. Ibid.

8. Singer, "Famine, Affluence, and Morality," 229–43.

9. Ibid., 233.

knowing which children should be saved first, and by which rescuers. Miller faults Singer for treating the poor as no better than victims and not giving them credit for being able to solve the problem of their poverty themselves.

Miller then examines Thomas Pogge's viewpoint.[10] While he does acknowledge that unlike Singer, Pogge does not treat the poor as mere victims, he also challenges Pogge's ambition to change the world order to ensure the equality of all.

He concludes by espousing the idea, found in John Rawls's work, that everyone ought to be able to enjoy a certain minimum number of human rights, with the corollary of a responsibility for protecting third parties:

> [. . .] whatever global justice means, it does not mean global equality—of resources, opportunity, welfare, etc.—so we are not required to change the global order in such a way that inequalities between societies are leveled completely. On the other hand, I have defended the idea of a global minimum that is due to every human being as a matter of justice, a minimum best understood as a *set of basic human rights. Since many societies are presently unable to guarantee these rights to* their own members, it appears that the responsibility to protect them may fall on outsiders.[11]

We will return later to this new concept of the *responsibility to protect*, which for better or worse has been in the news lately under the label of R2P.

John Rawls: Toward Political Liberalism That Does Not Exclude Global Redistribution of Wealth

Claiming that the theory of justice *as fairness* propounded by John Rawls falls under both political liberalism and economic liberalism is probably taking a questionable shortcut. I subscribe to this contention, however, because his two-part concept of *a priori* justice seems to me to have the merit of starting a public debate that I find to be crucial: do we, yes or no, wish to put political freedom (the first element of his principle of justice) first, or should economics have the final word? Later I will summarize his thesis.[12] For the moment, I would like to briefly mention the second element of his principle of justice, the *difference principle*, the nature and goal of which is described as fair distribution of wealth to the least advantaged people.[13]

10. Pogge, "Priorities of Global Justice." 22.
11. Miller, *National Responsibility and Global Justice*, 231.
12. See Part V, Chapter I The Rawlsian Legacy.
13. Rawls indicates, "Assuming the framework of institutions required by equal liberty and fair equality of opportunity, the higher expectations of those better situated are just if and only if they work as part of a scheme which improves the expectations of the least advantaged members of society. The intuitive idea is that the social order is not to establish and secure the more attractive prospects of those better off unless doing so is to the advantage of those less fortunate." See also *ibid.*, pp. 91 and 157, "[. . .] The two principles of justice (in serial order) 1. The principle of greatest equal liberty 2. (a) The principle of (fair) equality of opportunity (b) The difference principle." Rawls, *Théorie de la*

This is a capitalist notion, because it is based on the protection of private property. Yet it aims to compensate for the harshness of the market, which enables Denis Müller to say that Rawls "is trying to escape the traps of neo-liberalism."[14] It seems to me that his idea of justice is close to what could be called the welfare state.[15]

His theory awakened great hopes at the global level as a way to fight worldwide poverty, so I thought it would be useful to bring up the contributions of the most well-known proponents of globalism, Charles Beitz[16] and Thomas Pogge,[17] who was just mentioned.

However Rawls explained in *The Law of Peoples*[18] that his theory of justice is not applicable "as is" at the global level.

He specifically criticized Beitz for advocating a kind of global justice that would imply responsibility "without end"[19] for wealthy countries, and Pogge for not being able to explain to him how Pogge's suggestion of starting a global fund to help the poor (General Resource Dividend, or GRD)[20] differed from the duty to assist, which he, Rawls, had favored. He did not hide his difference from Pogge in the areas of taxation and administration.

> Depending on how the respective targets and cutoff points are defined, the principles could be much the same, with largely practical matters of taxation and administration to distinguish between them.[21]

So has the dream of globalism reached an impasse, and does it risk being relegated to the ranks of pipe dreams?

This is impossible to foresee. In any case, the topic seems to be an enduring one, given the number of universities that teach "global justice," such as the Harvard Kennedy School of Government (HKS) in Cambridge, Massachusetts. One of the professors there, Mathias Risse, was invited to National University of Singapore in the fall of 2013 and took the opportunity to ask this small Southeast Asian nation to participate in global efforts to help the poorest of the poor.[22]

---

justice, 106.

14. Müller, "Rawls, John Bordley," 1181.

15. Esping-Andersen, *The Three Worlds of Welfare Capitalism*, cited by Bertrand, Benjamin, "Etat-providence et libéralisme redistributif: entre 'nouveau' et 'néo libéralisme.'"

16. Beitz, *Political Theory and International Relations*.

17. Pogge, "An Egalitarian Law of Peoples," This reference is given by Rawls himself in *The Law of Peoples*, note 47, 115.

18. Rawls, *The Law of Peoples*, 116.

19. Ibid., 117.

20. Ibid., 118 n53, and 119.

21. Ibid., 119.

22. Risse, *From Third World to First—What's Next?*

Its pitfalls are many, however. In particular the secular irenic[23] risk of global political acculturation[24] cannot be ignored, and is what puzzled me in my general introduction to this study.

Amartya Sen's "Capabilities" As an Alternative to John Rawls's Model

The Origin and Formulation of Capabilities

A Chink in the Transcendental Approach to Justice

As an economist and philosopher,[25] Amartya Sen has been like a wind of change blowing among justice theoreticians such as John Rawls. For him, the important thing is to fight against injustice rather than to deal in transcendental justice that seeks a perfectly fair world. This can only mean that justice is contingent and contextual.

> What is presented here is a theory of justice in a very broad sense. Its aim is to clarify how we can proceed to address questions of enhancing justice and removing injustice, rather than to offer resolutions of questions about the nature of perfect justice.[26]

Thus he intends to develop a new idea of justice that clearly leans toward practical reasoning.[27] The task at hand is "determining whether a particular social change would enhance justice," an undertaking which he calls

> central to making decisions about institutions, behaviour and other determinants of justice, and how these decisions are derived cannot but be crucial to a theory of justice that aims at guiding practical reasoning about what should be done.[28]

Right from the start, he rejects any objection that might stand in the way of this pragmatic stance.

---

23. Lechot, "Irénisme" [Irenicism], 633–34.

24. Vujik indicates, "[. . .] the global project for a uniform, consumerist human race unified by the market and global advertising takes the form of a secular religious project, which aims through the promise of a global society of widespread happiness and material well-being to 'escape the bounds of history' much as religion presents itself as a message that 'transcends history.' The political, economic, and cultural global project contains the germ of a re-spiritualization of politics, for contrary to the theses [. . .] of Fukuyama and Gauchet, this is not an 'exodus from religion' that would affect the fate of the West; quite the contrary, it is a need for religion, a need that is increasingly felt on the impoverished outskirts and the global margins, which are clamoring for more justice and equality." Vujik, *La démocratie globale*, 6.

25. http://www.economie.gouv.fr/facileco/amartya-sen.

26. Sen, *L'idée de Justice*, 13.

27. Sen indicates, "[. . .] guiding practical reasoning about what should be done [. . .]." Sen, *L'idée de Justice*, 14

28. Ibid.

The assumption that this comparative exercise cannot be undertaken without identifying, first, the demands of perfect justice, can be shown to be entirely incorrect [. . .]."[29]

He then develops a new theory of "social choice"[30] to set against the transcendental justice of, for example, Hobbes, Kant, and Rawls.

A transcendental approach cannot, on its own, address questions about advancing justice and compare alternative proposals for having a more just society, short of the utopian proposal of taking an imagined jump to a perfectly just world. Indeed, the answers that a transcendental approach to justice gives—or can give—are quite distinct and distant from the type of concerns that engage people in discussions on justice and injustice in the world (for example, iniquities [sic] of hunger, poverty, illiteracy, torture, racism, female subjugation, arbitrary incarceration or medical exclusion as social features that need remedying).[31]

A Pluralistic Vision of Justice

Going back to his roots in India, Sen is eager to emphasize both Eastern and Western pluralism with respect to the very idea of justice.[32]

With this in mind, he claims the right to consult values other than those developed by English culture and its offshoots, which leads him to openly express his differences from his famous Harvard University colleague John Rawls. He criticizes Rawls's theory of justice for favoring equality over freedom.

He then turns to Isaiah Berlin, in particular, who distinguished between two kinds of freedom, specifically formal or "negative" liberty, and real or "positive" liberty (with the latter having been adopted by real libertarian doctrine[33]).

The "positive" sense of the word "liberty" derives from the wish on the part of the individual to be his own master. I wish my life and decisions to depend on myself, not on external forces of whatever kind. I wish to be a subject, not an

---

29. Ibid. (This point is analyzed in Chapter 4, "Voix et choix social" [Voice and social choice], Sen, *L'idée de Justice*, 121–50.)

30. Ibid., 126–28 (here he takes into account the impasses expressed by Condorcet's paradox and Arrow's "impossibility theorem").

31. Ibid., 131.

32. Ibid., 19–20.

33. Van Parijs indicates, "We can apply the term *real libertarian* to the position that [. . .] most energetically supports [. . .] real liberty [. . .] and most especially—since we say we are concerned with liberty for all— [. . .] the real liberty that falls to those who have the least of it." Van Parijs, *Qu'est-ce qu'une société juste?*, 225.

object; to be moved by reasons, by conscious purposes, which are my own, not by causes which affect me, as it were, from outside.[34]

Berlin, a native of Riga (Latvia) turned British philosopher, also had something to say about negative liberty, which he defined as follows.

> I am normally said to be free to the degree to which no man or body interferes with my activity. Political liberty in this sense is simply the area within which a man can act unobstructed by others.[35]

We can see right away that by promoting real (or positive) liberty and not simply formal (or negative) liberty, Amartya Sen is attempting to value the aspects of life that are important to each individual, with all his or her own unique characteristics and therefore in all his or her diversity.

It is important to add that what underlies Berlin's and Sen's approaches, philosophically speaking, is the total rejection of an *a priori* vision of a good life.

Berlin distances himself from thinkers who "knew what constituted the best life for Men," such as

> Plato, Aristotle, the Bible, the Talmud, Maimonides, perhaps Saint Thomas Aquinas and the other medieval Scholastics [. . .].[36]

We note that it is not without a modicum of cynicism that, in a striking turn of phrase, Berlin dares to view these thinkers as no more than a simple elite possessed of a "metaphysical eye [. . .]."[37]

> Perhaps a world of eternal truths and values perceptible to the magical eye of the true thinker does exist; it definitely belongs only to an elite to which, I fear, I have never been admitted.[38]

The Meaning and Mechanisms of the Capabilities

It was in the context of his work for international organizations such as the UNDP[39] and the World Bank that Amartya Sen developed his "capability approach," a concept that was clarified and supplemented by others such as "empowerment" and the "Human Development Index" (HDI).[40]

---

34. Berlin, *Four Essays on Liberty*, 122, cited by Reboud, Valérie, *Amartya Sen*, 33.
35. Ibid., 131.
36. Jahanbegloo, *En toutes libertés*, 52.
37. Ibid.
38. Ibid., 53.
39. United Nations Development Programme, www.undp.org.
40. Reboud, indicates, "The idea that poverty is multidimensional, as brought out by the capability approach, is picked up in the HDI, which is calculated every year for all countries and seeks to evaluate

I would say that the concept is "under construction" and that its author is a little hesitant about the idea of a formalism he feels would be ineffective. In fact, he wants to leave room for a range of opinions, in the hope of promoting a new democracy on a worldwide level.

> Democracy has to be judged not just by the institutions that formally exist but by the extent to which different voices from diverse sections of the people can actually be heard.[41]

There are many definitions that try to make this new concept intelligible, issuing either from the writings of Sen himself or from UNDP and World Bank reports. I will choose three of them that will enable me to bring out its "building blocks."

A person's "capabilities" are understood as a condition in which

> a person is really able to do the things that she would choose to do and has reason to choose to do.[42]

In a more dynamic world, the new concept is stated as follows.

> freedom to promote objectives we have reasons to value.[43]

The third definition creates the concept's real framework by connecting "freedom" with "functionings."

> The capability of a person stands for the different combinations of functionings the person can achieve; it reflects the freedom to achieve functionings.[44]

What does Sen mean by these two essential elements, "freedom" and "functionings," (which I have called the building blocks of the "capability" concept) that we have retained from the three definitions above?

For Sen, I repeat, freedom is positive or real freedom. More specifically, it is understood as the human being's ability to set priorities to achieve one or another, or even all, of his or her functionings.

"Functionings" refers to the objectives of a viable and valued life, according to the first definition; or that there are "reasons to value," according to the second.

---

the quality of life in each of these nations. Quality of life is assessed using three indicators: health, education, and income. The HDI measures the probability that an individual in a given country will not experience need in one of these three areas. So its value is between 0 and 1. An HDI value close to 1 means that the national population has a good quality of life (as measured y these three criteria). This is the case in industrialized countries." Reboud, "Amartya Sen, quel "modèle économique?," 74.

41. Sen, L'idée de Justice, 17.
42. Ibid., 309.
43. Sen, Repenser l'inégalité, 12, cited by Benicourt, "Amartya Sen," 438.
44. PNUD 1997 [UNDP 1997], 13, cited by Benicourt, "Amartya Sen," 439.

Part IV: Justice and Responsibility

The functionings can be divided into "beings" and "doings."[45] These latter refer to an individual's "states" and the "activities" or "actions" he undertakes. Basic "beings" consist of ensuring adequate nourishment, and living in decent conditions and good health. "Doings"—also called "additional choices," such as "political freedom," "guaranteed human rights," "respect for oneself," and, to take Adam Smith's example, "appearing in public without shame"[46]—target greater well-being.

In order to understand Sen's "capability approach," we must add at least two clarifications.

First, it deals with a potential, a possibility the individual has to achieve his personal objectives, that is, those that are important to him.

Second, Sen does not want to use even one single *a priori* criterion for well-being.[47] To borrow a phrase from the utilitarians, this is not a matter of maximizing utilities:

> [. . .] because of the nature of the evaluative space, the capability approach differs from utilitarian evaluation (more generally 'welfarist' evaluation) in making room for a variety of human acts and states as important in themselves (not just *because* they may produce utility, nor just to the *extent* that they yield utility).[48]

Consequently, what counts is the value the individual places on the achievement of a "being" or "doing," that is, of a functioning. And the benchmark absolutely may not be pleasure, desire, or happiness, as it is with utilitarians.

Why?

Sen explains it this way.

> The utility calculus can be deeply unfair to those who are persistently deprived, for example, the usual [. . .] deprived people[49] [. . .] tend to come to terms with their deprivation, because of the sheer necessity of survival, and they may, as a result, lack the courage to demand any radical change [. . .]. The mental metric of pleasure or desire is just too malleable to be a firm guide to deprivation and disadvantage.[50]

Some examples here will help explain the "capability" concept.

---

45. Benicourt, indicates, "It is [. . .] I believe, a good move, in better capturing the totality of functionings—the doings and the beings—that make life worthwhile, and which are to be reflected in the person's well-being." Benicourt, "Amartya Sen," 443.

46. Ibid., 439–40.

47. Ibid., 436.

48. Ibid., and quotation of Sen, *Capability and Well-Being*, 30–53.

49. Quite disrespectfully referred to as "underdogs."

50. Benicourt, "Amartya Sen," 437 and quotation from Sen, Amartya, *Development As Freedom*, 62–63.

Chapter III: Intragenerational Ethics

The first two shed some light on the distinction that must be made between formal (or negative) liberty and positive (or real) liberty; the third specifies the characteristics of the various functionings, called "beings" and "doings," respectively.

Take Sen's case of two people dying of hunger.[51] The first has chosen to fast, the second has nothing to eat to assuage his hunger. The first had a choice, and therefore real freedom to do something other than to not eat, while the second was prevented from eating.

What we are seeing at work here is an argument about the choices an individual has.

> The freedom included in the notion of capability thus proceeds from a "counter-to-fact" reasoning that consists of asking whether it would have been possible to do otherwise or choose something other than what was in fact done or chosen.[52]

A second example features two bicycle owners, A and B.[53] The first is in good health and the other has just had a disabling accident. The bicycle is important to each, not because of its market value but as an ecologically-friendly mode of transportation, or "green mobility" solution. Their life circumstances have created a difference in freedom between the two, since only A now has the positive or real liberty to travel by bicycle. In terms of "conversion of goods," A has the real freedom to convert his physical ability to pedal a bicycle into a "doing" (functioning) in order to move from one place to another. In contrast, B does not enjoy this physical mobility, and if he wishes to travel from his home to his job, must convert a different thing into a "doing," for example, by spending some of his assets to travel by taxi.

For the third example, I will make use of data supplied to me by Renaud de Watteville, the manager of Swiss Fresh Water, during the interview transcribed under Part VI of this study.[54] To clarify, I will interpret the information with the specific goal of making the difference between the two types of functionings, "beings" and "doings," even more understandable.

In a poverty-stricken village in Senegal, the water available to residents is of poor quality. The water comes from a distant source and is transported by cart, canoe, or car. Its cost, though modest, makes it difficult for everyone to acquire. The women and young girls of the village are often the ones who transport it, by dint of very hard work.

The villages long to improve their well-being and would like to have high-quality water available.

Having been informed of the existence of a new technology for converting polluted water into potable water (by the method known as reverse osmosis), they begin

---

51. Reboud, "Amartya Sen," 47.
52. Ibid.
53. Ibid., for the reference to the bicycle, though I have changed the information somewhat.
54. Stücki, De Watteville, *"Garantir l'accès à l'eau.*

the process for acquiring the machine of their dreams,[55] which will have potable water flowing right in the village square. (For the purposes of my example, it does not really matter whether the machine must be purchased, leased, or obtained through a loan.[56])

The villagers are ready to make a personal commitment to become watermen and waterwomen, or what I will call managers, and operate the machine. For this purpose, they will take the necessary time and acquire the skills needed to produce and sell the precious liquid.[57]

Their expertise (or real freedom) will be converted into several functionings, that is, into "being" (access to potable water) and "doing" (a job and the responsibility of managing it well). It should be noted that the skills acquired will have another benefit, which is to free up time for the young girls in the village, who normally cannot attend school because they must bring water from far away. This school time represents a higher functioning, that is, a "doing."

A sociologist would probably add that the "miracle machine" will radically change village life because it makes "empowerment" possible—that is, the power to call on the energy needed to improve well-being. The same social sciences expert would supplement his comments by warning against the conflicts that could arise in the village due to the managers' altered social position. Indeed, if they are able to sustain the business, even making it prosper, there is a risk that others will be envious. This may be the price that has to be paid for better-quality water!

This example shows the two above-mentioned essential characteristics (or building blocks) of the "capability" concept.

First, the managers are directly involved in operating the machine. They believe in the need to improve their well-being and that of the other villagers. (While this belief is self-evident to a Westerner, it is not necessarily so obvious in non-industrialized countries.) They enjoy the real freedom of producing potable water using a machine (which is purchased, leased, or taken on loan) that is operational only if the managers have appropriate training (use and maintenance of the machine, bookkeeping, etc.). Then they convert their knowledge into basic functionings and higher functionings.

In my opinion, Swiss Fresh Water's experiment in Senegal, in an extremely disadvantaged sociocultural situation, is of interest from the standpoint of contingent justice that has capabilities as its criterion. In the real world, a project that enables the beneficiaries to help improve their own way of life seems very encouraging to me, at a time when many development experts are seeing negative results for experiments tried over the past few decades.

Are such very small-scale solutions viable and do they have a bright future? What is at issue with this question is the "capability" concept's scope.

55. Ibid.
56. Ibid, with financing by the NGO supplied during the first year of the machine's use.
57. Ibid.

CHAPTER III: INTRAGENERATIONAL ETHICS

What Is the "Capability" Approach's Scope As a Tool for Our Time, for Potable Water?

In my opinion, by choosing to value the human being, through the "capability" approach, more than is done by utilitarian, Rawlsian, or libertarian theories, Amartya Sen has opened a crack in the edifice of Western theories of justice.

Notwithstanding all of that, is this approach relevant to developing countries and those most affected by the potable water problem?

Institutional responses by the UNDP and the World Bank, in reports that not unenthusiastically echo Sen's theories, imply that this is the case.[58]

Yet should we worry that, like Adam Smith's theories, Sen's will find it difficult to make a connection between ethics and economics, let alone to go so far as to find a harmonious balance between them?

Indeed, some of Sen's readers are sorry to say that his criteria do not work in economics,[59] and many detractors[60] have already criticized him for wanting to take all differences between people into account, which—as the Nobel laureate in economics himself concedes—could lead to "total confusion."[61] Some even accuse him of eliciting a weak consensus.[62]

Comments by critics such as Philippe Van Parijs, for example, which highlight the real economic difficulties of achieving positive liberty for everyone, also deserve mention. Here I will simply reproduce one of them.

> It is very possible [. . .] that some regulations that constrain market operation, some subsidy and tax policies, create rigidities and imbalances that in no way can be justified by an increase in real freedom for the most destitute. This is possible for each of these regulations and for each of these policies. But the converse is true as well. In each case, we need to be open to what experience and research allow us to assume about the probable impact of implementing or stopping the measure [. . .].[63]

---

58. Benicourt, "Amartya Sen," 440.

59. Ibid., 441.

60. Ibid., 443, quoting Sugden, Robert who indicates "Sen is remarkably optimistic about the chances of finding general agreement on the ranking of many functioning vectors [. . .]."

61. Ibid., 444, with quotation of Sen, Amartya, *Repenser l'inégalité*, 117.

62. Bénicourt indicates, "What is striking about Sen is the weak consensus of sorts that he elicits: international organizations such as the UNDP and the World Bank, non-governmental organizations, unorthodox and orthodox economists alike, sociologists, and philosophers—all see him as an 'alternative.' By never taking a concrete, unequivocal position, Sen may gain everyone's support, but he also puts an end to debates, differences of opinion, and in the end, the discussion about what tangible steps must be taken to eliminate poverty." Ibid., 445.

63. Van Parijs, *Qu'est-ce qu'une société juste?*, 228.

In the efforts of the 1998 Nobel laureate in economics, I myself see an opening for a "Habermassian" discussion that should be encouraged. His very concept of democracy (as cited above[64]), which differs from our Western ideas, tends in this direction.

I believe that with his "capability" concept, he has shown that it is possible to set a criterion for a contingent justice capable of meeting tangible needs against the criteria for transcendental—that is, perfect—justice. Has he not thereby brought to the table an interesting alternative to the "preferential option for the poor" criterion, one that can improve the status of the destitute at the "bottom of the pyramid"?

Let us hazard a guess that the conceptual tool, which Sen himself did not want to be rigid and unchangeable, can feed the imagination of those who are sensitive to development issues and the problems of poverty.

The Connection between the Human Right to Potable Water and Global Responsibility

In 2005, the delicate issue of the connection between responsibility and human rights was taken up by an international colloquium with the evocative title *La responsabilité, face cachée des droits de l'homme* [Responsibility, the hidden face of human rights].[65]

At this event, Jean-Louis Genard[66] brought out—in what I feel was a very relevant way—the need to emphasize different aspects of responsibility and project them onto the structure of human rights, especially "I-responsibility" and "you-responsibility."

For him, the former presupposes a "capacity for initiative" or "possibility of beginning,"[67] and the latter "a responsibility that can be considered from the perspective of the vulnerability of others."[68] This frame of reference allows us to differentiate between responsibility related to rights/freedoms and that related to rights/claims.

This distinction is very enlightening at a time when internationalists find themselves in opposition over the question of knowing whether the human right to water should be included with the economic, social, and cultural rights of United Nations Covenant I,[69] or rather with the civil and political rights—and therefore freedoms—of Covenant II.[70]

The disagreement represents none other than the break between a liberal and a social notion of democracy. Thus, if I revisit the theories about justice and global responsibility that were discussed earlier, I believe I can theorize that globalists Charles Beitz and Thomas Pogge would probably favor classifying the new human right to

---

64. See Part IV, Chapter III, The Meaning and Mechanisms of the Capabilities.
65. Dumont, et al., *La Responsabilité, face cachée des droits de l'homme*.
66. Genard, "Les métamorphoses de la responsabilité," 144.
67. Ibid., 143.
68. Ibid.
69. International Covenant on Economic, Social and Cultural Rights.
70. International Covenant on Civil and Political Rights.

water with Covenant I, and liberals such as John Rawls and David Miller would place it under Covenant II.

In a more concrete sense, and of course outlined rather broadly, this means that the former accept the idea of considering poor countries as creditors with claims against the rich countries, the latter being responsible for sharing their wealth with the most destitute and, if we follow Pogge's line of reasoning, for helping them industrialize by means of a worldwide fund. For the latter, it means that poor countries must be solely responsible for their own industrialization. However, in this second case, nothing rules out a duty to assist on the part of already industrialized countries which, incidentally, John Rawls and David Miller explicitly recommended.

As we can see, these are two completely different perspectives. Which will win out?

I myself think that while this conceptual distinction has the merit of a certain amount of clarity, the real world requires a practical solution. In fact it is urgent that pragmatic answers be found, particularly those advised by Amartya Sen, to encourage "less advanced" countries to move toward ever-greater autonomy. There would of course be a social cost, as was experienced by the industrialized countries over a century ago, and of which Singapore serves as a living example today.

I personally support considering the new human right to water as a beginning of the possibility, in the sense of Kant's transcendental philosophy, for non-liberal societies to escape their penury. So I am on the rights/freedoms side.

The Responsibility to Protect

A Trio of Duties: Respect, Protect, and Fulfill the Human Right to Water

Responsibility is an ethical phenomenon that cannot be confined to any one discipline, whether it be law, sociology, philosophy, or theology. From the standpoint of Kant's transcendental philosophy, this ambiguous concept can be considered, at the very least, as the

[. . .] condition of possibility for implementing rights.[71]

By conferring the status of a human right on water in July 2010, the UN General Assembly raised this natural resource to an axiological level that gave it value worth defending. By the very fact of making it a human right, the UN caused a new correlation to emerge, a normative interdependence between potable water and human beings.

However, we must still understand this normative interdependence in order to give it a viable profile. So again, it is worth analyzing, clarifying, and refining.

In fact, not all has yet been said.

---

71. Dumont, et al., *La responsabilité, face cachée des droits de l'homme*, VI.

PART IV: JUSTICE AND RESPONSIBILITY

It seems to me that the ethical field is still very open, even though some attempts at a normative—that is, legal—crystallization can already be seen here and there, as we will note in the portion of this study that treats of South Africa.[72]

Let us recall that the right to water is a *"ius in statu nascendi,"* a right in the nascent state, as proclaimed by water internationalist Laurence Boisson de Chazournes in August 2012.[73]

In my opinion, now is the time—in advance of the law that is falling into place little by little—to think about the values that will underpin it, values that could be theological, as we have seen in Part III, but could also be of another order.

In 2002, the Committee on Economic, Social and Cultural Rights (CESCR) sought to formulate them based on the work of an American researcher that had won its confidence[74] and outlined them in General Comment No. 15.[75] As Lucius Caflisch notes in a very detailed legal commentary entitled *Le Droit à l'eau, un droit de l'homme internationalement protégé?*[76] and published in 2010, they correspond to the obligations of

> [. . .] respecting the right to water and not hindering the exercise of it, preventing third parties from interfering with it, and taking steps to enable the full exercise of this right.[77]

The related formula, which we will see in the discussion on the legal structure of the human right to water,[78] is this, which I prefer in its elegant and precise English formulation: "duties to respect, to protect, to fulfill." This is the "trio of duties" mentioned in the heading of that section.

These duties or responsibilities being for the moment free of legal constraints, we can shed some light on them from an ethical standpoint. From this angle, I find that they form a whole, in the sense that respect is the ethical motive for a duty to protect, with its corollary being implementation.

So what we are concerned with here is the motive of responsible action, namely, *respect*.

---

72. See Part IV, Chapter III, Implementing the Human Right to Water in South Africa.
73. Boisson de Chazournes, "Le droit à l'eau et la satisfaction des besoins humains," 967–81.
74. Shue, *Basic Rights,* 52, cited by Hofer, "Wasserversorgung im Spannungsfeld von Menschenrecht."
75. Committee on Economic, Social and Cultural Rights, "General Comment No. 15: The Right to Water (Arts. 11 and 12 of the International Covenant on Economic, Social and Cultural Rights)."
76. Caflisch, "Le droit à l'eau—un droit de l'homme internationalement protégé?."
77. Ibid., 389.
78. See Part IV, Chapter III, Implementing the Human Right to Water in South Africa.

CHAPTER III: INTRAGENERATIONAL ETHICS

Respect As the Motive for the Ethical Duty to Protect

The concept of respect often evokes fear, deference, or the distance from which we are to relate to an important figure. Thus, for example, when Pope Benedict XVI announced his resignation from the papacy,[79] German Chancellor Angela Merkel ended her tribute to the Supreme Pontiff by stating her respect for him.[80]

In the potable water context, fear is misplaced. On the contrary, here respect means the consideration due to one in need, which also means giving that person a face in the sense used by philosopher Emmanuel Lévinas. Further yet, this kind of respect gives an individual his full dignity, that of a human being capable of responsibility, one whom adversity does not prevent from "counterattacking" in a creative way against "a lack of being," as Guillaume de Stexhe so strongly states.[81]

Given its protean nature, the concept of respect deserves a closer look.

Respect As Seen by Immanuel Kant and Paul Ricœur

In an attempt to better understand the word "respect" in its specifics, I will consult Immanuel Kant and Paul Ricœur. Though at first sight their positions on this subject differ, they reveal the essence of where humans fit into this concept.

What did these two philosophers say?

For Kant, respect or "reverence" included both fear and inclination.

> Reverence is properly awareness of a value which demolishes my self-love. Hence there is something which is regarded neither as an object of inclination nor as an object of fear, though it has at the same time some analogy with both.[82]

He immediately rejected respect's analogy with inclination and stressed that the object of respect is the law.

> All reverence for a person is properly only reverence for the law.[83]

So the fundamental moral law would be a duty for everyone not to exploit others—which is the famous categorical imperative in its second version.

> Act in such a way that you always treat humanity, whether in your own person or in the person of any other, never simply as a means, but always at the same time as an end.[84]

79. February 11, 2013.
80. Merkel indicates, "He has my highest respect," speech given on February 12, 2013.
81. De Stexhe, "Devoir, pouvoir?", 111.
82. Kant, *Fondements*, 95 (footnote).
83. Ibid.
84. Ibid., 143.

What did Paul Ricœur have to say about respect?

As I see it, he gave the concept of respect new meaning and legitimacy, bringing it up-to-date for the twenty-first century. He developed it in a passage of *Oneself as Another* on the topic of "Solicitude and the Norm."[85]

First, he showed that respect is specifically dialogic in structure, because it brings together two people, the agent and the patient. Next he stated that Kant's imperative placed these two people in a relationship of total dissymmetry, as evidenced by the power that one has with respect to the other.[86]

It is this very dissymmetry that can be seen at work in the example I will give later of a government that decides to turn off the water supply of a consumer who can no longer pay the bill because of his poverty.

Then, well aware that for Kant, the Golden Rule was of only secondary importance,[87] Ricœur wanted to bring out the human side by drawing a connection between the concept of solicitude and Kant's imperative.

> In order to bring out the tension hidden in the Kantian statement, it seems opportune to base our discussion on the Golden Rule, as it represents the simplest formula that can serve as a transition between solicitude and the second Kantian imperative.[88]

Thus, in my opinion, Ricœur humanized the second version of Kant's categorical imperative.

Conclusion

In the context of potable water's ethical challenges, these two philosophical visions that Paul Ricœur wanted to reconcile fully justify the need to match a responsibility to protect with an obligation to respect, with such an obligation revealing itself to be the real motive[89] and even the subjective principle itself of the desire[90] to undertake responsible political action. To state this another way, for the government, an obligation to respect would mean refraining from causing harm, or in a word, satisfying the universal principle "do no harm" that is contained in the negative formulation of the Golden Rule.[91] Knowing whether a government can be led or even forced to go further still by satisfying the positive formulation of the Golden Rule remains an open question, notwithstanding two exceptional cases that will be covered in a moment.

85. Ricœur, "Soi-même comme un autre," 254.
86. Ibid.
87. Ibid., 259.
88. Ibid.
89. Fuchs, *Comment faire pour bien faire?*, 178.
90. Kant, *Fondements*, 140.
91. See Part V, Chapter I.

I would theorize that both Kant's imperative and the Golden Rule represent the very foundations of the duty to "respect" suggested by the UN experts for enforcement of the right to water—in other words, that the duty to respect originates in an ethical, or even theological, principle.

Potable Water's Future As Seen by the UN and South Africa

"From Text to Action":[92] From the UN CESCR Guidelines to Responsible Government Action

In order to solve the problems institutions face, would it not be desirable for them to take into account the Kantian concern for finding just principles for just action?[93]

At the very least, a humanitarian organization such as the International Committee of the Red Cross (ICRC) can attest to the relevance of doing so. It chose to base its actions on seven principles, three of which have played a key role and still do today, namely "humanity," "impartiality," and "neutrality."[94] Respect for these principles has the virtue of ensuring that the institution, which was founded in 1863,[95] will endure.

Is the trio of duties we have just mentioned—the concepts "respect, protect, [and] fulfill the exercise of the human right to water" hammered out by the UN experts—called upon to play a similar role as a catalyst and encourager of countries, to ensure lasting protection for the billion individuals who today have serious difficulties obtaining access to water?

Even though I left the question unanswered earlier, we cannot rule it out, since two nations have actually squarely faced the issue of better water management for their citizens. I am thinking of Singapore, which I have already mentioned,[96, 97] and a large African country, South Africa.

Let us briefly state that these two countries are comparable insofar as they have each mobilized their forces to solve serious ethnic and religious problems while at the same time devoting more attention to the issue of water management. At present, both

---

92. Ricœur, *Du texte à l'action*.

93. Fuchs indicates, "We understand that here it is not a matter of knowing what must be done, but the principle according to which it must be done. Kant's work is formal. If we succeed in determining the just principle that should govern our relationships, the content of the ensuing acts will be good." Fuchs, *Comment faire pour bien faire?*, 176, end. See also Fuchs who indicates, "Here we find, transposed into the philosophical register, the very same principle of justification by faith that is central to Luther's theology. Justification ensures the formal condition of salvation, the moral consequences of which will necessarily be good." Fuchs, *Comment faire pour bien faire?*, 177 n21.

94. The other four principles are independence, voluntary service, universality and unity. See Moreillon, *Du bon usage de quelques principes fondamentaux de la Croix-Rouge*.

95. The ICRC was founded in 1863, www.icrc.org, and the 20th international conference of the Red Cross, at which the seven principles were adopted by resolution, was held in Vienna in 1965.

96. See Part III, Section II, Chapter II, Examples of Philanthropic Acts.

97. Tortajada, et al., *The Singapore Water Story*.

are inarguably seeing an improvement in the latter, which is helping to put them in an enviable economic position among the countries of Asia and Africa, respectively. However, we must note that South Africa's troubles are not over yet, because poverty, destitution, and violence remain major government and public concerns despite the abolition of apartheid.

Implementing the Human Right to Water in South Africa

When the South African government underwent a radical transformation in 1994 after its first black president in history, Nelson Mandela, took office, its back was to the wall. A real desire for democracy and a better life were in the air at that time.

Divisions between rich and poor were particularly glaring, so the new political authorities had a duty to try and find solutions that would help a hard-pressed third of South Africa's population of twenty-three million, which fraction was mostly black and living in rural areas, to survive.

Water appeared as a critical topic that was raised as early as 1990 by the ANC (African National Congress) party, which later came to power in 1994. In my opinion, the future president's party took charge of the situation in a very extraordinary way, by putting forward the idea of covering the essential water needs of the most destitute people free of charge.

In a white paper, the ANC introduced the highly innovative concept of "Free Basic Water" (FBW). This very practical political manifesto proposed free distribution of twenty-five liters per person per day, which was said to represent the minimum amount of water necessary for survival. It is interesting to note that the World Health Organization (WHO) has set this minimum at between fifty and one hundred liters.[98]

I believe I am not mistaken in stating that the impact of FBW was a decisive factor in the rebuilding of South African society, not to underestimate the very courageous transition from the apartheid regime to democracy led by the Truth and Reconciliation Commission[99] headed by the 1984 Nobel Peace Prize winner, Anglican Archbishop Desmond Tutu.[100]

It is appropriate to note that the steps for implementing FBW were indeed taken, and were completed in record time.

First, the human right to water was enshrined in article 27, para. 1b of the South African Constitution of 1996.[101] Second, shortly after this Constitution went into effect, the parliament passed two laws—the National Water Act[102] was quickly approved

---

98. WHO (World Health Organization). Compare with different data in the Xámok Kásek case.

99. Fiechter-Widemann, *Pardon, catharsis de la violence extrême*.

100. Doctor *honoris causa*, University of Geneva, June 5, 2009.

101. Constitution of the Republic of South Africa, article 27, para. 1(b) reads, "Everyone has the right to have access to [. . .] (b) sufficient food and water [. . .]."

102. Republic of South Africa, National Water Act.

in 1997, and the Water Services Act[103] in 1998. This legislation incorporated the principles of article 7 para. 2 of the Constitution, namely to "respect, protect, promote and fulfill" human rights. Finally, the government decree implementing the FBW concept was issued at the dawn of the second millennium.

I find it relevant to give an overview here of the South African legal strategy, which consisted of applying the three constitutional principles of "respect, protect, fulfill"[104] to potable water access.

A Logic of Responsibility for Implementing the Right to Water in South Africa

The following three examples will illustrate the real difficulties faced by the authorities responsible for making the three duties suggested by the CESCR a reality, as provided in South Africa's Constitution.

1. *Respecting the right to water means refraining from cutting off water services.*

South African courts have already adjudicated upon several cases in which the government was punished for its failure to respect the right to water.[105]

Most of these instances involved decisions made by municipalities to cut off a consumer's water service for non-payment of a bill, or because of defective infrastructure.

Consequences for those on the receiving end of such actions are serious: they are forced to try to obtain water from a polluted source, which will inevitably be harmful to their health and life.

2. *The State's responsibility to protect does not imply that it must furnish water at no cost, but at an affordable price.*

The ANC proposed FBW for South Africa in the 1990s mainly because black populations had no water service at all.

Today, however, it is widely acknowledged—even from a human rights standpoint—that because the infrastructure is very expensive, the consumer must help cover the costs. The UN's former Special Rapporteur on the human right to safe drinking water and sanitation, Catarina de Albuquerque, was quite clear on this point.

> There are many misunderstandings. Some people think the right to water means that potable water should be free for everyone. That is not true. It means that the government must create an environment that favors fulfillment of a right to healthful water close by and at an affordable cost, and that no one can be deprived of it simply because they are poor. Others say that if we recognize this right, it means that the private sector cannot be involved in

---

103. Republic of South Africa, Water Services Act.
104. Constitution of the Republic of South Africa, article 7, para. 2.
105. Winkler, "Respect, Protect, Fulfill," chapter 14.

water distribution. That is also untrue. The government must ensure that the right to water is respected, regardless of whether the service provider is public or private.[106]

So supplying water at an affordable price is the task a State must undertake to fulfill its duty to protect. In particular, if the government delegates water service to a private company, it will ensure that said company does not raise water prices beyond a certain level. An international standard of from 3 to 5 percent of income has been proposed.[107]

In practice, in South Africa and many other countries in Africa, Latin America, and Asia, it has been observed that when water service is delegated to a private company, water prices often rise to levels that far exceed this standard. For example, in Johannesburg, after a law authorizing municipalities to sign water franchises went into effect, prices were seen to have doubled as a result of the privatization, and even tripled in Queenstown. For some consumers, this meant that over one-fifth of their income had to go to pay for water.[108]

This reality clearly explains why privatization of water and water services is beset by such sharp criticism and even polemic.

Such social tensions must be taken seriously, and it is precisely because of their duty to protect that governments must set up appropriate regulations creating the necessary barriers to abusive practices contrary to the human right to water. We will come back to this point shortly.[109]

3. *"Free Basic Water" (FBW): From Concept to Implementation*

Inga Winkler's academic work entitled *Respect, Protect, Fulfill: The Implementation of the Human Right to Water in South Africa*[110] provides valuable information about the often chaotic progress in implementing the remarkable innovation of which I spoke so highly earlier.

In practice, perfectly targeting the "most destitute" among poor populations has turned out to be a complicated and almost impossible matter for the authorities. Of course some reasonable criteria were selected, such as delivering six thousand liters per month to a household of eight. It was determined, however, that dividing the water perfectly was in fact extremely difficult, since some households had sixteen members or more, and others had fewer than eight. Was there any sense of solidarity between those who had more and those who had less? In some cases, probably, but in general those who received more did not hesitate to sell the extra!

---

106. De Albuquerque, "Droit à l'eau."
107. Winkler, "Respect, Protect, Fulfill."
108. Ibid., 12 and n58: South African Human Rights Commission
109. See Part IV, Chapter III, Multinationals and Tensions.
110. Winkler, "Respect, Protect, Fulfill,"

Given the complexity of the real world, the FBW regulation was also favorable to less needy populations, which meant that those benefitting from it added up to nearly fifteen million residents out of South Africa's population of twenty-three million.

This conclusion also reveals another paradox: the poorest people do not even have access to the twenty-five liters recommended by the FBW.

> In particular the poorest in society are excluded from the implementation of FBW.[111]

Yet Winkler reassures us.

> However, the policy has been overall progressing and the number of poor people benefiting from it is also constantly rising.[112]

For my part, I will note that the Department of Water Affairs and Forestry (DWAF) authorities have observed that for a strong country with a flourishing economy, such as South Africa, the public cost/benefit ratio would be affordable even if water were distributed to the poorest people at no cost.

> [. . .] the cost associated with providing free basic water to poor households is not large for a country of our economic size and strength.[113]

So I believe that this is an example of how a government can be described as responsible, especially if it ensures that its poorest residents receive a minimum level of protection.

Is the Isolated Case of South Africa a Good Model?

We have just reported on the enormous difficulties faced in practice by a State—even one as strong as South Africa—trying to meet its obligations to respect, protect, and fulfill the right to water.

What happens in countries with fewer resources?

Could a supranational authority punish a nation that transgressed in the matter of these three duties to "respect, protect, and fulfill" the human right to water?

The work of Swiss legal scholar Christian Hofer, which in particular includes a doctoral dissertation[114] and an article published in 2012,[115] provides some very specific pieces of information about this problem.

---

111. Ibid., 12 and n58: South African Human Rights Commission.
112. Ibid., 12 n59, see Department of Water Affairs and Forestry (DWAF)'s site.
113. Ibid., 26, DWAF Strategic Framework 2003 n73.
114. Hofer, *More Market in Water Supply.*
115. Hofer, "*Wasserversorgung [Supplying water].*"

Part IV: Justice and Responsibility

The answer is that for the moment, such a supranational authority does not exist, and perhaps never will. Only the international cooperation mentioned in article 2, para. 1 of the UN's Covenant I, or ICESCR,[116] can be cited. It decrees as follows.

> Each State Party to the present Covenant undertakes to take steps, individually and through international assistance and co-operation, especially economic and technical, to the maximum of its available resources, with a view to achieving progressively the full realization of the rights recognized in the present Covenant by all appropriate means, including particularly the adoption of legislative measures.

Now it must be said that such international cooperation is practically nonexistent.

Should we bemoan this fact? Here, we are stepping into the territory of international politics, which is beyond the scope of this study. At most, I can mention the risk of totalitarianism, about which we already theorized earlier when discussing Hans Jonas's imperative of responsibility.[117]

Financial Responsibilities

Nations and international stakeholders are increasingly convinced that the resource "water" faces a serious threat in our times. Over the past few decades, extremely detailed agreements have been put in place by talented jurists, political experts, and economists to handle complexities in this area. Nevertheless, efforts to negotiate issues and settle disputes related to water still continually run up against a very wide range of positions, such as those mentioned in connection with privatization of water and especially those surrounding the financing of water-supply and wastewater-treatment infrastructure.

An essay by Mara Tignino and Dima Yared, published in the *Revue québécoise de droit international*,[118] gives a very trenchant analysis of this, concluding that it would be deceitful to hide the fact that the financial stakes are immense.

At the third World Water Forum in Kyoto in 2003, the International Working Group on Financing Water Infrastructure, chaired by Michel Camdessus, reported that annual expenditures for water services in developing countries, currently 75 billion dollars, would have to be increased to nearly 180 billion dollars in order to achieve the MDG for water and sanitation. As this figure would be difficult to reach by means of public financing alone, some governments are increasingly turning to the private sector to find partners that can offer them access to the necessary financial resources.

---

116. International Covenant on Economic, Social and Cultural Rights.
117. See Part IV, Chapter II, How Jonas's Philosophy was Received.
118. Tignino and Dima, *La commercialisation et la privatisation de l'eau*, 159–95.

CHAPTER III: INTRAGENERATIONAL ETHICS

Multinationals and Tensions Related to Global Responsibility

During my study, I saw in both Europe and Asia that "privatization" was civil society's catch phrase in campaigns for universal access to potable water. It was a kind of magic word used to demonize any attempt by a private company, whether small or large, domestic or multinational, to do business in the area of potable water treatment or services.

Here, again, we see emotions taking over from reason.

I wondered: Why should a contract of private law be rejected out of hand simply because of what it is, if it takes environmental issues into consideration and provides for an environmental impact study that both meets sustainable development criteria and will be completed prior to any actual fieldwork to improve potable water access?

Controversy over "Privatization"

To gain a better understanding of the stakes in this ticklish controversy, I have chosen to call upon five figures from the economic, academic, and political realms. All five of them have taken a critical look at the concept of "privatization."

First, I will borrow the definition of this concept developed by Josef Stiglitz, a Nobel laureate in economics. Next, I will try to understand the possible connection between *privatization* and *potable water* as explored by academic Erik Orsenna, who did a three-year in-depth study of water and let the results flow from his eclectic pen in a lively work called *L'Avenir de l'eau*.[119] He will be seconded by former Ambassador Benoît Girardin, who has worked for the Swiss Federal Department of Foreign Affairs in Pakistan as well as Madagascar and various other African countries.

Finally, the question of water's price and its relation to privatization will be elucidated through explanations by two politicians, one from the Middle East and one from South Africa.

The General Concept of "Privatization" in a Globalized World

What is "privatization"?

Josef E. Stiglitz, who was awarded the Nobel prize in economics in 2001, gave the following definition of privatization in his book *Globalization and Its Discontents*:[120]

> converting state-run industries and firms into private ones.[121]

---

119. Orsenna, *L'avenir de l'eau*.
120. Stiglitz, *La grande désillusion*.
121. Ibid., 102.

This former vice-president of the World Bank made a point of noting that there are two main reasons for the great skepticism with which privatization has been—and still is—greeted in poor countries; namely, jobs and corruption.

> Privatization has been so widely criticized because [. . .] [it] often destroys jobs rather than creating new ones.[122]

and

> Perhaps the most serious concern with privatization, as it so often has been practiced, is corruption. [. . .] If a government is corrupt, there is little evidence that privatization will solve the problem. After all, the same corrupt government that mismanaged the firm will also handle the privatization. In country after country, government officials have realized that privatization meant that they no longer needed to be limited to annual profit skimming. By selling a government enterprise at below market price, they could get a significant chunk of the asset value for themselves rather than leaving it for subsequent officeholders. [. . .] [W]ithout the appropriate legal structures and market institutions, the new owners might have an incentive to strip assets rather than use them as a basis for expanding industry.

Even though privatization is struck a serious blow by these two concerns, Stiglitz takes pains to bring out its positive aspects when procedures are followed. He says, for example, that

> [. . .] in general, competing private enterprises can perform [certain] functions more efficiently.[123]

In my eyes, it is therefore important to be aware not only of the real obstacles to effective privatization, but also of any remedies that have been used and have continued to hold attention at the highest levels. For example, in a chapter on corporate social responsibility[124] Mireille Delmas-Marty writes in her 2013 book *Résister, Responsabiliser, Anticiper* [Fight back, hold accountable, second-guess][125] that what companies need to do is ensure that the impact of their actions is acceptable from a societal and environmental standpoint. According to this legal scholar and member of the Paris Academy of Moral and Political Sciences, two of the most important ways to do this are the annual reports issued by TNCs,[126] and also their codes of conduct.

---

122. Ibid., 106.
123. Ibid, 107–09.
124. The concept of "corporate social responsibility" is often known by its acronym, CSR.
125. Delmas-Marty, *Résister, Responsabiliser, Anticiper*.
126. TNC is the acronym for Transnational Corporation.

The former increase the visibility of TNC actions by reporting to the stakeholders[127] and shareholders.[128]

The latter make specific commitments. Model codes of conduct have been making the rounds for several decades, but there has been resistance to standards that were too strict, especially from the International Chamber of Commerce (ICC).[129] Be that as it may—and it is important to stress this—the idea of "corporate responsibility exists in international law,"[130] in particular thanks to the United Nations Global Compact of 2000, which was instigated by the UN Secretary-General at the time, Kofi Annan, with the goal of

> [...] bringing together private stakeholders that so desired in search of shared solutions for achieving the millennium development goals.[131]

Privatization in the Context of Potable Water

Both Erik Orsenna and Benoît Girardin broached the subject of "privatization" for potable water, taking a critical look at it and stressing right from the start that water is not free. Erik Orsenna's explanation, brilliant in its simplicity, is worth citing here.

> Water is [...] less and less often a *gift* of nature. It is nearly always a manufactured *product* (treatment) and, simultaneously, a *service* (distribution);[132] it cannot be free because it becomes a manufactured product through treatment and a service through its distribution. The production and service have a cost. A good that has a cost cannot be considered *free*. But when it is as important as water, it is necessarily a resource that should be shared, a *common* good.

After meeting many politicians from around the world and speaking with numerous company directors, Erik Orsenna noted the impossibility of deciding for or against "privatization." He proved to be rather pessimistic about politicians who, because of the electoral system, cannot make long-term commitments. Let us hear what he had to say.

> When a municipal team sees the end of its term approaching, the temptation to reduce bills, to the detriment of the facilities, is very great.[133]

127. Delmas-Marty indicates, "[...] the company's *stakeholders* or partners, such as its employees, clients, suppliers, and community-based organizations." Delmas-Marty, *Résister, Responsabiliser, Anticiper*, 153.

128. Ibid.

129. Ibid., 142.

130. Ibid., 143.

131. Ibid. and 143, quotation from Ascencio, H., *Le Pacte mondial et l'apparition d'une responsabilité internationale des entreprises*.

132. Orsenna, *L'avenir de l'eau*, 399.

133. Ibid., 401.

Yet his viewpoint is more nuanced than that. Of course he recognizes that government entities can fall prey to

> [. . .] ailments common to every administration in the world: excess, an absence of sanctions, workers who all too readily bend to the will of elected officials, electioneering concerns.[134]

But he does refrain from advising full speed ahead to privatization.

> As for considering that there is an urgent need to privatize everywhere, that would mean making light of the abuses peculiar to the corporate world, since companies are driven and obligated to make a profit, which leads to permanent upward pressure on prices.[135]

Benoît Girardin considers that there are a number of types of "privatization," and he does not rule them out in principle, with the following proviso: it is imperative for public authorities relying on private enterprises to manage water supply lines to choose solutions that protect the interests of local communities.

He advises political communities that good solutions include subcontracting to private companies through public service concessions. He says that the duration or volume handled should be limited and, to guarantee sustainable management, the contracting authorities should encourage the use of emphyteutic leases that

> [. . .] are capable of encouraging sustainable management, increasing interest in improvements, and avoiding lax maintenance or even a *de facto* permanent appropriation.[136]

To avoid making it seem as if these two, the academic and the diplomat, are the only ones who adequately recognize the full ambiguity of the term "privatization," on April 7, 2014, I made contact with Professor Alexander J. B. Zehnder, a scientific expert from the EPFL (Swiss Federal Institute of Technology in Lausanne). He was giving a lecture on water for this institution's alumni in Singapore, entitled "How Does the Global Water Situation Affect Singapore?" Backed by the weight of his internationally-recognized scientific authority, he lamented that companies are increasingly less interested in going into water management and services in "failed" States, since the related risks are greater than with, for example, mining.

In 2007, Swiss legal scholar Christian Hofer wrote a dissertation along these same lines,[137] and this is also the viewpoint championed by Switzerland and its Department of Foreign Affairs.[138]

---

134. Ibid., 400.
135. Ibid.
136. Ibid.
137. Hofer, *More Market in Water Supply*.
138. Münger indicates, "[. . .] there are also misunderstandings about this right to water, especially where the private sector's involvement in potable water services and sanitation is concerned.

Zehnder again focused attention on the need to take the human factor into account, since in the context of PPPs (Public Private Partnerships), the people affected by any increase in the price of water do not hesitate to take to the streets.

How Much Should Potable Water Cost? The Crucial Question

Like the scarcity and privatization issues that affect water, its price is so critical to the debate that human beings probably never will find a definitive and satisfactory answer.

Every civilization of every era will have to answer this for itself.

It would seem that at least two very different political leaders have been inspired by the voice of reason: a professor of environmental sciences at Hebrew University of Jerusalem, and a South African official in charge of the Department of Water Affairs and Forestry.

The former, Professor Hillel Shuval, expressed himself in these terms concerning water-related tensions between Israel and Palestine, which were reduced thanks to a water sale agreement.

> [. . .] if you monetize the conflict, it makes it less emotional. If water is seen as a commodity, not as milk, it shows that there is not enough there to go to war.[139]

The latter, former South African Minister of Water Affairs and Forestry Ronald Kasrils, said:

> In South Africa we treat water as both a social and an economic good. Once the social needs have been met, we manage water as an economic good, as is appropriate for a scarce natural resource. Some non-governmental organizations and international organized labor oppose what they call the "commodification" of water and thus oppose cost recovery. We are concerned about this because absence of cost recovery leads to inadequate funding for infrastructure development and the resulting overuse leads to local shortages and service breakdowns which impact most heavily on the poor.[140]

We can deduce from this that if politicians can agree on the price of water, the dialogue may lead to peace—at least as far as the water issue is concerned—between politically divided countries. Within a country such as South Africa, which still faces the threat of serious social conflicts between white and black populations, a modus

---

[. . .] Discussions on this issue have focused too heavily on international companies, forgetting the importance and development potential of the domestic private sector and small local entrepreneurs, for example, operators in Mauritania's small towns. [. . .] Currently, this local private sector is often the only party present to ensure minimal service in underprivileged urban areas." Münger, "Les défis de l'eau requièrent-ils la mobilisation?"

139. Segerfeldt, *Water for Sale*, 40.
140. Ibid., 117–18.

vivendi seems workable if the water resource is equitably distributed (that is, with essential needs distributed free or at very low cost, but amounts exceeding the 25 to 30-liter basic service sold at a rate that might cover the huge costs of the infrastructure).

The UN's Challenges for Real Access to Water and Sanitation

Three years after the United Nations declared water to be a new human right, on July 24, 2013, the international community passed a resolution proclaiming November 19 "World Toilet Day." However, there is still a long and difficult road ahead before the effects of the appeals made by the churches and the Dublin principles are felt by one third of humanity who still have no access to sufficient water in quality and quantity, and sanitation.

This was the conclusion reached by the Deputy Secretary-General of the United Nations, Jan Eliasson, on May 2, 2013, in a speech titled "Our New World, Challenges for Peace, Development and Human Rights" delivered at National University of Singapore (NUS). He was one of the architects of peace who supported the project proposed by Singapore's sanitation-focused Jack Sim,[141] and won an important diplomatic victory on July 24, 2013, when the UN General Assembly passed the resolution in support of sanitation for all.[142]

Eliasson also made another important point in his speech. Stressing that education was one of the MDGs[143] on which the most progress had been made, he lamented that in contrast, water and sanitation goals were far from having been met. That was why he was explicitly inviting the private sector to join government efforts in this area.

The observation that the UN's values seem to be suffering from a loss of credibility is impossible to sweep under the rug, especially since new violations of the main human rights are seen every day.

The UN is not alone on the hot seat.

Christian Häberli, one of the participants in the second W4W colloquium on March 20, 2012, arrived at the same conclusion. He feels that World Trade Organization (WTO) agricultural policy still does not adequately take the human right to food into account. Some, and specifically the Swiss and Brazilian churches in their 2005 statement, believe that the human right to food implicitly includes the human right to water.

This viewpoint is based on article 11 para. 1 of the ICESCR, which states,

> The States Parties to the present Covenant recognize the right of everyone to an adequate standard of living for himself and his family, including adequate

---

141. Jack Sim created the World Toilet Organisation in 2009 and worked for four years to convince Singaporean authorities, and then the UN mission in New York, of the importance of creating World Toilet Day. See *The Straits Times,* July 25, 2013, A10. www.straitstimes.com.

142. http://sanitationdrive2015.org/call-to-action.

143. Millennium Declaration, para III. Goal 7, Target 7. C.

food, clothing and housing, and to the continuous improvement of living conditions [...].[144]

Of course Häberli, an agricultural specialist, acknowledges that the new provisions in the WTO Agreement on Agriculture (AoA)[145] of 2001 aim to protect non-commercial sectors such as food and the environment.[146] On the other hand, he considers that in practice this guarantee does not achieve satisfactory results, as proven by the serious world food crisis of 2007-2008.

So in Häberli's estimation, the WTO has done only "half of the work," because while improving the rules of competition by curtailing opportunities for export subsidies, it built a "firewall" around the human right to food. He specifically warns against the absence of regulations for international food aid.

> Overall it appears that present international trade and investment rules are ill-suited to address food trade issues which have a negative impact at the national and house-hold levels. These shortcomings can be said to violate the right to food laid down in human rights treaties. What is clear however is that we are in presence of a job half-done [...]. Actually, some significant loopholes could be getting even bigger, impairing both global and national food security especially in times of high food prices.[147]

He invites all stakeholders to coordinate their efforts in order to put both the human right to food and the human right to water into effect.

> WTO and other trade agreements have improved the opportunities for efficient agricultural producers however they have not even addressed the Right to Water. There are no commitments under the Services part of market access negotiations (GATS).
>
> This is where I think research and policy at the national and international levels is most urgently needed. The international human rights obligations all of our governments have subscribed to in New York must guide this search for solutions. All stakeholders must join this interrogation. We all must contribute here.[148]

The desire he is expressing is that we take a critical yet constructive approach to these efforts.

---

144. International Covenant on Economic, Social and Cultural Rights, article 11 para. 1.

145. http://www.wto.org.

146. WTO Agreement on Agriculture preamble indicates, "[...] commitments under the reform program should be made in an equitable way among all Members, having regard to non-trade concerns, including food security and the need to protect the environment," cited by Häberli, *God, the WTO—and Hunger*, 93.

147. Häberli, Christian, *Water, Vital Need and Global Justice*.

148. Ibid.

PART IV: JUSTICE AND RESPONSIBILITY

Does a Global Water Ethic Have Anthropological Roots?[149]

Paul Ricœur uses the conciliatory language of practical wisdom, from which I hope to draw my inspiration to say what, in the final analysis, a "global responsibility" means to me.

We all know the slogan "think globally, act locally," which is attributed to contemporary French theologian and legal scholar Jacques Ellul. However, referring to philosopher Immanuel Kant, why not say "dare to act globally" in preference to "act locally"?

Indeed, the verb "to dare" evokes risk, the effort of moving beyond the common view.

So to me, daring to "think" global responsibility means taking concrete steps to encourage interaction across political boundaries, especially in order to act against the poverty and injustice experienced by those with inadequate access to water.

Among such steps, three appear to me to be essential, namely: first, informing people about the current national and international situation; second, participation by citizens in their own countries; and third, travel.

Informing is the intellectual process of thinking locally and globally; participation by citizens in their own countries is acting locally, which sometimes has a global impact (for example, when voting for development aid); and travel within and outside of national borders is how humans encounter the Other.[150]

To those who would object that travel is not possible for everyone, I would respond that today it is possible to approach the Other in all parts of the world either through information technologies—e-mail, Twitter, Skype, and the like—or by hosting the Other who does travel in one's home. To the objection of language differences, I would say that English is increasingly becoming the lingua franca. In fact, it must be observed that even Chinese president Xi Jinping and Japanese prime minister Shinzo Abe speak English, not to mention small children in Bhutan, who have been learning the language of Shakespeare since the reign of their fourth king (1972-2006). To anyone citing the difficulty that citizen participation is not available to everyone, my answer would be that yes, it is true that many political regimes still obstruct this today. However, I would also reply that the Western vision need not be imposed by force, but could be suggested or even called into question in discussion forums.[151]

Implicit in my suggestion is the importance of creating human ties, those which teach us to cooperate and be connected to each other. This really does mean a learning

---

149. Müller indicates, "The Protestant ethic [. . .] has good reason to rediscover the anthropological roots of the ethical question [. . .]. The ethical requirement is indissociable from the concrete human being to which it refers." Müller, "Morale," 942.

150. Many writers have celebrated travel (Nicolas Bouvier and Claude Lévi-Strauss, not to mention George Orwell and many others).

151. A multitude of entities monitor democracy and global democracy. A global consensus will not be reached in the near future, see Miller, "Die Idee globaler Demokratie, Eine Kritik."

process that is not always easy—learning various languages, learning about the history of one's country and the world, and about democracy in the literal sense, which means becoming informed and engaging in debate in order to vote better and elect better candidates.

Is the foregoing a digression from the issue of universal access to water, which the UN and Christian churches call a human right?

Not at all.

This is why we now find ourselves at the heart of the matter: in my opinion these three things—becoming informed, engaging in citizen participation, and approaching the Other—are the necessary ingredients for a global potable water ethic that is anthropologically rooted and not based solely on metaphysics or eschatology.

Becoming Informed about Current Events and History

First, it is indisputable that the font where the human right to water was christened is found in New York, and that the founding text was written in English on July 28, 2010. Needless to say, the voluminous documentation leading up to the decision was also written in English, and many of the forums held during the decision process were also in the language of Francis Bacon. (To be clear, I am of course not unaware of the role played by interpreters.)

Second, it is equally indisputable that the new human right to potable water was born of a logic that, mainly for historical reasons related to World War II, gave rise to the human rights corpus in the modern sense, as discussed in Part III of this study. It is also the product of a logic introduced especially by the Brundtland Commission on sustainable development (see Part I, Chapter IV). Finally, it came into being in the context of water-related social confrontations, especially in Cochabamba, Bolivia.[152]

Participating as a World Citizen to Foster Connection

Third, it cannot be denied that democracy is taking on an increasingly global dimension, and global citizens want to have a say in their own well-being, especially where access to potable water is concerned. Some people call this the global democracy of civil society. I have called this issue to mind here and there. Make no mistake: I am not defending activism in and of itself. On the contrary, what I am standing up for is the importance of everyone being a responsible citizen in his or her own country. In Switzerland, we unquestionably have the opportunity to express ourselves at the ballot box, not only on local issues but also on questions of global import,[153] several times each year (even, I may add, if we are living outside of the country). We have made

152. See Part III, Section II, Chapter II, Is Resentment a Motive for Action.
153. Rousseau, indicates, "the right of voting [on public affairs] makes it my duty to study them." Rousseau, *Du contrat social,* 41.

decisions about water a number of times. For example, in 1988 the transition from private to public water management in the Canton of Geneva was confirmed,[154] and in 2012 the right to water was enshrined in Geneva's Constitution.

Following in Paul's Footsteps: Traveling to See the Face of the Other

As I see it, whether we encounter the Other by Skype, by welcoming him into our home, or by seeking him out in the farthest reaches of the globe, this I-you relationship is of crucial importance in awakening the sense of reciprocity, a topic which I will conceptualize later with the help of Paul Ricœur and his "superabundance of love."

As far as reciprocity is concerned, was not the Apostle Paul the first to teach Christians about it, this man who braved the most dangerous voyages to join his brothers and sisters in Christ and make faith in God known to them?[155]

Mini-Conclusion

Once again, the international community has made every effort to think through concepts such as the duty to respect, protect, and fulfill the right to water; but by and large it still finds itself rather powerless when it comes to putting them into practice.

It is patently obvious that there is no form of international oversight capable of ensuring that "failed" States will implement legislation to prevent excessively high water prices. Frequent abuses have been seen when the provision of water services is entrusted to private companies. It is with the very goal of blocking such abuses that the UN experts' guidelines and the South African example ought to be brought into play.

There are alternatives, if we can keep from balking at discussion and standing on dogmatic positions. In this respect, I side with Christophe Hofer and the Swiss Department of Development and Cooperation in maintaining that when a public authority is unable to fulfill its obligations without the private sector's help, the alternative option of private water management need not be rejected out of hand without a closer look.

Still, legal mechanisms absolutely must be set up to ensure that the private enterprises comply with the duties to respect and protect suggested by the Committee on Economic, Social and Cultural Rights in General Comment no. 15. South African legislation and jurisprudence are quite clear on this point and, according to my information, provide a model that is unique in the world, and therefore one to be followed.

---

154. Constitution of Geneva, October 14, 2012, article 158, reads, "Water supply and distribution are a public monopoly held by Services Industriels de Genève."

155. For example, see I Thess 1:8.

CHAPTER III: INTRAGENERATIONAL ETHICS

Conclusion

Summarizing these many sections I have just devoted to Justice and Responsibility would be an exercise in tedium.

I will say, however, that their goal was to document humanity's efforts to achieve better justice here below. And, I would like to point out, it was in fact a deep sense of injustice, arising from the observation of the poverty associated with scarce or polluted potable water, that led me to undertake my research.

When beginning this dissertation, I did not even dare to hope that there would be a real example on Earth of the application of certain Western values such as justice and individual responsibility, values which I considered as necessary in principle for access to potable water and sanitation.

Instead, not only did I find a concrete example, but it enabled me to understand what requirements the human right to water might imply in temporal reality. It took being there in person to see, on the spot, that a radical transformation of society is indeed the heavy price that must be paid in order to attain a kind of social justice that offers high-quality potable water in sufficient quantity for everyone. Singapore, which was called underdeveloped in the 1960s, is the country that has undergone this transformation.

The project was born of the dream of a Singaporean attorney educated in Great Britain. Will it last?

At first sight, Lee Kuan Yew's successors would seem to bear the responsibility for this. It is also their responsibility to take stock of the effort demanded of the public, to weigh successes against failures, and then to promote their experience among Singapore's younger generations, who are the beneficiaries of the resulting prosperity—without having had to make any sacrifices themselves, I must stress. In the final analysis, it is their duty to share the methods by which they gained their knowledge with other nations that are still struggling in terms of development.

Taking a second look, however, shows that the West should also share in this responsibility, if only by acknowledging that in less than fifty years, Singapore has successfully emerged from the poverty in which it was mired when it became independent in 1965.

Examination of these issues absolutely must continue, based on this example.

Too many countries are truly destitute, a condition that becomes obvious where easy access to potable water and sanitation, as well as the lack of water treatment infrastructure, are concerned.

What can be done?

Avoiding the traps of neoliberalism and an excessively utopian dream of globalization, the global citizen, together with the international political and economic world, does have in hand the conceptual tools for living in greater harmony.

With regard to universal access to potable water, it seems the road will still be long, since industrialization of "less advanced" countries is a process that has a high social price, let alone the financial cost.

So I decline to consider global justice and global responsibility as "givens." I feel that while the reflections of the greatest thinkers of our time, such as John Rawls or Amartya Sen, are of course precious resources, we still must continue our search for yet another source of justice.

Part V

The Theological Structure of Potable Water's Challenges

Introduction

What Kind of Justice Should Apply to Universal Access to Potable Water?

PAUL RICŒUR POSTULATES TWO fields of application for justice—or rather, more precisely, as he often stated it, for the "common sense precepts of justice." He distinguishes between justice as solicitude and justice as equality. These two types of justice cover, respectively, interpersonal relationships ("I–you"), and all of humanity ("I–he").

He starts from the Aristotelian premise that corrective justice must be separated from distributive justice.

The first distributes things according to a simple arithmetic equality, while the second takes into account the real differences between the nature of people and of the things to be shared.[1]

Ricœur is highly skeptical of the second. For him, the idea of distribution conceals an important ambiguity. How can we determine "just shares" without becoming

---

1. For a summary of these differences, see Dermange who indicates, "Equal [. . .] does not mean that everyone ought to receive the same share, but that 'proportional' justice ensures an equal relationship to each person's contribution, in a proportion equation A/B = C/D, in which A and B are people and C and D are the portions they receive." See also Ricœur, *Soi-même comme un autre*, 235: "It is the unequal that we deplore and condemn. Aristotle [. . .] [in a] stroke of genius [. . .] [gave] a philosophical content to the idea received from the tradition. On the one hand, Aristotle finds in the equal the character of intermediateness between two extremes [. . .]. In fact, where there is sharing, there may be too much or not enough. The unjust man is one who takes too much in terms of advantages [. . .] or not enough in terms of burdens. On the other hand, he carefully marks out the type of intermediateness, namely *proportional equality,* that defines distributive justice. Arithmetic equality is not suitable, he holds, because of the nature of the persons and of the things shared. [. . .] Distributive justice then consists in equalizing two relations between, in each case, a person and a merit. It therefore rests on a proportional relation with four terms: two persons and two shares." Dermange, *Le Dieu du marché*, 20.

mired in "a nest of inextricable difficulties"?[2] In particular, he wonders, if distributive justice advocates equality, is it not characterized by "a mutual disinterest for the interest of others," an "idea that we find in Rawls"?[3]

So, Ricœur holds, it is necessary to conceive of yet another kind of justice as solicitude, that is, "a belonging that extends all the way to that of an infinite *mutual indebtedness* [. . .]."[4]

By one of those rhetorical devices of which he is a master, Ricœur pleads for:

> [. . .] "saving" equality, philosophically and ethically. Equality, however it is modulated, is to life in institutions what solicitude is to interpersonal relations.[5]

Here are two clearly distinct "face to face" encounters or two types of "each": first, the *each* that Ricœur says *grammatically* assumes equality's distributive character,[6] which relates to all humanity; and second, the *each* as the *face* of the "other than oneself," which falls within the interpersonal realm of solicitude.

My own interpretation of Ricœur's position is that the first, impersonal kind of "each" is practiced within the institutional context of contingent justice, while the second is that of love and justice of another order, the kind recommended by Jesus Christ: "Love your neighbor as yourself."

We will discuss this other type of justice first, via the Golden Rule. Then, revisiting the system used in Part IV for the temporal world, and with help from John Calvin and Dietrich Bonhoeffer, I will move from supererogatory justice as a logic of normativity to a logic of implementation, that of responsibility from a theological perspective.

---

2. Ricœur, *Soi-même comme un autre*, 235.
3. Ibid., 236.
4. Ibid.
5. Ibid.
6. Ibid.

Chapter I

Solicitude and Love as a Means to Supererogatory Justice

The Golden Rule Concept

IN A MOMENT, I will invoke a more detailed argument to postulate that the Golden Rule—an ancient norm if ever there was one—could today, in a surprising way, open up a new ethical direction for human action, especially for the challenges of potable water. First, though, I will mention its origins and formulation and then undertake to pin down its content and scope.

Origin and Formulation of the "Golden Rule"

German humanist and exegete Albrecht Dihle wrote a significant, detailed study on this moral behavioral rule, which he believes goes back to the dawn of time.

> [. . .] the criterion according to which the Golden Rule determines the value of an action turns out to be an integral part of the oldest and most primeval concept of morality that we can actually detect in literature.[1]

He finds, however, that it was not formulated until late, and that it has appeared in two guises since the beginning of the Christian era.

The first is the negative statement of the rule furnished by Rabbi Hillel Ha Zaken. It was supposedly his answer to the strange, even insolent request by a scoffer who wanted to learn the whole Torah while standing on one foot.[2] The rabbi answered the challenge with a clever and concise reply.

> Whatever is hurtful to you do not do to any other person. That is the whole of the law.

The second, positive form goes back to ancient times, according to Dihle. It is mentioned in the New Testament as well, being found in both the Sermon on the Mount and the Sermon on the Plain. In Matthew 7:12, it is written as

---

1. Dihle, *Die Goldene Regel*, 11.
2. Ibid., 8.

Part V: The Theological Structure of Potable Water's Challenges

[i]n everything do to others as you would have them do to you; for this is the law and the prophets.

In Luke 6:31, we find

[d]o to others as you would have them do to you.

Dihle is careful to clarify that Christianity cannot claim the positive statement of the Golden Rule as its own, since the famous Greek orator Isocrates[3] had already referred to it.[4] Dihle further states that this maxim was already known to the philosophers Aristotle and Seneca, and greatly valued by emperors such as Alexander Severus and Marcus Aurelius. This led the German scholar to conclude that

> [. . .] the author of the *Historia Augusta* (Alex. Sev. 51) considered Alexander Severus's predilection for the Golden Rule to be a sign of syncretism between Judaism, Pythagoreanism, and Christianity.[5]

It is important to note that the simplest expression of these maxims fell from the lips of the English in the fifteenth or sixteenth century, under the evocative name of the Golden Rule.[6] Dihle also does not hesitate to speak of a lexical formula that falls within the art of sophistry.[7]

So should we take the same position as Kant, who felt that this rule was merely "trivial"?[8]

I think not, despite the sobriquet "golden," to which some bitter souls might react at first sight by saying that it glitters rather too brightly.

On the contrary, scientific works such as those by Dihle, Ricœur, and du Roy,[9] which reintroduce a rule that was nearly forgotten for a century,[10] seem to me to offer some thoughts useful to our globalized world and a global potable water ethic.

---

3. Isocrates (436–338 BC), cited by Du Roy, *La Règle d'Or*, 80.
4. Dihle, *Die Goldene Regel*, 113.
5. Ibid., 10.
6. Du Roy, 15, citing Goodmann, *The Golden Rule*, 9.
7. Dihle, *Die Goldene Regel*, 127.
8. Kant indicates, "Let no one think that here the trivial '*quod tibi non vis fieri, etc.*' *[alteri ne feceris(*)]* can serve as a standard or principle. For it is merely derivative from our principle, although subject to various qualifications: it cannot be a universal law since it contains the ground neither of duties to oneself nor of duties of kindness to others [. . .]." Kant, *Fondements*, 144, note.

(*) Author's note: I have added the terms chosen by Alexander Severus here. The Latin reads "that which you do not want done to you, [do not do to others]."

9. Du Roy, Olivier, French theologian.
10. Du Roy, *La Règle d'Or. Le retour d'une règle oubliée*, 94.

CHAPTER I: SOLICITUDE AND LOVE AS A MEANS TO SUPEREROGATORY JUSTICE

The Meaning and Mechanisms of the Golden Rule

A Historical Look at the Elements of the Golden Rule

Protagonists

First let us define the protagonists brought together by the Golden Rule. Then we will go on to elucidate the connections between them.

It is usual to speak of the "agent-recipient" or "agent-patient" pair, with the first term identifying the individual who is acting and the second denoting the one suffering or being acted upon, according to the Latin etymology of "patient." A more intersubjective expression speaks of the "ego" and the "alter ego," with this duo breathing a little more soul into the Golden Rule, as we shall see later. For his part, Paul Ricœur talks about "I" and "you," which he contrasts to the "it" of institutions.

So when fighting for survival or engaged in a conflict, Man finds himself facing the Other, his understanding of whom is mediated by the latter's face and body.

The Lex Talionis[11]

The scope of what the maxim covers seems limitless, since both Rabbi Hillel Ha Zaken and Christ specified in their formulations of the Golden Rule that it encompasses all of the Law. So we need to refer to the Torah for explanations. Leviticus 24:17-21 gives us the main points.

> Anyone who kills a human being shall be put to death. Anyone who kills an animal shall make restitution for it, life for life. Anyone who maims another shall suffer the same injury in return: fracture for fracture, eye for eye, tooth for tooth; the injury inflicted is the injury to be suffered. One who kills an animal shall make restitution for it; but one who kills a human being shall be put to death.

These instructions are also known as the *lex talionis,* which is often summed up by the equivalency "an eye for an eye, a tooth for a tooth." It implies vengeance.

We may allow Dihle's interpretation that the Golden Rule is based on a logic of equivalency similar to that of the *lex talionis;* however, it represents the other side of the coin because it rules out vengeance. In effect, in order to break the circle of violence, "do unto others what they have done unto you" is abolished.

To say it another way, in the *lex talionis* the Other is the one against whom the same measure must be taken in an act of vengeance.

---

11. Etymology: in Latin, *talis* means "of such a kind" or "such."

Part V: The Theological Structure of Potable Water's Challenges

Leibniz's Intuition of Reciprocity[12]

In contrast, in the "ego and alter ego" pair, the Other also seeks reciprocity but of a completely different kind, as Leibniz[13] worked out. In this case reciprocity involves empathy, which tends to reverse the partners' roles, with the agent trying to see himself with the Other's eyes or put himself in the Other's shoes:

> Put yourself in others' place, and you will have the right point of view for judging what is just or not.[14]

Interpersonal Relationships in Ancient Times

Dihle makes a point of noting that the Golden Rule has another face besides equivalence. For him, it consists, again, of an interpersonal relationship.

> While its formulation requires a rational analysis of interpersonal acts, which would not be expected until a relatively late date, its effectively moral way of making judgements shows that it is rooted in very ancient retaliatory ways of thinking.[15]

Dihle stresses that this intersubjective relationship was already appearing in the Torah, since prohibition of the prescribed vengeance was supplemented by the rule of loving one's neighbor (which furthermore is found again later in the Gospels):

> You shall not take vengeance or bear a grudge against any of your people, but you shall love your neighbor as yourself [. . .].[16]

However, according to Dihle, this love of one's neighbor cannot be understood as a relationship of one individual to another, since in the time of Leviticus it was the group—the family—that was the basic cultural unit. Since each of its members had an interest in protecting the Other, each became the Other's neighbor.

> Where conflicts of vital interests were settled exclusively between extended family groups, within the group the interests of an individual and his neighbor necessarily coincided.[17]

---

12. *Le Petit Larrousse* indicate, "Leibniz (1646-1716) was a German jurist, scholar, diplomat, and philosopher. A Lutheran, he had an "ambition to rise above Christianity's religious and philosophical differences." *Le Petit Larousse illustré*, 1505.

13. Du Roy, *La Règle d'Or. Le retour d'une règle oubliée*, 32.

14. Leibniz, "Méditation sur la notion commune de justice" 122–24, cited by Du Roy, *La Règle d'Or. Le retour d'une règle oubliée*.

15. Dihle, *Die Goldene Regel*, 12.

16. Lev 19:18.

17. Dihle, *La Règle d'Or. Le retour d'une règle oubliée*, 119.

Chapter I: Solicitude and Love as a Means to Supererogatory Justice

The Golden Rule's Mechanisms Seen through a Ricœurian Lens

Is the Golden Rule an Endoxon for Our Brothers and Sisters Who Thirst?

I have chosen to consult Paul Ricœur, who eased the transition from modernity to post-modernity, or in other words, made a key contribution for our time, by seeking to reinterpret the Golden Rule and give it a new scope.

In a masterly demonstration in the eighth study of his *Oneself as Another*,[18] the French philosopher first offered a post-Kantian formalization of the Golden Rule. Then, in *Amour et Justice*,[19] he postulated that this rule is left behind by the rule of love in a logic of superabundance. Finally, he made a surprising connection between the Golden Rule and John Rawls's difference principle.[20]

In my opinion, his reasoning may have very timely significance for conceptualizing the Other than Oneself, the brother or sister, as a suffering human being and the object of a kind of benevolence or solicitude that has been reworked in the context of unequal access to potable waters.

At the beginning of his argument, Ricœur revisits the negative formulation of the Golden Rule and clarifies that, for him, it "[. . .] appears to be part of the *endoxa* acclaimed by Aristotle's ethics, one of those received notions that the philosopher does not have to invent, but to clarify and justify." He then refers to the positive formula as found in the Gospels of Matthew and Luke, and justifies it by the "motive of benevolence that prompts us to do something on behalf of our neighbor."[21]

The Parable of the Good Samaritan

In his turn, Dihle would not have opposed this last interpretation, being one who in reading the Gospels saw the maxim's highly cosmopolitan scope expressed in the parable of the Good Samaritan. Indeed, Christ's parable, reported in the book of Luke,[22] shows that human beings are brothers and sisters in suffering and that political or religious affiliation cannot be a reason for refusing to give or receive help.

> In expanding to become a relationship with all people—a step that was not obvious to late Judaism—the commandment to love one's neighbor gains, in the Christian tradition, that same humane broadness that it also had in the philosophical ethic of Hellenism—in which, however, it was shaped by different requirements.[23]

---

18. Ricœur, *Soi-même comme un autre*.
19. Ricœur, *Amour et Justice*.
20. Rawls, *Théorie de la justice*, 92.
21. Ricœur, *Soi-même comme un autre*, 255.
22. Luke 10:25–37.
23. Dihle, *La Règle d'Or. Le retour d'une règle oubliée*, 111.

Part V: The Theological Structure of Potable Water's Challenges

This neighbor, the Other in the interpersonal relationship, who is also another person worthy of respect, is the focus of Ricœur's concern. The philosopher's interest in the Other, which he demonstrated with greater conviction after encountering Lévinas's philosophy,[24] was evident in his working life, especially through his attention to the problems of undocumented persons and his commitment to fight the death penalty,[25] but most especially in his capacity as a philosopher and ethicist.

His entire work *Oneself as Another* is marked by the "fundamental" or earlier ethics we have already discussed,[26] especially Aristotle's (teleological), Bentham's (utilitarian), and Kant's (duty-based or deontological).

We will now explore Ricœur's abovementioned eighth study, which took a new look at Kant's imperatives, to justify the Golden Rule from an ethical standpoint.

The Kantian Legacy: A New Formalism for the Golden Rule

As a keen observer who respected Kant's work, Ricœur first tried to explore why the German philosopher and author of the famous categorical imperative (stated three different ways, as noted above), which "isolates the moment of universality,"[27] kept his distance from the Golden Rule. This was likely, says Ricœur, because of "the imperfectly formal character of the rule. It can no doubt be held to be partially formal, in that it does not say what others would like or dislike to have done to them. It is imperfectly formal, however, to the extent that it refers to liking and disliking; it thereby introduces something on the order of inclinations."[28]

Next, Ricœur tried to understand the connection that Kant created with his second imperative, which I repeat here.

> Act in such a way that you always treat humanity, whether in your own person or in the person of any other, never simply as a means, but always at the same time as an end.[29]

He undertakes to interpret it with the help of two key terms: *humanity*, and *person as an end in itself*.[30] He stresses that for the purposes of his demonstration, *humanity* must be defined "not in the extensive or enumerative sense of the sum of human beings but in the comprehensive or fundamental sense of that by reason of which one is made worthy of respect [...]."[31]

---

24. Fiasse, *Paul Ricœur*, 88.
25. Ibid., 130.
26. See Part II, Chapter I.
27. Ricœur, *Soi-même comme un autre*, 240.
28. Ibid., 259–60.
29. Ibid., 258 n1 (trans. Delbos [IV, 429], 295).
30. Ibid., 259.
31. Ibid., 260.

Chapter I: Solicitude and Love as a Means to Supererogatory Justice

Ricœur tries to enter into his eminent predecessor's logic by noting that Kant had to use the term *humanity* in his second formulation of the imperative in order to make it consistent as a continuation of the first version, which guided "the principle of autonomy from unity, which does not take persons into account, to plurality."[32] However, Kant inserted a "secret discontinuity"[33] by suddenly introducing the idea of end in itself and *persons as ends in themselves*, whereas "the test of universalization, essential in affirming autonomy, continues with the elimination of the opposite maxim: never treat humanity *simply as a means*."[34] Otherness "is prevented from deploying itself by the universality that encircles it, by the viewpoint of the idea of humanity,"[35] an idea which is then taken in the sense of all human beings.

However, this unusual intrusion distinguishing "my person" from "the person of others" would certainly introduce an idea of plurality, which Ricœur is eager to demonstrate by saying that "the Golden Rule and the imperative of the respect owed to persons do not simply have the same field of exercise, they also have the same aim,"[36] which is "to establish reciprocity wherever there is a lack of reciprocity."[37]

Ricœur adds that by introducing "the very idea of persons as ends in themselves" along with "the notions of 'matter,' of 'object,' and of 'duty,' [. . .]," something new is said that *clarifies* and *purifies* the "deepest intention" of the Golden Rule.[38]

> What is said here that is new is precisely what the Golden Rule states on the level of popular wisdom, before it is sifted through the critique. For it is indeed the deepest intention of this rule that now emerges clarified and purified. What indeed is it to treat humanity in my person and in the person of others as a *means* if not to exert *upon* the will of others that power which, full of restraint in the case of influence, is unleashed in all the forms that violence takes, culminating in torture? And what is the occasion for this progressive violence of power exerted by one will upon another if not the initial dissymmetry between what one does and what is done to others?[39]

Even though Ricœur doubts, as he continues his argument, that "Kant succeeded in distinguishing, on the ontological plane where he situates himself, the respect owed to persons from autonomy," he believes he has thereby revealed and underscored "this subtle discordance within the Kantian imperative" and considers that it is "legitimate to see in this imperative the formalization of the Golden Rule, which obliquely

---

32. Ibid., 258–59.
33. Ibid., 259.
34. Ibid., 261.
35. Ibid., 263.
36. Ibid., 262.
37. Ibid.
38. Ibid., 261.
39. Ibid.

designates the initial dissymmetry out of which flows the process of victimization in opposition to which the Golden Rule sets forth its demand for reciprocity [.]"[40]

At this stage, Ricœur acknowledges that he has "done violence to the Kantian text,"[41] but wishes to reassure the reader by maintaining that the advantage of this reasoning was that it gave the second formulation of the categorical imperative "its entirely original character,"[42] such that it "ceases to appear as a copy of the universality at work in the principle of autonomy [. . .]."[43] Thanks to this line of thought he "[allowed] the voice of solicitude to be heard, behind the Golden Rule, the voice which asked that the plurality of persons and their otherness not be obliterated by the globalizing idea of humanity."[44]

The Christian Legacy: Love and the Golden Rule

In *Oneself as Another*, Paul Ricœur warned his readers that he wanted to offer the work in the service of philosophy, and therefore would refrain from displaying his Christian commitment.[45]

In contrast, his perspective in *Amour et Justice* differed in that he clearly stated his intent to draw a connection between theological and philosophical matters and to introduce the "self in the mirror of the Scriptures."[46]

As we have just seen, Ricœur read the Golden Rule in light of the Kantian imperatives to reveal this rule's intrinsic quality of "reciprocity."

In *Amour et Justice*, he set about demonstrating that this maxim can be read in two ways.[47]

First, it can be understood via the utilitarians' self-serving formula *do ut des*, or "I give so that you might give." Second, it can also be transformed into a paradigm of selflessness, in light of the well-known commandment to "love your neighbor as yourself," and then, to save "the Golden Rule from an always possible perverse interpretation,"[48] into

> Give because it has been given unto you.[49]

---

40. Ibid., 263–64.
41. Ibid., 262.
42. Ibid.
43. Ibid.
44. Ibid., 264.
45. Ricoeur indicates, "The ten studies that make up this work assume the bracketing, conscious and resolute, of the convictions that bind me to biblical faith." Ricoeur, *Soi-même comme un autre*, 36.
46. Ricœur, "Le soi dans le miroir des Ecritures," 45–74.
47. Ricœur, *Amour et justice*, 39.
48. . Ibid.
49. Ibid.

CHAPTER I: SOLICITUDE AND LOVE AS A MEANS TO SUPEREROGATORY JUSTICE

So love must be understood as part of a logic of superabundance, whereas Justice can correspond only to a logic of equivalence.

Yet Ricœur does not want to stop there. He even surprises us by stating that under the law of love, "love your neighbor as yourself," the Golden Rule's logic of superabundance does not go far enough for Jesus Christ. This is what we discover in Luke 6:32-34 when Christ warns against the weakness of a logic of reciprocity.

> If you love those who love you, what credit is that to you? For even sinners love those who love them. If you do good to those who do good to you, what credit is that to you? For even sinners do the same. If you lend to those from whom you hope to receive, what credit is that to you? Even sinners lend to sinners.

So what must be done? Simply, the unimaginable, as we read in Luke 6:35.

> But love your enemies, do good, and lend, expecting nothing in return.

Here Ricœur waxes lyrical, speaking of a "hymn to love,"[50] which is a "hyper-ethical expression of a broader economy of the gift."[51]

He hastens to relativize the absoluteness of the law of love by asking philosophy and theology to formulate a moral judgment capable of rectifying every unstable equilibrium by means of an original concept mentioned above, the economy of the gift.

In my opinion, it is this compassion and generosity that should speak to us. According to Ricœur, they are feasible even if not everyone can be called upon to have one of "those unique and extreme forms of commitment"[52] shown by Saint Francis, Gandhi, and Martin Luther King, Jr.

He concludes with almost mystical enthusiasm, as follows:

> Thus we may affirm in good faith and with a good conscience that the enterprise of expressing this equilibrium in everyday life, on the individual, judicial, social and political planes, is perfectly practicable. I would even say that the tenacious incorporation, step by step, of a supplementary degree of compassion and generosity in all of our codes—including our penal codes and our codes of social justice—constitutes a perfectly reasonable task, however difficult and interminable it may be.[53]

---

50. Ibid., 33.
51. Ibid.
52. Ibid., 38.
53. Ibid., 42.

Part V: The Theological Structure of Potable Water's Challenges

*The Rawlsian Legacy: The Golden Rule
and the Difference Principle*

I think it would now be interesting to know what Paul Ricœur thought about *A Theory of Justice*[54] by John Rawls.

Though he touches on it only briefly while reflecting on practical wisdom in politics[55] and the necessary role of institutions "if justice is truly to deserve the name of fairness,"[56] his assessment is pointed. In Rawls's "difference principle," he glimpses a "fine internal tear within the rule of justice"[57] in favor of the Golden Rule.

We recall that this "difference principle" represents the last part of the idea of justice in John Rawls's work. Rawls provides two principles of justice, given in lexical order.[58] The first is the principle of liberties, such as political liberties, freedom of speech and liberty of conscience, freedom of the person and the right to hold property, in short, those liberties that "are defined by the concept of the Rule of Law."[59] The second is called the "difference principle" (or, by economists, the "maximin principle," much to John Rawls's dismay),[60] and deals with social and economic inequalities.

While the first principle's freedoms absolutely must be equal for everyone, in the second principle Rawls has to resort to two "moments"[61] to make social and economic inequalities acceptable.

To summarize, these two divisions of John Rawls's "difference principle" are as follows.

A/ social and economic inequalities must result in a choice of "positions of authority and responsibility"[62] achieved in a context of fair equality of opportunity.[63]

---

54. Rawls, *Théorie de la justice*.

55. Ricœur, *Soi-même comme un autre*, 291.

56. Ibid.

57. Ibid., 292.

58. Ricoeur indicates, "This lexical or lexicographic order is easy to comment on: the first letter of any word is *lexically* first, in the sense that no compensation on the level of succeeding letters would erase the negative effect that would result from substituting any other letter in place of the first; this impossible substitution gives the first letter an infinite weight. Nevertheless, the order that follows is not without weight, since the letters that come after make the difference between two words having the same beginning. The lexical order gives a specific weight to all the components without making them mutually substitutable." Ricoeur, *Soi-même comme un autre*, 273 n1.

59. Rawls, *Théorie de la justice*, 92.

60. Rawls indicates, "Economics may wish to refer the difference principle as the maximin criterion, but I have carefully avoided this name for several reasons. The maximin criterion is generally understood as a rule for choice under great uncertainty [. . .], whereas the difference principle is a principle of justice. It is undesirable to use the same name for two things that are so distinct." Rawls, *Théorie de la justice*, 115

61. Ricœur, *Soi-même comme un autre*, 272.

62. Rawls, *Théorie de la justice*, 92.

63. Thus, to give an example of my own, a doctor of modest means who has obtained his degree in a country offering an inexpensive course of study, but then decides to earn his living as a

B/ social and economic inequalities must be organized in such a way as to enable the victims of economic and social consequences arising from a lower position to benefit as much as possible from the economic and social advantages produced by those who benefit from a higher position.

John Rawls states this "difference principle" as follows:

> One applies the second principle by holding positions open, and then, subject to this constraint, arranges social and economic inequalities so that everyone benefits.[64]

Or, to state this in the same terms as Ricœur's interpretation: with the difference principle, Rawls wants to equalize "as far as possible inequalities related to differences of authority and responsibility [. . .]."[65]

I note that Ricœur found a link between this difference principle and the one expressed in the Golden Rule, since "the viewpoint of the most disadvantaged is taken as a term of reference." Now, he says, if "the maximin principle, considered by itself, could [. . .] be reduced to a refined form of utilitarian calculation,"[66] then consideration of the most disadvantaged "rests in the last analysis on the rule of reciprocity, close to the Golden Rule, the aim of which is to redress the initial dissymmetry related to the power an agent exercises over the patient of his action, a dissymmetry that violence transforms into exploitation.[67]

Even though the maximin principle is inherently a distributive justice principle, like the "preferential option for the poor" discussed in Part I, Chapter IV, Ricœur's original analysis would seem to imply that Rawls's theory of justice "slips" over into the "justice as solicitude" camp.

Is the Golden Rule a Tool for Our Time in Terms of the Ethical Challenges of Potable Water?

There is a suspicion in non-democratic and non-industrialized countries that human rights, especially the human right to potable water, are part and parcel of a larger set of Western values. I must emphasize that this mistrust is not purely academic. While traveling in Africa and Asia, I myself have seen on many occasions that if I were to be so bold as to mention human rights, I would be risking bodily harm.

Philosopher Paul Ricœur clearly discerned this suspicion about the universal validity of human rights, which to him are

---

singer-songwriter and therefore to change his social position, must accept a lower income than if he had continued to practice medicine.

64. Rawls, *Théorie de la justice*, 92.
65. Ricœur, *Soi-même comme un autre*, 272.
66. Ibid., 292.
67. Ibid.

Part V: The Theological Structure of Potable Water's Challenges

[. . .] the fruit of the cultural history belonging to the West [. . .]. It is as though universalism and contextualism overlapped imperfectly on a small number of fundamental values, such as those we read in the universal declaration of the rights of man and of the citizen.[68]

For the present-day discussion about water, especially the right to potable water, Ricœur probably would have tried to dismiss the accusation of ethnocentrism[69] that might come back to haunt the UN declarations. I think he would have reasserted his view that

[. . .] on the one hand, one must maintain the universal claim attached to a few values where the universal and the historical intersect, and on the other hand, one must submit this claim to discussion [. . .]. Nothing can result from this discussion unless every party recognizes that other potential universals are contained in so-called exotic cultures.[70]

He supported the opinion that this necessary discussion is the one held face to face with the Other, the one of alterity as handled in accordance with the minimal potentialities of the Golden Rule, or better yet, with full hearts and overflowing generosity in accordance with the "logic of superabundance." Regardless of the protagonists' positions on human rights as an international legal corpus, this "otherness" ought to be able to be expressed.

We must recall that this discussion cannot be held in the absence of the right of assembly and freedom of association—those liberties that John Rawls placed above all others and which, unfortunately in my opinion, were relegated to the UN's Covenant II.[71]

---

68. Ibid., 335.

69. Ricoeur indicates, "This legislation is indeed the product of a singular history that is broadly that of Western democracies. And to the extent that the values produced in this history are not shared by other cultures, the accusation of ethnocentrism is shifted toward the declarative texts themselves, which have nevertheless been ratified by all the governments on this planet." Ricoeur, *Soi-même comme un autre*.

70. Ibid., 336.

71. Here I would simply like to make a comment that I find interesting in light of the new "human right to water." As it has turned out, "human rights" specialists have not yet been able to agree as to whether this new arrival ought to be considered an implicit part of the "right to life" set forth in article 3 of the Universal Declaration of Human Rights (hereafter UDHR) or an implicit part of the "right to food" established in article 25 of the same document. The debate is an important one, because if the right to water were part of the right to life, it would be one of the civil and political rights enumerated in articles 1 through 21 of the UDHR. On the other hand, if the right to water were understood as part of the right to food, it would be classified with the economic, social, and cultural rights listed in articles 22 through 27 of the UDHR. It should be noted that the two covenants were derived from the UDHR of 1948 and were adopted in 1966. They did not enter into effect until almost ten years later, two months apart—Covenant I (abbreviated ICESCR) concerning economic, social, and cultural rights on January 3, 1976, and Covenant II (abbreviated ICCPR), concerning civil and political rights, on March 23, 1976. The surprising thing about them is that they reverse the order of the UDHR articles. Covenant I is devoted to economic, social, and cultural rights, whereas Covenant II deals

Chapter I: Solicitude and Love as a Means to Supererogatory Justice

What I am trying to underscore here is that semantics is important and that attention must be paid to the sensibilities of "vulnerable" countries. Failure to do so would mean exposing ourselves to pointless conflicts. In my opinion, the serious issue of poverty and the lack of access to water for nearly a third of humanity therefore cannot be resolved by a dogmatic attitude that understands human rights and the human right to water as the only truth.

Since the road to democracy and a minimal level of well-being is still long for the world's "southern" countries, alternatives must be found in the meantime. Do we need a paradigm shift? If so, why not take the Golden Rule as a common denominator for a global potable water ethic?

Now let us hear what theology has to tell us about the attitude expected of human beings with regard to nature, and consequently, to water.

---

with civil and political rights. Did this situation, which in my opinion we must term an anomaly, arise solely for reasons of timing, since the ICESCR was ratified by the necessary thirty-five countries before the ICCPR? This is a plausible explanation, but I am not convinced. Indeed, we know that it took some intense negotiations to set up the two covenants, so they did not see the light of day until nearly twenty years after the UDHR was signed. I believe the answer is to be found in the political compromises that had to be made during the Cold War in order to reach a consensus to which John Rawls certainly would not have subscribed. As far as Rawls was concerned, putting the liberties first was non-negotiable. As we saw earlier, he stated his principle of justice in lexical order. So for him, reversing the order of priority of the freedoms and economic rights would have been out of the question. The Rawlsian order means that attacks on the basic liberties that are the same for everyone protected by the first principle cannot be justified or compensated by greater social and economic advantages. These freedoms have a central area of application within which they cannot be limited or challenged unless they conflict with other basic liberties. That is also why none of them is absolute, but even if they must be modified to form a system, this system should be the same for everyone.

Chapter II

"Thinking" Water Differently—Theologically

The Responsibility to Protect Water As Seen from a Theological Perspective

ACCOMPANYING ME ON THIS theological journey will be two European theologians and an American medievalist. The perhaps formidable task of the first two will be to refute the thesis of the third, who considers Christianity to be at the root of the current ecological crisis.

John Calvin and Man Responsible for Nature before God

Nature Respected and Protected

French reformer John Calvin, who lived in Geneva for many years and played a key role in shaping that city's future, outlined Man's responsibility to Creation early on, in both his *Institutes of the Christian Religion*[1] and his various commentaries on the books of the Old Testament, especially *Commentaire des cinq livres de Moïse*.[2]

Though American ways of thinking have been reshaping human awareness of nature since the late nineteenth century, I find it necessary to avoid eclipsing this very important theological source, a body of work that does not limit itself to being a masterful reorganization of ecclesiastical, political, and social life in Geneva, as I intend to show below.

In his treatise *La pensée économique et sociale de Calvin*,[3] Calvin commentator André Biéler brought out the reformer's viewpoint concerning the relationship that humankind should have with nature in general and the earth in particular, so I will be referring to his work several times.

---

1. Calvin, *Institution de la religion chrétienne*.

2. Calvin, *Commentaire des cinq livres de Moïse*, cited by Biéler, *La pensée économique et sociale de Calvin*, 522.

3. Biéler, *La pensée économique et sociale de Calvin*.

Chapter II: "Thinking" Water Differently—Theologically

I feel justified in noting that while Calvin's legacy to Geneva, his adopted city, was an institutional apparatus with effects that are still felt today, he was also eager to pay unconditional and respectful tribute to nature, as he strongly stated in language replete with all the virtues of the rhetorical arts.

He had two main reasons for doing so. First, he saw nature as an irrefutable proof of God's existence. Second, since nature alone is not sufficient to meet humanity's needs, it must be systematically treated and cultivated in order to avoid famines.

Calvin on the Power of God

Let us read John Calvin, who admired nature and metaphorically called it the "theater of God's glory." Note in passing the verve and force of his words.

> So then let us not be so blind in looking upon the skies, as not to perceive the lively image of God's majesty and of the wonderful power that he sheweth there. For it were better for us that our eyes were picked out, than to have the fruition and sight of the goodly works except we proceed to turn them to our behoof [benefit], by mounting up to the author of them. The brute beasts shall bear no blame for their having of the light: and that is because they have no reason to know the workmaster. But on our part, it is certain that there may need none other thing to condemn us before God, and to take all excuse from us, but that besides our eyes, he hath also given us some reason and understanding, to comprehend the wonderful things that he sheweth us both above and beneath.[4]

He notes that everyone, scholar and peasant alike, is capable of understanding the "wonderful wisdom, [of] both heaven and earth"—

> [. . .] not only those more abstruse things, which are the subjects of astronomy, medicine, and the whole science of physics, but those things which force themselves on the view of the most illiterate of mankind, so that they cannot open their eyes without being constrained to witness them.[5]

Calvin on Creation: An Incomplete Work

However, the time devoted to contemplation is brief in Calvin's discourse, the main objective of which, as we have just seen, is to show God's power. This God does not intend to allow his creature to become lazy and idle. No, it must work the ground and cultivate it to avoid barrenness and scarcity. We can find Calvin's leitmotif of labor in

---

4. Calvin, "96 sermon sur le livre de Job," 434.
5. Calvin, *Inst.*, I, V, 2.

many commentaries, for example those on Isaiah and the Pentateuch. In the first, he does not hesitate to attribute famines to the lazy.

> Let us not therefore ascribe barrenness and famine to any other causes than to our own fault [. . .].[6]

In the second, he clarifies:

> Moses now adds, that the earth was given to man, with this condition, that he should occupy himself in its cultivation. Whence it follows that men were created to employ themselves in some work, and not to lie down in inactivity and idleness. [. . .] Wherefore, nothing is more contrary to the order of nature, than to consume life in eating, drinking, and sleeping, while in the meantime we propose nothing to ourselves to do. Moses adds, that the custody of the garden was given in charge to Adam, to show that we possess the things which God has committed to our hands, on the condition, that being content with a frugal and moderate use of them, we should take care of what shall remain.[7]

This strikingly modern Calvinistic teaching has the virtue of acquainting us with the legacy of ancient traditions concerning three points that, in my mind, can shed some light on the bases we are seeking for a global potable water ethic.

Calvin wished to instruct us not only about managing and protecting the earth, but also especially about serving others.

First, he reminds us that the earth is entrusted to humankind as a gift from God and Man must be accountable for it, as is written in Genesis 2:15.

> The Lord God took the man and put him in the garden of Eden to till it and keep it.

Therefore, a human being must accept that he is merely a holder of the land. It is as God's steward and the steward responsible to future generations that he must work to make it bear fruit.

> Let him who possesses a field, so partake of its yearly fruits, that he may not suffer the ground to be injured by his negligence; but let him endeavor to hand it down to posterity as he received it, or even better cultivated. Let him so feed on its fruits that he neither dissipates it by luxury, nor permits [it] to be marred or ruined by neglect. Moreover, that this economy, and this diligence, with respect to those good things which God has given us to enjoy, may flourish among us; let every one regard himself as the steward of God in all things which he possesses. Then he will neither conduct himself dissolutely, nor corrupt by abuse those things which God requires to be preserved.[8]

---

6. Calvin, *Commentaires Esaïe, sur Es.* 30:23, cited by Biéler, *La pensée économique et sociale de Calvin*, 427.

7. Calvin, *Commentaire des cinq livres de Moïse*, 18.

8. Biéler, *La pensée économique et sociale de Calvin*, citing Calvin, 356.

Second, however, he notes that under the terms of God's commandments given in Exodus 23:10–11, Man must not overuse or exhaust the land that he is putting to legitimate use:

> For six years you shall sow your land and gather its yield; but the seventh year you shall let it rest and lie fallow [. . .].

Calvin uses surprisingly vivid terms to make this commandment to protect the earth stand out:

> To this precept [God] alludes, when he declares by the Prophets that the land "enjoyed her Sabbaths," when it had vomited forth its inhabitants, (2 Chronicles 36:21;) for since they had polluted it by violating the Sabbath, so that it groaned as if under a heavy burden, He says that it shall rest for a long continuous period, so as to compensate for the labor of many years.[9]

Sound Management of the Earth and Consideration of Brothers and Sisters in Need

Finally, according to Calvin, sound management of the earth cannot fail to include consideration of our brothers and sisters in need.

> Wherefore [God] undoubtedly inculcates liberality and kindness, and the other duties, whereby human society is maintained; and hence, in order that we may not be condemned as thieves by God, we must endeavor, as far as possible, that every one should safely keep what he possesses, and that our neighbor's advantage should be promoted no less than our own.[10]

It is true that Calvin does not specify the neighbor's portion, but as his commentator Biéler stresses, he did not consider this a matter of accepting community of goods like the Anabaptists, who wanted to shake off the yoke of the State. Quite the contrary: the political order seemed to him to be essential and he energetically denounced the turmoil the Anabaptists caused.

Here is the passage by Calvin that André Biéler cites to show the importance that the reformer accorded to political order.

> But this place hath need of a sound exposition, because of fantastical [fanatical] spirits, which do feign a commonality or participation together of goods, whereby all policy or civil government is taken away; as in this age the Anabaptists have raged, because they thought there was no Church unless all

---

9. *La pensée économique et sociale de Calvin*, citing Calvin, 357.
10. Ibid., 353, citing Calvin, *Commentaire des cinq livres de Moïse*, 18, covering Exodus 20:15.

men's goods were put and gathered together, as it were, in one heap, that they might all one with another take thereof.[11]

Dietrich Bonhoeffer and Man's Responsibility before God in Light of the Biblical Commandment to Love

A Gift of Persuasion

Who better than German theologian Dietrich Bonhoeffer, who was a member of the Resistance during World War II and was imprisoned for his participation in the plot to overthrow Hitler, to help continue John Calvin's reflections?

Is he not a true witness of the suffering human being? Cannot the attention he devoted to the excluded and the powerless also relate to those aspiring to gain access to potable water under conditions worthy of humankind?

In my opinion his testimony, which is based on a solid and unshakable trust in God, remains highly relevant today in a globalized world that is rapidly changing and searching for values.

The proof of this is the enthusiastic response he still elicits, particularly from young Germans, who are being swept off their feet by his poetry set to music on YouTube. This is especially true of the magnificent poem entitled in its English translation "Powers of Good" (and in French, *Puissances Bienveillantes*).[12] I note that the German title, *Von Guten Mächten Umgeben* ["surrounded by good powers"] is more expressive because it really does evoke a protective force.

However, there is another text that is even more relevant for a global water ethic, because it has to do with the recurring problem of poverty.

If I am to believe a footnote in *Résistance et Soumission*[13] this text shook the world as far away as the Roman Catholic community in Brazil. The note explains that "this text played an important role among liberation theologians such as Gustavo Gutiérrez, who cited it in *The Power of the Poor in History*.[14]

It reads as follows.

The View from Below

> There remains an experience of incomparable value. We have for once learnt to see the great events of world history from below, from the perspective of the outcast, the suspects, the maltreated, the powerless, the oppressed, the reviled—in short, from the perspective of those who suffer. The important

---

11. Ibid., 354, citing Calvin, *Commentaires sur le Nouveau Testament*, covering Acts 2:44.

12. Bonhoeffer, *Résistance et soumission*, 492.

13. Ibid.

14. Gutierrez, *Force historique des pauvres*, 219 and n. 72. See also Brown, *Liberation Theology*, ed. note.

thing is that neither bitterness nor envy should have gnawed at the heart during this time, that we should have come to look with new eyes at matters great and small, sorrow and joy, strength and weakness, that our perception of generosity, humanity, justice and mercy should have become clearer, freer, less corruptible. We have to learn that personal suffering is a more effective key, a more rewarding principle for exploring the world in thought and action than personal good fortune. This perspective from below must not become the partisan possession of those who are eternally dissatisfied; rather, we must do justice to life in all its dimensions from a higher satisfaction, whose foundation is beyond any talk of "from below" or "from above."[15]

Why is it so persuasive?

I think there are two reasons that Bonhoeffer's pen is so powerful. First of all, it was aided by a rhetorical mastery quite capable of shaking us out of our routine and making us uncomfortable. Then again, and most especially, it was prompted by the German theologian's own human suffering. Bonhoeffer was experiencing in the flesh an unequal struggle against the forces of the Gestapo, and living the extreme humiliation of one who had been condemned to die and knew that his days were numbered.

So let us reread his elegantly poetic hymns and his profoundly lyrical prose!

Moving past the palpable suffering expressed in every syllable, the reader is then led beyond what can be expressed in words toward horizons that invite him or her to defend that which is most human in humankind and to discover, with astonishment and gratitude, that he or she is filled with compassion for the sufferer.

Of course, Bonhoeffer says, no one can truly understanding the suffering of another. No one can substitute himself or herself for the sufferer:

> [. . .] we can share in other people's sufferings only to a very limited degree.[16]

However, though we cannot understand, we can "act with responsibility" by not

> waiting and looking on [. . .]. The Christian is called to sympathy and action [. . .] by the sufferings of his brethren, for whose sake Christ suffered.[17]

Such is Bonhoeffer's recommendation, though he does not ask anyone to be superhuman.

> We are certainly not Christ; we are not called on to redeem the world by our own deeds and sufferings, and we need not try to assume such an impossible burden.[18]

---

15. Bonhoeffer, *Résistance et soumission*, 40.
16. Ibid., 37.
17. Ibid., 36.
18. Ibid.

Part V: The Theological Structure of Potable Water's Challenges

What Is the Christian's Responsibility?

So what responsible action can the Christian be asked to take when faced with suffering in general, and the suffering of those who are thirsty in particular?

Here, again, Bonhoeffer moves us through his keen insight into human nature.

> We must allow for the fact that most people learn wisdom only by personal experience. This explains, first, why so few people are capable of taking precautions in advance—they always fancy that they will somehow or other avoid the danger, till it is too late. Secondly, it explains their insensibility to the sufferings of others; sympathy grows in proportion to the fear of approaching disaster.[19]

He then continues, lucidly, by listing humankind's characteristic psychological justifications:

> [. . .] lack of imagination, of sensitivity, and of mental alertness.

Without judging, he notes that from a Christian standpoint, this means that

> [. . .] large-heartedness [. . .] is lacking.[20]

We tend to compensate for this with

> [. . .] a steady composure, an ability to go on working, and a great capacity for suffering.[21]

Like other exceptional men and women in history, Bonhoeffer himself possessed this large-heartedness. As Paul Ricœur notes, however, we cannot all engage in extreme forms of commitment. We cannot all be Nelson Mandela,[22] the "giant of history" honored by U. S. President Barack Obama in his December 10, 2013 speech in Soweto at the funeral of South Africa's first black president.

A Medievalist Battles Judeo-Christian Theologians

As stated above, I would like to take another little breather and defuse a controversy first raised in 1967 by an American medievalist named Lynn White, Jr. The reason I am giving him space here is that his text entitled "The Historical Roots of our Ecological Crisis"[23] is freely accessible to all on the Internet and therefore continues to attract

---

19. Ibid.
20. Ibid.
21. Ibid.
22. Ricœur indicates, "We cannot all demonstrate "those unique and extreme forms of commitment" shown by Saint Francis, Gandhi, and Martin Luther King, Jr." Ricœur, *Amour et Justice*, 38.
23. White, "The Historical Roots of Our Ecologic Crisis," 13–24.

attention, as confirmed by the article that Swiss philosopher and historian Jacques Grinevald devoted to it in 2010.[24]

Once again, I will turn to the two theologians to guide my thoughts in refuting White's thesis.

Anthropocentrism versus Physiocentrism

Lynn White saw Christianity as the origin of all the evils suffered by today's world, especially those related to environmental degradation, which *ipso facto* includes potable water.

He began his article with a historical presentation of the development of Western sciences and technology, noting in particular that the use of water power "by 1000 a.d. at the latest" for

> [. . .] industrial processes other than milling grain[25]

was an important factor that allowed the West to begin dominating the world. Lynn White saw the foundation for this dominance in the Hebrew Bible's creation narrative, which establishes that God gave Man the power to rule over nature.

He continued his analysis by comparing the creation stories of other religions and enthused about animist traditions that saw each tree and river as an invisible being to protect.

He next declared that Christianity was wrong to reject animism[26] and so irreparably to breach the protective screen that this form of religion provided to prevent the exploitation of nature.

He concluded from this that

> [e]specially in its Western form, Christianity is the most anthropocentric religion the world has seen.[27] [. . .] Christianity [. . .] not only established a dualism of man and nature but also insisted that it is God's will that man exploit nature for his proper ends.[28]

He did remain hopeful, however, that Christianity will turn to the only conceivable model, that espoused by Saint Francis of Assisi, the monk who knew how to talk to birds. He proposed that Saint Francis, as the founder of a new religion of nature, be made the patron saint of ecologists.

---

24. Grinevald, *La thèse de Lynn White*, 39–67.
25. White, "The Historical Roots of Our Ecologic Crisis," 16.
26. Le *Petit Larousse illustré*, gives for "animism" following definition, "A form of religion that attributes a soul to animals, phenomena, and natural objects." Le *Petit Larousse illustré*, 92.
27. White, "The Historical Roots of Our Ecologic Crisis," 19.
28. Ibid., 19–20.

Part V: The Theological Structure of Potable Water's Challenges

We can see that there is a vast gulf separating John Calvin and Lynn White, the latter probably never having made the effort to read even a few pages of the reformer's work, let alone his passages on God's Creation that I cited earlier,[29] which are marked by a deep respect for nature.

It is possible to put a name to this distance, which sets the anthropocentric view of Man's relationship to nature against a physiocentric doctrine that is not so very far removed from the one Albert Schweitzer, the early twentieth-century theologian and physician, expressed in one of his books entitled *Civilization and Ethics*.[30]

To me, though, the fundamental difference between White and Schweitzer is that the latter does not accuse Christianity for what the world has become. Quite the contrary: he very modestly and non-judgmentally notes that by paying too little attention to the beauty in every manifestation of life, even being blind to it, Man probably misses out on real life.

Schweitzer knew how to translate this love of life into a disarming lyricism, as shown by this excerpt from his above-mentioned book.

> A man is truly ethical only when he obeys the compulsion to help all life which he is able to assist, and shrinks from injuring anything that lives. He does not ask how far this or that life deserves one's interest as being valuable, nor, beyond that, whether and how far it can appreciate such interest. Life as such is sacred to him. He tears no leaf from a tree, plucks no flower, and takes care to crush no insect. If in summer he is working by lamplight, he prefers to keep the window shut and breathe a stuffy atmosphere rather than see one insect after another fall with singed wings upon his table.[31]

Now we need to take a look at Lynn White as set against Dietrich Bonhoeffer.

Christianity versus the French Revolution as the Root of the Current Ecological Crisis

For his part Dietrich Bonhoeffer, whose language could be colored by boundless poetry, as we have seen, could also be unyielding and sharp when it came down to Judeo-Christian apologetics.

In a passage of his *Ethics* entitled "Inheritance and Decay,"[32] it is possible to discover a most excellent theological source for demolishing Lynn White's argument, for three reasons.

Bonhoeffer first tried to understand how, through such major events as the Reformation and the French Revolution, Man ended up substituting himself for the God

---

29. See Part V, Chapter II, John Calvin and Man Responsible.
30. Schweitzer, Albert, *Civilization and Ethics*.
31. Ibid., 247.
32. Bonhoeffer, *Ethique*, 65 ff.

CHAPTER II: "THINKING" WATER DIFFERENTLY—THEOLOGICALLY

of Abraham and Jacob. He then updated Martin Luther's doctrine of the two kingdoms[33] with a view to convincing Western Man to live out a responsible commitment to the community, in faith.

Of course, Bonhoeffer said, once Western Man had been released from under the clerical thumb by Luther, he was able to discover his own abilities in space and time, which gave him new energy and enabled him to develop technology.

Up to this point, I can see that Dietrich Bonhoeffer and Lynn White might have agreed, since both saw Christianity as favorable ground for the rise of industrialization.

However, Bonhoeffer differed from the American medievalist in attributing the source of a nihilism destructive to Man's future not to Christianity, but to the French Revolution, which

> [. . .] was the laying bare of the emancipated man in his tremendous power and his most terrible perversity.[34] Reason became a working hypothesis, a heuristic principle, and so led on to the unparalleled rise of technology. This is something essentially new in the history of the world.[35]

Furthermore,

> [i]t was an entirely new spirit that evoked [the technical science of the modern Western world], and it will continue only so long as this spirit continues. This is the spirit of the forcible subjugation of nature beneath the rule of the thinking and experimenting man. Technology became an end in itself. It has a soul of its own. Its symbol is the machine, the embodiment of the violation and exploitation of nature.[36]

Where does his reasoning lead?

For him, thinkers at the time of the French Revolution, wishing to create

> [. . .] a new unity of mind in the west,[37]

were incapable of supporting the rapid development of science and technology by providing the preconditions for a responsible, lasting human commitment to them.

He even added that two negative factors, or what might be called "undesirable partners," aggravated this lack. These, he said, were nationalism and the emergence—alongside a bourgeoisie engaged in intense economic activity—of

---

33. Jehle, *Karl Barth,* 126, citing Lau, who indicates, "According to Luther, every Christian is a citizen of two worlds, the kingdom of God on the right and the kingdom of God on the left. In the realm on the right hand of God, Christ himself reigns through Word and Sacrament. Here the instructions of the Sermon on the Mount are valid. In the realm on the left hand of God (here, of course, God is also ultimately reigning, which really has to be considered), the emperor rules with the sword." Lau, *Die Religion in Geschichte und Gegenwart,* 1945 ff.

34. Bonhoeffer, *Ethique,* 73.

35. Ibid.

36. Ibid.

37. Ibid., 76.

Part V: The Theological Structure of Potable Water's Challenges

[. . .] the masses, the fourth estate. All it stood for was simply the masses and their misery.[38]

In support of his conviction of the dangers of nationalism and the uncontrolled emergence of the masses, Bonhoeffer evoked the horrors of the Revolutionaries' Terror:

The emancipation of the masses leads to the reign of terror of the guillotine.[39]

So according to him it would indeed have been the French Revolution, not Christianity, that led to unchecked, irresponsible use of the environment. He said that by setting aside Christianity, and with it the doctrine of the two kingdoms mentioned above, the Revolutionaries not only consigned the Judeo-Christian God to oblivion, but also made him the target of increasingly pronounced hostility. Mere atheism, understood as denying the existence of God, gave way to a ruthless war on the very notion of a transcendental idea.

Can we not find a strange and symptomatic echo of the German theologian's warnings about nationalism and uncontrollable human forces in the studies done by Nicole Gnesotto and Giovanni Grévi in *Le monde en 2025*?[40] For example, in reading this report by the Institute for Security Studies in Paris, I was struck by the presence of real anxiety about a multipolar world that has protectionist tendencies and is threatened by a population explosion, especially in Africa in non-democratic countries that are said to be "failing," or "hindered."[41]

There is no doubt in my mind that Lynn White's brief article initiated an unequal battle against Calvin's and Bonhoeffer's works—though it is not necessarily a losing one for Lynn White's adherents, for two reasons. First, the impressive media machine of the Internet is capable of weakening even the greatest edifices! Second, Swiss ecologists are giving White, who held a degree from Harvard and was a highly respected professor in California, a new platform and a new audience.[42]

For my part, I am very glad that said ecologists have respected the democratic principle of discussion and have published a piece antithetical to White, "Pour en finir avec Lynn White" [Let us be done with Lynn White] in a work entitled *Crise écologique, crise des valeurs? Défis pour l'anthropologie et la spiritualité* [Ecological crisis, crisis of values? Challenges for anthropology and spirituality]. This article was written by Jean Bastaire, who in consternation cried out,

---

38. Ibid., 75.
39. Ibid., 77.
40. Gnesotto and Grevi indicate, "[. . .] eventual paralysis of international institutions, a growing number of disparities, and the emergence of nationalist or protectionist views could lead to a more contentious form of multipolarism that would see the major powers fighting over resources, markets, and spheres of influence." Gnesotto and Grevi, *Le monde en 2025*, 280.
41. Tchamo, *Justice distributive ou solidarité à l'échelle globale?*, 196.
42. Grinevald, *La thèse de Lynn White*, 4.

[. . .] this caricature has become unbelievably popular, and it is high time for Christians to reinstate the truth.[43]

Repentance and Works for the Love of Our Neighbor

Introduction

John Calvin was concerned about the human condition and presented it to us in strong, sharply-worded language, as attested by the following passage.

> But since no man in this terrestrial and corporeal prison has strength sufficient to press forward in his course with a due degree of alacrity, and the majority are oppressed with such great debility, that they stagger and halt, and even creep on the ground, and so make very inconsiderable advances,—let us every one proceed according to our small ability, and prosecute the journey we have begun. No man will be so unhappy, but that he may every day make some progress, however small.[44]

For him, however, reason and human will alone do not suffice for our "course," and we must serve God alone.

> Now, let those who are of opinion that the philosophers have the only just and orderly systems of moral philosophy, show me, in any of their works, a more excellent economy than that which I have stated. When they intend to exhort us to the sublimest virtue, they advance no argument but that we ought to live agreeably to nature; but the Scripture deduces its exhortation from the true source, when it [. . .] enjoins us to refer our life to God the author of it [. . .].[45]

For Calvin, the issue was one of direction—of directing behavior, or even redirecting it and changing course if one has chosen the wrong path.

Calvin on Water

In *Institutes of the Christian Religion*, I found a brief passage that may provide part of the answer to the question of how Calvin "thought" water. I am referring to the section about the use of indifferent things, or *adiaphora*, in his text devoted to Christian liberty.

---

43. Bastaire, *Pour en finir avec Lynn White*, 69.
44. Calvin, *Inst.*, III, VI, 5.
45. Ibid., III, VI, 3.

Part V: The Theological Structure of Potable Water's Challenges

He said that *adiaphora* are "external things, which in themselves are indifferent."[46] We call them morally neutral.

Now water, in particular, is a thing external to human beings.[47]

What did Calvin say about it? Did he consider water to be morally neutral, or rather something that is good or bad and therefore has an axiological value?

It is interesting to read that he counted not only good wine, but also "purer and sweeter water than others"[48] among the *adiaphora*. So he recognized that meeting a vital need is not the only purpose of high-quality water; it also has the characteristic of adding an agreeable sensation, even pleasure, to the act of drinking. In other words, he tied clean water to well-being.

He also gave an opinion about foods, both those necessary to meet our needs and those that give pleasure:

> Now if we consider for what end he has created the various kinds of aliment, we shall find that he intended to provide not only for our necessity, but likewise for our pleasure and delight.[49]

So one of Calvin's concerns was to establish a clear quality scale for potable water and food.

This provides a few clues useful to my thesis.

Before starting my investigation, I postulated that there is a difference between water with a moral value and water with no moral value, with the first needing to be able to satisfy baseline essential needs and the other used to ensure well-being.

From reading the very short passage in *Institutions of the Christian Religion* concerning potable water, as cited above, I infer the following, which we must acknowledge is tautological. On the one hand, there is a "purer and sweeter water than others" that, like good wine, falls into the category of *adiaphora*. On the other hand, there is a less pure and less sweet kind of water that suffices to meet the vital need to drink, but is not morally neutral.

There is no question that in the sixteenth century, Calvin was not asking himself whether it was necessary to conceptually distinguish between water as an essential need and water as a source of well-being. He had no need to do so. In my opinion, however, it is useful and even indispensable to keep this concept of *adiaphoron* in mind to redirect modern thoughts about potable water. I myself will use it to justify a human right to water in the strict (or absolute) sense, to water that would not be an *adiaphoron* but would have a moral value for the amount needed for survival. Water without a moral value, high-quality water that contributes to well-being, would be an

---

46. Ibid., III, XIX, 7.
47. If we set aside the fact that the human body is about 65 percent water.
48. Calvin, *Inst.*, III, XIX, 7.
49. Ibid., III, X, 2.

Chapter II: "Thinking" Water Differently—Theologically

adiaphoron, and I would classify it as a human right in the broad (or relative) sense. The synoptic table given in Part VI, Section 6 echoes this distinction.

It is also appropriate to take a look at Calvin's peremptory stance concerning all things that we do enjoy now or may in the future, not limited to water that is pleasant to drink or the delicious foods and dainty dishes he suggests we prepare.

In a passage of *Institutions of the Christian Religion* that uses highly metaphorical language to describe the wonders of Creation, he had a dual purpose. Not only did he wish to make mankind aware of the diversity and beauty of these marvels; he also intended to draw our attention to the fact that God, their author, provides them even though they are not necessary.

> But shall the Lord have endued flowers with such beauty, to present itself to our eyes, with such sweetness of smell, to impress our sense of smelling; and shall it be unlawful for our eyes to be affected with the beautiful sight, or our olfactory nerves with the agreeable odour? What! Has he not made such a distinction of colours as to render some more agreeable than others? Has he not given to gold and silver, to ivory and marble, a beauty which makes them more precious than other metals or stones? In a word, has he not made many things worthy of our estimation, independently of any necessary use?[50]

He continued his line of reasoning by inviting human beings to acknowledge that we are the lucky recipients, and to accept them as gifts from God. He did not fail to note that this gratitude is not self-evident.

In particular, he lamented that some people abuse Christian liberty by stubbornly persisting in using only necessary things.

> Nor can we avoid even those things which appear to subserve our pleasures rather than our necessities.[51]

Calvin found evidence of excessive scrupulousness in our act of allowing ourselves to be caught up in battles with our conscience, like the person who

> [...] will afterwards be unable with any peace of conscience to drink [...] purer and sweeter water than others. In short, he will come to think it criminal to step over a twig that lies across his path.[52]

This attitude, he said, approaches superstition and can have serious consequences for those who become enslaved to it. Not only are they "hurried by despair into a vortex of confusion,"[53] but furthermore "those things which were naturally pure become contaminated [...]"[54] to them, as the Apostle Paul stressed in Romans.

50. Ibid.
51. Ibid., III, X, 1.
52. Ibid., III, XIX, 7.
53. Ibid.
54. Ibid., III, XIX, 8.

Part V: The Theological Structure of Potable Water's Challenges

> I know and am persuaded in the Lord Jesus that nothing is unclean in itself; but it is unclean for anyone who thinks it unclean.[55]

Calvin also found it very unfortunate that these individuals "in perplexities"[56] do not recognize that external things are "gifts of God" which they ought to "receive with thanksgiving," gifts that are

> [. . .] sanctified to our use. [1 Tim 4:5] I mean a thanksgiving proceeding from a mind which acknowledges the beneficence and goodness of God in the blessings he bestows.[57]

The question that springs to mind is, are the gifts free? Can Man use them as he pleases? Or are there rules governing the correct use of them, a moral use?

Calvin's answer is crystal clear. Man can claim them, but the way he looks at them is changed, transformed, provided that he considers all of them gifts from God.

By completely changing his way of looking at things, Man can give up his position as one who dominates to adopt the posture of a human being subject to God's law. This will enable him to enjoy these things fully, but moderately, or to use Calvin's expression, with "sobriety." He is also called to employ them as a responsible steward who will have to answer for their appropriate use.[58]

To gain an even better grasp of Calvin's attitude to external things, I consulted a passage of *La Morale selon Calvin*[59] [Morality according to Calvin] by Genevan theologian Eric Fuchs. He cites a text that he says is characteristic of our reformer in its ambiguity. While the prose is truly "magnificent," according to Fuchs, it is not without a warning against any exuberance, which is "absolutely typical of the Calvinistic, and more broadly the Protestant, ethic."

Let us see for ourselves:

> Ivory and gold, and riches of all kinds, are certainly blessings of Divine Providence, not only permitted, but expressly designed for the use of men; nor are we any where prohibited to laugh, or to be satiated with food, or to annex new possessions to those already enjoyed by ourselves or by our ancestors, or to be delighted with musical harmony, or to drink wine. This is indeed true; but amidst an abundance of all things, to be immersed in sensual delights, to inebriate the heart and mind with present pleasures, and perpetually to grasp at new ones,—these things are very remote from a legitimate use of the Divine blessings. Let them banish, therefore, immoderate cupidity, excessive profusion, vanity, and arrogance; that with a pure conscience they may make

---

55. Rom 14:14.
56. Calvin, *Inst.*, III, XIX, 8.
57. Ibid.
58. Parable of the talents as found in Matt 25:14–30.
59. Fuchs, *La morale selon Calvin*, 60.

a proper use of the gifts of God. When their hearts shall be formed to this sobriety, they will have a rule for the legitimate enjoyment of them.[60]

The fundamental point for Calvin was that not only do we receive these things as gifts from God, we also need to care for our neighbor.

We are to freely use [these things] [. . .] to honor God and serve our neighbor.[61]

How are we to serve him? Do we jump into charitable works, and glory before God in their importance?

Here, again, Calvin gave a warning. No matter how hard Man tries to do good, it is impossible for him to compete with God. Fuchs says it this way.

Thus, for Calvin, the works of unbelievers have no value except that given to them by God himself in his providence. Here we must understand this as "no value before God," because the person who does the works is not motivated solely by the desire to please God. To please God, putting our works above ourselves as our homage to God is exactly what we must not do; rather, we must be willing to lay ourselves open to the power of God's love. God justifies the believer, that is, the person who lives based not on what can be seen and counted, but on the alterity of a word, a promise, a Spirit.[62]

In other words, it is only through faith and repentance that human works can have value in God's sight.

Works for the Love of One's Neighbor, the Delicious Fruits of Repentance[63]

As the Israelites were traveling through the desert, Moses enjoined his people to keep their eyes on the bronze serpent.[64] He was encouraging them to rise above the vicissitudes of the present by keeping the Promised Land in view.

I believe Calvin employed a similar technique in *Institutions of the Christian Religion*. Being one who himself endured physical suffering, he was too realistic to close his eyes to human misery.

---

60. Calvin, *Inst.*, III, XIX, 9.
61. Fuchs, *La morale selon Calvin*.
62. Ibid., 57.
63. I note that the French translators of Calvin's Latin text sometimes use the word *repentance* and sometimes the word *pénitence*, from which I deduce that these two words can be considered synonyms.
64. Num 21:9 reads "So Moses made a serpent of bronze, and put it upon a pole; and whenever a serpent bit someone, that person would look at the serpent of bronze and live."

Part V: The Theological Structure of Potable Water's Challenges

> [. . .] this life, considered in itself, is unquiet, turbulent, miserable in numberless instances, and in no respect altogether happy; and [. . .] all its reputed blessings are uncertain, transient, vain, and adulterated with a mixture of many evils [. . .].[65]

Having recalled this mortal condition, he set the goal: to serve God and consider life, no matter how hard it is, as a gift from God.

> [. . .] and in consequence of this [we] at once conclude that nothing can be sought or expected on earth but conflict, and that when we think of a crown we must raise our eyes towards heaven.[66]
>
> Our life in this world is a gift of the Divine clemency, which, as we owe to him, we ought to remember with gratitude [. . .].[67]

Both Moses, more than three millennia since, and Calvin, over five hundred years ago, invited those who were willing to listen to stop focusing on the human condition and allow themselves to be guided by God. In biblical language, such a change in attitude translates into repentance or conversion.

Calvin's View of Repentance in the Broad Sense

What is interesting to read in *Institutes of the Christian Religion* is that repentance does not have the narrow sense ascribed to it by the French dictionary *Le Petit Larousse*, which calls it a "painful regret for one's errors, one's sins."[68] In contrast, Calvin consulted the Hebrew and Greek etymologies to find the meaning.

> The Hebrew word for repentance denotes conversion or return. The Greek word signifies change of mind and intention.[69]

Based on these two linguistic resources, Calvin interpreted repentance as follows:

> A true conversion of our life to God [. . .] and with true penitence [a] return into his right way [. . .].[70]

He did not stop at merely defining it, but went on to explain it in light of Paul's second letter to the Corinthians.[71] Paul had noted that repentance produces certain fruits:

---

65. Calvin, *Inst.*, III, IX, 1.
66. Ibid.
67. Ibid., III, IX, 3.
68. *Le Petit Larousse Illustré*, 921.
69. Calvin, *Inst.*, III, III, 5.
70. Ibid.
71. 2 Cor 7:11 reads, "For see what earnestness this godly grief has produced in you, what eagerness to clear yourselves, what indignation, what alarm, what longing, what zeal, what punishment! At every point you have proved yourself guiltless in the matter."

Chapter II: "Thinking" Water Differently—Theologically

These things are carefulness [*sollicitude* or "concern" in Calvin's original French], excuse, indignation, fear, vehement desire, zeal, [. . .].[72]

Calvin did not hesitate to expound upon the flavor of these fruits. While at first he stressed how necessary it is for a believer to be "affected with a serious sense of displeasure because he has sinned against God," he then interpreted Paul's verse very liberally, in my opinion, stating,

> [n]ow, it may also be understood what are the fruits of repentance. They are, the duties of piety towards God, and of charity toward men, with sanctity and purity in our whole life.[73]

Calvin's stimulating interpretation takes us far from a maudlin version of Christianity that focuses on contrition. No, here we find energy and drive.

> He [Paul] appears to me to have used the word desire to denote diligence in duty and alacrity of obedience. [. . .] Similar to this is the meaning of zeal, which he immediately subjoins [. . .].[74]

Does not this brief exegesis illuminate the point that repentance provides Man with an opportunity to reconcile with himself, find meaning in his life, and be able to live a life worth living?

I can very easily imagine that a Christian wishing to commit to a humanitarian cause, such as showing concern on behalf of those who are disadvantaged where water is concerned, would consider it important to take such an interpretation of the Bible as the basis for explaining the causes and motives of his or her action—the very same as those for repentance, which can give the action its full value.

For unbelievers, the terms *desire* and *zeal* can be updated into modern secular language as *motivation,* a concept that appeared in the twentieth century and is connected to the term *process,* which translates the modes of acting.[75]

Calvin's Works Born of Repentance

In a city grappling not only with the plague brought from Asia[76] but also with economic challenges, Geneva's water problem was no doubt a major and unavoidable concern for the city officials responsible for the municipality's fate in Calvin's day. While I did not find any evidence in the work of this Frenchman from Picardy that

---

72. Calvin, *Inst.,* III, III, 15.
73. Ibid., III, III, 16.
74. Ibid., III, III, 15.
75. http://www.barbier-rd.nom.fr/motivation.htm, 4.
76. Ghemawat indicates, "Even the sub-1 percent globalization of the Middle Ages was enough for the Black Death, transmitted by rats from Asia, to ravage Europe—and reshuffle the ranks of trading cities." Ghemawat, *World 3.0,* 117.

he undertook any definite action in this direction, I do find the creation of social institutions at his instigation and under his leadership to be excellent examples of the "delicious fruits of repentance" and therefore, in my opinion, a wellspring of ideas for our reflection on a water ethic.

Why?

One cannot fail to recognize Calvin as the author of a pioneering body of work, a tireless crafter of improvements to the health, education and welfare of the residents of Geneva, a city decimated by the ravages of a globalized pandemic before the term even existed—the plague mentioned a moment ago. To his credit, he helped develop the Hospice Général (which had been founded by Genevan political authorities shortly before Calvin's arrival) to care for the body and promoted education by creating a public school, the Collège and Académie. There is more: he also successfully tried to further well-being. He improved the living standard through his efforts against begging and by creating work and jobs,[77] the basis for the economy, which moreover continued to grow after he passed away.

Geneva's social life was radically altered—for the better, I hasten to add. No one could question this change in direction.

I note that it is possible to find a direct connection between Calvin's social work in Geneva and the thoughts of Nobel economics laureate Amartya Sen that led to the Human Development Index (HDI), an economic indicator recognized by the UN in 1990 that measures well-being in the various countries of the world. The HDI uses statistics on *life expectancy, literacy,* and *standard of living,* a trio that Calvin had already suggested for the Genevans.

Conclusion

Christianity's heritage seems to me to offer some tools for our consideration of how better to face humanity's new challenges in the twenty-first century. For example, I suggest that we create a global water ethic based on the commandments invoked by both John Calvin and Dietrich Bonhoeffer.

For Calvin, Man has a real responsibility to manage nature, which includes both land and water, in an appropriate and context-sensitive way.

Bonhoeffer felt that we have a responsibility to the most destitute. Is not *The View from Below,* which he wrote while in prison, still equally powerful when applied to Indian paupers living in slums who, unlike city residents, must spend their meager resources to buy the water essential for their survival from tanker trucks?

As for Lynn White's radicalism, it seems to me that it should be read with the greatest caution, because such an attitude carries within it the seeds of uncontrollable violence.

---

77. Biéler, *La pensée économique et sociale de Calvin,* 156 and 158.

Chapter II: "Thinking" Water Differently—Theologically

I myself agree with the distance at which José A. Prades, Robert Tessier, and Jean-Guy Vaillancourt held physiocentrism in their presentation at a 1992 colloquium at Montreal University, entitled *L'éthique de l'écodécision: fondements et pratiques* [The ethics of ecodecision: grounds and practices].

> The radicalism ensuing from the shield that physiocentrism places before reality would also endanger some of the modern Western world's major attainments, especially the democratic ideal, which would be overshadowed as it melted into the nature of human beings crushed by the rules they would have to follow in the name of a highly questionable ideology. Under these conditions, comprehensive and consistent anthropocentrism appears to be the most suitable and safest basis for environmental policy and ethics for our times.[78]

Regardless of the positions taken by one side or the other, what I find to be essential is openness to discussion, as recommended by Karl-Otto Apel.[79] Theological ethics can be a crucial source of help, as stressed by Arthur Rich, citing German ethicist Helmut Thielcke.

> The task of theological ethics is to show, in the final analysis, "what it is all about." So it need not make decisions itself, or relieve someone who is following a given ethic from this duty.[80]

This ethic could be that of the Golden Rule, which enjoys universal consensus; and, for Christians, it could be the law of love.

This would result in a return to a more personalized commitment, one closer to the face of others, without always leaving the burden of responsibility for the poorest of the poor to someone else. Let us remember Christ's words, "I was thirsty, and you gave me something to drink."[81]

These are the powerful words that can call us to repentance, to conversion, to a change in direction toward responsible action.

These are the kinds of commitments we will discuss next.

---

78. Prades et al., *L'éthique de l'écodécision*.
79. Apel, *Diskurs und Verantwortung*.
80. Thielcke, *Einführung in die christliche Ethik*, 241.
81. Matt 25:35.

Part VI

Strategies for Mitigating Water Poverty

Some Original Testimonies

Introduction

A PREREQUISITE FOR TALKING about strategy is becoming aware of the need to act in a certain direction, and to coordinate the actions with this goal in mind.

With regard to mitigating poverty related to potable water issues, I wished to consult men and women who are convinced of potable water's value and can communicate their conviction.

I will briefly introduce the five interviews I have devoted to this topic, after first reporting comments by Mikhail Gorbachev, the emblematic president of Green Cross. He says that the vital resource of water is perhaps going to force us to do our utmost to ensure that its real value is increasingly taken into account and that all of our forces, even the weakest, will be combined so that effective water management becomes the highest priority of all.

On his institution's twentieth anniversary, after the fall of the Soviet Union and in a laudable act of resilience, he spoke up. Not content to simply utter one more appeal, he gave some numbers, which instead of hearing we will read.

> But the truly bad news is that water consumption is growing even faster than the population—twice as fast in the twentieth century. As a result, today one-third of the world's population lives in countries that experience water stress. It is estimated that this proportion will grow to two-thirds by the year 2025.[1]

---

1. Gorbatchev, *Allons-nous attendre d'avoir soif pour mesurer la valeur de l'eau?*.

He concluded his article by citing Benjamin Franklin, who said, "when the well is dry, we know the worth of water," a moving quotation reminiscent of Saint-Exupéry's cry of despair in *Wind, Sand and Stars*.[2]

The first two interviews are from an ecumenical and interfaith perspective. One illustrates the real-life commitment of a Swiss Protestant charitable organization, the other opens a virtual dialogue between an American Catholic academic and a distinguished political figure from the Arab world. To clarify, I constructed the second exchange based on the texts of speeches given by these two participants at the second Workshop for Water Ethics (W4W) held on March 20, 2012[3, 4] and transcribed in the proceedings. I therefore take full responsibility for the content.

The last three interviews seem to me to be helpful in starting a dialogue about the future of water in general, in connection with both the geopolitical aspects of transboundary aquifers and the opportunities that philanthropists have seized in order to facilitate access to water. The final interviewee will be a surprise guest.

Interview with a Representative of a Swiss Protestant Diaconal Ministry

Preamble

One of the main purposes of this interview is to show that strategies for mitigating water poverty cannot be solely scientific and technical in nature; they must also go hand in hand with an institutional system that is adapted to a particular place and the people who live there.

The models presented are not theoretical; they have been applied in the real world. They demonstrate two important points, in particular. First, participation by all community members is required. Duly informed, they can make helpful decisions about managing their assets well. Second, each member knows that he must adapt his behavior to the rules accepted by everyone, and that along with the rules come effectively enforced penalties for violations. Indeed, the very survival of the community depends on compliance with the law.

Evelyne Fiechter-Widemann

Valentin Prélaz, thank you for accepting my request for an interview in your capacity as an employee of Swiss Church Aid, generally known by its French and German acronyms EPER and HEKS.[5]

2. See Part III, Section II, Chapter I.
3. El Hassan, *"Eau, besoin vital [Water, Vital need]."*
4. Permission to publish has been granted for all persons interviewed.
5. EPER stands for "Entraide Protestante Suisse," and HEKS for "Hilfswerk der Evangelischen

Part VI: Strategies for Mitigating Water Poverty

In a moment I will ask you to tell us about the motivations and qualifications that enable you to do your wonderful job. For the time being, though, I need to explain why your statement plays a pivotal role in my dissertation.

As you know, between 2006 and 2009 I was on the EPER Foundation's board. It was in the context of this service as a legal adviser that I was made aware of the development issues tied to potable water. I also noted FEPS's[6] commitment to this cause, when it joined the Catholic churches in Brazil as a cosigner of the 2005 Ecumenical Declaration on *Water As a Human Right and a Public Good*."[7]

I discovered that the information on this subject available through the Geneva Protestant Church[8] was relatively limited, and I felt the need to know more. So, with the support of the University of Geneva's Faculty of Theology, I decided to examine ethical modes that might favor fair access to potable water and sanitation in the so-called "developing" countries.

Appended to this study, I am providing a report I wrote about a trip to southern Africa that I was privileged to take with you, as an observer, from March 24 to April 3, 2011. In it, I recount how we met with the local people in charge of the various EPER projects you supervised.[9] While the report was helpful in organizing this interview, your paper for your Certificate of Advanced Studies (CAS) from the Swiss Federal Institute of Technology in Lausanne (EPFL) was a useful source for the conversation itself.[10]

The purpose of the interview is to show how we can develop strategies for making the poorest and most vulnerable people aware of the value of potable water, and for persuading them to take appropriate steps to preserve and protect it.

So it is not a question solely of building bridges between North and South; we must also note the importance of the concepts of empowerment and the human-rights-based approach, popularized by the United Nations during the last decade. EPER subscribes to these, as you had occasion to inform me before the trip to Zimbabwe and South Africa.

Now I will move on to the interview itself.

You have chosen to enter a profession that requires frequent travel in distant lands to bring local residents knowledge that will help their health, education, and economic development—or, in other words, to try to free them from poverty.[11]

Kirchen Schweiz."

6. FEPS stands for "Fédération des Eglises protestantes de Suisse."

7. Ecumenical Declaration, ibid.

8. "Eglise protestante de Genève" [an association of the Protestant churches of Geneva], often known by its acronym, EPG.

9. Fiechter-Widemann, *Looking for water with EPER/HEKS*, Appendix hereafter.

10. Prélaz, *Linking Disaster Risk Management*.

11. This is another reference to the human development index triad.

Part VI: Strategies for Mitigating Water Poverty

What skills and personal qualities are necessary when approaching peoples whose customs and cultures are so different from ours? Can you also tell me about the causes and motives that led you to work for EPER?

Valentin Prélaz

Thank you for your renewed interest in the diaconal ministries of Switzerland's Protestant churches.

I spent a good part of my teen years in Africa, since my father was in charge of projects for the Swiss Department of Development and Cooperation (DDC).[12] I graduated from the French high school in Antananarivo (Madagascar) before coming back to Switzerland for college.

After this early schooling, I decided to begin studies at Bern University of Applied Sciences. Once I had earned my bachelor's degree in agronomy, forestry, and food sciences, I applied for humanitarian positions. For three years, between 2001 and 2003, I worked for the ICRC,[13] at first as the head of delegation in Angola, then as an agronomist in Afghanistan, and finally as a delegate in Liberia. These experiences left an indelible mark on me, I was so distressed by the violent things I had seen.

I felt I needed a career change. So I spent two years at the Swiss Centre for Agriculture Extension as an agronomist, then I was hired by Swiss Church Aid, where I still work. In the fall of 2010, I had an opportunity to specialize in climate-change issues and poverty at the EPFL, while keeping my job. For me, it was a chance to write a thesis in English entitled *Linking Disaster Risk Management, Climate Change and Poverty Reduction*.[14]

EFW

Was potable water one of your major concerns?

Valentin Prélaz

Certainly. But I will say right off that this issue cannot be dealt with in isolation, which is exactly what led me to broaden my interdisciplinary base. Today, the issue of climate change is absolutely central, especially to water.

It must be noted that populations subject to water stress do not always understand why it has been raining less over the past several years and more and more wells are going dry.

---

12. www.deza.ch.
13. ICRC stands for the International Committee of the Red Cross.
14. Prélaz, *Linking Disaster Risk Management*.

PART VI: STRATEGIES FOR MITIGATING WATER POVERTY

Educational efforts are becoming critical in this regard, which is why I suggested that Swiss Church Aid ought to arrange some training sessions on climate change. To my great joy, they were very successful.[15] As I explain in my thesis, it is this very area in which action by non-governmental organizations can be the most efficacious. NGOs actually have a harder time being effective on other, equally serious issues such as AIDS and poor governance.

I also suggested asking at-risk populations to consider taking their fate into their own hands and changing strategies. The new strategies are planned in courses taken by rural residents, people who depend entirely on the produce of their lands for subsistence.

EFW

It was in an attempt to understand what these strategy changes meant that I wanted to make the trip to southern Africa. During our first interview in July 2010, you told me that the people of Zimbabwe remained unconvinced of the need to give up their traditional flood irrigation method. You explained that Africans, in this case African women, also remained very attached to their custom of hand-carrying water from the river, despite the fact that this method is very hard work.

Valentin Prélaz

That is correct. I also told you about irrigation systems that are more sustainable than wells. Of those, we prefer the following four. First there is drip irrigation, which uses very little water or labor. Second comes pumping, which is especially appropriate during the dry season and is done in dried-up river beds to retrieve water less than two meters underground. Small dams are also used, which allow water to be saved and used after the rainy season. Finally, windmills used with boreholes are a well-known alternative.

I also think it is very important to suggest to the farmers that they develop a crop other than maize, which requires a great deal of water. We have to explain to them that a change in strategy is necessary and that by substituting millet for maize, they will save a lot of water. But on each of my official visits, I see far too little progress in this respect.

If you would like to know more about these strategies, you can take a look at page 6 of my thesis,[16] where I give a table showing the impact that drought and failed wells can have on humans and animals.

15. Prélaz indicates, "Between the 5th and the 9th of October 2010, HEKS/EPER along with Bread For All (BFA) conducted a Zimbabwe context analysis [. . .] and a Community Risk Assessment (CRA) in 2 rural villages in Matobo District [. . .]." Prélaz, *Linking Disaster Risk Management*, 3.

16. Ibid., 6.

Part VI: Strategies for Mitigating Water Poverty

EFW

Your study very clearly shows the dramatic consequences of a lack of water, when wells can no longer meet demand.

In this table, you systematically explain the increase in disease and mortality rates in both human beings and animals. You also show that famine and a decline in financial resources endanger social life which, if there are food and water shortages, will have to deal with a rise in crime, such as more theft and domestic violence.

Many people find this gloomy assessment discouraging.

What I saw was a joyful crowd that welcomed us with Zimbabwean songs and dances a few meters from Makhasa Dam. Then it fell silent to actively take part with all due seriousness in a sort of district assembly.

About a hundred men and women of the village had gathered outside. The agenda included a meeting with EPER's representatives—you and Juliana Manjengwe of Harare—and people from Christian Care, an NGO represented by Duduzile Sikosana. I learned there that this NGO was founded in 1967 by the Zimbabwe Council of Churches, and that it is one of the largest organizations working to ensure food security within the country.[17]

At this meeting, I was pleasantly surprised that women spoke as freely as the men, and the men listened respectfully to their contributions.

Valentin Prélaz

That was in fact one of the high points of my official visit to Zimbabwe. You probably remember that the topic of water was discussed there in two contexts, namely the farmers' concerns about irrigation, and sanitation issues.

EFW

Yes. After the meeting you even asked some of the participants to show me the dam that had been built by the English when Zimbabwe was still called Rhodesia. I saw that, unfortunately, it had received only very basic maintenance, but Christian Care had provided financial resources so that some of the pipes could be changed out and a siphon installed.

I also recall hearing some participants say that they were considering building latrines near their meeting place.

For me, this last point raised a lot of questions. Near the meeting place, I had seen a large brand-new building, which I was told was an enormous public toilet facility built by World Vision. I was curious to know why it was so little used by the local people.

---

17. Fiechter-Widemann, *Looking for Water with EPER/HEKS*. See appenix.

Part VI: Strategies for Mitigating Water Poverty

Valentin Prélaz

I think that for this sensitive subject of personal hygiene, the native local residents want to build this type of facility themselves using volunteers.

EFW

It is an eminently cultural problem, then. But I saw that the latrines made available to us were primitive. So it is essential to teach the public about hygiene and provide them with logistical resources.

In this respect, do you think that the UN's resolution of July 17, 2013[18] proclaiming November 19 as World Toilet Day will move this subject to the top of the political agenda for governments like Zimbabwe's?

Valentin Prélaz

I dare to hope so.

This issue of sanitation is an opportunity to clarify what is understood by "empowerment," as you brought up while introducing our interview.

In fact, the UN added the concept of the human-rights-based approach (HRBA) to it about a decade ago.

EFW

What is that?

Valentin Prélaz

The HRBA concept aims to facilitate dialogue between two categories of people, the Duty Bearers and the Rights Bearers.

On the one hand you have the authorities, the Duty Bearers, who must be made aware of their responsibilities; and on the other, the Rights Bearers, the residents. The former might be the national, provincial, or local government, and the latter rural societies, for example, those that are demanding better access to water and sanitation.

EFW

Can you tell me whether you were able to determine if HRBA could work in Zimbabwe?

---

18. Resolution "Sanitation for all."

Part VI: Strategies for Mitigating Water Poverty

Valentin Prélaz

I would say, first, it should be noted that in Zimbabwe and in rural areas, traditional customs prevail. For example, the traditional chiefs have the right to distribute land to someone who has the necessary skills and resources to cultivate it. The same goes for water. If a farmer wants to dig a well or drill a borehole, he has to get permission from the local government.

EFW

Yes, I was struck by the fact that a community president was present at each of your official visits. As a non-specialist observer, I had the feeling that the community members were taken seriously by the village chief. That fits in very well with an HRBA approach.

Valentin Prélaz

One might think so. You also probably remember that during each of these visits, the public was reminded of the articles of a set of regulations called a "constitution." So, obviously, the discussions had to do with the penalties to be meted out or incurred if these regulations were to be broken.

EFW

I was surprised by the term "constitution" chosen for this kind of legal text by the rural communities, for example the Centre Bambanani Ward. In fact it is not a legal text of public law determining the basic rights and powers of the public authorities. It exists simply to ensure that each villager owns a cow within a certain amount of time! I allude to this in my report entitled "Looking for water with EPER/HEKS."[19]

To keep things on a legal level, I noted the excellent associative structure developed in South Africa's Limpopo Province by the head of the Itireleng Development and Educational Project (hereafter IDEP), Matome Malatji.

You will probably agree with me that we find the concept of "Rights Bearers" we were just mentioning in the bylaws of the federation of rural associations called the Mopani Farmers Union, named after a municipality in Limpopo Province.[20] I cite

---

19. Fiechter-Widemann, *Looking for water with EPER/HEKS*.

20. Ibid. (See also report by Prélaz who indicates, "Today, less than 10 percent of households have piped water in their homes, 38 percent rely on communal taps for access to water and 19.5 percent on dams, rivers and springs for water [. . .]. Only few emerging small scale farmers rely on boreholes [. . .]. Prélaz," *Water Infrastructures Improvement-Project Proposal*, 1).

article 4 paragraphs 1-4 of the bylaws (also called a "constitution") entitled "Aims and Objectives."

- To build a voice of the emerging farmers in the district enabling farmers to access resources and information for local economic development—food security.
- To identify skills gaps of the farmers and lobby relevant institutions and government departments to empower farmers with such skills.
- To ensure that the needs of the farmer's communities are prioritized in the integrated development plans (IDPs) of both local and district municipalities to boost the local economy, food security and better livelihood for the poor farmers.
- To ensure the active participation of the farmers in the transformation land [sic] and agrarian policies such that they favor the poor farmers.[21]

But let me ask about the reality of the relationships between the local communities, that is, the "Rights Bearers" who approved the text of their "constitution," and the government. Does the latter in fact fulfill the "Duty Bearers" role?

I am posing the question because reading the following passage from your report left me with food for thought.

> Matome Malatji deplores the government's lack of willingness to grant access to land as it had promised. In ten years, only 3 percent of the land has been redistributed to the farmers. The former owners often burn the trees and break the pipes when they leave their property. This is what we will see in the field (see below, second visit).[22]

Valentin Prélaz

This is obviously a sensitive point. But you had also noted that the government is making an effort by "setting up a program to combat poverty in rural and disadvantaged regions."[23]

EFW

Any progress is good progress. In any case, I returned from the trip to southern Africa, particularly South Africa, convinced that a spark of vitality does exist in the poorest regions of Africa, and it deserves to be fed.

---

21. Ibid., 29.
22. Ibid., 22.
23. Ibid.

PART VI: STRATEGIES FOR MITIGATING WATER POVERTY

If I have understood correctly, you are no stranger to setting up "framework conditions" like the Mopani Farmers Union "constitution" in the rural communities we visited; and they were put in place as part of efforts to prevent hunger.

My 2011 report, which is appended, refers to this. Here is an excerpt.

> IDEP director Matome Malatji compels respect by his precise and resolute speech. At the beginning of the session, he recalled the history of IDEP, which was created in 1988 but has been especially active since 1994. IDEP has set up eight associations, which themselves are members of a federation called the Mopani Farmers Union (hereafter MFU). Its primary objective is to combat hunger and acquire the means to do so, which consist in particular of providing training and support to about 1220 farmers. This includes not only raising the rural population's awareness of climate and ecological challenges, but also offering training in effective water management and overseeing irrigation systems to improve the use of water, a scarce resource in this region due to low rainfall.
>
> IDEP and EPER organize workshops on a regular basis. IDEP also organizes farmers assemblies at which current events are discussed and problems identified. This attests to IDEP's "catalyst" philosophy, an approach that aims to make small farmers aware of their responsibilities and attentive to their own needs. This is what is known as "empowerment" or "People's Participatory Planning and Action" (PPPA).[24]

Valentin Prélaz

What you are saying is motivating in terms of leading other projects. But as you could see, the challenges, especially in Zimbabwe (where Helvetas, which specializes in water issues, has no presence), are enormous and these poor populations are dependent on international aid, especially the women.

EFW

Yes. I especially recall the discussion you had with EPER employee Juliana Manjengwe in Zimbabwe about the decision the Swiss parliament had just made with regard to its development aid.

You stressed the fact that any reduction decided upon by the Swiss legislature would directly affect the projects. In that particular instance, you were relieved to hear that Switzerland had even increased its contribution to development aid to raise it to 0.5 percent of gross national income.[25]

24. Ibid., 23.

25. The Swiss Department of Development and Cooperation indicates, "In February 2011, Parliament decided to increase its official development assistance (ODA) to 0.5 percent of gross national

PART VI: STRATEGIES FOR MITIGATING WATER POVERTY

Valentin Prélaz

That is correct.

EFW

It is time for us to end our talk. In my opinion, this first interview has shown that it is possible to give value to water, but that awareness of this value with an eye to effective management requires a long-term effort in connection with a demanding strategy.

An awareness of this vital resource's real worth is the *sine qua non* for meeting the goal.

So it is not a question of willingness. It is important to bring together many stakeholders, who must all be convinced of water's value. While both a community's leaders and its members must be counted among these, they will also often need outside expertise, and therefore short-, medium-, or long-term assistance. Such aid can come from NGOs such as EPER, which I will hereafter call donors. It comes at the cost of a real effort by both donors and recipients, for example, those we visited.

I stress that in order for an NGO to be able to act effectively in countries such as those of southern Africa, and to establish its credibility, especially with donors, it must be able to rely on capable employees not only to set up the conversations with the recipients, but to provide reports containing accurate data. I saw that for the most part, these reports were very well written by the indigenous residents. Was this "accountability," in the form of an ability to give an accounting of how the aid supplied was used? I am beginning to think so.

The fact remains that those who supply NGO funds must themselves be aware of water's value. I must concede that to understand this, a visit to countries facing water stress is an irreplaceable experience. Not only is it impossible to travel in the bush without water bottles; the unassuming accommodations also do not have running water. In fact, it is not rare to have to fetch water for cooking, flushing, and bathing from a tap located outside the building. Carrying these water supplies in large tubs is no picnic.

Your experience as an ICRC delegate in some of the most dangerous war zones on the planet, and your expertise in tropical agronomy, which you continue to expand on a regular basis, have probably given you all the tools you need for your job. EPER appreciates these qualities of yours.

---

income (GNI). This level was reached in 2015. Under the expenditure stabilisation programme decided by the Federal Council for the period from 2017 to 2019, Switzerland's ODA will be slightly lower according to current estimates, at around 0.48 percent of GNI. This remains short of the 0.7 percent target set by the UN and recognised by Switzerland." https://www.eda.admin.ch/deza/en/home/sdc/strategy/legal-bases/message-international-cooperation-2017-2020/fuenf-rahmenkredite.html.

PART VI: STRATEGIES FOR MITIGATING WATER POVERTY

Interfaith Dialogue on Water (Catholic and Muslim Perspectives)

Preamble

Making everyone aware of water's value was a central focus of the previous interview, which dealt at length with supervising water management and the relevant reports to be supplied by the recipients of development aid. In English, the term "accountability" is aptly used to signify this type of management oversight, whereas Canadian French speakers have translated it very well by *redevabilité*.

The value that should be attributed to water will also be at the heart of this next interview, but from a different perspective.

It is undeniable that, historically speaking, religious motives have played a considerable role in the problem of fresh water. That is why I wanted to create a fictitious interfaith dialogue between two people who spoke at the second W4W colloquium held in Geneva on March 20, 2012.

A virtual[26] interfaith dialogue between El Hassan bin Talal, Prince of Jordan©, and Dr. Christiana Peppard, Assistant Professor of Theology and Science at Fordham University in New York, moderated by Evelyne Fiechter-Widemann in 2013

Evelyne Fiechter-Widemann

Your Royal Highness, I am pleased to open this virtual interfaith dialogue with Dr. Christiana Peppard, an admirer of Jordan who has traveled in your beautiful country and published an article on the water of the Jordan River in 2013.[27]

I welcome you both to this unique encounter. Thank you for allowing me to moderate it.

At the W4W colloquium on March 20, 2012,[28] you both defended water as a mediator for peace and a guarantor of social ties, not only convincingly but also scathingly, one of you with the use of a video. The wealth of information in your presentations prompted me to suggest a virtual interview at this time, which seems to me to be an appropriate way to gain a better understanding of the real-world issues.

---

26. The adjective "virtual" requires an explanation here. It refers strictly to the technique of using an imaginary dialogue, not to any technical aspect in the modern sense of information technology. At the W4W colloquium held on March 20, 2012, Dr. Peppard spoke in person, while El Hassan bin Talal, Prince of Jordan, contributed via video conference. The purpose of the imaginary dialogue is to provide a synthesis of the two viewpoints.

© Important notice: HRH Prince El Hassan bin Talal of Jordan is the copyright holder of his contribution to the virtual interfaith dialogue.

27. Peppard, "Troubling Waters."

28. Peppard, *Water, Vital Need,* and El Hassan bin Talal, *Prince of Jordan.*

PART VI: STRATEGIES FOR MITIGATING WATER POVERTY

El Hassan bin Talal, Prince of Jordan

I am all the more willing to speak here given that I was a moderator at the World Conference of Religions for Peace. I was given the task of working with nine families of believers.[29] I should mention that I chaired the United Nations Secretary-General's Advisory Board on Water and Sanitation (UNSGAB),[30] following HRH Willem-Alexander of the Netherlands in that office.

Christiana Peppard

Religions and cultures are vast resources for considering how human societies have regarded water: what kind of thing it is, what sort of value it ought to have. One aspect of my work focuses especially on how water is regarded in Catholic social teaching (CST) in the present day, and how this is linked to theological and ethical commitments as well as practical implications.

EFW

As I listened to your presentations, it seemed to me that one of the main concerns for both of you was implementing mechanisms to ensure that the poor have resources for basic subsistence, with potable water being essential in this regard. Can you each say something in turn on this point?

Christiana Peppard

In my capacity as a Professor responsible for disseminating Catholic Social Teaching (CST), I offer a reminder that the Catholic Church endeavors to promote the concept of the "preferential option for the poor" to ensure that they have access to potable water when it often becomes too expensive or scarce for them.

I also stress the danger of media disinformation about the complex issue of potable water, as I mentioned at the W4W colloquium in March 2012. Indeed, I was not the only one to have been surprised by the announcement in the press at the time that part of the Millennium Development Goals had been met, specifically point 7c. This was far too optimistic, since the indicators selected not only included industrialized areas but also weighted urban areas more heavily than rural ones.[31]

---

29. Ibid.
30. www.unsgab.org.
31. Peppard, *Water, Vital Need*.

Part VI: Strategies for Mitigating Water Poverty

El Hassan bin Talal, Prince of Jordan

I welcome your reaction to this announcement, which in my opinion is not likely to serve the cause of the most destitute. To use the example of the Middle East, recent decades have propelled the issue of potable water to the forefront of social concerns. I would like to share these numbers, which speak volumes.

> In the Arab world, 300 million people may have to live with only 500 m³ per person per year by 2025. This amount is below the water poverty threshold, which is usually considered to be 1000 m³ per person per year.[32]

EFW

Of course this represents the amount of water available per person in general—that is, reserves, not the amount that is accessible and actually used, which in France for example is about 150 liters of water per day and 55 m³ per year, while residents of a country such as Jordan must get along on 100 liters per day.

Christiana Peppard

In recent years, people living in the industrialized Western countries have come to learn a bit more about water stress and scarcity, due to problems of aquifer depletion and drought in their own regions. However, it is the case that many people are not well aware of their watersheds, or the infrastructure that facilitates their access to water, or global problems pertaining to water. Unfortunately this kind of knowledge often comes only after a water-related tragedy of significant proportions.

El Hassan bin Talal, Prince of Jordan

The problem is that even the affected populations are not yet truly aware of the many factors that decrease the availability of potable water. For example, they are often unaware of the extent to which population growth and urban development will make the need to change our water-related behavior increasingly urgent. However, scholars in the Islamic world do have the tools to meet these new challenges, as evidenced by the studies in the excellent anthology entitled *Water Management in Islam*.[33]

---

32. El Hassan bin Talal, *Prince of Jordan*.
33. Faruqui, et al., *La gestion de l'eau selon l'Islam*.

PART VI: STRATEGIES FOR MITIGATING WATER POVERTY

EFW

This is indeed a valuable resource for understanding how Islam can help clarify concepts and build bridges between different religious beliefs, which play a decisive role in such a delicate and complex issue as water management.

The book's authors are themselves from different cultural and religious backgrounds. They gathered at a colloquium in Amman in 1998 as representatives of three institutions: the International Development Research Centre (IDRC)—a Canadian public corporation—, the International Water Resources Association (IWRE), and the Inter-Islamic Network on Water Resources Demand and Management (INWRDAM).[34]

This document highlights the fact that even though "the Prophet [. . .] discouraged the selling of water,"[35] scholars of Islam suggest following the 1992 Dublin Statement's recommendations that water be considered an economic good. They stipulate that water must certainly be regarded as a gift from God, and therefore has no price, but there is a possible exception to this principle. In fact, if water is treated and therefore represents the result of work, the person who did the work must be compensated for his labor:

> [. . .] treated water can be traded because the organization responsible for the treatment has spent money and invested work in it (added value or reward for work). This ruling can encompass water from treatment plants, water privately transported and stored, and any water to obtain which work, infrastructure, and knowledge have been invested.[36]

Christiana Peppard

So now we are touching on the thorny issue of knowing whether a price can be put on fresh water, and whether its distribution can be delegated to the private sector. For its part, the Catholic Church insists that water cannot be solely a commodity that would be controlled for the benefit of a few to the detriment of many.[37] It recognizes, however, that although private entities must not be excluded in principle from providing water distribution services, they must "meet the requirements of a common good."[38]

---

34. Ibid., 7 and 195.
35. Ibid., 132.
36. Ibid.
37. Peppard indicates, "[. . .] fresh water is a 'good of creation' that is meant for the benefit of all. This means that it must be shared equitably around the world, and it must be preserved for future generations. By extension fresh water cannot be treated primarily or exclusively as a commodity. It cannot be controlled for the benefit of a few at the expense of many." Peppard, *"Water, Vital Need."*
38. Ibid, n5.

Part VI: Strategies for Mitigating Water Poverty

In a letter sent to the 2003 World Water Forum, the Holy See stated that water is one of these common goods:

> [. . .] the PCJP [Pontifical Council for Justice and Peace] expressed great hesitation about the unrestrained commodification of fresh water, stating that water is precisely a "common good of humankind" under the principle of the universal destination of the goods of creation, and adding that "the few, with the means to control, cannot destroy or exhaust this resource, which is destined for the use of all."[39]

El Hassan bin Talal, Prince of Jordan

I can only approve. Islam also considers water to be a common good.

EFW

Having heard your views, I will take this opportunity of again bringing up the excellent book you mentioned, *Water Management in Islam,* which goes into this topic in detail. I think it is important to quote a relevant passage.

> Water is first and foremost a social good in Islam—a gift from God and a part of, and necessary for, sustaining all life.
>
> Water belongs to the community as a whole—no individual literally owns water.
>
> The first priority for water use is access to drinking water of acceptable quantity and quality to sustain human life, and every human being has the right to this basic water requirement.
>
> The second and third priorities for water are for domestic animals and for irrigation.
>
> Humankind is the steward of water on earth.[40]

But one thing is bothering me and I will now ask you both: Is it possible to reconcile the views of the Christian and Muslim faiths, which express great reluctance to put water under the influence of market mechanisms, even in the face of the urgent real-world situation as evoked by the striking numbers for MENA[41] countries as mentioned a moment ago?

---

39. Peppard, "Fresh Water and Catholic Social Teaching," 338.
40. Faruqui, et al., *La gestion de l'eau selon l'Islam,* 53.
41. MENA is the acronym for Middle East and North Africa.

Part VI: Strategies for Mitigating Water Poverty

Should not the predicted increase in water stress be an incentive for politicians everywhere in the world, regardless of their religious faith, to create an effective water-management system? This implies huge financial investments, mainly for infrastructure, including facilities to treat wastewater for reuse.

It is said that nearly 200 billion dollars will need to be invested to provide universal access to water by 2025.[42]

El Hassan bin Talal, Prince of Jordan

This view is in fact clearly present in Muslim communities. Here is their stance, as I stated it in March 2012.

> Although water belongs to no one, water suppliers' costs must be covered. At the same time, it is up to the governments to ensure a fair relationship between the cost and the service.[43]

With regard to wastewater treatment, Faruqui mentions a 1978 decision by Saudi Arabia's Council of Learned Islamic Scholars, which says,

> Treated wastewater can theoretically be reused [. . .], provided that it presents no health risk.[44]

Christiana Peppard

Here, fairness is the key value for guiding a policy of fair water prices. This point was extensively discussed at the 2012 W4W colloquium, particularly in the presentations given by Emmanuel de Lutzel[45] and Paul Dembinski.[46]

Ethical forms of regulation will be crucial for pricing water. As HRH pointed out, for any water system, there is need to cover the costs associated with the treatment and provision of water. But who pays? And why?

Paying for infrastructure is often considered to be different from charging for water itself, which many traditions understand as a gift from God or an ethical entitlement due to each person. In fact the human right to water is a notion that again centralizes some of these debates.

Many scholars and advocates—myself included—are committed to the idea of fairness, but what that means in practice is highly variable. I advocate the importance of culturally sensitive understandings of "fairness" when considering water prices.

---

42. Tignino and Yared, "La commercialisation et la privatisation," 160.
43. El Hassan bin Talal, *Prince of Jordan*, and Siler, *Water Management in Monotheistic Religions*.
44. Faruqui, et al., *La gestion de l'eau selon l'Islam*, 33.
45. De Lutzel, *"Droit à l'eau [The Right to Water]."*
46. Dembinski, *"Eau, besoin vital [Water, Vital Need]."*

Part VI: Strategies for Mitigating Water Poverty

For example: What amounts of water should be provided for free, and what amount (or for what purposes) should be under the domain of the market? What institutions are responsible for providing clean, potable water? And since water tends to be a natural monopoly, are there ways to protect against corruption in water management?

EFW

Your thesis concerning the finiteness of water also speaks to me.

You mention at one point in your essay that even though the market and technology have often had a favorable role in meeting water and food needs, it has now become necessary to change our current unsustainable behavior due to the finite nature of water.

> In sum, while the assumed (but not ubiquitously proven) efficiency of the market may have some kind of place in achieving sustainability in key resources, and technology will provide important types of advances in those domains, neither the free market nor technological innovation (nor some combination of the two, unfettered from an ethical framework) will solve the problems of water management and distribution.[47]

I would like to explain that this need to promote sustainability was clearly defended by the five hundred experts who met in Dublin in January 1992, who laid down four principles in their statement for the June 1992 Rio conference.

I devoted a few lines to these principles earlier (Part II, Chapter III, no. 2). As a reminder, they addressed water's fragility, the need to have users participate in its management, and the importance of women's role in this area. The need to prevent water wasting by agreeing to consider it an economic good was a key argument.

El Hassan bin Talal, Prince of Jordan

Allow me to put in a word for the principles I recommend, summarized by the acronym "WISE." You will find the details in the proceedings of the 2012 W4W colloquium.

We must note how greatly inequalities in water access have increased in the MENA region in recent decades. Some countries are water- and energy-poor, while others enjoy ready access to these two resources. If these countries were to cooperate to find a strategy for improving water management, with energy and technological innovation playing a key role, such a wise path could ensure peace.[48]

---

47. Peppard, "Fresh Water and Catholic Social Teaching."
48. El Hassan bin Talal, *Prince of Jordan*.

PART VI: STRATEGIES FOR MITIGATING WATER POVERTY

EFW

It goes without saying that water's value is central to Islam.[49]

Dr. Peppard, when you say that water is *sine qua non* and *sui generis*,[50] you are emphasizing that it is an essential condition for the very existence of human beings and the ecosystem, and there is no substitute for it.

So your purpose is to make it clear that water is *universally* central.

If I have understood you correctly, you give it a universal ethical value. I myself subscribe to this concept of an ethical value for water, but in a more narrow sense, namely only insofar as covering essential needs is concerned. This amounts to saying that I believe in the ethical value of the potable water necessary to survival, but any other water—fresh or not—is an *adiaphoron* in the sense used by Calvin, as I explained in a chapter of my dissertation.[51] With regard to water that is pleasant to drink, or needed for hygiene or any other use such as agriculture, industry, or navigation, it is our human attitude toward it that must be ethical, given our role as responsible stewards who must answer for the proper use of these assets.[52]

This leads me to ask both of you what you think of the UN's adoption of the new human right to water in 2010.

El Hassan bin Talal, Prince of Jordan

I believe that this predicate adds value and importance to water. It shows that governments should concern themselves with making improved water management a priority—which implies that some of them will need to ask for help with technology and human resources if they run into difficulties, and that those asked should respond positively.[53]

EFW

And you, Dr. Peppard?

---

49. Ibid., no. 9.
50. Peppard, *Water, Vital Need and Global Justice*.
51. See Part V, Chapter II, no. 2.2.
52. Parable of the talents as told in Matt 25:14–30.
53. El Hassan bin Talal, *Prince of Jordan*.

Part VI: Strategies for Mitigating Water Poverty

Christiana Peppard

I agree with what HRH has just expressed. The language of human rights provides a moral vocabulary for considering water; it helps to make visible this problem of water access and fundamental human needs.[54]

But I confess that I still have some questions about how effective the articulation of this right will be in achieving the goals of sufficient clean, fresh water and sanitation for all. There is still the question of what institutions or entities are empowered to provide water; who pays for the services associated with water; and whether unethical behaviors can be avoided. As important, too, is the fact that many cultures and religions regard water in very different kinds of ways. While most agree that water is of course essential for life—that is, it is universal—it is also clear that cultural and religious understandings of water are not uniform. That is, there is much cultural diversity regarding how water is understood and what values it is seen to carry. The human right to water attempts to speak in a universally accessible moral language, and that is important. But it is not a perfect language, and it does not provide a road map for meeting the goals contained therein.

El Hassan bin Talal, Prince of Jordan

It is made even more complex by cultural and religious issues.

EFW

In this regard, I think it would be useful to point out that the book you quoted, *Water Management in Islam,* makes an important contribution to the water issue, especially where the role of women is concerned.

It mentions that people living in MENA[55] countries, who are facing an actual scarcity of water, must try to innovate both technically and in the cultural and religious realms, especially in terms of how women are seen. In order for the female half of the human race to have a substantial voice in water management, the cultural and religious barriers that often keep women from acquiring knowledge and expertise absolutely must be removed: this is a matter of survival. I note that the authors of this book insist on the need to

> conduct a wide-ranging pilot study to integrate religious elements into a comprehensive programme of public education and awareness projects to encourage conservation and reuse [of water], with particular emphasis on women

---

54. Peppard, "Fresh Water and Catholic Social Teaching," 341 n46.
55. MENA is the acronym for Middle East and North Africa.

and girls, who are often left out of such programmes because their religious learning does not occur in mosques or schools.[56]

El Hassan bin Talal, Prince of Jordan

I hasten to stress the importance of pilot projects now underway that aim to involve—in addition to the domestic sector—the agricultural, industrial and institutional sectors as well, with this last assuming responsibility for the difficult reforms to be undertaken. Here I am again making reference to Faruqui.[57]

Christiana Peppard

Our exchange indicates specific points of connection between water-related values in Islam and Catholic social teaching. This is a very promising and fruitful area for further reflection and conversation. How might such values—of fairness, respect for others, respect for creation as a gift from God—be brought into discourse on water management? This is an important question and challenge for scholars, religious people, politicians, water managers, and development experts.

EFW

Another participant from the 2012 colloquium, Professor Laurence Boissons de Chazournes, would probably agree with you. She feels that,

> [. . .] promoting the right to water in international human rights law helps shape an egalitarian discourse about access to water.[58]

There is no doubt that this overview of the values you both promote has been all too brief.

But I am convinced that the quality of both of your presentations at the W4W colloquium in March 2012 will likely encourage an approach grounded in the *value* of water and in *values*—one that is often difficult to imagine in scientific works, a point stressed by the authors of the anthology *Water Management in Islam*, which I will cite once again here in the words of Professor Asit K. Biswas, one of the co-authors of *The Singapore Water Story*.[59]

> However, examining values is not easy. Most scientists and even development professionals avoid examining religion or values in the context of their work

---

56. Faruqui, et al., *La gestion de l'eau selon l'Islam*, 56.
57. Ibid., 57.
58. Boisson de Chazournes, *"Eau, besoin vital [Water, Vital Need]."*
59. Tortajada, Cecilia, et al. *The Singapore Water Story*.

to avoid discord and keep discussion "objective." However, where science, development, and values intersect, the issue cannot be avoided.[60]

Participants in the 1998 Amman colloquium added that as a prerequisite to discussion, a consensus must be found that would aim to perceptibly demonstrate.

> [. . .] that followers of different belief systems have much to learn from each other.[61]

Christiana Peppard

I absolutely share your point of view, as my study on Jordan proves.[62]

EFW

So water lets us discover the richness of each of our cultures.

It is important to state that there is no lack of international platforms for reflecting on water, such as the annual Water Week in Stockholm[63] or biennial Water Week in Singapore,[64] to help anyone who is interested gain a better understanding of the complexities of water issues. On the religious level, we should note that for over ten years the World Council of Churches has been making efforts to educate its members about water as a gift from God, and it has set up an "Ecumenical Water Network."[65]

Your Royal Highness, Dr. Peppard, thank you for this productive exchange on today's potable water challenges, and for having both noted the central element of human love, as represented by HIMA[66] for Muslims and the love of one's neighbor for Christians.[67]

Mini-Conclusion

European writer Antoine de Saint-Exupéry, who had never known thirst before his plane crash, was forced to test the limits of human endurance in the desert.[68]

---

60. Faruqui, et al., *La gestion de l'eau selon l'Islam*, 8–9.
61. Ibid., 9.
62. Peppard, "Troubling Waters."
63. www.worldwaterweek.org.
64. http://www.siww.com.sg.
65. http://eau.oikoumene.org.
66. From Akkadian, a language spoken over five thousand years ago. See El Hassan bin Talal, Prince of Jordan, *Water, Vital Need and Global Justice*.
67. Peppard, "Fresh Water and Catholic Social Teaching, 336 n29."
68. De Saint-Exupéry, *Terre des hommes*, 149.

Part VI: Strategies for Mitigating Water Poverty

Already in the time of Abraham, desert peoples were daily facing a scarcity of water, and they learned how to live under these specific conditions. In my opinion it is important for them to have a voice in any discussion on potable water management. Their wisdom can help guide other peoples that have more recently come face-to-face with water stress issues. They have in fact been thinking for centuries about the laws needed to ensure fair access to the vital resource of water.

As an example, consider the people of Oman and the magnificent *aflaj* irrigation systems they invented over four thousand years ago, based on the concept of water as a common good.

Here I will again cite *Water Management in Islam*. I find the following passage to be promising as far as encouraging intercultural and interfaith dialogue.

> There is no contradiction between what Islam says about water management and the emerging international consensus on the issue, as reflected by recent accords such as the Dublin Principles[69] or the UN Water Convention.[70] In fact, the Islamic water management principles are not unique. Some of the same principles could be derived by studying other faiths, their holy books, and the lives of their prophets. As one delves into Islam, one encounters values common not only to the other two Abrahamic religions, Christianity and Judaism, but also to many other world-views and religions. But clean water has always been scarce in the Middle East where Islam emerged and where for many centuries most Muslims lived, whereas water has only recently begun to become scarce in regions such as Europe [. . .]. Hence, the rules governing water management are probably more specific and detailed in Islam than in most other religions.[71]

I confess that I have great respect for these desert peoples in general, but especially for those I have met personally, whether in Jordan, Ethiopia, Zimbabwe, or South Africa.

In their company, I have begun to understand what water really represents as a vital need.

To me, the image of the well seems to be a key element supporting the idea of the ethical value of water needed for survival. In particular, it supplies a clue to the sensitive and controversial question of what price to assign or not to assign to water. We must remember that residents of arid regions have already accepted, some hundreds of years ago, the concept of the market value of the well—with the counterbalancing idea that its owner was to distribute his water at no charge to anyone who had none and risked dying of thirst without this gift.[72]

---

69. Dublin Statement.

70. I believe this refers to the UN Convention on the Law of the Non-navigational Uses of International Watercourses, which entered into effect on August 17, 2014.

71. Faruqui, et al., *La gestion de l'eau selon l'Islam*, 58.

72. Faruqui, Naser, et al., indicate "The Prophet once said, 'he who purchases the Ruma Well

The image brings out the values of humanity, solidarity, and compassion. It truly sets apart that which is necessary to life. It enables us to postulate that the quality and quantity of water that has an ethical value will not necessarily be free, except to those for whom it is impossible to satisfy this vital need "here and now."

In any case, I recall the wise men of the East who, observing the development of the phenomenon of water, saw the need to "think" a system of water pricing.

> The success of water pricing as a water demand management initiative will depend on promoting 'a new cultural appreciation that water is a limited resource for which people of the area must pay.'"[73]

How much should water consumers pay, and how? How will institutions fulfill their regulatory role?

That is the challenge and, not to mince words, the stakes are war and peace, as with any radical change dictated by circumstances. As HRH Prince Hassan reminded us in March 2012, international cooperation is required.

> If we are wise, a path to peace may open before us. For that to happen, we must transcend our geographical boundaries and seek to cooperate in order to find a solution in the form of a strategy for the future.[74]

My next guest, Ambassador Benoît Girardin, will also invite us to cross borders and cooperate internationally.

Interview with a Swiss Diplomat: "Thinking" Dry Wells

Preamble to the Interview with Ambassador Benoît Girardin

When "thinking" the value of water, we must include not only the visible water on the earth's surface, but also and most especially the invisible water in aquifers, which by definition are underground.

This topic had already been brought up during the question-and-answer session at the first W4W colloquium in 2011,[75] and was comprehensively and systematically revisited by Ambassador Benoît Girardin at the third W4W colloquium on March 19, 2013.[76]

The interview I wish to conduct with him has two purposes.

---

and offers its water to Muslims free of charges will be granted paradise." Faruqui, et al., *La gestion de l'eau selon l'Islam*, 132 (Ahmad 524, source: *Hadith Encyclopedia*). This implies that wells and their water can be traded.

73. Ibid., 136.
74. El Hassan bin Talal, *Prince of Jordan*.
75. *Proceedings of the First W4W Interdisciplinary Colloquium*. Appendix 5a hereafter.
76. Girardin, *Fair Management of Transboundary Aquifers*.

Part VI: Strategies for Mitigating Water Poverty

Its first aim is to reveal vulnerability, which has not yet been sufficiently taken into consideration by either global citizens or politicians. The second is to ask the ethical question of how governments will collaborate with regard to a vital resource that may exist beneath multiple countries and so becomes the object of shared responsibility that must be negotiated together.[77]

Evelyne Fiechter-Widemann

Mr. Ambassador, I welcome you, not only as one of the founding members of W4W but also as the current president of a private university in Rwanda, Africa.

I cannot help but be surprised by the variety and heavy demands of your new career as a young retiree from Swiss diplomacy. Your duties at PIASS, the Protestant Institute of Arts and Social Sciences in Butare, in addition to those of your position as a Lecturer at the Geneva School of Diplomacy and International Relations, require you not only to travel frequently, but also to continually update your knowledge. And you delight in sharing it! The proof of this lies in the publication in 2012 and 2014 of an essay on "Ethics in Politics,"[78] and in your recent research on the issue of transboundary aquifers.

Your training at the Faculty of Theology, leading to a doctorate in 1977, must have developed your need and desire to be of service to others.

Benoît Girardin

If I can help clarify the "global water ethic" concept that you are advancing by applying it to groundwater, I will be delighted.

EFW

Thank you for being willing to answer my questions. Not only did your talk last March 19 about the wealth of potable water buried beneath the earth's crust amaze me, it also made me want to know more. Can you start us off by setting the stage?

Benoît Girardin

With pleasure, especially since these ever-so-precious reserves of potable water are being endangered with every day that passes because many political players are unfamiliar with them.

---

77. Dermange indicates, "Natural resources are global or shared, therefore their liabilities must also be subject to shared management, and this becomes a question of ethics." Dermange, *"Le pôle justice sociale [The Social Justice Focus]."*

78. Girardin, *Ethics in Politics.*

Part VI: Strategies for Mitigating Water Poverty

EFW

You're scaring me! Is it too late to do anything about it?

Benoît Girardin

No, of course not, but it's important to size up the challenge.

At the third W4W colloquium on March 19, 2013, I wanted to draw people's attention to the fact that we still have a very inappropriate understanding of aquifers' true limits when it comes to meeting the vital need for potable water, whether for humans, animals, plants, or the ecosystem in general. Things have gone on as if these were unlimited reserves with guaranteed quality, and the political framework was ill-prepared to help us face the situation.

In fact, the first interstate convention concerning an aquifer was not recorded until 1950. It was signed by Luxembourg and Germany because government officials and some civil society groups had become aware of the consequences that building a dam in Luxembourg might have for the aquifer.[79]

EFW

You have honed your skills as a negotiator in the international arena over a long period of time, and I see them shining through here. To begin with, though, could you explain to me what a transboundary aquifer is? Is this some amount of water that is found underground beneath two countries, or even several political entities?

Benoît Girardin

Exactly. But what is also important to remember is that this groundwater is especially vulnerable because it is accessible via springs and by pumping. It is all the more fragile because those who use it are only vaguely aware (or feign ignorance) of the risk of exhausting this resource and preventing its regeneration by excessively polluting it. Lapalisse would say that if the aquifer is not systematically replenished, it will run out.

EFW

That reminds me of the shock I felt in January 2010 when I discovered the Azraq reed marsh in northern Jordan. This tiny stretch of water is the remnant of a vast wetland. Upon inquiry, I learned that the causes of this ecological drama date back to the 1960s,

---

79. Girardin, *"Gestion juste des aquifères transfrontaliers [Fair Management of Transboundary Aquifers]."*

when unlimited pumping from the Azraq aquifer began in order to meet the needs of Amman and Irbid, which were growing by leaps and bounds then and still are today.

So the oasis has ceased to exist. All that remains today is a pale shadow of its past splendor when birds came by the thousands to drink, though it is still a tourist destination managed by the Royal Society for the Conservation of Nature."[80] I do need to clarify that this is not a transboundary aquifer, being in the heart of Jordan. However, I find the example relevant, especially because it shows the authorities' inability, as things now stand, to act against those who pump water illegally.

Benoît Girardin

This really is an instance where it was too late to recharge a water area to protect it, and where there is an obvious lack of governance.

So you can easily understand what I want to convey, which is that the water ethic, which you state is "global," must include water in both its surface and underground expanses, throughout time, and planet-wide.

EFW

Jordan's case is certainly not unique. Tell me, is the international community just standing by with its arms folded?

Benoît Girardin

I have to say that, for the moment, results are very modest. The current trend is to manage the natural resource of water in the context of a territory defined by political boundaries, even though it does go beyond those boundaries—but invisibly.

In the summary of my talk, you can find a few significant dates that speak for themselves. The issue was first broached about sixty years ago, but it was not until December 2008 that the UN General Assembly passed a resolution to protect aquifers, when it signed nineteen articles that had been developed by UNESCO's International Hydrological Programme and the UN International Law Commission and were intended to provide a framework for managing transboundary aquifers."[81]

---

80. http://www.rscn.org.

81. Girardin, *"Gestion juste des aquifères transfrontaliers."*; and Resolution of the United Nations on the Law of Transboundary Aquifers.

PART VI: STRATEGIES FOR MITIGATING WATER POVERTY

EFW

I note that only bilateral treaties were made between 1950[82] and 1978.[83] I also see that on a multilateral level, the May 21, 1997 UN Convention on the Law of the Non-navigational Uses of International Watercourses[84] wisely included the aquifer issue in article 2a.[85] However, this agreement did not enter into effect until August 17, 2014.

Benoît Girardin

So you can see that Switzerland and France have played something of a pioneering role in this area with the January 1, 1978, agreement between the Republic and Canton of Geneva and the Upper Savoy *(Haute-Savoie)* Prefecture.[86] Truth to tell, a dire situation was developing. The aquifer was threatened with depletion, which "prompted the attempt to reach an agreement to preserve it."[87] In fact, "the aquifer's level had dropped by seven meters, and one-third of the entire layer of water had disappeared in twenty years."[88]

For legal scholars and publicists,[89] in particular, it can be interesting to note that the sacrosanct principle of sovereignty was called into question and limited by the realities of the situation, and later "thanks to patiently built trust."[90] When the 1978 agreement had to be revised, the Genevan and French governments accepted a real institutional change. They delegated authority to local government entities. For the Republic and Canton of Geneva, this was SIG.[91] For France it was three border-area communities, namely the Annemasse Regional Metropolitan Area Community, the Community of Geneva-Area Municipalities, and the Municipality of Viry.[92]

---

82. Girardin, *"Gestion juste des aquifères transfrontaliers."*

83. Ibid.

84. Convention on the Law of the Non-navigational Uses of International Watercourses.

85. Ibid., article 2(a) reads, "'Watercourse'" means a system of surface waters and groundwaters constituting by virtue of their physical relationship a unitary whole and normally flowing into a common terminus."

86. *Arrangement relatif à la protection, à l'utilisation et à la réalimentation de la nappe souterraine franco-suisse du Genevois.*

87. Girardin, *"Gestion juste des aquifères transfrontaliers."*

88. Ibid.

89. *Le petit Larousse illustré* reads, "A legal scholar specializing in public law." *Le petit Larousse illustré*, 877.

90. Girardin, *"Gestion juste des aquifères transfrontaliers."*

91. SIG is the French acronym for the Geneva Industrial Services, which is in charge of supplying water and electricity.

92. Girardin, *"Gestion juste des aquifères transfrontaliers,"* and the *Convention relative à la protection, à l'utilisation, à la réalimentation et au suivi de la nappe souterraine franco-suisse du Genevois.*

PART VI: STRATEGIES FOR MITIGATING WATER POVERTY

EFW

As many Genevans probably are, I was unaware that water was such an issue in French-speaking Switzerland and the neighboring part of France. The presence of Lake Geneva blinds us to it!

Benoît Girardin

Let's not forget that the lake does provide part of the city of Geneva's supply. Yet outside our own region, the stakes of managing transboundary aquifers in the rest of the world are much higher and more serious.

Other examples show this too, and it is worth sharing them here. Of course I chose to mention only four of the 273 aquifers counted by UNESCO,[93] but those I selected seemed to me to be the most representative. First, I looked at the Guarani aquifer, which lies beneath Brazil, Argentina, Uruguay, and Paraguay and has a capacity of 40,000 km³. While these four countries did sign an international agreement in 2010, unfortunately it is relatively general and difficult to implement.

We can also mention the vast Nubian sandstone aquifer system that connects Egypt, Sudan, Libya, and Chad. It has been the subject of some agreements between the relevant countries. For the moment, none has been reached for the Iullemeden aquifer underlying Mali, Niger, and Nigeria. This particular water source cannot easily be recharged and is being rapidly depleted. Another overused aquifer is located in the Punjab between Pakistan and India.

EFW

I have a question about Lake Chad, which you were just mentioning in the context of the Nubian aquifer. Is it not at a double disadvantage, since the lake itself has lost an enormous amount of surface area in a few years?

At least, that is what is stated in the 2003 *Atlas mondial de l'eau*, which provides some interesting data.[94] It talks about a project of unprecedented scope in this region that would involve "partly altering the course of a tributary of the Ubangi, a large river in the Central African Republic, to transfer its water into a tributary of the Chari River by means of canal nearly 300 km long."[95]

---

93. Girardin, *"Gestion juste des aquifères transfrontaliers."*
94. Diop and Recacewicz, *Atlas mondial de l'eau*, 61.
95. Ibid.

Part VI: Strategies for Mitigating Water Poverty

Benoît Girardin

So there are possible solutions to help us confront this worrisome reality. You know how vulnerable these regions are, though, especially due to geopolitical tensions and the associated wars. As mentioned in the report you just cited,

> [t]his replenishment of the lake cannot happen, however, without the agreement of both the Republic of the Congo and the Democratic Republic of the Congo, which are downstream along the Ubangi. Saving Lake Chad could be an opportunity for increased regional cooperation . . . or a source of renewed conflict.[96]

In fact, we have inherited a vision of national sovereignty that is too uncompromising.

EFW

Yes, it is that famous American doctrine of Harmon's that I mentioned earlier[97] while discussing the selfish use of water. It seems still to have some adherents, though in the end the United States gave it up.

But for a more optimistic view of the issue, I wonder if the UN General Assembly's proclamation of the "International Year of Water Cooperation" in 2013 actually encouraged collaboration between countries. What do you think?

Benoît Girardin

I'm sure it did, even if it was just "a drop in the ocean," if I may be permitted the expression!

EFW

Now I would like to talk with you a bit about some ethical considerations, which you also mentioned in your report.

One passage in particular speaks to me. It concerns countries that make a mockery of their responsibilities, for example, by pulling large amounts of water from a transboundary aquifer with impunity, or even polluting it. In this way they seriously damage the resource, paying no heed to the "polluter pays" rule about which Professor Anne Petitpierre-Sauvain spoke at the first W4W colloquium on March 22, 2011.[98]

---

96. Ibid.
97. See Part III, Section II, Chapter II, no. 3.4.
98. Petitpierre-Sauvain, "*Rôle et portée du principe du pollueur-payeur [The Role and Reach of the 'Polluter Pays' Principle]*.

PART VI: STRATEGIES FOR MITIGATING WATER POVERTY

Benoît Girardin

This is exactly the kind of behavior that the 1997 UN Convention on the Law of the Non-navigational Uses of International Watercourses is intended to punish.

EFW

So let's come back to one international agreement that you mention in detail in your report, namely the one concerning the aquifer in the Geneva region. I have almost concluded that you are elevating the procedure set up in 2007 to the level of a real model for integrated water resources management. In your opinion, what are its main virtues?

Benoît Girardin

It's a model to the extent that both parties recognized their shared responsibility to the future and to sustainability. They chose a pragmatic approach and applied it all the way down to the level of managing the details, and they accepted limits on their national sovereignty. The proof of this is that bilateral supervision, that is, mutual accountability,[99] was put in place. For the details, I refer you to the document of March 19, 2013.[100]

EFW

Then do you think that this procedure and this type of limited sovereignty could be a source of inspiration in managing other aquifers throughout the world?

Benoît Girardin

I think we could indeed be satisfied if the political authorities responsible for the use of groundwater were to choose the methodology used for the Geneva-area aquifer as a frame of reference.

But I would like to say a few more words to stress two points relating to fairness and governance.

For me, one criterion for "equitable and reasonable use of the aquifer resource" could be frugality. This criterion would encourage the countries to see to it that "the volumes used do not exceed the recharge volumes."[101]

---

99. *Redevabilité* in French. See Petitpierre-Sauvin, "Rôle et portée du principe pollueur-payeur dans la gestion de l'eau."
100. Girardin, *"Gestion juste des aquifères transfrontaliers."*
101. Ibid.

Part VI: Strategies for Mitigating Water Poverty

Of course, good governance is necessary to ensure that this resource is used frugally. This could be achieved by bilateral monitoring of the implementation of intergovernmental agreements concerning transboundary aquifers.

To be clear, in my opinion this type of monitoring of aquifer management turns out to be necessary both in the specific case of France and Geneva, and in the world at large. In the first case it can operate in a bilateral mode. In the second, multilateral or regional arbitration could be used to keep "survival of the fittest" in check when it seems likely to prevail. Consequently,

> [i]t may prove to be wise to turn to an independent multilateral or regional third party that is involved beginning with the joint evaluation of steps taken and risks.[102]

Obviously, as with all questions of social justice, the many different geographical configurations are not the only factors that will play a role; there will of course also be political, economic, social, and cultural aspects to consider.

EFW

In this regard, I think it is relevant to mention the case of South Africa, where a severe water shortage is expected due to accelerating urbanization and a population explosion. In my opinion, this country ought to have in hand the requisite institutional tools for peaceful management of the Karoo aquifer, which lies beneath the desert of the same name (Karoo means "land of thirst") and is shared with Lesotho. This resource was recently discovered through work done by UNESCO.

Benoît Girardin

So, like me, you have noticed the enormous need of effective governance of aquifers' waters.

EFW

Yes, and I even think that they give us some hope for this precious natural resource's future. It is important to keep in mind that these transboundary aquifers have given jurists and hydrogeologists an opportunity to work together to "create a common language in the formulation of new sets of laws on water resources. This has resulted in a concrete example of efficient cooperation between the bodies of the UN System,"[103] culminating in the Law on Transboundary Aquifers that the UN General Assembly

---

102. Ibid.
103. http://www.unesco.org/water/new/aquifères_transfrontaliers.shtml, p. 2.

adopted by consensus on December 11, 2008, in resolution A/RES/124. The UN documentation lauds this resolution as

> [...] a concrete step forward towards the peaceful sharing of groundwater resources. Until today there was no instrument of international law that could provide a complete set of recommendations and guidelines for the sustainable and peaceful management of transboundary aquifers.[104]

Benoît Girardin

To add to your remark about the legal aspect, it seems vital, especially for aquifers, that principles or "codes of ethics" be taken into account when negotiating international conventions.

EFW

In fact I was going to ask you about ethics where managing transboundary aquifers is concerned, because I did not clearly understand what you meant in your report when you said "the devil is in the details."

Benoît Girardin

We need to fine-tune to encourage sustainable and interdependent or shared management, that is, some "checks and balances."[105] For me, political entities that have agreed to commit to a negotiation process must defend their country's interests, of course, but they must also be able to agree on certain values to give the agreement a chance to be fair. Here is what I said on the subject.

> The key players must be represented at the table to express their interests and risks, so as to be able to understand the other party's interests and fears.[106]

EFW

May I react to that? We can bring up treaties such as the one imposed on Ethiopia by Egypt—or rather, by the British colonial power—in 1902, concerning management of the Blue Nile. Under pressure from Great Britain, Abyssinian Emperor Menelik II had to agree that Egypt and Sudan possessed inordinate rights to the water, to Ethiopia's detriment.

104. Ibid.
105. Girardin, *"Gestion juste des aquifères transfrontaliers."*
106. Ibid.

Part VI: Strategies for Mitigating Water Poverty

Benoît Girardin

Yes, this is an old example of geopolitics, but there are others that confirm the viewpoint expressed by Marc Zeitoun in his talk at the W4W colloquium on March 19, 2013. He said that treaties are—often wrongly—assumed to promote fairness, because they are signed by all parties.[107]

EFW

I can see that your scientific expertise brings a new perspective to water's global challenges. Indeed, thanks to UNESCO's recent work on transboundary aquifers and their inclusion in the UN General Assembly's 2008 resolution, a certain amount of optimism is gaining a foothold, which contrasts sharply with the fear-mongering we so often hear.

Of course, governance for aquifers will be a very long-term undertaking, and as yet there is barely even any awareness of the dangers this underground resource is facing.

I note that the detailed section of the recently ratified Convention on the Law of the Non-navigational Uses of International Watercourses of May 21, 1997 mentions a system of sanctions adequate to protect both the visible and invisible "water" resource.

We still need to consider an important subject that raises controversy and even awakens passions,[108] namely the practice of zero-cost water. I discussed this in another chapter,[109] in particular with respect to the 1992 Dublin Statement. I clearly stated that as you see it, this option can lead only to harmful consequences.

> Experience shows that the practice of zero-cost water has led to devastating overuse and monopolizing by players who are capable of learning to use expensive technologies and then implementing them.[110]

So is the alternative really the prospect of a potable water shortage, as expressed on a tragic note by the "dry wells" metaphor and brought to light by the concrete example of the scheduled disappearance of the Azraq wetland? Or will the international community take the necessary steps, and quickly? We must encourage it to do so.

---

107. Zeitoun, "*Hydropolitique internationale [International Hydro-politics]*." He talks about "naïve assumptions about cooperation."

108. Paquerot, *Eau douce*, 226, citing Lord Selborne, who indicates, "Recognizing water as an economic good, now expressed in many declarations and in the policies of major lenders and donors, has generated heated political debate, much fear [. . .]. Some claim that fostering the notion of water as a commodity moves public perception away from the reality of water as a common good and from a sense of shared duty and responsibility." Lord Selborne, *L'éthique de l'utilisation de l'eau douce*, 32.

109. See Part II, Chapter III, no. 2.

110. Girardin, *"Gestion juste des aquifères transfrontaliers."*

Part VI: Strategies for Mitigating Water Poverty

Aside from new technologies proposed by Singapore for the infinite re-use of water,[111] there is no way to find a substitute for it in most regions of the world, as Christiana Peppard so topically stressed at the March 2012 W4W colloquium.[112]

Thank you, Mr. Ambassador, for sharing your stimulating insights.

Interview with an Administrator Who "Thinks Water Remotely"

Earlier I spoke of philanthropy.[113] The next interview seems to me to be an example of what this word might mean to us in the twenty-first century, in the context of water *as a vital need*, or to put it more simply, the potable water needed for survival.

Evelyne Fiechter-Widemann

Participants in the three colloquia organized by W4W between 2011 and 2013[114] have been able to follow the progress of your "Swiss Fresh Water" project almost from the beginning. I think it's important to mention it in my study as an example of a project that was developed based on an ethical choice.

Allow me to introduce you, Renaud de Watteville. You are a member of the Order of Saint John and the Rotary Club. In 2008 you founded the "Swiss Fresh Water" company (hereafter SFW), which has received Lausanne Région's[115] PERL[116] Trophy, a Liechti Foundation prize bestowed in 2009, and support on various occasions from Switzerland's federal government for its innovative project involving a machine for desalinating seawater and brackish water.

Before getting into the more technical details, can you tell me what led you to promote "potable water kiosks" for small villages, especially in Africa?

Renaud de Watteville

You'll find me very enthusiastic about my project, and I'm thinking mostly of the future and new developments. But you're right, let's go back to the beginning of what must truly be called an adventure. I'm highly motivated largely because of two real-life situations that really upset me.

---

111. Tortajada, et al., *The Singapore Water Story*, 26.
112. Peppard, *Water, Vital Need and Global Justice*.
113. See Part III, Section II, Chapter II, no. 2.3.
114. For the *Proceedings of the W4W Interdisciplinary Colloquia* held from 2011 to 2013, see Appendices hereafter.
115. www.lausanne.ch/perl.
116. PERL is the acronym for Prix Entreprendre Région Lausanne [the Lausanne region entrepreneurship prize].

Part VI: Strategies for Mitigating Water Poverty

Here are the circumstances behind my commitment to the world's most destitute people, and to helping them gain access to potable water.

One time I was in Madagascar in a sort of hotel in a tiny village along the Mozambique Channel, and I was quite naturally drinking bottled water. My eyes were instinctively drawn to some Malagasy villagers digging holes in the dune to get at the water that was in it. Then, without really paying too much attention, I saw that they had found brackish water and were drinking it. All of a sudden something clicked. I had just realized how different their lot was from mine, even just in our ability to quench our thirst and meet a vital need.

Some months later, a friend came back from a trip to Haiti and told me what he had seen there while swimming in an acquaintance's pool. He had noticed that the outside wall of the pool, which was built on the edge of the property, was sweating, and the water was running down into the public street. Imagine how surprised and amazed he was to see local residents bringing cups and trying to collect the water flowing from the wall. It made his blood boil and he had to find a way to do something concrete in the face of this humanly unacceptable situation.

He decided to have a fountain built for local residents who had no access to water. It soon became the cause of vehement disputes. Then my friend had to intervene and hand the fountain over to the head of the village, who had the authority to restore social peace.

My travels to various places led me to believe that it was absolutely necessary to do something to face up to injustices of this kind and, if possible, prevent violence. Perhaps my Protestant training and the fact that I'm the son of a doctor of theology contributed to my sense of commitment to others less fortunate than I.

So then I came up with the project of a production system for low-cost potable water for underprivileged villages in Africa and Asia. I fairly quickly found a group of people who could help make it a reality. It would take too long to name them now, so I'll refer you to the interview I gave on March 19, 2013, at the third W4W colloquium.[117]

EFW

Were you thinking of selling the water right from the start?

---

117. Ypsilantis, *Ethique globale de l'eau*, interviews of Evelyne Fiechter-Widemann, HE Benoît Girardin and Renaud de Watteville by Sarah Dirren. Babylone, broadcast on March 25, 2013, RTS (Radio Télévision Suisse). http://download-audio.rts.ch/espace-2/programmes/babylone/2013/babylone/20130325_full_babylone_1a43cd83-1988-4dc7-aab4-c560de2300b-128k.mp3.

Part VI: Strategies for Mitigating Water Poverty

Renaud de Watteville

Obviously, I asked myself the ethical question, "Is selling water good?" This is summarized in the proceedings of the first W4W colloquium, which was held on March 20, 2011.[118]

EFW

I think it is relevant to cite an excerpt from your article here.

The number of sides to this problem is infinite [. . .].

Let us consider a concrete example.

We are sitting here at a table, having a discussion and drinking water. We are a hundred meters from Lake Geneva, which provides free potable water. In Geneva, tap water probably costs about 0.5 centimes per liter, and yet we buy bottled water at 4 francs for 3 deciliters or 12 francs per liter. Why?

Is it the taste? All three taste good. Marketing? Well, maybe a little! Convenience? Probably! (It is delivered, pre-packaged, served, etc.). And that is fine. Work deserves pay, it is our choice, our pleasure, and we are free to do it.

On the other hand, what if we no longer have the choice, for example, if a third party pollutes the lake or the water is diverted for commercial purposes or geopolitical ends? That would force us to either buy water or move away to survive. On the day when our families have no more to drink, we will rise up and fight [. . .].[119]

Renaud de Watteville

As you can see, I was speaking in extremes. But it's a reality we have to face out there. For example, the machines I put up in Senegal cost something. I had to invest money and find sponsors such as the Rotary Foundation.

The important thing, though, is to sell this water at an affordable price. The goal of selling it is to finance all or part of the machine, plus maintenance and local wages. If producing water becomes a "win-win" business at the local level, then the solution will not only improve public health but also create jobs, ensuring the system's sustainability.

EFW

Can you explain to me how you manage to make the sale of water fair and equitable?

---

118. De Watteville, *"Est-il bien de vendre de l'eau [Is Selling Water Good?]."*
119. Ibid.

Part VI: Strategies for Mitigating Water Poverty

Renaud de Watteville

A lot of forethought went into setting up a system I felt was justifiable, and I'm still testing it. Some assessments and corrective action will probably be needed, but you have to start somewhere.

A fair price is the one that makes it possible to meet the objectives I described while allowing for a good rate of penetration by water in the population.

Water has always had a cost. First, there is a direct cost for treatment and supply. Then there's the indirect cost, such as the time young girls have to spend going for water and carrying the precious liquid home, which causes them to miss school. Other indirect costs are, for example, the medical costs of treating diseases caused by unhealthful water, and the cost of the wood needed to boil it.

In our case, in Senegal, potable water is often imported and has been transported for hours by cart, canoe, or car. It is usually sold for 2 euro cents per liter for water of uncertain quality.

In contrast, the water produced by our machine costs about 0.2 to 0.4 euros cents per liter if you consider depreciation and maintenance, and if you produce a significant amount, up to 4,000 liters per day.

Working with the village and regional authorities, we set the selling price at 1.4 euro cents per liter in order to generate sufficient earnings to pay wages and provide projects for the community. So this price is much lower than the lowest cost for imported water and still covers maintenance for the system, ensuring that it will last.

But I very quickly saw that in the poorest small villages, the people at the bottom of the population pyramid and children did not have easy access to water. So we decided to start free distribution of water at the school and the community clinic.

It also turned out that the small villages needed special support. They did not have sufficient sales to justify a water treatment system. To help meet this need, we created the Access To Water Foundation. Its role is to finance the facilities that are on loan, and the village makes a commitment to pay 75 percent of the sales revenue into a blocked bank account to pay for the following year's maintenance.

This process is already supported by Rotary Club, the Soroptimists and the Order of Saint John. A number of these projects are currently being prepared.

EFW

I see in the summary given in the proceedings of the W4W of March 19, 2013, that the Rotary Water Booster concept has three goals:

- provide small villages with access to affordable and safe drinking water;

- help start up a local water kiosk that becomes self-sustaining thanks to trained, responsible locals, who provide annual reports on the water boosters; and
- provide visibility for the one-time donor, whose gift through Rotary can have a lasting impact on the community that receives the aid.

Renaud de Watteville

That is exactly right. Now I'd like to give you a few technical and economic details.

Technically speaking, the desalination machine supplied by SFW is moderately priced, sturdy, and easy to use. It's powered by electricity from solar panels or the local electrical power grid. Brackish or polluted water is purified by a reverse osmosis system that removes residues such as salt, arsenic, fluoride, heavy metals, viruses, and bacteria.

To make upkeep economical, a unique decentralized maintenance system is set up for each machine, and also for groups of machines, along with a local business concept known as a "water package."

EFW

What is a water package?

Renaud de Watteville

It's a one-year fixed-term comprehensive contract that includes the machine lease, maintenance, and the ability to produce and sell a certain amount of water—between 500,000 and 1,000,000 liters—each year.

It is interesting to note that the project's sponsors, such as the Rotary Foundation and the Access To Water Foundation,[120] insist that the contract setting the water's price be negotiated with the local authorities. To repeat, in Senegal that price is 1.5 euro cents per liter. This is high enough to yield a profit for the machine's manager while covering wages as well as operating and technical expenses.

To clarify, if the manager isn't able to pay the amount set in the comprehensive contract, local banks guarantee remittance through a loan paid directly to SFW.

EFW

Legally speaking, then, a "water package" is a contract of a type all its own, with some elements of a lease agreement, a contract for services, and a sale contract.

---

120. Access to Water Foundation, www.accesstowaterfoundation.org.

Part VI: Strategies for Mitigating Water Poverty

Renaud de Watteville

If you say so!

I'd like to add an important point about supervision of the operation.

A decentralized maintenance system has been set up. Each machine is connected to remote technology (GSM and Internet) to provide data, and Swiss Fresh Water does the monitoring from Switzerland. We also refer to this system as "telemetry."

EFW

These technical details are a great addition to the examples I gave at the beginning of my study to make the concept of vulnerability clearer in the context of water. Your project seems to have done a good job of incorporating the three factors I mentioned there—health, education, and economics.[121]

Indeed, in Swiss Fresh Water's case, high-quality water contributes to health, village residents are part of the project and are trained to maintain the water kiosk, and finally, the water packages are of economic benefit to the recipients, who can obtain the financial means to manage the resource and find jobs.

Renaud de Watteville

I'm glad to have convinced you on both the practical and conceptual levels.

It's true that the number of jobs is still very small, but I'm optimistic. I want to stress that since 2011 this project, which is financially supported by the Rotary and Access To Water Foundations, has provided potable water to more than 20,000 people. Its success is due to the fact that the recipients' specific needs are taken into account.

EFW

The fact that Switzerland is also supporting you through the DDC's water initiatives department is quite a plus as well. I wish you all success as you go on with this wonderful program.

Now, another interviewee is volunteering, and I just cannot say no!

A Virtual Interview with the Protagonist, "Thinking Water"

Water

You've thought about me every day for several years, and reflected on concepts that may concern me.

---

121. See Part I, Chapter III, no. 4.

Part VI: Strategies for Mitigating Water Poverty

So I would like to have a say.

Evelyne Fiechter-Widemann

That had never occurred to me! Well, why not? I've already "virtually" interviewed some talented men who are no longer with us today, so yes, I'm duty-bound to let you speak. But just for a few minutes.

Water

Well you're not very generous. In my opinion, even several years of your human time would not be enough to handle my case, which is, after all, unique. Thanks for indulging me, just the same.

I will structure my statement around three points. One is related to time and future generations, another to your global ethic of water, and third and last I would like to end on a poetic note.

First, I note that you're not a climatologist or glaciologist and that you focused on the new "human right" status that the international community decided to give me. Though brief, your thoughts on future generations and Hans Jonas's appeal through his *imperative of responsibility* interest me. On this subject, let me say the following.

I can't resist calling your attention to the fact that you human beings can certainly take steps on a personal level to stop pouring all your waste into my rivers, especially those plastic bottles that are choking them to death. Far-reaching methods are needed if you're going to clean up all pollution of every kind in rivers, streams, and lakes. Moving this item to the top of the agenda would be in the interests of the entire international community—which, if it succeeds in this Herculean task, will have acted responsibly and found one of the answers to your concern about future generations.

Yet not enough is being done yet, as you well know.

As your scientists remind you every day, you depend on rains and droughts, which they can measure in increasingly sophisticated ways. If you continue to be oblivious to the issue of climate change, you run the risk of the well running dry tomorrow. However, noting that scientists themselves—whether government[122] or independent experts—do not present a united front on this serious issue, I will say no more about it.

My second comment has to do with the water ethic within which you want to include the human right to water, albeit in a restrictive way. Let's be perfectly clear. No matter what you do, I will never be part of a system.

So you want to summarize your study in the following *water synopsis* table.

---

122. www.notre-planete.info/actualités/3812-rapport-5-changement-climatique-GIEC.

PART VI: STRATEGIES FOR MITIGATING WATER POVERTY

I. Water Use					
Water *as a vital need* (the amount necessary for survival[1a])	Water as *well-being* (Water of the necessary quality and quantity for drinking, food preparation, personal hygiene, clothing, household, garden, and sanitary needs[2b])	Agriculture and industry Luxury swimming pools, car wash, golf Obligation to use non-potable water	Transport	Energy	Eco-systems

II. Global Water Ethic[3c]	
Essential/absolute ethic Water has a moral value (not an *adiaphoron*[4d])	Functional/relative ethic Water as *adiaphoron*
Potable water, as a *human right* • 2005 churches' Declaration on Water As a Human Right and a Public Good and 2006 ecumenical statement • UN General Assembly's resolution of July 28, 2010	Water, as an *economic good*
• Dublin Statement of 1992, as a human right and economic good	

ICCPR	ICESCR	
Human right to water in the narrow sense (*stricto sensu*) Bases: • Natural right to life • Sixth commandment • Golden rule (negative formulation)	Human right to water in the broad sense (*lato sensu*) Bases: • Human dignity • Eighth commandment • Golden Rule (positive formulation)	Bases: • Eighth commandment • Golden Rule (positive formulation)

Deontological Ethic		Eudaemonistic Ethic	Utilitarian Ethic
Free potable water (or human right in the narrow sense/A). Recipients: Persons in extreme poverty	Potable water at a reasonable price[5e] (or human right in the narrow sense/B)	Potable water at a reasonable price[6f] (or human right in the broad sense) Non-potable water: Obligation to use non-potable (less expensive) water for toilets and gardens Citizen participation in the cost of water treatment	Price of water set using criteria yet to be determined (see Benoît Girardin[7g] and Part IV, Chapter III) Goals: Avoid waste; avoid pollution of surface water, aquifers, and the ecosystem; re-use wastewater, water treatment system.

Justice-in-itself/ natural law	Distributive justice		Corrective justice

Expected effects of fair and responsible management (stewardship) of water:[8h] guarantee the number of m³ per person per year needed to avoid water stress.[9i]

Part VI: Strategies for Mitigating Water Poverty

1a. Between 7.5 and 15 liters per person per day, according to www.who.int/water_sanitation_health: "How much water is needed in emergencies," technical note 9, updated July 2013, p. 2.

2b. Between 20 and 70 liters per person per day, according to www.who.int/water_sanitation_health, ibid (Maslow's hierarchy).

3c. For the abbreviations used in this table, see the List of Abbreviations; for statements and resolutions, see the Table of Contents.

4d. Adia*phoron* and *adia*phora: See Part V, Chapter II, Calvin on Water.

5e. For suggestions concerning "reasonable price," see Ramseier, *Potable Water in Geneva*, ; and De Watteville, *Guaranteeing Access to Water Is One of The Rotary Foundation's Six Strategic Focuses*.

6f. Ibid.

7g. Girardin, *Does Water Have a Cost, and If So, What?*

8h. See Part III, Section I, Chapter I, Calvin's *Natural Law* as a Political Legacy and Basis for the Human Right to Water, and the role of governing authorities according to Calvin.

9i. See Part I, Chapter II and Part VI, interview with El Hassan bin Talal, Prince of Jordan.

Well, why not? Maybe you'll be able to convince your readers that the "human rights" perspective is no cure-all and that they will have to use many other strategies to protect me. In this respect, I have clearly understood that you're not an economist and are merely outlining solutions.

But there is one thing bothering me. Have you truly thought about what this all could mean, where I'm concerned? Have you reread what Swiss Protestant ethicist Arthur Rich wrote at the end of last century about the etymology of the word "ethos"?

EFW

Yes, I recall the passage from his book, *Business and Economic Ethics: The Ethics of Economic Systems*.

> The term "ethics" is derived from the Greek word "ethos." [. . .] It originally meant "usual seat," then the place where one lives and thus is at home. From that the abstract use of "ethos" in the sense of "habit," "convention," "tradition," and finally "custom" can be understood.[123]

Water

Yes, I like this definition and find that it suits me perfectly.

---

123. Rich, *Ethique économique*, 37.

Part VI: Strategies for Mitigating Water Poverty

Indeed, it is thanks to me that a place can be lived in and life can unfold there. All of the archeology and ethnology museums talk about peoples settling around watercourses. In the desert, nomads traveled for many kilometers before stopping at an oasis, where water was abundant and revitalized men and animals, where the Arabian and Bactrian camels could refill their humps.

EFW

May I remind you that I'm writing a dissertation, not a children's story.

Water

Didn't Christ himself say "Let the little children come to me"?[124]

EFW

Yes, but—

Water

All right, then, let's be more scientific.

The reason I like Arthur Rich's definition so much is that it clearly puts me at the heart of your life, amidst hearth and home and, I would even say, in your private life.

Now, what never ceases to amaze me is that people think so little of me, especially when I'm almost invisible, hiding in the aquifers. Why have I been so violently abused, especially since industrialization? Why did eighteenth-century moralist and economist Adam Smith allow himself to say that diamonds are not necessary but have a high value, and water is necessary but without value?

What I am demanding now is that my value be proclaimed in a loud and ringing voice.

EFW

Yes, but which value do you mean? An ethical value, or an economic value?

Water

That's a human debate that I don't want to get mixed up in. I've noticed that to you, I have an ethical value only when I'm covering vital needs for people in a state of

---

124. Mark 10:14.

Part VI: Strategies for Mitigating Water Poverty

extreme poverty, which is what you call water as a human right in the narrow sense/A, but otherwise I'm morally neutral as an *adiaphoron,* as you indicated in your instructive table.

I, on the other hand, think that you people of Earth could make more room for me in your educational systems, from nursery school on up to the most advanced universities.

Indeed, the latter institutions direct their students to study the "Human Development Index," which is all the rage with its triad relating, first to health with the concept of "life expectancy," then to education with the "literacy rate," and finally to economic development through the "standard of living."[125]

Now, there is no health without water, no opportunity for study without water—because a sick, thirsty student will not be very ready to think—, and no economic development without water. Period.

Have I made myself clear?

EFW

Now don't get angry.

Water

Yes I am angry, and my wrath has only just begun to abate since the countries ratified and eventually put into effect the Convention on the Law of the Non-navigational Uses of International Watercourses[126] of May 21, 1997—which contains, in particular, a principle you mentioned in your interview with Hugo Grotius: "do no harm."

EFW

I understand, and Lucius Caflisch,[127] one of the principal architects of this international convention that was twenty years in the making, could only agree with you.

Water

Be that as it may, a great deal remains to be done. If both governments and global citizens will finally heed the warnings from the UN and NGOs that specialize in protecting my identity, and work very closely together toward this goal, as advocated by the International Year of Water Cooperation in 2013, then you can keep alive the hope

---

125. Human Development Index, http://www.hdr.undp.org.
126. Convention on the Law of the Non-navigational Uses of International Watercourses.
127. Caflisch, "Le droit à l'eau—un droit de l'homme internationalement protégé?," 385–94.

Part VI: Strategies for Mitigating Water Poverty

that future generations will thank you for having set the planet to rights. Philosopher Hans Jonas would not contradict me, since he was the one who came to my defense in *The Imperative of Responsibility*.[128]

EFW

I get the feeling you'd like to end on a more lyrical note.

Water

Yes, and here is my prose poem.

I am everywhere, though scarcely seen nor sensed: colorless, odorless, silent but for when my drops join forces in the rain, to fall—perhaps—torrentially. Then might my fateful raging be unleashed to carry off bridges and frail structures in my path.

My catalog of duties marches on: to quench the thirst of humankind, of beasts, and plants; to beautify all nature with my falls; to take the guise of rivers used for transport, and fertilize their plains to make them grow so you may eat their fruits, and water there your thirsty flocks and herds; to power industry's machines, which I inspired; to clean the home where each night you retire; to help the mother see her newborn babe by washing away birth's blood. The list stretches to infinity.

Therefore, I claim, my life's my own, though Man has ever tried to tame me down. Long thought a common good, or shared resource, I'm disappearing in some places now. There, people—taking notice—change my name, rechristening me an economic good. But, at the same time, I've become a human right in the twenty-first century.

So I sense my hour has come. But why my falling star?

As I work on, no rest in sight, my forces lessen day by day. Statistics say, polluted, I sow death and illness all around. Some the limpid waters would restore: scientists, striving to protect Lake Geneva. But others thoughtlessly toss in mountains of waste: the Ganges is a toxic flood. And experts say, by far, it's not alone.

Now as I'm well aware, since century's close, my fate's been thought to be of more concern. Thank you, globalization. But when all's said and done, will it be found that I've been cared for well enough to give eight billion people here on Earth a good and pleasant life? My fate is in your hands. Be careful, lest I take revenge.

---

128. Jonas, *Le principe responsabilité*.

PART VI: STRATEGIES FOR MITIGATING WATER POVERTY

EFW

I seem to hear you speaking with the moving accents of eco-philosopher Aldo Leopold's thinking mountain.[129] Many, many thanks for this surprising but oh-so-acerbic exchange!

Conclusion

My field survey and interviews are the scaffolding that helped me to construct and support my thoughts on the ethical challenges of potable water in today's world.

I felt that it was the men and women who answered my questions who would make it possible to back up my thesis that ethical water, that is, the water necessary to meet vital needs in cases of extreme poverty, would have no chance of being legitimately defended for the good of all without some serious work being done in such sensitive areas as women's role in water management and governments' dual role in promoting better governance and peace.

In short, I found that if we stop at proclaiming water days and initiating other water awareness campaigns, our efforts will be in vain and an exercise in futility, regardless of the good intentions behind them, unless they are accompanied—in practice and everywhere down to the smallest corner of the planet—by a search for the conditions that must be met if we are to attain what I would call the winning trio for a potable water ethic: women, governance, and peace.

We will have to agree to three kinds of efforts.

The first is to increase the number of both individual and community operations targeting greater respect for and attention to women, so they will have access to an education that can make them credible partners in water management. In this regard, two universal conventions should be welcomed, namely the Convention on the Elimination of All Forms of Discrimination against Women[130] of December 18, 1979, and the Convention on the Rights of the Child of November 20, 1989.

The second effort is a systematic war on corruption to ensure better governance; the third is to train youth and adults in peace and reconciliation.

These are not merely empty words. They were uttered most convincingly by my partners in conversation who, I would like to stress, are reputable people and represent different cultures and religious beliefs.

Though these statements have shown that the road from word to action is still long and full of pitfalls, I find them to be signs of hope, as long as they are heard.

---

129. Leopold, *Almanach d'un comté des sables*.

130. Convention on the Elimination of All Forms of Discrimination against Women, 13; and Convention on the Rights of the Child, 3.

General Conclusion

A CONCLUSION IS MEANT to be a synthesis. In this case, it will have three parts.

First, I will mention where the project got started and its maturation over time, which I experienced as an investigatory process that aimed to validate the main concepts that have recently appeared for the emergence of a global potable water ethic.

The second part, which is longer, will be the heart of the conclusion, as the time has now come to say how the human right to water could either tend towards justice or turn out to be normatively too weak to fight injustice, due to its ambiguity.

The closing statements will try to provide a glimpse of a revisited Golden Rule's potential to be a message of hope for life in abundance.[1]

A Place for Reflection and Integration: Geneva's Autonomous Faculty of Protestant Theology Faces up to Globalization's Challenges

I chose to question the relevance of the "human right" to water at the Autonomous Faculty of Protestant Theology in Geneva. In my mind, this was an ideal place to undertake an exploration that would be open to the chosen topic's interdisciplinary nature. It is also an appropriate venue in which to try to understand why the Swiss and Brazilian churches chose to collaborate and issue the Ecumenical Declaration on *Water As a Human Right and a Public Good* in 2005.

This university faculty is also a place for international dialogue, as it proved by offering a MOOC[2] on reformer John Calvin in the fall of 2013.

For decades, with the aid of its professors, assistants and students, it has shown itself to be open to society through its public conferences, media interviews, and on-line presence. Aside from its main areas of expertise, such as theology, philosophy, and ethics, it has shown itself to be capable of developing talent in economics, politics, and sciences by readily inviting these fields' foremost specialists from Europe, the Middle East, and the United States to participate in seminars for its own students as well as courses open to the general public.

---

1. Ecumenical Declaration on Water reads, "Water is a gift of God, which he offers to all so that they may use it responsibly for fullness of life," Ecumenical Declaration, ibid, no. 1, §1.

2. MOOC is the acronyme of Massive Open Online Course.

It provides a place to assimilate ideas, so to speak, and to use a trendy term. "Assimilation" (the term *intégration* in French)[3] is understood as a way to avoid ending up with a set of vague concepts—such as those born of globalization, for example. So it is that today, individuals tempted to give in to the distractions of a flood of information are invited to find a place where they can refocus and ponder their human condition. However, assimilation *(intégration)* absolutely does not equate to fundamentalism *(intégrisme)*. On the contrary, dialogue is in order here so we can face up to totally new challenges that require a state of mind appropriate for discovering new avenues of exploration.

Other Platforms Taken into Consideration

So I was able to proceed with my study in this atmosphere of academic freedom, taking the measure not only of the Faculty of Theology's seminars, but also of several countries outside of Europe, in order to combine theory with practice. I was able to meet with representatives of every inhabited continent who were motivated by the same shared passion: finding solutions to guard against an uncertain future brought about by poor water management, in which millions of people would be left helpless by increasingly frequent and devastating floods, or forced to relocate due to drought and insufficient potable water.

In Singapore, I met with professors from the Swiss Federal Institute of Technology, economists, politicians, philosophers, and entrepreneurs who had come to visit the city-state because of its status as what must today be called a water "hub."[4] Indeed, outside of international conferences, it has become a platform where a professional civil society provides not only the most useful expertise for facing water's huge challenges, but also the evidence of men and women committed to working for the public good.

Does a deep gulf exist between civil society's world and that of the UN, which decided to number potable water among the human rights? I believe that bridges must be built between these two poles to facilitate constructive thought.

The New Human Right to Water: Justice or Sham?

It seems very justified to me to credit both UN and civil society stakeholders with a burning desire for justice, seconded by an ethical mission to redirect human activity that is struggling with the challenges of water in general and potable water

---

3. Cuvillier, *Nouveau dictionnaire philosophique*, 100.

4. Orsenna indicates, "Originally, the English word 'hub' meant the part around which a wheel turns. The sense of the word has expanded. It now means any point toward which radii converge, any center of a network." Orsenna, *L'avenir de l'eau*, 83.

in particular. This is what has caused and motivated them to alert public opinion about potable water issues and to translate their concerns into declarations and draft conventions.

I have dared to bring up the question of a sham, which is certainly an iconoclastic one, because the reality of water inequality in many countries deserves constant attention along with a tireless rethinking of the political choices made.

The example of South Africa, which has succeeded in enshrining an ethical value, the human right to water, in its Constitution in order to put it into effect, is unquestionably a ray of hope for this country's disadvantaged populations that live in extreme poverty. They now have in hand a legal instrument for laying violations of this right before the courts. But as we have seen, even in South Africa, in practice a yawning gap still exists between intentions and actual access to the basic water supply needed for survival.

I feel, however, that we should not be discouraged by this news. Quite the contrary. South Africa has shown itself to be a pioneer in an area of extreme importance to humanity's future. It has demonstrated its ability to defend the transcendental value of life.

And all in the name of what principles?

All indications are that Aristotle's natural law, the different forms of which we saw in Part III, is making a comeback, complete with grand entrance, after having been relegated to the background during the Enlightenment and up until the end of World War II. It is this natural law that serves as the basis for the new human right to water.

And, as we saw in Part IV, it is the search for justice that motivates action.

I would like to address this question of justice in two phases. First I will reread Aristotle, guided by Michel Villey, who has already been frequently called upon for this study.

Then I will compare the UN tools and Swiss constitutional law on points pertaining to the human right to life and human dignity, with reference to the two international covenants that have already been mentioned a number of times—the ICCPR[5] and the ICESCR[6]—and the Swiss federal Constitution. (I explained earlier[7] why I insist on citing Covenant II before Covenant I, notwithstanding the United Nations' choice of order.)

---

5. International Covenant on Civil and Political Right.
6. International Covenant on Economic, Social and Cultural Rights.
7. See Part V, Chapter I, no. 3.

General Conclusion

Justice, the Concept Forged by Aristotle

Ancient philosopher Aristotle was the one who created the conceptual pairing of justice and law or right,[8] via the Greek word *dikaion*. As Michel Villey notes,

> [i]n Greek, it is the single word *dikaion* that we sometimes translate as *juste* [just] and sometimes as *droit* [law or right]. Our European languages have not been able to separate themselves from the ancient languages on this point: the ministry of "justice" is concerned with the law. *Recht* [law or right] remains morphologically tied to *Gerechtigkeit* [justice]."[9]

By adding the qualifier *physikon*, he even created the concept of natural justice, as we explained earlier.[10]

Western thinkers—in their capacities as theologians, philosophers, and legal scholars—redefined this justice-in-itself over the centuries, in the forms of natural law, obedience to God, and modern natural law. We can ultimately find traces of it in today's concept of human rights, and consequently in that of the human right to water. On this point I refer the reader back to Part III, Section I.

Aristotle also pointed out, admirably in my opinion, that it is judges and rulers who are most likely to put this kind of justice into practice.

> This is why, when people dispute, they take refuge in the judge; to go to the judge is to go to justice; for the nature of the judge is to be a sort of animate justice; and they seek the judge as an intermediate, and in some states they call judges mediators, on the assumption that if they get what is intermediate they will get what is just. The just, then, is an intermediate, since the judge is so.[11]

Moreover,

> [t]he magistrate on the other hand is the guardian of justice, and, if of justice, then of equality also. [. . .] so that it is for others that he labours, and it is for this reason that men, as we stated previously, say that justice is 'another's good' [. . .].[12]

It is important to point out that, as I noted earlier,[13] Calvin also saw the vocations of these two types of magistrates, the former representing the judiciary and the latter political power, as the key to fair application of the law—or, as we call it today, responsibility or good governance.

---

8. Villey indicates, "The idea of *droit* [law or right] goes hand in hand with that of *justice*." Villey, *Le droit et les droits de l'homme*, 39.

9. Ibid.

10. See Part III, Section I.

11. Aristote, *Ethique à Nicomaque*, chapter V [1132 a 20], 244.

12. Ibid., chapter V, 1132 b 1, 257.

13. See Part III, Section I, Chapter I.

General Conclusion

The Human Right to Water in the Narrow and Broad Senses

"[I]ntuitions without concepts are blind," said Immanuel Kant.[14]

To explain my own point of view, I propose that we distinguish between a human right to water in the narrow sense and a human right to water in the broad sense (see the table given in the last interview of Part VI).

The former, which I also call the *narrow concept,* would be based on the natural law of the right to life, and the latter, or *broad concept,* on human dignity. This is the distinction that I postulated at the beginning of my study in Part II (Section I, Introduction), for which I believe I have discovered a concrete application as we will see in a moment.

The *narrow concept* would apply to the minimum amount of water needed for survival, and therefore would correspond to the sixth commandment (which forbids killing). According to Calvin's broadly construed interpretation of this instruction from Moses' Tables of the Law, we are to do our utmost to avoid hurting others, as summed up in the slogan "do no harm."

The *broad concept* would concern the minimum amount of water necessary for life with dignity. It has to do with the eighth commandment (prohibition of stealing). Calvin's free interpretation of this prescription goes beyond simply forbidding theft to state that it means "faithfully [. . .] to preserve to every man what justly belongs to him"[15] and not to "deny them those kind offices, which it is our duty to perform to them."[16]

From an economic standpoint, the human right to water in the narrow sense means potable water supplied free of charge in cases of extreme poverty.[17] The *argumentum a contrario* suggested for the concept of *adiaphoron* in Part V, Chapter II makes the potable water needed for survival a moral value that underlies this assertion.

As far as the human right to water in the broad sense is concerned, water is to be supplied at a reasonable price, except for a free or subsidized supply available to people living in extreme poverty. This is the perception of a pure, sweet, water, which according to Calvin is pleasant and contributes to well-being, and according to me reinforces the theory of a human right in the broad sense. Since this kind of potable water is an *adiaphoron,* without a moral value in and of itself, nothing stands in the way of trading it as an economic good in accordance with the ways and means of distributive justice for household needs.

From a legal perspective, more specifically that of public or constitutional law, I will cite two sources.

14. Kant, *Critique de la raison pure,* 77.
15. Calvin, *Instit.,* II, VIII, 45.
16. Ibid.
17. Which I have called the human right in the narrow sense/A. See chart Part VI/6.

General Conclusion

As I indicated at the close of my virtual interview with Hugo Grotius (Part III, Section I, Chapter II), the two UN covenants defending freedoms (right to life) and social rights (right to food) are the ICCPR and the ICESCR, respectively. For me, the former corresponds to the human right to water in the narrow sense, and therefore to free water for the most disadvantaged people; and the latter to the human right to water in the broad sense, that is, water to be supplied at a reasonable price so that one may be fed, housed, and clothed under sanitary conditions.

The other source is Swiss constitutional law, which distinguishes between ideal freedoms and political rights. The first, such as the right to life in article 10 of the Swiss Constitution[18] are "self-executing," that is, they need no law in order to be enforceable;[19] and the second create a positive obligation for the State, that is, a right to assistance, but only in cases of extreme insecurity, according to article 12 of the Constitution (as an exception to the general principle of article 41[20]):

> Persons in need and unable to provide for themselves have the right to assistance and care, and to the financial means required for a decent standard of living.[21]

I find the systematics of Swiss constitutional law to be interesting on two counts. First, it demonstrates that in an industrialized rule of law state such as Switzerland, it is not necessary to enshrine a human right to water in the Constitution, since the right to life as provided by the ICCPR is assured and translates into a prohibition on any untimely water shutoff. Second, in order to preserve human dignity, as guaranteed by article 7 of the Constitution, persons living in such extreme poverty that they cannot pay their water bill or provide for themselves may receive public assistance.

These two legal sources—the first from international public law and the second from Swiss constitutional law—form the premise of my demonstration. They will allow me to answer, in a moment, the question that led me to write this study, that is, whether the human right to water proposed by the UN and civil society is more akin to justice or a sham.

First, however, I need to lay out the suspicions of a sham that will weigh in the balance to confirm my answer.

---

18. Constitution fédérale suisse states, "Every person has the right to life." Constitution fédérale Suisse, Article 10.

19. Grisel, *Droits fondamentaux*, 5.

20. Constitution fédérale suisse states, "No direct right to state benefits may be established on the basis of these social objectives." Constitution fédérale suisse states, article 41 para. 4

21. Ibid., article 12.

GENERAL CONCLUSION

Will the Human Right to Water Drown in a Sea of Confusion or a Political Storm?

My suspicions have to do with two indices that could present an obstacle to enforcing the human right to water, namely globalization and poor governance in "failed" states.

Globalization

Globalization, which was discussed in part one, is responsible for the blurring of such concepts as *human rights, humanitarian,* and *philanthropy,* to which we must add the new *human right to water.*

It also confuses the issue of markets and the economy, which makes the average citizen very uneasy indeed.

The globalized market is malfunctioning, and as a result is attacked daily. Such criticisms are not always unfounded, as former CNRS director Henri Bourguinat[22] notes. However, the fact remains that its fiercest opponents, such as dictators Kim Jong-Un of North Korea and Robert Mugabe of Zimbabwe, do not offer any viable alternatives for the populations they dominate and keep in extreme poverty.

As was so masterfully demonstrated by theologian and economist Adam Smith's work, which is still surprisingly relevant as shown earlier in this study,[23] it will probably be impossible for economics and ethics ever to reach a consensus.

Be that as it may, anti-market fundamentalism in various forms is a formidable stumbling block for the issue of universal access to water. The (perhaps unintended) effect of the slogans that go along with it is to block efforts to eradicate the very real scourge of water wasting, especially in agriculture. The waste can be ended only through an economic approach to water management in combination with oversight by a rule of law government capable of imposing penalties on water wasters. Financial expert Henri Bourguinat is baffled by such hatred of the market.

> After all, why should we think that the same people who yesterday mistakenly sang the praises of the planned economy/heavy industry pair are called to become today's pundits? The question begs to be asked, especially if one analyzes the predominant attitude towards markets and the often dogmatic feeling of rejection they inspire.[24]

---

22. Professor emeritus of economic sciences at the University of Bordeaux IV and former director of the Centre National de Recherche Scientifique [French National Science Research Center].

23. See Part III, Section II, Chapter III, no. 2.

24. Bourguinat, *Les intégrismes économiques,* 87.

GENERAL CONCLUSION

"Failed" States Challenged to Provide Infrastructure for Universal Access to Water

It is immediately apparent to anyone that expensive facilities are necessary to make potable water if no unpolluted spring or aquifer is available, and that equally costly infrastructure is needed to remove wastewater. What people underestimate, however, is the degree to which personal freedom must be curtailed to ensure equal access to water for all, if everyone is to lay aside old customs and join the modern twenty-first century world. The example of Singapore is telling in this regard, as discussed earlier.

So requiring a third-world country to commit to this path, which can be no sinecure for either the government or the people whose living conditions it is supposed to be improving, is a purely utopian gesture.

In fact, there is no supranational judicial body to rule on such things. In the example I gave earlier of a rural community in Paraguay,[25] the Inter-American Court of Human Rights did indeed order the government to pay damages, and even imposed social measures to improve the well-being of the Kásek community, but did not require the defendant to build infrastructure either to supply water or to treat wastewater. Had the government done so, it is not too far-fetched to suppose that the Court would not have informed the complainants about the sacrifices that would have to be endured for such a social transformation. So the ruling could at best be nothing more than a short-term measure, even supposing that it were properly carried out.

In contrast, it is not impossible to foresee that if, in the relatively near future, officials trained to provide good governance and supported by a public that had reached civic maturity were to choose to take charge of draconian reforms, then dreams of universal access to water could become a reality.

Is the "human right" tool well adapted to realities in the field when it comes to implementing such reforms?

Are there not still too many men and women, especially in the developing world, who are trapped in an unwholesome obscurantism, or simply still in a less advanced state of civilization[26] that prevents them from seeing real opportunities for a better life in which the water would again be not only clear, but also and especially of good quality? Are there not still too many governments that lack the necessary vision to end water pollution, which is caused mostly by an absence of eco-friendly wastewater treatment systems, and to teach their people not to throw their refuse into seas, lakes, rivers, and streams?

These are the doubts that I think are relevant and should be made known to the parties most concerned, and which presumed prerogatives invoked in the name of human rights would mask.

---

25. Xákmok Kásek.
26. I am thinking of Papuans in particular.

So this essay represents an attempt to meet human beings where they are, in the midst of their uncertainties, gropings, and fears. The finest international declarations[27] have perhaps not yet, or at least not sufficiently, been able to convince them to change their attitude and truly put the water problem at the top of their list of daily priorities.

A Theoretical Answer Tempered by Two Concrete Examples that Give Reason to Hope

Now I am able to defend the thesis that the human right to water in the narrow sense falls within the province of natural law or its various forms such as modern natural law or, again, is taken into account in the slogan "do no harm," not to mention the negative formulation of the Golden Rule and the second version of Kant's categorical imperative.[28]

I have no doubts whatsoever that this human right to water in the narrow sense corresponds to Justice, more specifically Justice-in-itself. It can be enforced by any government in the world without additional legislation, for example following the model of the Swiss Constitution, or even in the absence of a constitution, since this is a universal natural right, a point that the Stoic Cicero would not argue.[29]

If, on the other hand, a poorly interpreted human right to water in the broad sense aims to obligate every government on the planet to supply high-quality water to everyone, thereby forcing them to build expensive infrastructure, I would say that we would face major practical and institutional obstacles that would leave the potential recipients of the water completely destitute. In this case, I think it would not be unjustified to suppose that the new human right to water is nothing but a mirage, a sham.

It is true that, in practice, the examples of South Africa and Singapore that I have described in my study allow us to remain somewhat optimistic about potable water's future. Will these examples catch on, or, in a spirit of practical wisdom, should we settle for French theologian Jacques Ellul's slogan, "think globally, act locally"?

I think I have successfully demonstrated throughout this study that as I see it, the "human right" tool for potable water is not, on its own, up to the task. The risk is that the most destitute people will place too much hope in it. I myself recommend an urgent search for other tools, including the principle of accountability, to be used by "failed" states to provide good governance. Let us note that "accountability" is simply one form of justice, the one advocated by Pascal in one of his most striking "thoughts":

---

27. Considerable progress has been made since 1972 and the environmental awakening in Stockholm, via the introduction of sustainable development principles in Rio de Janeiro in 1992, the Millennium Development Goals in 2000, and the creation of the new human right to water in 2010.

28. Kant indicates, "Act in such a way that you always treat humanity, whether in your own person or in the person of any other, never simply as a means, but always at the same time as an end." Kant, *Fondements* [IV, 429] 295.

29. Cicero, see Part III, Section I, Chapter I.

"We must [...] combine justice and might, and for this end make what is just strong, or what is strong just."[30]

The Moment of Truth

The moment of truth has now snuck up on us, as it were, as far as freedom is concerned—more specifically, the political freedom that I consider to be undeniably linked to the issue of potable water. Did not John Rawls, in his theory of justice *as fairness,* give it priority over his difference principle, which moves toward economic equality among human beings? Did not Paul Ricœur, too, remind us of the drama of the industrial era, which made a mockery of the freedoms won in the context of "historical struggles as ancient as those of the urban communities in Italy, Flanders, and Germany for self-determination"?[31]

What, then, is to be said about the choice made by the international community when it adopted the two covenants of 1966 (Covenant I, or ICESCR; and Covenant II, or ICCPR), which revealed a changing priority in the order of the human rights set forth in the Universal Declaration of Human Rights of 1948, as noted in Part III?[32] Now potable water is both a political and an economic issue, and the question as to whether the human right to it should be placed, conceptually, under Covenant I (dealing with economic, social, and cultural rights) instead of Covenant II (civil and political rights) has not been answered unanimously one way or the other, either among international legal scholars or within the churches.[33]

In my opinion, the global challenges of potable water offer the international community a really excellent topic of discussion for initiating a worldwide public debate. Will it seize the opportunity to once again make political freedom the top priority and thereby bring about a sort of conversion?

A Revisited Golden Rule: Give Because It Has Been Given Unto You!

In response to the legal systematics and reference to a justice of equivalence that have enabled me to give a rational answer to the question I asked, an echo rings out—not

---

30. Pascal, *Pensées,* 137.
31. See Part III, Section II, Chapter III.
32. See Part III, Section I, Chapter II.

33. Schäfer indicates, "Whereas BR-CH [the abbreviation for the Brazilian/Swiss Ecumenical Declaration on Water As a Human Right and a Public Good of April 22, 2005, co-initiated and jointly supported by the Federation of Swiss Protestant Churches] sees the human right to water as being included in the right to adequate food, the World Council of Churches [which in February 2006 adopted the Statement on Water for Life] remains vague and includes the right to water under the right to life ('an integral part of the right to life,' Resolution b)." Schäfer, "Brasilianisch-schweizerische," 2, under the heading "Zugang zu Wasser ist ein Menschenrecht" [Access to water is a human right].

canceling out my answer but instead transcending it—from Ricœur's *economy of the gift*, the surprising concept that opens the way for a new, almost subversive interpretation of the Golden Rule. It is no longer a question of merely "do unto others what we would have them do unto us," but rather much more.

The French philosopher's new formula, inspired by the Gospels, offers a new expression of the act of giving, which no longer implies simple reciprocity, but speaks to pushing compassion to its limits, to "giving because it has been given unto us."

In short, we have passed into the realm of supererogatory justice and love, the kind illustrated by the parable of the Good Samaritan as reported in Luke 10:25-27.

Living up to Christ's commandment to love is of course not within the reach of every human being, even those who have demonstrated "those unique and extreme forms of commitment,"[34] such as Hugo de Grotius, Martin Luther King, Jr., Dietrich Bonhoeffer, Nelson Mandela, and Aung San Suu Kyi, but Ricœur believes that it is achievable here on Earth.

> Thus we may affirm in good faith and with a good conscience that the enterprise of expressing this equilibrium in everyday life, on the individual, judicial, social and political planes, is perfectly practicable. I would even say that the tenacious incorporation, step by step, of a supplementary degree of compassion and generosity in all of our codes—including our penal codes and our codes of social justice—constitutes a perfectly reasonable task, however difficult and interminable it may be.[35]

Do not some of the facts back him up, such as the two examples of South Africa and Singapore given above? To these cases we should add the work of the International Red Cross Movement and its Geneva Conventions, which confer special protection on water in times of war.

Is the hope of seeing authorities from every country, in concert with global citizens, concerning themselves with "giving because it has been given unto them" so that we can live in greater harmony, within reach? I will let the Apostle Paul answer for me.

> And now faith, hope, and love abide, these three; and the greatest of these is love.[36]

---

34. Ricœur, *Amour et Justice*, 38.
35. Ibid., 42.
36. I Cor 13:13.

Looking for Water with EPER/HEKS

Visits to Rural Communities in Zimbabwe and South Africa

Evelyne Fiechter-Widemann

Former member, EPER Foundation Board

© EFW/Geneva 2011

March/April 2011

Contents

Acknowledgments | 347

A. Zimbabwe | 349
    1. EPER's First Partner, Christian Care | 349
        1.1 The Vilakalidli Garden | 350
        1.2 Bambanani Ward Centre | 351
        1.3 Makhasa Dam | 352
    2. EPER's Second Partner, the Fambidzanai Permaculture Centre | 354
    3. Training for Better Governance | 356

B. South Africa | 357
    1. Khanya College | 357
    2. Itireleng Development and Educational Project | 358
        2.1 Framework Conditions for Current Hunger-Prevention Projects | 358
        2.2 Site Visits | 359
            2.2.1 Mzilela Gardening Project | 359
            2.2.2 Balloon Farm in Trichardsdaal | 360
            2.2.3 Khomananihitirha Farmers Association | 360
            2.2.4 Nursery in Maruleng | 360

C. Conclusion | 362

Acknowledgments

WHILE SERVING ON THE EPER/HEKS (Swiss Church Aid) foundation's board from 2006 to 2009, I was inspired to undertake an academic study on the ethical challenges of water at the University of Geneva, in the Autonomous Faculty of Protestant Theology.

Thanks to EPER/HEKS's management, especially Esther Oettli, manager of the International Division, I had the privilege of meeting Valentin Prélaz, the head of Swiss Church Aid's Lausanne-based Protestant aid program for southern Africa. After interviewing him about his projects, I shared my interest in acquiring a better understanding of water-related issues, especially the difficulties that southern African populations face in gaining access to potable water. He spontaneously agreed to let me participate in one of his official supervisory visits to Zimbabwe and South Africa from March 24 to April 3, 2011.

Being able to hold an on-site dialogue with the recipients of humanitarian aid provided by this Protestant NGO was an unforgettable experience.

In one tangible demonstration of this very warm exchange, a woman taking part in a large assembly at Makhasa Dam in Zimbabwe gave me a bag containing about a kilogram of small broad beans. Over a hundred people had gathered and, after spontaneous dancing accompanied by stirring songs, met for about two hours.

I offer warm thanks to EPER/HEKS and its representatives, especially those who agreed to add an extra passenger to their team, namely Valentin Prélaz for the entire trip and employees Juliana Manjengwa in Zimbabwe and Donna Andrews in South Africa.

I could hardly fail to be moved by the memory of the simple and unaffected welcome I received throughout the ten-day trip, both in Zimbabwe from the partners at Christian Care and Fambidzanai Permaculture Centre, and in South Africa from Oupa and the managers at IDEP (Itireleng Development and Educational Project). I was able to share in the joys and also the real concerns of the communities we visited.

These acknowledgments would be incomplete if I neglected to thank Laurence-Isaline Stahl Gretsch, the head of Geneva's History of Science Museum, for her layout work on this report.

Looking for Water with EPER/HEKS[1]

Visits to Rural Communities in Zimbabwe and South Africa

A. Zimbabwe

EPER [Swiss Church Aid] collected feedback from rural communities in Zimbabwe (Matobo District, located in the southern province of Matabeleland)[2] on Monday and Tuesday, March 28 and 29, 2011.

The schedule for these two days was packed, given the long distances that had to be traveled and the need prepare for the community meetings with the partners, Christian Care's Bulawayo Office on Monday and Fambidzanai Permaculture Centre on Tuesday.

I will limit myself to giving a general picture of the visits we made with these two partners, bearing in mind that Valentin Prélaz has filed a detailed report with EPER's management in Switzerland.

1. EPER's First Partner, Christian Care

I would like to mention the wonderful welcome we received in Maphisa from Christian Care's employees. This organization was founded in 1967 by Zimbabwe's Council of Churches and is one of the largest of the country's institutions concerned with food security. Its objectives include improving access to water and public health, education, and organic farming.

The project head, Duduzile Sikosana, had prepared a packet with the schedule for the day, the activity report for January through March 2011, and a glossary in the local language, Ndebele (a Bantu language). She was assisted by David, who is responsible for food security, and Pastor Everson Ndlovu, who takes charge of development

---

1. Hereafter referred to as EPER.

2. Prélaz indicates, "this district is considered as a semi-arid/arid area." Prélaz, "Linking Disaster Risk Management," 3.

and education and who presided over the discussions all day without showing the least sign of fatigue—an impressive performance.

The Vilakalidli garden (March 28, 2011).

1.1 The Vilakalidli Garden

The community that hosted us was represented by about twenty people, mostly women. The very lively discussion covered mainly water-supply and livestock issues. I am pleased to note that the women expressed themselves freely.

Access to Water

Concerning the first topic, the pictures speak for themselves. The subject was pumping water to irrigate the field, which was too dry due to a lack of rain. One of the participating women explained to me that during the dry season, the river runs underneath the sand and one must dig a hole to reach the water.

A manual pumping system was recently installed, but unfortunately turned out to be inadequate because the women tired too quickly. Furthermore, the pipes that should have been used for pumping had been damaged by heavy rains the previous fall.

During the meeting, mention was made of the search for an alternative solution. On behalf of the community, the woman in the red hat (see below) requested that a diesel pump be supplied.

Valentin Prélaz pointed out that two conditions would have to be met for such a piece of equipment to be furnished:

- a supply of diesel would have to be secured;
- arrangements for regular maintenance of the system would have to be made.

Protecting Livestock

The other point addressed had to do with livestock. Managing stock is difficult, not only because some animals die due to a lack of medication, but also because they are highly coveted and are sometimes stolen. However, the members of the community are so proud of owning cattle that they are redoubling their efforts to avoid such losses. To my great surprise, an on-the-spot poll by Valentin Prélaz revealed that the farmers prefer them by far to goats or chickens: it is a real question of honor and social standing! An article in the July 31, 2011 edition of the *Bulawayo24 News* confirms that owning cattle, which are an important source of income, is a sign of power and authority in Ndebele culture.

1.2 Bambanani Ward Centre

Our host community sent nearly as many men as women to the meeting on Monday, March 28, 2011. Discussions focused mainly on the new constitution adopted by its members. By constitution[3] is meant a document containing corporate bylaws, which

3. [French footnote omitted.]

specify the annual contributions likely to cover the costs of vaccinating the livestock and the methods of managing the animals so as to increase their numbers. This constitution seems to play a positive role in a very real way: several villagers have been able to acquire ownership of a cow over time.

The final goal is of course for every member of the village to own a cow after a few years.

Governance

The difficulty lies in electing a committee to take charge and call meetings regularly. As things stand, it seems that governance is not optimal and that enforcement of the constitution is spotty. At least, that is what Valentin Prélaz and Juliana Manjengwa implied, without actually spelling it out. But I see the regular monitoring by EPER employees as an encouragement for the communities to move forward with their projects.

1.3 Makhasa Dam

A community of about a hundred people awaited us with many songs and dances at the Makhasa Dam, built in 1951.

New pipes and a siphon system were installed by Christian Care ... resulting in well-kept gardens.

It was truly a joy to meet this community, which is so grateful to Christian Care and EPER. We were offered many gifts, including seeds.

The many speeches, often impassioned, were very informative and interspersed with songs. The open-air gathering beneath a tree (which I may go so far as to call the "palaver tree") was attended by young and old, men and women alike. In addition to CF (conservation farming), gender[4] issues and AIDS-related topics were an important part of the discussion.

An Awareness of Women's Role

It seemed clear from the discussion that the men had become aware of women's important role as far as both CF and health issues were concerned. However, as Valentin Prélaz noted in his report, a gulf still exists between the new laws supporting access to economic resources and the cultural customs that subordinate women.[5]

Another topic mentioned was how the constitution was being applied especially effectively in the area of organic farming. Many people (even some of the men) spoke up to say that a good 50 percent of the crop is now raised by "katchopo" (conservation farming), and 50 percent by traditional means.

Among the projects mentioned were education, mobility (request to purchase a mountain bike), and the construction of latrines near the community's regular meeting place. We had seen a number of such facilities in the area during our short trip from the meeting place to the location of some fields we were visiting at nightfall.

Anecdote and Questions

I asked one of the participants, who had come along in the car driven by Juliana Manjengwe, about a brand-new large building that I pointed out. He answered that it contained latrines built by World Vision, but that he himself built others for the community at nearly no charge.

Is this anecdote not food for thought? Are our organizations doing too much? Would it not suffice to make the people we want to help aware of the importance of access to public health facilities, then let them provide it using their own methods?

Debriefing and Goodbyes

After a debriefing at the Christian Care center, we said an emotional goodbye to that organization's representatives and spent the second night in the Agricultural Development Authority's guest house, which has faucets and toilets but not water (at least, not any more). The precious liquid must be fetched from a hosepipe several meters beyond the house, or from a cistern out front.

---

4. [French footnote omitted.]
5. Prélaz, ibid., 4.

The guesthouse, which has no running water.

Two aides, Juliana, Valentin and Evelyne.

2. EPER's Second Partner, the Fambidzanai Permaculture Centre

The Fambidzanai foundation was created in 1988. (Fambidzanai means "walking together.") Its main objective is to develop and promote organic farming and demonstrate its viability through numerous projects in the field as well as training courses and seminars.

On Tuesday, March 29, 2011, the two representatives of the center that we met took us to visit several gardens as well as a resource center under construction. Since my study was focusing on how communities water their crops, at this point I will mention three types of irrigation: water brought from the river, and irrigation aided either by a windmill that works a pump, or by manual pumping.

A sixty-year-old woman was working in the first garden while a young woman went to get water from a river five minutes away.

Seven holes had been dug in which to plant mango, avocado, and orange trees. The Fambidzanai Centre plans to provide a water pump soon.

In the second garden, a windmill and bore hole system supplies the water (at a cost of between 10 and 15 thousand dollars).

I was amazed to see that the farmers do not use the available hoses to water the crops directly; instead, they fill buckets, carry the water to the plants, and pour it out.

At the third site, a manual water pump is used.

3. Training for Better Governance

The various debriefings conducted by our hosts after the site visits revealed that the issue of accountability by aid recipients is absolutely crucial.

I could see that project monitoring was not a mere formality. EPER, for example, must use all the diplomacy it can muster to encourage the communities to comply with the rules set in their constitutions. It does have a field officer whose job is to verify compliance with the rules that are so necessary for the survival of the populations in question. However, without Juliana Manjengwa's invaluable and efficient work, and the semiannual visits by the program head from Switzerland, the constitution might well go unheeded.

I will round out my observations by noting that the visits also usually include workshops, for example those jointly arranged by EPER and BFA (Bread For All) in October 2010 on the topic of global warming, the risk of drought, and the challenges posed by AIDS.[6] These sessions are extremely important as tools for both communication and training with the goal of fighting poverty.

B. South Africa

As in Zimbabwe, we had many meetings, which took place on March 31 and April 1, 2011.

1. Khanya College

The moment we arrived in Johannesburg we were welcomed by Donna Andrews, an EPER employee, and had a long discussion with Oupa, an activist from the apartheid days. He said he was very frustrated with what was currently happening in his country, despite the smooth transition from apartheid to democracy under charismatic President Nelson Mandela (a statue of whom we saw at the Johannesburg airport) and the outstanding work done by the Truth and Reconciliation Commission[7] to ensure the healthy rebuilding of South African society.

6. Prélaz, ibi., 3.
7. Fiechter-Widemann, "Pardon, catharsis de la violence extrême".

He hastened to list the problems, for example:

- the financial crisis and considerable foreign exchange losses
- termination of EPER support (planned for the end of 2012)
- the gap between South Africa's 1996 constitution and reality

Oupa was very committed to supporting a winter school[8] to teach activists their rights, especially the right to resist.

2. Itireleng Development and Educational Project (IDEP)

The Itireleng Development and Educational Project (hereafter referred to as IDEP) is EPER's partner in the Mopani District (located in Limpopo Province, whose 5.7 million residents are among South Africa's poorest people).[9]

2.1 Framework Conditions for Current Hunger-Prevention Projects

IDEP director Matome Malatji compels respect by his precise and resolute speech. At the beginning of the session, he recalled the history of IDEP, which was created in 1988 but has been especially active since 1994. IDEP has set up eight associations, which themselves are members of a federation called the Mopani Farmers Union (hereafter MFU).[10] Its primary objective is to combat hunger and acquire the means to do so, which consist in particular of providing training and support to about 1220 farmers. This includes not only raising the rural population's awareness of climate and ecological challenges, but also offering training in effective water management and overseeing irrigation systems to improve the use of water, a scarce resource in this region[11] due to low rainfall.

IDEP and EPER schedule workshops on a regular basis. IDEP also organizes farmers assemblies at which current events are discussed and problems identified. This attests to IDEP's "catalyst" philosophy, an approach that aims to make small farmers aware of their responsibilities and attentive to their own needs. This is known as "empowerment" or "People's Participatory Planning and Action" (PPPA).[12]

---

8. www.khanyacollege.org.za.

9. See report by Prélaz, who indicates, "Today, less than 10% of households have piped water in their homes, 38% rely on communal taps for access to water and 19.5% on dams, rivers and springs for water. (…) Only few emerging small scale farmers rely on bore holes (…)." Prélaz, "IDEP and HEKS EPER", 1.

10. See the appended Constitution of the Mopani Farmers Union.

11. Prélaz, Valentin, ibid., 2.

12. Prélaz, ibid.

It should be noted that in addition to the legal framework provided by the associations and the federation, the government has set up an anti-poverty program in rural and disadvantaged areas such as the region covered by IDEP.[13]

Matome Malatji deplored the government's unwillingness to grant access to land as it had promised. In ten years, only 3% of the land has been redistributed to the farmers.[14] The former owners often burn the trees and break the pipes when they leave their property, as we saw in the field (see below, second visit).

A long discussion of a water supply project supported by a Genevan attorney followed. A group of heirs he was representing had offered to donate 15,000 francs for a project, if possible the building of two bore holes, which are a way of drilling for access to water. But the two young women working for Matome Malatji, with the lovely names of Mokhadi and Kedibone, explained that this would be very expensive in South Africa. Valentin Prélaz asked them to contact at least three companies so the work could be awarded to the one offering the best price.

2.2 Site Visits

2.2.1 Mzilela Gardening Project

This association has approximately three hundred members. Lazarus Moger is the manager.

Moger is a young retiree (he worked in a mine until 2007) who has become the manager of a plot of about 222 hectares. He proudly showed us his fields of beans. He also grows a large number of fruit trees, especially mangoes, and employs many small farmers, including his son. His fields are well tended, with working irrigation. He himself installed a water pumping system.

Moger was awarded a prize from the municipal government for his management of the land. He explained that together with the neighboring farmers, he is required to produce 20 metric tons of fruits and vegetables per year for Pick n Pay; failure to do so would result in termination of the contract. He noted an urgent need for new tractors, as his were defective. To end the visit, we were asked to complete the usual form[15] attesting to our visit.

---

13. Southern Africa Regional Programme 2007–2009 and its extension until end of 2012, see Prélaz, ibid., 3. This report also mentioned the following stakeholders: Department of Agriculture, Department of Land Affairs, Department of Labour, Department of Health and Social Development, District Municipality, etc.

14. Restitution Land Rights Act, Cooperatives Act.

15. All of the communities had us fill out such a form.

2.2.2 Trichardsdaal Balloon Farm

The South African farmers reclaimed this farm after a years-long legal battle. Despite having been paid by the government, the former owner absolutely refused to leave. He was finally separated from his property in 2010, but not without first having destroyed the pipe system! Such serious clashes show the difficulty of getting beyond the issue of apartheid in the real world, even though it was banned in 1990.

2.2.3 Khomananihitirha Farmers Association

This delightful half-hectare farm was run by a woman in her forties. She gives preference to organic methods and teaches this type of farming to the association's other forty-nine members. She talked about the difficulty of obtaining water.

She shows visitors a hollow where two palm trees have been planted; she hopes to build a small dam there. She also plans to plant a *marula* tree, a species typical of South Africa, next year. She noted that in addition to the association farmers, her four sisters help her a great deal.

2.2.4 Nursery in Maruleng

Four women and a man, all of a certain age, greeted us next to an enormous termite nest. The very humble man was the municipal secretary; he spoke enthusiastically about current projects. He explained that he had formerly worked in a mine.

He told us of his wish to help the land he administers prosper and how grateful he is that the visitors were taking an interest in his water problems. He wanted to build a bore hole so that women would not have to go so far to get water in buckets from the river. This would enable them to take better care of the garden.

Seedlings in the greenhouse were covered with ashes to deter locusts.

A Ray of Hope

EPER employee Donna Andrews[16] spoke passionately about the Mopani Farmers Union, of which the projects mentioned above are illustrative. She concedes that resources and potential vary widely. But she thinks that this IDEP-supported union is an innovation in South Africa and that its philosophy and structure foster true solidarity among farmers. She has high hopes, is certain even, that this system will make it possible for the "new farmers" to have a better life. Thanks to the MFU, the association's member farmers are leaving the multitudinous ranks of the unemployed (48%) and can live life with dignity. They are in control of their own future, and so can avoid becoming welfare recipients.

16. Of Cape Town.

C. Conclusion

I returned to Switzerland having been both enriched by striking images of water problems, like the one the cover page of this article, and persuaded that despite the difficulties, we must tirelessly continue our dialogue with the African partners.

Both the partners and the communities with which we met were cooperative and anxious to improve their living conditions by training themselves as best they could to face their challenges. I note that, very often, I saw in them a sense of responsibility and commitment, with the desire to be completely free to take up the challenges of daily living.

Such freedom can be won through the associations they have created.

However, obstacles of all sorts—institutional, political, climatic and economic—are such that help is always welcome. For example, they were very thankful for the support they were receiving, and also expressed their great hopes of being able to count on assistance from EPER for a long time to come.

Modest though it may be, Switzerland's contribution is essential, because it provides real encouragement to fight for a better future in a climate where water is especially unpredictable, but real potential exists.

Here I would like to state my admiration for those who share their expertise with the African people, the employees of this charitable organization of the Swiss churches. They are helping to bring these people closer to us, ultimately to become true brothers and sisters for whom we can and must show concern.

This trip to Zimbabwe and South Africa in the spring of 2011 helped me decide to focus mainly on Africa when I write my dissertation on the topic of justice for water, a project I mentioned in the introduction to this report.

Evelyne Fiechter-Widemann

Bibliography

Abel, Olivier, et al., eds. *Jean Calvin et Thomas Hobbes: Naissance de la modernité politique [John Calvin and Thomas Hobbes: the birth of political modernity].* Genève: Labor et Fides, 2013.

———. "La responsabilité incertaine [Uncertain responsibility]." *Esprit 1994/11.* http://olivierabel.fr/ethique-et-politique/la-responsabilité-incertaine.php.

Agi, Marc. *Christianisme et droits de l'Homme [Christianity and human rights].* Paris: Des Idées et des hommes, 2007.

Aksoy, Emine E. "La notion de dignité humaine dans la sauvegarde des droits fondamentaux des détenus [The notion of human dignity in the protection of prisoners' basic rights]." In *Prison policy and prisoner's rights, Proceedings of the Colloquium of the IPPF."* Stavern, Norway, 25-28 June 2008. Nijmegen: Wolf legal, (2008) 45–61.

Al Jayyousi, Odeh. *Water As a Human Right: Towards Civil Society Globalization.* In Biswas, Asit, K. et al., *Water As a Human Right for the Middle East and North Africa*, 121–31. London: Routledge, 2008.

Alexandrowicz, Charles. "Le droit des nations aux Indes orientales, (XVIe, XVIIe, XVIIIe siècles (fin) *[The law of nations in the East Indies (sixteenth, seventeenth, eighteenth centuries (end)].* Annales. Economies, Sociétés, Civilisations* [Annals. Economies, Societies, Civilizations] 19 (1964) 869–84. http://persee.fr/doc/ahess_0395-2649_1964_num_19_5_421228.

Alloa, Emmanuel. "La phénoménologie comme science de l'homme sans l'homme [Phenomenology as a science of Man without Man]." *Tidschrift voor Filosofie* 72 (2010) 79. philpapers.org/rec/ALLLPC.

Annuaire français de droit international 43 (1977).

Apel, Karl-Otto. *Diskurs und Verantwortung. Das Problem des Uebergangs zur postkonventionnellen Moral* (translated into French as *Discussion et responsabilité*) *[Discussion and responsibility: The problem of transitioning to postconventional morality].* Paris: Cerf, 1996.

Arendt, Hannah. *Condition de l'homme moderne [The human condition].* Translated by Georges Fradier. Paris: Calmann-Lévy, 1983.

———. *La vie de l'esprit, I. La pensée [Life of the mind, I. The mind].* Paris: PUF, 1981.

Aristote. *Ethique à Nicomaque [Nichomachean ethics].* Translated by Richard Bodeüs. Paris: Flammarion, 2004.

———. *Métaphysique.* Translated by Marie-Paule Duminil et Annick Jaulin. Paris: Flammarion, 2008.

Arnsperger, Christian, and Philippe Van Parijs. *Ethique économique et sociale [Economic and Social Ethics].* Paris: La Découverte, 2003.

BIBLIOGRAPHY

Arrangement relatif à la protection, à l'utilisation et à la réalimentation de la nappe souterraine franco-suisse du Genevois [Arrangement for the protection, use, and recharging of the Franco-Swiss aquifer in the Geneva area], signed by the Republic and Canton of Geneva and Upper Savoy Prefecture, which entered into effect on January 1,1978. http://www.internationalwaterlaw.org/documents/regionaldocs/franko-swiss-aquifer.html.

Ascencio, Hervé. "Le Pacte mondial et l'apparition d'une responsabilité internationale des entreprises." In *Le Pacte mondial des Nations Unies 10 ans après*, edited by Boisson de Chazournes, Laurence and Emmanuelle Mazuyer, 183. Bruxelles: Bruylant, 2011.

Autin, Albert. *L'Institution chrétienne de Calvin [Calvin's Institutes of the Christian Religion]*. Paris: Malfère, 1929.

Baillat, Aline. " La gouvernance de l'eau à la lumière du 6ème Forum mondial de l'eau." *Actes du 2ème colloque interdisciplinaire organisé par le W4W, Eau Besoin Vital et Justice Globale* (Mars 2012). http:www.ville-ge.ch/mhs/anima_2012_eau.php; in English :"Governance for Water in Light of the Sixth World Water Forum." http:www.fiechter.name/w4w.

Banque, Mondiale. "Private Participation in Infrastructure Database." (Status July 2012). http://ppi.worldbank.org.

Baranes, William. " De l'injuste au juste." In *De l'injuste au juste*, edited by Marie-Anne Frison-Roche and William Baranes. Paris: Dalloz, 1997.

Bastaire, Jean. "Pour en finir avec Lynn White *[Let us be done with Lynn White]*." In *Crise écologique, crise des valeurs? Défis pour l'anthropologie et la spiritualité*, edited by Dominique Bourg and Philippe Roch, 69–76. Geneva: Labor et Fides, 2010.

Becchi, Paolo. "Our Responsibility Towards Future Generations." In *Efficiency, Sustainability, and Justice to Future Generations*, edited by Klaus Mathis, 77–96. Lucerne: Springer, 2011.

Beitz, Charles. *Political Theory and International Relations*. Princeton: Princeton University Press, 1979.

Ben-Ghiat, Ruth. "Un cinéma d'après-guerre: le néoréalisme italien et la transition démocratique." *Annales, Histoire, Sciences Sociales* 63 (2008) 1215–48. http://www.cairn.info/revue-annales-2008-6-page-1215.htm.

Benicourt, Emmanuelle. "Amartya Sen: une nouvelle ère pour le développement?" *Tiers-Monde* 47 186 (2006) 433–47. http://www.persee.fr/doc/tiers_1293-8882_2006_num_47_186_5639.

Berlin, Isaiah. *Four Essays on Liberty*. Oxford: Oxford University Press, 1969.

Bertrand, Benjamin. "Etat-providence et libéralisme redistributif: entre 'nouveau' et 'néo libéralisme'." Master's thesis. Montréal:Université du Québec, 2012.

Beza, Theodore. *Du droit des magistrats (1574) [On the rights of magistrates]*. Scholarly edition by Robert R. Kingdon. Geneva: Droz, 1970.

Bieler, André. *La pensée économique et sociale de Calvin [Calvin's economic and social thought]*. Geneva: Georg, 2008.

Bioy, Xavier. "La dignité, question de principes *[Dignity: Questions on principles]*." In *Justice, éthique et dignité [Justice, ethics, and dignity]*, edited by Simone Gaboriau and Hélène Pauliat, 47–86. Limoges: Pulim, 2006.

Birnbacher, Dieter. *La responsabilité envers les générations futures [Responsibility toward future generations]*. Paris: PUF, 1994.

Biswas, Asit K., and Cecilia Tortajada. "Editorial: Infrastructure and Development." *International Journal of Water Resources Development* 30 (2014) 3–7.

———. "Water Supply of Phnom Penh: an Example of Good Governance." *International Journal of Water Resources Development* 26 (2010) 157–72.

Boisson de Chazournes, Laurence. *Fresh Water in International Law*. Oxford: Oxford University Press, 2013.

———. "Le droit à l'eau et la satisfaction des besoins humains: notions de justice [The right to water and meeting human needs: Notions of justice]." In *Unité et diversité du droit international. Ecrits en l'honneur du professeur Pierre-Marie Dupuy [The unity and diversity of international law. Papers in honor of Profes[sor Pierre-Marie Dupuy]*, 967–81. La Haye: Nijhoff, 2014.

———."Eau, besoin vital et justice glogale : perspective juridique." *Actes du 2ème colloque interdisciplinaire organisé par le W4W, Eau Besoin Vital et Justice Globale* (Mars 2012). http :www.ville-ge.ch/mhs/anima_2012_eau.php ; in English: "*Water, Vital Need and Global Justice: A Legal Perspective.*" http :www.fiechter.name/w4w.

Boisson de Chazournes, Laurence, and Emmanuelle Mazuyer, eds. *Le Pacte mondial des Nations Unies 10 ans après [The UN Global Compact ten years later]*. Brussels: Bruylant, 2011.

Boltanski, Luc. *La souffrance à distance [Distant suffering]*. Paris: Métailié, 1993.

Bonhoeffer, Dietrich. *Ethique [Ethics]*. Translated by Lore Jeanneret. Genève: Labor et Fides, 1965 (translation into French of *Ethik*, Munich: Kaiser, 1949) paragraph headed "Les droits naturels de la vie et de l'esprit," 149 n1. English: see Bonhoeffer, Dietrich, *Ethic*. Translated by Neville Horton Smith, New York: Macmillan, 1955, paragraph headed "The Natural Rights of the Life of the Mind," 186 n. 1.

———. *Résistance et soumission, Lettres et notes de captivité [Letters and papers from prison]*. 1970. Translated by Bernard Lauret with the collaboration of Henry Mottu. Genève: Labor et Fides, "Œuvres de Dietrich Bonhoeffer" 8, 2006.

Bonino, Serge-Thomas. *À la recherche d'une éthique universelle, Nouveau regard sur la loi naturelle [In search of a universal ethic, a new look at natural law]*. Commission théologique internationale. Paris: Cerf, 2009.

Bony, Paul. "Une lecture de l'épître aux Romains: l'Evangile, Israël et les Nations [A reading of the Epistle to the Romans :the Gospel, Israel and the nations]. Revue catholique de formation permanente [Catholic review for continuous professional development], Esprit & Vie, no 82. Paris: Cerf, 2003.

Bourg, Dominique, and Philippe Roch, eds. *Crise écologique, crise des valeurs? Défis pour l'anthropologie et la spiritualité*. Genève: Labor et Fides, 2010.

Bourguinat, Henri. *Les intégrismes économiques. Essai sur la nouvelle donne planétaire. [Economic fundamentalisms. Essay on the world's new deal]* Paris: Dalloz, 2006.

Bouvignies-Bouchindhomme, Isabelle. "Hobbes sans Calvin? [Hobbes without Calvin?]" In *Jean Calvin et Thomas Hobbes. Naissance de la modernité politique*, edited by Olivier Abel, et al., 115–36. Genève: Labor et Fides, 2013.

Bovay, Claude. "Pauvreté *[Poverty]*." In *Encyclopédie du protestantisme*, edited by Pierre Gisel and Lucie Kaennel, 1053–54. Paris-Genève: Cerf-Labor et Fides, 1995. [2nd edition: Paris-Geneve: Quadrige-PUF-Labor et Fides, 2006].

Brandt. *L'obsolescence de l'offre religieuse [Obsolescence in what religion has to offer]*. Geneva: Slatkine, 2010. [2nd edition: Paris-Genève: Quadrige-PUF-Labord et Fides, 2006].

Brooks, David B. "Human Rights to Water in North Africa and the Middle East: What is New and What is Not; What is Important and What is Not." In *Water as a Human Right for the*

Middle East and North Africa, edited by Asit K. Biswas, et al., 19–33. London and New York: Routledge, 2008.

Brown, Robert McAfee. *Liberation Theology: An Introductory Guide.* Westminster: John Knox, 1993.

Bühler, Pierre. "Ethique et droit dans la théologie protestante." In *Ethique et droit,* edited by François Dermange and Laurence Flachon, 143–59. Genève: Labor et Fides, 2002.

———. "Prédestination et Providence [Predestination and Providence]." In *Encyclopédie du protestantisme,* edited by Pierre Gisel and Lucie Kaennel, 1096–111. Paris-Genève : Cerf-Labor et Fides, 1995. [2nd edition: Paris-Genève: Quadrige-PUF-Labor et Fides, 2006].

Caflisch, Lucius. "Le droit à l'eau—un droit de l'homme internationalement protégé? [Is the right to water an internationally protected human right ?]" In *L'eau en droit international,* edited by Société Française pour le Droit International, 385–94. Paris: Pedone, 2011.

Calvin, Jean. *Commentaire des cinq livres de Moïse [Commentary of the Pentateuch],* 1564, Op. Calv., t. XXIV et XXV.

———. *Commentaires Esaïe, sur Es. 30:23 [Commentary on Isaiah, covering Isaiah 30 :23],* cited by André Bieler. *La pensée économique et sociale de Calvin [Calvin's economic and social thought].* Reprinted, Genève: Georg, 2008.

———. *Commentaires sur le Nouveau Testament, [Commentaries on the New Testament].* French edition of 1561. Paris, 1854.

———. *96e sermon sur le livre de Job, sur Job 26:8–14 [Ninety-sixth sermon on the book of Job, covering Job 26:8–14].* Op. Calv., t. XXXIV.

———. *L'Institution chrétienne.* Translated by Marie de Védrines et Paul Wells. Aix-en-Provence, Charols: Excelsis, 2009.

———. *Institution de la religion chrétienne.* Edition nouvelle publiée par la Société Calviniste de France. Genève: Labor et Fides, 1955.

Calvo-Mendieta, Iratxe, et al. "Entre bien marchand et patrimoine commun, l'eau au cœur des débats de l'économie de l'environnement [Between a marketable good and a shared resource :Water at the heart of environmental economy debates]." In *L'eau mondialisée, la gouvernance en question [Globalized water: A question of governance],* edited by Graciela Schneier-Madanes, 61–74. Paris: La Découverte, 2010.

Camus, Albert. Excerpt from his acceptance speech for the Nobel prize for literature, December 10, 1957. http://www.nobelprize.org/nobel_prizes/literature/laureates/1957/camus-speech-f.html.

Canto-Sperber, Monique. *L'inquiétude morale et la vie humaine [Moral disquiet and hunan life.* Paris: PUF, 2001.

Cassin, René. *Les guerres de 1914-1918 et de 1939-1945 et le combat pour la dignité humaine [The wars of 1914-1918 and 1939-1945 and the struggle for human dignity].* Marseille: Centre littéraire d'impression provençal, 2008.

Chongkittavorn, Kavi. "Is the ASEAN Community withering?" *The Straits Times,* September 25, 2013, A 21.

Cicéron. *De republica libri [On the republic],* III, 17, quotation on Wikipedia.

Combemale, Pascal. *Introduction à Marx [Introduction to Marx].* Paris: La Découverte, 2010.

Comte-Sponville, André. *Petit traité des grandes vertus.* Paris: PUF,1995.

Conseil de l'Europe [Council of Europe]. "Le principe du respect de la dignité de la personne humaine [The principle of respect for human dignity]." In *Actes du séminaire UniDem,* organisé à Montpellier du 2 au 6 juillet 1998 en coopération avec le Pôle universitaire européen de Montpellier et du Languedoc-Roussillon et la Faculté de droit, Commission européenne pour la démocratie par le droit [Proceedings of the *UniDem* seminar held in Montpellier, July 2-6, 1998, in cooperation with the European university cluster of Montpellier and Languedoc-Roussillon and the School of Law - European Commission for Democracy through law], 26–44. Strasbourg: du Conseil de l'Europe, 1999.

Constitution fédérale Suisse. *Recueil Systématique* [Systematic Compendium of Swiss Federal Law], 101. http://www.admin.ch/ch/f/sr/c101.html. April 18, 1999.

Constitution genevoise du 14.10.2012, Recueil systématique, RS 131.234. http://www.admin.ch/ch/f/rs/131_234/a42.html.

Constitution of the Republic of South Africa, December 18, 1996 http://www.wipo.int/wipolex/en/details.jsp?id=6455.

Convention on Access to Information, Public Participation in Decision-Making and Access to Justice in Environmental Matters (Aarhus Convention), June 25, 1998, https://treaties.un.org/pages/ViewDetails.aspx?src=TREATY&mtdsg_no=XXVII-13&chapter=27&lang=en&clang=_en.

Convention on the Elimination of All Forms of Discrimination Against Women, A/RES/34/180, New York, December 18, 1979. http://www.ohchr.org/EN/ProfessionalInterest/Pages/CEDAW.aspx.

Convention on the Law of the Non-navigational Uses of International Watercourses (A/51/49) adopted by the General Assembly of the United Nations at its 51st session, New York, entry into force August 17, 2014. http://legal.un.org/ilc/texts/instruments/english/conventions/8_3_1997.pdf.

Convention on the Rights of the Child, A/RES/44/5, New York, November 20, 1989. http://www.ohchr.org/EN/ProfessionalInterest/Pages/CRC.aspx.

Convention on Wetlands of International Importance especially as Waterfowl Habitat (Ramsar Convention), February, 2, 1971, United Nations Treaty Series, 14583.

Convention relative à la protection, à l'utilisation, à la réalimentation et au suivi de la nappe souterraine franco-suisse du Genevois, *[Agreement concerning the protection, use, recharging, and monitoring of the Franco-Swiss aquifer in the Geneva area]* signée entre la Communauté d'Agglomération de la Région Annemassienne, la Communauté de Communes du Genevois, la Commune de Viry et la République et canton de Genève, ayant pris effet le 1er janvier 2008. http://www.unece.org/env/water/meetings/legal_board/2010/annexes_groundwater_paper/Arrangement_French_Swiss.pdf.

Coyras, Timothée. *"Lévinas et le primat inconditionné de l'autre." Actu Philososphia* (March 2009). http://www.actu-philosophia.com/spip.php?article95.

Cullet, Philippe, et al. *Water Governance in Motion: Towards Socially & Environmentally Sustainable Water Law.* New Delhi: Cambridge University Press, 2010.

Cuviller, Armand. *Nouveau dictionnaire philosophique [New Philosophical Dictionary].* Coulommiers-Paris: Armand Colin, 1964.

D'Humières, Patrick. *Le développement durable va-t-il tuer le capitalisme? Les réponses de l'éco-capitalisme [Will sustainable development kill capitalism? Eco-capitalism answers].* Paris: Maxima, 2010.

De Albuquerque, Catarina. "Droit à l'eau : passer de la théorie à la mise en œuvre." Conférence du 11 septembre 2010 relayée par A.G.L.E.A.U. (alerte générale de l'eau), [Lecture given on September 11, 2010, as reported by AGLEAU]. *agleau.blogspot.com/2010/09/catarina-de-albuquerque-precise-pour.html.*

De Bèze, Théodore. *Du droit des magistrats* (1574). Edition critique par Kingdon, Robert R. Genève: Droz, 1970.

De Frouville, Olivier. "Une conception démocratique du droit international [A democratic conception of international law]." *Revue européenne des sciences sociales* XXXIX-120 (2001) 101–44. http://ress.revues.org/659.

De Grotius, Hugo. *Le Droit de la guerre et de la paix [The right of war and peace]*. *Prolégomènes [The preliminary discourse]*, §XI. Translated by P. Pradier-Fodéré.1867. Paris, PUF, 1999, 12. Cited by Forthomme, Bernard, "La prédestination est-elle une aventure ?" In *Jean Calvin et Thomas Hobbes. Naissance de la modernité politique [John Calvin and Thomas Hobbes: the birth of political modernity*. Edited by Olivier Abel, et al., eds. Genève: Labor et Fides, 2013, 24.

———. *Mare liberum [The freedom of the seas]*, which is chapter n°XII of *De Jure Prædæe commentaries [Commentary on the law of prize and booty]*. See de Grotius, Hugo, *De la liberté des mers [The freedom of the seas]*. Translated by Antoine de Courtin (1703), Caen: Université de Caen/Centre de philosophie politique et juridique (Bibliothèque de philosophie politique et juridique, Textes et Documents) 1990. Cited by Forthomme, Bernard, "La prédestination est-elle une aventure ?" In *Jean Calvin et Thomas Hobbes. Naissance de la modernité politique [John Calvin and Thomas Hobbes: the birth of political modernity*. Edited by Olivier Abel, et al., eds. Genève: Labor et Fides, 2013.

De Lutzel, Emmanuel. "Droit à l'eau: Quelles solutions, avec quels acteurs?" *Actes du 2ème colloque interdisciplinaire organisé par le W4W, Eau Besoin Vital et Justice Globale* (Mars 2012). http :www.ville-ge.ch/mhs/anima_2012_eau.php; in English: The Right to Water: What Solutions, Whose Action?" http :www.fiechter.name/w4w.

De Saint-Exupéry, Antoine. *Terre des hommes [Wind, sand and stars]*. Paris: Gallimard, Collection Folio, 1939.

De Stexhe, Guillaume. "Devoir, pouvoir? La responsabilité dans les limites de la simple humanité [Duty, power? Responsibility within the limits of simple humanity]." In *La responsabilité, face cachée des droits de l'homme [Responsibility, the hidden face of human rights]*. Hughes Dumont, et al. 107ff. Bruxelles: Bruylant, 2005.

De Tétaz, Jean-Marc. "Droit naturel [Modern natural law]." In *Encyclopédie du protestantisme*, edited by Pierre Gisel and Lucie Kaennel, 376–77. Paris-Genève : Cerf-Labor et Fides, 1995.

Delmas-Marty, Mireille. *Résister, Responsabiliser, Anticiper [Fight back, hold accountable, second-guess]*. Paris: Seuil, 2013.

Dembinski, Paul. "Eau, besoin vital et Justice globale: la quête du juste prix". *Actes du 2ème colloque interdisciplinaire organisé par le W4W, Eau Besoin Vital et Justice Globale* (Mars 2012). http :www.ville-ge.ch/mhs/anima_2012_eau.php; in English: "Water, Vital Need and Global Justice: Search of a Fair Price." www.fiechter.name/w4w.

Department of Development and Cooperation (Switzerland). "*Etude de l'empreinte hydrique suisse – Illustration de la dépendance de la Suisse à l'égard de l'eau*" *[A study of Switzerland's water footprint : An illustration of Switzerland's water dependence]*(2012). https://www.eda.admin.ch/content/dam/deza/fr/documents/publikationen/Diverses/209748-wasser-fussabdruck-schweiz_FR.pdf.

———. "Water 2015, Policy Principles and strategic guidelines for integrated water." https://www.eda.admin.ch/content/dam/deza/en/documents/themen/wasser/25138-integrated-water-resource-management_EN.pdf.

BIBLIOGRAPHY

Department of Water Affairs and Forestry (South African DWAF)'s site on Implementation Status of Free Basic Water Services, available at www.dwaf.gov.z./freebasicwater.

Dermange, François, and Laurence Flachon, eds. *Ethique et droit [Ethics and law]*. Genève: Labor et Fides, 2002.

Dermange, François, and Denis Müller. "*Utilitarisme [Utilitarianism]*." In *Encyclopédie du protestantisme*, edited by Pierre Gisel and Lucie Kaennel, 1457. Paris-Genève: Cerf-Labor et Fides, 1995.

Dermange, François. "Argent [Money]." In *Encyclopédie du protestantisme*, edited by Pierre Gisel and Lucie Kaennel, 43. Paris-Genève: Cerf-Labor et Fides, 1995.

———. "Calvin contre la puissance souveraine [Calvin against sovereign power]." In *Jean Calvin et Thomas Hobbes. Naissance de la modernité politique [John Calvin and Thomas Hobbes: the birth of political modernity]*, edited by Olivier Abel, et al., 75–96. Genève: Labor et Fides, 2013. [2nd edition: Paris-Genève: Quadrige-PUF-Labor et Fides, 2006].

———. "Développement durable." Cours donné à la Faculté de Théologie de Genève, automne 2012. (Unpublished).

———. *Le Dieu du marché, éthique, économie et théologie dans l'œuvre d'Adam Smith [The God of the market, ethics, economics, and theology in Adam Smith's work]*. Genève: Labor et Fides, 2003.

———. "*La diffusion du calvinisme. Réveils et mission [The spread of calvinism. Resurgence and missions]*." MOOC Courses, semaine 4. (11.11.13 au 15.11.13) https://class.coursera.org/calvin-001/wiki/view?page=syllabus.

———. "L'éthique de Calvin. Les avantages du modèle : une éthique de la responsabilité [Calvin's Ethics. The advantages of the model: an ethic of responsibility]." MOOC Courses, semaine n°3 (4.11.13 au 8.11.13), séquence n°5. https://class.coursera.org/calvin-001/wiki/view?page=syllabus.

———. "Mandeville, Bernard." In *Encyclopédie du protestantisme*, edited by Pierre Gisel and Lucie Kaennel, 865. Paris-Genève: Cerf-Labor et Fides, 1995. [2nd edition: Paris-Genève: Quadrige-PUF-Labor et Fides, 2006].

———. "*La responsabilité*." In *Introduction à l'éthique, penser, croire, agir*, edited by Jean-Daniel Causse and Denis Müller. Genève: Labor et Fides, 2009.

———. "Smith, Adam." In *Encyclopédie du protestantisme*, edited by Pierre Gisel and Lucie Kaennel, 1342–43. Paris-Genève: Cerf-Labor et Fides, 1995. [2nd edition: Paris-Genève: Quadrige-PUF-Labor et Fides, 2006].

———. "Le pôle Justice Sociale dans le développement durable: quelques enjeux de la discussion philosophique aujourd'hui". *Actes du 1er colloque interdisciplinaire organisé par le W4W, Trop ou Pas Assez d'Eau, Comment Bien Faire Avec Cette Ressource Vitale Capricieuse?* http :www.ville-ge.ch/mhs/anima_2011_eau.php; in English : "The Social Justice Focus in Sustainable Development : Some Challenges of the Current Philosophical Discussion." http :www.fiechter.name/w4w.

De Watteville, Renaud. "Est-il bien de vendre l'eau?" *Actes du 1er colloque interdisciplinaire organisé par le W4W, Trop ou Pas Assez d'Eau, Comment Bien Faire Avec Cette Ressource Vitale Capricieuse?* http:www.ville-ge.ch/mhs/anima_2011_eau.php; in English "Is Selling Water Good?" http:www.fiechter.name/w4w.

De Watteville, Renaud and Cédric Lombard. "Swiss Fresh Water: un système de dessalement de l'eau solaire pour les populations à faible revenu?" *Actes du 1er colloque interdisciplinaire organisé par le W4W, Trop ou Pas Assez d'Eau, Comment Bien Faire Avec Cette Ressource Vitale Capricieuse?* http:www.ville-ge.ch/mhs/anima_2011_eau.

php; in English: "Swiss Fresh Water: A Low-cost Decentralized Desalination System for Low-Income Populations?" http:www.fiechter.name/w4w.

Dihle, Albrecht. *Die Goldene Regel. Eine Einführung in die Geschichte der antiken und frühchristlichen Vulgärethik [The Golden Rule. An introduction to the history of ancient and early Christian popular ethics]*. Göttingen: Vandenhoeck & Ruprecht, 1962.

Dilthey, Wilhelm. "Introduction à l'étude des sciences humaines [Introduction to the human sciences]." In *Les grands textes de la philosophie [The great texts of philosophy]*, edited by Georges Pascal, 200–01. Paris: Bordas, 1963.

Diop, Salif and Philippe Recacewicz. *Atlas mondial de l'eau, Une pénurie annoncée [World water atlas, a shortage ahead]*. Caen: Autrement, Collection Atlas/Monde, 2004.

Dostoyevsky, Fyodor. *The Brothers Karamazov*. Translated by Constance Garnett. New York: The Modern Library, 1996.

Du Roy, Olivier. *La Règle d'Or. Le retour d'une règle oubliée. [The Golden Rule: The return of a forgotten rule]*. Paris: Cerf, 2009.

Dublin Statement on Water and Sustainable Development, January 31, 1992. http://www.un-documents.net/h2o-dub.htm.

Dufour, Alfred. *Droits de l'homme, droit naturel et histoire [Human rights, modern natural law, and history]*. Paris: Léviathan, PUF, 1991.

Dufourcq, Elisabeth. *L'invention de la loi naturelle [The invention of natural law]*. Montrouge: Bayard, 2012.

Dumas, André. "Réponse à Hans Jonas." Esprit, 438 (1974) 190–92. http://www.jstor.org/stable/24262955.

———. "Justification." Encyclopedia Universalis. http://www.universalis.fr/encyclopedia/justification/.

Dumont, Hugues, et al. *La responsabilité, face cachée des droits de l'homme [Responsibility, the hidden face of human rights]*. Bruxelles: Bruylant, 2005.

Dunant, Henry. *Un souvenir de Solferino.* Berne: Croix-Rouge, 1964.

Dupuy, Jean-Pierre. *Avions-nous oublié le mal? Penser la politique après le 11 septembre [Had we forgotten evil? Thinking politics after September 11]*. Paris: Bayard, 2002.

Ecumenical Declaration on Water As a Human Right and a Public Good, Ed. Fédération des Eglises protestantes de Suisse FEPS, Bern, April 22, 2005. http://www.kirchenbund.ch/sites/default/files/publikationen/pdf/common-text-1.pdf).

Edelman, Bernard. *"La dignité de la personne humaine, un concept nouveau [The dignity of the human being]."* Recueil Dalloz, 185, 1997.

El Hassan bin Talal, Prince of Jordan. "Eau, besoin vital et Justice Globale" *Actes du 2ème colloque interdisciplinaire organisé par le W4W, Eau Besoin Vital et Justice Globale* (Mars 2012). http :www.ville-ge.ch/mhs/anima_2012_eau.php; in English:" Water, Vital Need and Global Justice." http:www.fiechter.name/w4w.

———. "Water Management in Monotheistic Religions", http://www.ce.utexas.edu/prof/mckinney/ce397/Topics/Religion-Clark.pdf.

Encyclopédie Larousse. *"Bien."* http://www.larousse.fr/encyclopedie/divers/bien/26802.

Encyclopaedia Universalis. Paris: Encyclopaedia Universalis France, 1968.

Esping-Andersen, Gøsta. *The Three Worlds of Welfare Capitalism*. Princeton: Princeton University Press, 1990.

Falkenmark, Malin. *"No Freshwater Security without major Shift in Thinking."* Stockholm International Water Institute (SIWI) Sweden (2000). http://hdl.handle.net/10535/5149.

Falque, Max, ed. *L'eau entre réglementation et marché [Water between regulation and the market]*. Paris: Johanet, 2014.

FAO: Voluntary Guidelines to support the progressive realization of the Right to Adequate Food in the Context of National Food Security, November 24, 2004. http://www.fao.org/docrep/009/y7937e/y7937e00.htm.

Faruqui, Naser, et al. *La gestion de l'eau selon l'Islam*. Ottawa et Paris: Les Presses de l'Université des Nations Unies, Crdi-Karthala, 2003.

Federal Constitution of the Swiss Confederation, April 18, 1999, Classified Compilation, RS 101 https://www.admin.ch/opc/en/classified-compilation/19995395/index.html.

Fiasse, Gaëlle. *Paul Ricœur, De l'homme faillible à l'homme capable [Paul Ricœur, from fallible man to capable man]*. Paris: PUF, 2008.

Fiechter, Eric, and Nicolas Zbinden. "La médiation en Suisse: les raisons d'un manque d'impact" *[Why mediation has had little impact in Switzerland]*." *Plaidoyer 1* 3 (2013) 23–26. https://www.asbs.sg/pdf/misc_03.pdf.

Fiechter-Widemann, Evelyne. "Pardon, catharsis de la violence extrême? [Forgiveness: can it bring catharsis in cases of extreme violence ?]" Mémoire présenté à la Faculté de Théologie, Genève (2001). http://www.fiechter.name/publications.

———. "A la recherche de l'eau avec l'EPER/HEKS, Visites de communautés rurales au Zimbabwe et en Afrique du Sud." http: www.fiechter.name/w4w; in English: "Looking for water with EPER/HEKS, Visits to Rural Communities in Zimbabwe and South Africa " (March 2011) http: www.fiechter.name.

———. "Eau comme droit humain, Eau comme bien public, Eau comme bien économique."*Actes du 1er colloque interdisciplinaire organisé par le W4W, Trop ou Pas Assez d'Eau, Comment Bien Faire Avec Cette Ressource Vitale Capricieuse?* (Mars 2011). http://www.ville-ge.ch/mhs/anima_2011_eau.php; in English: "Water As a Human Right, Water As a Public Good, Water As an Economic Good." http: www.fiechter.name/w4w.

———. "Eau, besoin vital et Justice Globale: perspective éthique." *Actes du 2ème colloque interdisciplinaire organisé par le W4W, Eau Besoin Vital et Justice Globale* (Mars 2012). http :www.ville-ge.ch/mhs/anima_2012_eau.php; in English: "Water, Vital Need and Global Justice: Ethical Perspective." http : www.fiechter.name/w4w.

———. "La Responsabilité de protéger, comme condition de possibilité d'une Ethique Globale de l'eau." *Actes du 3ème colloque interdisciplinaire organisé par le W4W, Eau Besoin Vital et Justice Globale* (Mars 2013). http :www.ville-ge.ch/mhs/anima_2013_eau.php; in English: "The Duty to Protect As a Condition of Possibility for a Global Water Ethic." http : www.fiechter.name/w4w.

Fondation pour Genève, ed." *Cahier 1 Soft Gouvernance [Soft governance]*." Genève: L'Observatoire, 2007.

———. *"Cahier 2 Multi-stakeholders."* Genève: L'Observatoire, 2007.

———. *"Cahier 3 Responsabilité sociétale [Corporate responsibility]."* Genève: L'Observatoire, 2009.

———. *"Cahier 4 « Soft » Institutions."* Genève: L'Observatoire, 2010.

Forster, Marc. "The Quantum of Solace." Film (Switzerland 2008).

Forthomme, Bernard. "La prédestination est-elle une aventure?" In *Jean Calvin et Thomas Hobbes. Naissance de la modernité politique*, edited by Olivier Abel, et al. Genève: Labor et Fides, 2013.

Friedman, Thomas L. *The World is Flat. A Brief History of the Twenty First Century.* New York: Farrar, Straus and Giroux, 2005.

Fuchs, Eric, and Pierre-André Stucki. *Au nom de l'autre. Essai sur le fondement des droits de l'homme. [In the name of the Other. Essay on the basis of human rights].* Genève: Labor et Fides, 1985.

Fuchs, Eric. *Comment faire pour bien faire ?* [How can we do things right?] Genève: Labor et Fides, 1996.

———. *La morale selon Calvin.* Paris: Cerf, 1986.

Gaboriau, Simone et Hélène Pauliat, eds. *Justice, éthique et dignité.* Limoges: Pulim, 2006.

Galland, Frank. *Le Grand Jeu: Chroniques géopolitiques de l'eau,* Paris *[The Grand Game]*: CNRS, 2014.

Garapon, Antoine. *Raison du moindre Etat, Le néolibéralisme et la justice [The rationale for the least government: neoliberalism and justice].* Paris: Odile Jacob, 2010.

Gaziaux, Eric, and Laurent Lemoine. *La loi naturelle – Le retour d'un concept en miettes? [Natural law: the return of a concept in tatters?]* Revue d'éthique et de théologie morale [Journal of ethics and moral theology]. Paris: Cerf, 2010.

Genard, Jean-Louis. *La grammaire de la responsabilité [The Grammar of Responsibility].* Paris: Cerf, 1999.

———. "Les métamorphoses de la responsabilité [The metamorphoses of responsibility]." In *La Responsabilité, face cachée des Droits de l'Homme,* edited by Hughes Dumont, et al., 131–51. Bruxelles: Bruylant, 2005.

General Comment no. 15, The Right to Water (art. 11 and 12), January 20, 2003, E/C.12/2002/11. http://www.refworld.org/docid/4538838d11.html.

Gérard, Christophe. "*Herméneutique de la valeur (1). Distinctions élémentaires pour l'étude axiologique des textes. [Hermeneutics of value (1)]. Basic distinctions for the axiological study of texts]*" In *Qu'est-ce qui fait la valeur des textes?* Edited by Christine Chollier. Reims: Presses Universitaires de Reims, 2011.

Ghemawat, Pankaj. "Shed caveman mentality." The Straits Times, July 20, 2013, D9.

———. *World 3.0, Global prosperity and how to achieve it.* Boston: Harvard Business Review Press, 2011.

Girardin, Benoît. "L'eau a-t-elle un coût? Et si oui, lequel? Considérations éthiques [Does Water have a Cost? And If so, What? Ethical considerations]." *Actes du 1er colloque interdisciplinaire organisé par le W4W, Eau Besoin Vital et Justice Globale* (Mars 2011). http://www.ville-ge.ch/mhs/anima_2011_eau.php; in English *"Does Water Have a Cost, and If So, What? Ethical Considerations."* http: www.fiechter.name/w4w.

———. *Ethics in Politics, Why it matters more than ever and How it can make a difference.* And its French translation, *"L'éthique: un défi pour la politique. Pourquoi l'éthique importe plus que jamais en politique et comment elle peut faire la différence."* Genève: Globethics.net, 2014.

———. "Gestion juste des aquifère transfrontaliers." *Actes du 3ème colloque interdisciplinaire organisé par le W4W, Ethique globale de l'Eau.* http://www.ville-ge.ch/mhs/anima_2013_eau.php; in English: *"Fair Management of Transboundary Aquifers."* (March 2013). http : www.fiechter.name/w4w.

Gisel, Pierre and Lucie Kaennel, eds. *Encyclopédie du protestantisme.* Cerf-Labor et Fides, Paris-Genève, 1995. [2nd edition: Paris-Genève: Quadrige-PUF-Labor et Fides, 2006].

Gnesotto, Nicole, and Giovanni Grevi. *Le monde en 2025 [The World in 2025].* Paris: Robert Laffont, 2007.

Goodmann, John. *The Golden Rule, or the Royal Law of Equity Explained*. Londres: Samuel Roycroft, 1688.

Gorbatchev, Michaïl. "*Allons-nous attendre d'avoir soif pour mesurer la valeur de l'eau? [Are we going to wait until we are thirsty to measure the worth of water ?]*" Quotidien de Suisse romande, Le Temps (2013). http://www.letemps.ch/opinions/2013/09/01/allons-attendre-soif-mesurer-valeur-eau.

Goyard-Fabre, Simone. *Les embarras philosophiques du droit naturel [The philosophical predicaments of modern natural law]*. Librairie Philosophique. Paris: Vrin, 2002.

———. "Les rapports du droit et de la morale aujourd'hui [The relations between right and morality today] ." In Dermange, François, and Laurence Flachon, eds. *Ethique et droit [Ethics and law]*. Genève: Labor et Fides, 2002.

Griffin, R.C. *Water Resource Economics. The Analysis of Scarcity, Policies, and Projects*. Cambridge, MA: The MIT Press, 2006.

Grinevald, Jacques. "La thèse de Lynn White, Jr (1966) sur les racines historiques, culturelles et religieuses de la crise de la civilisation industrielle moderne [Lynn White, Jr.'s thesis concerning the historical, cultural, and religious roots of the crisis in modern industrial civilization]." In *Crise écologique, crise des valeurs? Défis pour l'anthropologie et la spiritualité*, edited by Dominique Bourg and Philippe Roch, 38–67. Genève: Labor et Fides, 2010.

Grisel, Etienne. *Droits fondamentaux, Libertés idéales* [Fundamental rights, ideal freedoms]. Stämpfli: Bern, 2008.

Guttierez, Gustavo. *Force historique des pauvres*. In "Cogitatio Dei," 137. Paris: Cerf, 1986.

Haas, Guenther Horst. *The Concept of Equity in Calvin's Ethics*. Carlisle: Paternoster, 1997.

Habel, Norman, and Peter Trudinger. "Water: A Matter of Life and Death." In *Interface: A Forum for Theology in the World* 14 1, edited by Rev Dr Paul Babie. Adelaide, Australia: ATF Theology, 2011.

Häberli, Christian. "God, the WTO—and Hunger." In *Poverty and the International Economic Legal System, Duties to the World's Poor*, edited by Krista Nadakavukaren Schefer. Cambridge: Cambridge University Press, 2013.

———. "Water, Vital Need and Global Justice: *Economic Perspective. Right to Food and Right to Water: Are They the Same Challenge?*" Actes du 2ème *colloque interdisciplinaire organisé par le W4W, Eau Besoin Vital et Justice Globale* (Mars 2012). http :www.ville-ge.ch/mhs/anima_2012_eau.php.

Habermas, Jürgen. *De l'éthique de la discussion [Remarks on discourse ethics]*. Paris: Flammarion, 1992.

Haggenmacher, Peter. "La nouvelle physionomie du "Ius" et le remaniement du droit naturel." [The new physiognomy of "ius and the reworking of natural law], in *Grotius et la doctrine de la guerre juste [Grotius and the doctrine of just war]* (2013) 462–529. http://iheid.revues.org/627.

———. "Grotius, Hugo (1583–1645). In *Encyclopédie du protestantisme*, edited by Pierre Gisel and Lucie Kaennel, 556. Paris-Genève : Cerf-Labor et Fides, 1995. [2nd edition: Paris-Genève: Quadrige-PUF-Labor et Fides, 2006].

Hardin, Garret. "The Tragedy of the Commons." 1243–48. Science 162, 1968.

Hatting, Johan. "The state of the art in environmental ethics as a practical enterprise: a view from the Johannesburg document." In *Environmental Ethics and International Policy*, edited by Ten Have, Henk, A.M.J. Paris: Unesco, 2006.

Bibliography

Hegel, Georg Willhelm Friedrich. "*Principes de la philosophie du droit [Elements of the philosophy of right]*", part II, *La Moralité subjective (Moralität)* [Morality], section I: "Le projet (*der Vorsatz*) et la responsabilité (*die Schuld*)" [Purpose and responsibility], §115-118. Translated into French by Jean-Louis Vieillard-Baron. Paris: Flammarion, 1999.

Héraclite. *Fragments*. Translated by Jean-François Pradeau. Paris: Flammarion, 2004.

Hersch, Jeanne. "Quelques paradoxes des Droits de l'homme [Some paradoxes of human rights]." In *Festschrift zum 70. Geburtstag von Werner Kägi*, 183–92. Zürich: Schulthess Polygraphischer Verlag, 1978.

Hessel, Stéphane. *Indignez-vous [Time for outrage]*. Montpellier: Indigènes, 2010.

Hobbes, Thomas. *Leviathan*. Cited by Michel Villey, *Le droit et les droits de l'homme [The law and the rights of Man]*. Paris: Quadrige-PUF, 1983.

———. *Elementorum philosophiæ sectio tertia de Cive* (Paris, 1642), *Opera latina*, ed. Molesworth, London, 1839-1845, chapter III, §3, 198, reprint, Aalen, 1961, vol. 2, 133 ff., cited *De Cive*, see translation by S. Sorbière (1649), republished Paris, 1982, cited by Dufour, Alfred, *Droits de l'homme, droit naturel et histoire [Human rights, modern natural law, and history]*. Paris: Léviathan, PUF, 1991, 116, note 27 and 122, note 71.

Hoekstra, Arjen. *The water footprint of modern consumer society*. London: Routledge, 2013.

Hofer, Christian. "More Market in Water Supply: Understanding the International Human Rights Law Perspective." PhD diss., Rechtswissenschaftliche Fakultät der Universität Zürich, 2007.

———. "Wasserversorgung im Spannungsfeld von Menschenrecht und kommerzieller Nutzung [Supplying water in the area of tension between human rights and commercial use]." *Jusletter*, (2012). http://www.jusletter.ch.

International Covenant on Economic, Social and Cultural Rights, A/RES/2200 A (XXI), New York, December 16, 1966, https://treaties.un.org/doc/Publication/UNTS/Volume%20993/volume-993-I-14531-English.pdf.

Isocrate. *Eginétique*. Paris: Les Belles Lettres, 1928.

Jahanbelgloo, Ramin. *En toutes libertés. Entretiens (d'Isaiah Berlin) avec Ramin Jahanbegloo [Full freedom, interviews (by Isaiah Berlin) with Ramin Jahanbegloo]*. Paris: du Félin, 1990.

Jankelevitch, Vladimir. *Le paradoxe de la morale [The paradox of morality]*. Paris: Seuil, 1981.

Jaspers, Karl. "Conditions et possibilités d'un nouvel humanisme [On the conditions for a new humanism and its possibilities]. " Translated from German by Jeanne Hersch. In Rencontres internationales de Genève, tome IV, 1949, 211. Collection: Histoire et société d'aujourd'hui. Neuchâtel: La Braconnière, 1949.

———. "Pour un nouvel humanisme" [In support of a new humanism]. In *Rencontres internationales de Genève* [International Encounters in Geneva], vol. IV, 1949, 215. Collection: Histoire et société d'aujourd'hui [History and society today], Neuchâtel, La Braconnière, 1949, eighth interview dated September 10, 1949, 215.

Jehle, Frank. *Karl Barth: Une éthique politique, 1906-1968 [Ever against the stream: The politics of Karl Barth 1906-1968]*. Lausanne: d'En Bas, 2002.

Jobin, Guy. "Le paradigme de la responsabilité comme condition de l'éthique théologique. [The paradigm of responsibility as a condition of theological ethics]." Lecture given at Université Laval's Faculty of Theology and Religious Studies on October 24, 2002. *Laval théologique et philosophique [Theological and philosophical Laval]* 60 1 (2004), 134.

Jonas, Hans. *Le principe responsabilité. Une éthique pour la civilisation technologique.* [*The imperative of responsibility: In search of an ethics for the technological age*]. Translated by Jean Greisch. Paris: Champs essais, 1990.

Jonas, Hans and Ariane Favre. "Technologie et responsabilité. Pour une nouvelle éthique [Technology and responsibility: toward a new ethic]" Esprit 438 (1974), 163–90. http://www.jstor.org/stable/24262949.

Jovanovic, Miroslav. "Does globalisation take us for a ride?" In *Journal of Economic Integration* 25 3 (2010) 501–49. http://www.researchgate.net/publication/227489353_is_Globalisation_taking_us_for_a_Ride?

Kant, Immanuel. *Conjectures sur le commencement de l'histoire humaine* [*Conjectural beginning of human history*]. Translated by Ole Hansen-Love. Paris: Hatier, 2008.

———. *Critique de la raison pratique.* Translated by Jean-Pierre Fussler. Paris: Flammarion, 2003.

———. *Critique de la raison pure* [*A critique of pure reason*]. Translated by André Tremesaygues and Bernard Pacaud. Paris: Quadrige, PUF, 2012.

———. *Fondements de la métaphysique des mœurs* [*Groundwork of the metaphysic of morals*]. Translated by Victor Delbos, revised by A. Philonenko. Paris: Vrin, 2008.

———. *La religion dans les limites de la simple raison* [*Religion within the boundaries of mere reason*]. Translated by J. Gibelin. Paris: Vrin, 2010.

———. *Logique.* Translated by Louis Guillermit. Paris: Vrin, 2007.

———. *Métaphysique des mœurs II, Doctrine du droit, Doctrine de la vertu* [*Metaphysics of morals II, doctrine of right, doctrine of virtue*]. Translated by Alain Renaut. Paris: Flammarion, 1994.

———. *Qu'est-ce que les Lumières?* [*What is enlightenment?*]. Translated by Jean-François Poirier and Françoise Proust. Paris: Flammarion, 2006.

———. *Que signifie s'orienter dans la pensée?* [*What does it mean to orient oneself in thinking?*]. Translated by Jean-François Poirier and Françoise Proust. Paris : Flammarion, 2006.

———. *Vers la paix perpétuelle, esquisse philosophique* [*Toward a perpetual peace: A philosophical sketch*]. Translated by Jean-François Poirier and Françoise Proust. Paris: Flammarion, 2006.

La Fontaine, Jean de, *Le loup et le renard* [The Wolf and the Fox], Fable XI,6.

Lamy, Pascal, Director-General of the WTO, February 19, 2011, *Pragmatic Solutions need to be found now to enhance global governance,* speech given at the European University Institute in Florence, https://www.wto.org/english/news_e/sppl_e/sppl187_e.htm.

Lasserre, Frédéric, and Boutet, Annabelle. "Le droit international réglera-t-il les litiges du partage de l'eau? Le bassin du Nil et quelques autres cas (Note) [Will international law settle disputes about sharing water? The Nile basin and other cases (note)]." Etudes internationales 33 (3) (2002) 497–514. http://id.erudit.org/iderudit/704441ar.

Lau, Franz. *Die Religion in Geschichte und Gegenwart* [*Religion and history and in the present*]. Tübingen: Mohr Siebeck, 3rd éd., 1962.

Laurent, Pierre. *Pufendorf et la loi naturelle.* Paris: Vrin, 1982.

Lavelle, Louis. *Traité des valeurs, Théorie générale de la valeur* [*Treatise on values, general theory of value*], 1. Paris: PUF, 1951.

Lazerwitz, David. "The Flow of International Water Law: The International Law Commission's Law of the Non-Navigational Uses of International Watercourses." In *Indiana Journal of Global Legal Studies,* 1 1 (1993) 15.

Le Petit Larousse illustré. [The illustrated *Petit Larousse*]. Paris: Larousse, 2006.

Le Pourhiet, Anne-Marie. "Touche pas à mon préambule [Hands off my preamble." Le Figaro, 28 mai 2008. http://www.lefigaro.fr/debats/2008/05/24/01005-20080524ARTFIG00053-touche-pas-a-mon-preambule-.php.

Lechot, Pierre-Olivier. "Irénisme [Irenicism]." In *Encyclopédie du protestantisme*, edited by Pierre Gisel and Lucie Kaennel, 633–34. Paris-Genève: Cerf-Labor et Fides, 1995. [2nd edition: Paris-Genève: Quadrige-PUF-Labor et Fides, 2006].

Leclerc-Olive, Michèle, "Les notions de société civile, Usages et traductions." In *Les cahiers d'Artess* (2013). http://artess.hypotheses.org/73.

Lee Kuan Yew. *From Third World to First, The Singapore Story: 1965-2000*. New York: HarperCollins, 2000.

Leibniz, Gottfried Wilhelm. "*Méditation sur la notion commune de justice [Meditation on the common notion of justice]*." In *Le Droit et la Raison [Law and Reason]*, Edited by René Sève. Paris: Vrin, 1994.

Leiner, Martin. "Droit, Ethique et Justice. Annotations en relation avec l'ouvrage de Wolfgang Huber, *Gerechtigkeit und Recht*" [Law, ethics and justice. Annotations on Wolfgang Huber's work *Gerechtigkeit und Recht [Justice and law]*"]. In Dermange, François, and Laurence Flachon, eds. *Ethique et droit [Ethics and law]* Labor et Fides, Genève, 2002.

Lenoir, Frédéric. *Le temps de la responsabilité, Entretiens sur l'éthique [Time for responsibility. Interview on ethics]*. Paris: Fayard, 2013.

Leopold, Aldo. *Almanach d'un comté des sables [A sand county almanac]*. Translated by Anne Gibson. Paris: Flammarion, 2000.

Lévinas, Emmanuel. *Altérité et transcendance*. Paris: Librairie générale française, 4th édition, 2013.

———. *Humanisme de l'autre homme [Humanism of the other]*. Paris: Le Livre de Poche, Fata Morgana, 1972.

Liehard, Marc. "Le protestantisme et les droits de l'homme [Protestantisme and human rights]." In *Christianisme et droits de l'Homme,* edited by Marc Agi, 105–31. Paris: Des Idées et des Hommes, 2007.

London Protocol on Water and Health to the 1992 Convention on the Protection and Use of Transboundary Watercourses and International Lakes, (1999). https://treaties.un.org/doc/Publication/MTDSG/Volume%20II/Chapter%20XXVII/XXVII-5-a.en.pdf.

Lyons, Evelyne. "Conséquences sociales de la construction des barrages: quelles responsabilités et quels outils?" Actes du 3ème colloque interdisciplinaire organisé par le W4W, Ethique globale de l'Eau. http://www.ville-ge.ch/mhs/anima_2013_eau.php; in English: "*The Social Consequences of Building Dams: What Are the Responsibilities, What Are the Tools?*" (March 2013). http: www.fiechter.name/w4w.

Mahboob, Mahmood, and Filipe Santos. "The UBS-INSEAD Study on Family Philanthropy in Asia." UBS Philanthropy Services, INSEAD, Zurich, Singapore, Hong-Kong, (2011). http://sites.insead.edu/social_entrepreneurship/documents/insead_study_family_philantropy_asia.pdf.

Maillard, Nathalie. *La vulnérabilité, Une nouvelle catégorie morale? [Vulnerability: a new moral catagory?]* Genève: Labor et Fides, 2011.

Manon, Simone. "*Le mal radical. Kant. Arendt*, À propos du film "Hannah Arendt" de M. Von Trotta *[Radical evil. Kant. Arendt. Regarding M. von Trotta's film "Hannah Arendt]*." Philolog (2013). http://www.philolog.fr/le-mal-radical-kant-arendt-a-propos-du-film-hannah-arendt-de-m-von-trotta.

Marienstras, Richard. "Réponse à Hans Jonas." *Esprit*, 438 (1974) 185–90. http://www.jstor.org/stable/24262952.

Martens, Paul. "La dignité humaine: bonne à tout faire des cours constitutionnelles [Is human dignity a maid of all work for constitutional courts?]." In *Justice, éthique et dignité*, edited by Simone Gaboriau and Hélène Pauliat, 143–58. Limoges: Pulim, 2006.

Martin-Achard, Robert, et al. *La figure de Moïse [The figure of Moses]*. Genève: Labor et Fides, 1978.

———. "Israël et les nations, la perspective missionnaire de l'Ancien Testament." Cahiers théologiques 42, Delachaux & Niestlé S.A. (1959).

Mathis, Klaus, ed. *Efficiency, Sustainability, and Justice to Future Generations*. London: Springer, 2011.

Maurer, Jean-Luc. "Indonesia's Economic, Social and Political Development Process." Conférence du 21 août 2013, Singapour. http://lkyspp.nus.edu.sg/event/indonesias-economic-social-and-political-development-process-recent-achievements-and-challenges-for-the-future/.

Meadows, Donella H., et al. *The Limits to Growth: A Report for the Club of Rome's Project on the Predicament of Mankind*. New York: Universe, 1972.

Mehl, Roger, and Denis Müller. "Politique [Politics]." In *Encyclopédie du protestantisme*, edited by Pierre Gisel and Lucie Kaennel, 1073–90. Paris-Genève: Cerf-Labor et Fides, 1995. [2nd edition: Paris-Genève: Quadrige-PUF-Labor et Fides, 2006].

Melanchthon, Philipp. *Loci communes theologici, De lege* [Common places in theology, On law], 475–88. Opera, t. II, Basel, 1541.

Melançon, Simon. *La guerre de l'eau de Cochabamba, Bolivie: un problème de géopolitique et de territorialité [The water war in Cochabamba, Bolivia: a problem of geopolitics and territoriality]*. Québec: Département de géographie de la faculté de foresterie et géomatique de l'Université de Laval, 2005.

Miegge, Mario. "Althusius, Johannes." In *Encyclopédie du protestantisme*, edited by Pierre Gisel and Lucie Kaennel, 20. Paris-Genève: Cerf-Labor et Fides, 1995. [2nd edition: Paris-Genève: Quadrige-PUF-Labor et Fides, 2006].

———. "Capitalisme." In *Encyclopédie du protestantisme*, edited by Pierre Gisel and Lucie Kaennel, 184–00. Paris-Genève: Cerf-Labor et Fides, 1995. [2nd edition: Paris-Geneve: Quadrige-PUF-Labor et Fides, 2006].

Miller, David. "Die Idee globaler Demokratie: Eine Kritik [A critique of a global democracy." In *Die Idee der Demokratie – L'idée de démocratie*, edited by Brigitte Hilmer, 63–81. Basel: Schwabe, 2012.

———. *National Responsibility and Global Justice*. New York: Oxford University Press, 2007.

Millennium Declaration of the United Nations, III/19, September 8, 2000. Resolution A/RES/55/2/.

Mirandola, Giovanni Pico della. *De hominis dignitate [Oration on the dignity of Man]*. Translated by Yves Hersant. Cited by Bioy, Xavier. " La dignité: questions de principes." In *Justice, éthique et dignité*, 47–86. Limoges: Ed. Pulim, 2006.

Mirza, Monirul Qader, et al., eds. *Interlinking of Rivers in India: Issues and Concerns*. London: Taylor and Francis Group, 2008.

Monod, Jacques. "La science et ses valeurs [Science and its values]." In *Pour une éthique de la connaissance [For an ethic of the knowledge]*, 146. Paris: La Découverte, 1970. Cited by Russ, Jacqueline. *La pensée éthique contemporaine*. Paris: PUF, 1994.

Montesquieu. *De l'Esprit des Lois*. Paris: Garnier-Flammarion, 1979.

Moreillon, Jacques. "Du bon usage de quelques principes fondamentaux de la Croix-Rouge [Concerning the correct use of some of the fundamental principles of the Red Cross]." In *Etudes et essais sur le droit international humanitaire et sur les principes de la Croix-Rouge en l'honneur de Jean Pictet [Studies and essays on international humanitarian law and on the Red Cross principles in honor of Jean Pictet]*. Edited by Christophe Swinarski. Genève: Martinus Nijhoff, 1984.

Mourgeon, Jacques. "*Les droits de l'être humain destructeurs de la liberté.*" In *Territoire et Liberté, Mélanges Madiot*. Bruxelles: Bruylant, 2000.

Moyn, Samuel. *The Last Utopia, Human Rights in History*. Cambridge: Harvard University Press, 2010.

Mubiala, Mutoy. *L'évolution du droit des cours d'eau internationaux à la lumière de l'expérience africaine, notamment dans le bassin du Congo/Zaïre [Developments in law covering international watercourses in light of the African experience, especially in the Congo/Zaire basin]*. Paris: PUF, 1995.

Müller, Denis, and Simone Romagnoli. *Dietrich Bonhoeffer, Autonomie, suivance et responsabilité*. Paris: Revue d'éthique et de théologie morale, 2007.

———. "La loi 'naturelle' au risque de l'instabilité évangélique. Prescriptum protestant à un concept en miettes ['Natural' law at the risk of evangelical instability, a Protestant prescription for a concept in tatters]." Revue d'éthique et de théologie morale [Journal of ethics and moral theology], (2010/HS, 261) 11–30. http://www.cairn.info/revue-d-ethique-et-de-theologie-morale-2010-HS-page-11.htm.

———. "Morale [Morality]." In *Encyclopédie du protestantisme*, edited by Pierre Gisel and Lucie Kaennel, 940–60. Paris-Genève: Cerf-Labor et Fides, 1995. [2nd edition: Paris-Genève: Quadrige-PUF-Labor et Fides, 2006].

———. "Rawls, John, Bordley." In *Encyclopédie du protestantisme*, edited by Pierre Gisel and Lucie Kaennel, 1181–82. Paris-Genève: Cerf-Labor et Fides, 1995. [2nd edition: Paris-Genève: Quadrige-PUF-Labor et Fides, 2006].

Münger, François. "Les défis de l'eau requièrent-ils la mobilisation de tous les secteurs de la société dont le secteur privé?" *Actes du 1er colloque interdisciplinaire organisé par le W4W, Trop ou Pas Assez d'Eau, Comment Bien Faire Avec Cette Ressource Vitale Capricieuse?* http://www.ville-ge.ch/mhs/anima_2011_eau.php; in English: "Do Water's Challenges Require Mobilization of All Sectors of Society, including the Private Sector?" (March 2011). http:www.fiechter.name.

Neuberg, Marc. *La responsabilité, questions philosophiques [Responsibility: philosophical issues]*. Paris: PUF, 1997.

Nietzsche, Friedrich. *Eléments pour la généalogie de la morale [On the Genealogy of Morality]*. Translated by Patrick Wotling. Paris: Librairie Générale Française, 2000.

Noël, Patrick-Michel and Martin Paquet. "Un Québec zénonien, Charles Taylor et la commission de consultation sur les pratiques d'accommodement liées aux différences culturelles [Zenonian Quebec: Charles Taylor and the Bouchard-Taylor commission on accommodation practices for cultural differences]." In *Monde Commun*. Laval, Québec: Université de Laval, 2009.

Nussbaum, Martha C., and Amartya Sen, eds. *The Quality of Life*. Oxford: Clarendon, 1993.

Nye, Joseph. *Soft Power, The Means to Success in World Politics*. New York: Public Affairs, 2004.

Ordonnance du 23 novembre 2005 du Département fédéral [suisse] de l'Intérieur sur l'eau potable, l'eau de source et l'eau minérale [Ordinance of the Swiss Federal Department of

Home Affairs, dated November 23, 2005, version of January 1, 2014, concerning potable water, spring water, and mineral water]. *Recueil Systématique des lois fédérales suisses [classified compilation of Swiss federal laws].* RS 817.022.102. http://www.admin.ch/ch/f/rs/c817_022_102.html.

Orsenna, Erik. *L'avenir de l'eau, Petit précis de mondialisation II. [The future of water, little handbook of globalization II].* Paris: Fayard, 2008.

Ostrom, Elinor. *Governing the Commons, The Evolution of Institutions for Collective Action.* New York: Cambridge University Press, 1990. [2nd edition, New York, Cambridge University Press, 2008]

"Our Common Future" in http://www.un-documents.net/wced-ocf.htm.

Paquerot, Sylvie. *Eau douce: La nécessaire refondation du droit international [Fresh water: A necessary reworking of international law].* Sainte-Foy: Presses Universitaires du Québec, 2005.

Pascal, Blaise. *Pensées,* Paris: Flammarion, 1976.

Peppard, Christiana. "Fresh Water and Catholic Social Teaching: A Vital Nexus." *Journal of Catholic Social Thought* 9 2 (2012) 325–52.

———. "Troubling Waters: the Jordan River between religious imagination and environmental degradation." *Journal of Environmental Studies and Sciences* 3 2 (2013) 109–19. http://link.springer.com/article/10.1007/s13412-013-0116-1?no-access=true.

———. "Eau, besoin vital et justice globale : perspective théologique. Valorisation de l'eau : théologie, éthique et enseignement social de l'Eglise". *Actes du 2ème colloque interdisciplinaire organisé par le W4W, Eau Besoin Vital et Justice Globale* (Mars 2012). http :www.ville-ge.ch/mhs/anima_2012_eau.php; in English: "*Water, Vital Need and Global Justice: Theological Perspective. Valuing Water: Theology, Ethics and Catholic Social Teaching*." http : www.fiechter.name/w4w.

Petitpierre-Sauvain, Anne. "Rôle et portée du principe pollueur-payeur dans la gestion de l'eau". *Actes du 1er colloque interdisciplinaire organisé par le W4W, Trop ou Pas Assez d'Eau, Comment Bien Faire Avec Cette Ressource Vitale Capricieuse ?.* (Mars 2011). http :www.ville-ge.ch/mhs/anima_2011_eau.php; in English: "*The Role and Reach of the 'Polluter Pays' Principle in Water Management.*" (March 2011). http:www.fiechter.name.

Petters-Melo, Milena. "Cultural Heritage Preservation and socio-Environmental Sustainability: Sustainable Development, Human Rights and Citizenship." In *Efficiency, Sustainability, and Justice to Future Generations,* edited by Klaus Mathis, 139–61. Dordrecht: Springer, 2011.

Pflieger, Géraldine. *L'eau des villes, Aux sources des empires municipaux. [City water, at the wellsprings of municipal empires].* Lausanne: Presses polytechniques et universitaires romandes, 2009.

Pinsent, Masons. *Pinsent Masons Water Yearbook,* 2011-2012, 13th ed. (2011).

Piron, Sylvain. "*Congé à Villey [Giving Villey his notice].*" Atelier du Centre de recherches historiques (1/2008). http://acrh.revues.org/index314.html.

Pogge, Thomas. *An Egalitarian Law of Peoples.* Philosophy and Public Affairs (PAPA) 23 3 (1994). Reference given by Rawls, John. *The Law of Peoples.* Cambridge: Harvard University Press, 1999, note 47, 115.

———, ed. *Freedom from Poverty as a Human Right: Who Owes What to the Very Poor?* Oxford: Oxford Universtity Press, 2007.

———. "Priorities of Global Justice." In *Global Justice,* edited by Thomas Pogge, Oxford: Blackwell, 2001.

Postel, Sandra T., and Aaron T. Wolf. "Dehydrating Conflict." *Foreign Policy* 126 (2001) 60–67.

Prades, José, et al. "L'éthique de l'écodécision: fondements et pratiques ." In *Environnement et développement: Questions éthiques et problèmes sociopolitiques [Environment and development: Ethical questions and sociopolitical problems]*. Québec: Fides, 1994.

Préambule de la Déclaration des droits de l'homme et du citoyen de 1778, in: E. Fuchs et P.A. Stucki, *Au nom de l'Autre. Essai sur le fondement des droits de l'homme*, Genève: Labor et Fides, 1985.

Prélaz, Valentin. *Linking Disaster Risk Management, Climate Change and Poverty Reduction*. Thesis for the Certificate of Advanced Studies (CAS), EPFL, Lausanne, 2010 (unpublished).

———. IDEP and HEKS EPER, *Water Infrastructures Improvement-Project Proposal*, December 2010 (unpublished).

Rahnema, Madjid. *Quand la misère chasse la pauvreté [When destitution replaces poverty]*. Paris: Fayard/Actes Sud, 2006.

Ramseier, Stéphan. "L'eau potable à Genève." *Actes du 2ème colloque interdisciplinaire organisé par le W4W, Eau Besoin Vital et Justice Globale*. http :www.ville-ge.ch/mhs/anima_2012_eau.php; in English: "*Potable Water in Geneva*." (March 2012). http :www.fiechter.name/w4w.

Rapport de l'ONU, 2013, à propos des OMD ad. 7. C. http://www.un.org/millenniumgoals/environ.shtml.

Rapport mondial sur le développement humain 2006. "Au-delà de la pénurie: pouvoir, pauvreté et crise mondiale de l'eau." New York. https://www.scribd.com/doc/162032689/Au-dela-de-la-penurie-pouvoir-pauvrete-et-crise-mondiale-de-l-eauRapport-sur-le-developpement-humain-2006.

Rawls, John. *The Law of Peoples*. Cambridge: Harvard University Press, 1999.

———. *Théorie de la justice [A theory of justice]*. Translated by Catherine Audard. Paris: Points, 2009.

Reboud, Valérie. "Amartya Sen, quel 'modèle économique?'" In *Amartya Sen: un économiste du développement?* Edited by Valérie Reboud, 19-66. Lyon: Agence Française du Développement, 2008. http://www.genreenaction.net/IMG/pdf/FaitN30_Amartya_Sen.pdf.

Rendtorff, Trutz. "Modernité." In *Encyclopédie du protestantisme*, edited by Pierre Gisel and Lucie Kaennel, 921–34. Paris-Genève: Cerf-Labor et Fides, 1995. [2nd edition: Paris-Genève: Quadrige-PUF-Labor et Fides, 2006].

Renoux-Zagame, Marie-France. *Du droit de Dieu au droit de l'homme [From God's law to human rights]*. Paris: PUF, 2003.

Report of the United Nations Conference on the Human Environment, Stockholm, June 5-16, 1972, UN Doc. A/CONF.48/14/Rev. 1. http://www.un-documents.net/aconf48-14r1.pdf.

Report of the United Nations Water Conference, Mar del Plata, March 14-25, 1977, UN Doc. E/CONF.70/29, New York, 1977. http://www.internationalwaterlaw.org/bibliography/UN/Mar_del_Plata_Report.pdf.

Republic of South Africa, National water Act, Act No. 36 of 1998, available at www.dwaf.gov.za/Documents/Legislature/nw_act/NWA.pdf.

Republic of South Africa, Water Service Act, Act No. 108 of 1997, available at www.dwaf.gov.za/Documents/Legislature/a108-97.pdf.

Resolution A/RES/63/124, The Law of Transboundary Aquifers, December 11, 2008.
Resolution A/RES/64/292, The Human Right to Water and Sanitation, July 28, 2010.
Resolution A/67/L.75, Sanitation for All, July 17, 2013.
Resolution A/RES/55/2/, United Nations Millennium Declaration, para. III/19, September 8, 2000.
Resolution A/RES/217 (III), Universal Declaration of Human Rights, December 10, 1948.
Rich, Arthur. *Ethique économique [Economic Ethics]*. Translated by Anne-Lise Rigo an Irène Minder-Jeanneret. Genève: Labor et Fides, 1994.
Ricoeur, Paul. *Amour et Justice [Love and Justice]*. Paris: Points, 2008.
———. "Le concept de responsabilité" [The concept of responsibility]. In *Le Juste 1*. Paris: Esprit, 1995.
———. "La dignité humaine [Human dignity]." In J. F. Raymond, *Les enjeux des droits de l'homme* [The stakes of human rights], 236–37. Paris: Larousse, 1988.
———. *Le Juste*. Paris: Esprit, 1995.
———. "De la morale à l'éthique et aux éthiques *[From morality to the ethical and ethics]*." In *Un siècle de philosophie 1900-2000*. Paris: Gallimard, Centre Pompidou, 2000.
———. "Le soi dans le miroir des écritures." In *Amour et Justice [Love and Justice]* 43–74. Paris: Points, 2008.
———. *Soi-même comme un autre [Oneself as another]*. Paris: Seuil, 1990.
———. " La tâche de l'herméneutique: en venant de Schleiermacher et de Dilthey [The task of hermeneutics : as coming from Schleiermacher and Dilthey]." In Paul Ricœur. *Du texte à l'action, Essais d'herméneutique II [From text to action, Essays in Hermeneutics, II]*, 83–111. Paris: Seuil, 1986.
———. *Du texte à l'action*. Paris: Seuil, 1986.
Rio Declaration on Environment and Development, Rio de Janeiro, June 3-14, 1992, UN Doc. A/CONF.151/26. http://www.un.org/documents/ga/conf151/aconf15126-1annex1.htm.
Risse, Mathias. "*From Third World to First—What's next? Singapore's Obligations to the rest of the World From a Human Rights Perspective.*" Harvard Kennedy School (2014). https://research.hks.harvard.edu/publications/getFile.aspx?Id=1032.
Rousseau, Jean-Jacques. *Du contrat social [The social contract]*. Paris: Flammarion, 2012.
Ruffy, Victor. "Des parlements de jeunes pour l'eau, un programme de Solidarité Eau Europe." Actes du 3ème colloque interdisciplinaire organisé par le W4W, Ethique globale de l'Eau (Mars 2013). http://www.ville-ge.ch/mhs/anima_2013_eau.php; in English: "Youth Parliaments for Water, a Solidarité Eau Europe Program" (March 2013). http: www.fiechter.name/w4w.
Russ, Jacqueline. *La pensée éthique contemporaine [Contemporary ethical thought]*. Paris: PUF, 1994.
Samuelson, Paul A. "The Pure Theory of Public Expenditure." Review of Economics and Statistics 36 4 (1954) 387–89.
Sartre, Jean-Paul. *L'Être et le Néant [Being and Nothingness]*. Paris: Gallimard, 1943.
———. *L'existentialisme est un humanisme [Existentialism is a humanism]*. Paris: Gallimard, 1966.
Scanlon, John, et al., *Water as a Human Right?* Cambridge: IUCN, 2004.
Schäfer, Otto. "Brasilianisch-schweizerische 'Oekumenische Erklärung zum Wasser als Menschenrecht und als öffentliches Gut' und OeRK-Erklärung 'Wasser für das Leben,' ein Vergleich *[Brazilian and Swiss Ecumenical Declaration on Water As a Human Right*

and a Public Good and the World Council of Churches Statement on Water for Life, a comparison]." Bern: Fédération des Eglises protestantes de Suisse, 2006 (unpublished).

Schweitzer, Albert. *Civilization and Ethics: The Philosophy of Civilization, Part II.* Translated from German by C.T. Campion. London: A & C Black, 1929.

———. *La civilisation et l'éthique.* Translated by Madeleine Horst. Paris: Alsatia, 1976.

Segerfeldt, Fredrik. *Water for sale: how business and the market can resolve the world's water crisis.* Washington, DC: Cato Institute, 2005.

———. "Water for sale: how business and the market can resolve the world's water crisis". Brussels: Amigo Society, May 30, 2006. www.ein.eu/files/Segerfeldt_Amigo.pdf.

Selborne, Lord. "*L'Ethique de l'utilisation de l'eau douce: vue d'ensemble (2000)*]". UNESCO, Sous-commission de la COMEST. http://unesdoc.unesco.org/images/0012/001220/122049 F.pdf.

Sen, Amartya. *Capability and Well-Being.* In Nussbaum, Martha C. and Amartya Sen, eds. *The Quality of Life.* Oxford: Clarendon, 1993.

———. *Development As Freedom.* New York: Anchor, 1999.

———. *L'idée de Justice [The idea of Justice].* Translated by Paul Chemla. Paris: Flammarion, 2009.

———. *Repenser l'inégalité [Inequality reexamined].* Translated by Paul Chemla. Paris: Seuil, 2000.

Senarclens, Pierre. Cours sur la "Politique du développement." Faculté autonome protestante de Genève, le 31 octobre 2012 (unpublished).

———. *La politique internationale,* Paris: Armand Colin, Dalloz, 2002.

Shue, Henry. *Basic Rights: Subsistence, Affluence and U.S. Foreign Policy.* Princeton: Princeton University Press, 1980.

Siler, Clark. "*Water Management in Monotheistic Religions.*" (April 2008). http://www.ce.utexas.edu/prof/mckinney/ce397/Topics/Religion/Religion-Clark.pdf.

Singer, Peter. "Famine, Affluence, and Morality." *Philosophy and Public Affairs* 1 (1972) 229–43.

Siy, R. Y., Jr., *Common Resource Management: Lessons from the Zanjera.* Quezon City: University of the Philippines Press, 1982.

Smith, Adam. *Lectures on jurisprudence.* Edited by J.C. Bryce. Oxford: Oxford University Press, 1983.

———. *Recherches sur la nature et les causes de la richesse des nations [An inquiry into the nature and causes of the wealth of nations].* Translated by Germain Garnier. Paris: Flammarion, 1991. (When cited by Dermange, François: Smith, Adam, *An Inquiry into the Nature and Causes of the Wealth of Nations* [1776], edited by R. H. Campbell et al. Oxford: Oxford University Press, 1976.)

———. *Théorie des sentiments moraux [The theory of moral sentiments].* Translated by Michaël Biziou, Claude Gautier, and Jean-François Pradeau. Paris: Quadrige 2, PUF, 2011. (When cited by Dermange, François: Smith, Adam, *The Theory of Moral Sentiments* [1759], edited by A.L. MacFie and D.D. Raphael. Oxford: Oxford University Press, 1976.)

South African Human Rights Commission, *The Right to Water,* 44th Economic and Social Rights Report Series, 2002/2003 Financial Year 4 (Johannesburg, 2004).

Sophocle. *Antigone.* Translated by P. Mazon. Paris: Les Belles Lettres, 1950.

Spaemann, Robert. "Nebenwirkungen als moralisches Problem [Side effects as a moral problem]," *Philosophisches Jahrbuch* [Annual of philosophy], 1975. Cited by Ricœur, Paul, "Le concept de responsabilité." In *Le Juste 1,* Paris: Esprit, 1995.

BIBLIOGRAPHY

———. *Notions fondamentales de la morale.* Translated by Stéphane Robilliard. Paris: Flammarion, 1999.

Stahl Gretsch, Laurence-Isaline. "Notes." Actes du 3ème colloque interdisciplinaire organisé par le W4W, *Ethique globale de l'Eau* (Mars 2013). http://www.ville-ge.ch/mhs/anima_2013_eau.php; in English: "Notes" (March 2013). http: www.fiechter.name/w4w.

"Notes." (March 2013). http://www.ville-ge.ch/mhs/anima_2013_eau.php.

Statement on Water for Life by the World Council of Churches, Porto Alegre, Brazil, February 23, 2006, https://www.oikoumene.org/en/resources/documents/commissions/international-affairs/human-rights-and-impunity/statement-on-water-for-life.

Stiglitz, Joseph E. *La grande désillusion [Globalization and its discontents].* Translated by Paul Chemla. Paris: Fayard, 2002.

Stückelberger, Christoph. *Das Menschenrecht auf Nahrung und Wasser – eine ethische Priorität [The human right to food and water: An ethical priority].* Geneva: Globethics. net Focus, 2009.

Stücki, Christoph, and Renaud de Watteville. "Garantir l'accès à l'eau, l'un des six axes stratégiques de la Fondation Rotary." Actes du 3ème colloque interdisciplinaire organisé par le W4W, *Ethique globale de l'Eau* (Mars 2013). http://www.ville-ge.ch/mhs/anima_2013_eau.php; in English: "Guaranteeing Access to Water Is One of The Rotary Foundation's Six Strategic Focuses." (March 2013). http : www.fiechter.name/w4w.

Swiss Agency for Development and Cooperation (SDC) and WWF. *"L'empreinte sur l'eau de la Suisse pour la première fois mesurée [Switzerland's water footprint measured for the first time]."* rio20.ch/en/2012/03/switzerlands-water-footprint-is-measured-for-the-first-time.

Swiss Civil Code, December 10, 1907, Classified Compilation, RS 210, https://www.admin.ch/opc/en/classified-compilation/19070042/index.html.

Swiss Code of Obligations, March 30, 1911, Classified Compilation, RS 220, https://www.admin.ch/opc/en/classified-compilation/19110009/index.html.

Taylor, Charles. *Les sources du moi.* Translated by Charlotte Melançon. Paris: Seuil, 1998.

Tchamo, Daniel N. *Justice distributive ou solidarité à l'échelle globale? John Rawls et Thomas Pogge [Distributive justice or solidarity at the global level? John Rawls and Thomas Pogge].* Paris: L'Harmattan, 2012.

The Société des Eaux de l'Arve company (1866-1988). http://www.patrimoineindustriel.ch/ARCHIVES/PARISAFFICHETTES/PageVESSY.pdf.

The Straits Times, (September 2, 2013), B7. http:// www.straitstimes.com.

Thielcke, Helmut. *Einführung in die christliche Ethik [Introduction to Christian ethics].* München: R.Piper, 1963.

Tignino, Mara, and Dima Yared. "La commercialisation et la privatisation de l'eau dans le cadre de l'Organisation Mondiale du Commerce [Commercialization and privatization of water in the context of the WTO]." Revue québécoise de droit international, 19 2 (2006) 159–95.

Tignino, Mara. *L'eau et la guerre, éléments pour un régime juridique* [Water and War: Elements for a Legal Regime]. Bruxelles: Bruylant, 2011.

———. "L'eau et son rôle pour la paix et la sécurité internationales [Water and its role in international peace and security]." In "*Rapport mondial sur le développement humain 2006. Au-delà de la pénurie: pouvoir, pauvreté et crise mondiale de l'eau [World report on human development 2006. Beyond scarcity: power, poverty, and the world water crisis]."* http//hdr.undp.org/en/media/hdr_2006_fr-complet-pdf as well as in *Revue internationale de la Croix-Rouge*, 92 (879) (2010) 6. http://www.icrc.org/fre/assets/files/other/irrc-879-tignino-fre.pdf.

———. "L'eau et la guerre: une perspective juridique." *Actes du 3ème colloque interdisciplinaire organisé par le W4W, Ethique globale de l'Eau* (Mars 2013). http://www.ville-ge.ch/mhs/anima_2013_eau.php; in English: "Water and War: A Legal Perspective." (March 2013). http: www.fiechter.name/w4w.

Tomuschat, Christian. *Human rights, between Idealism and Realism*. New York: 2nd ed., Oxford University Press, 2008.

Tortajada, Cecilia, et al. *The Singapore Water Story, Sustainable Development in an Urban City-State*. London: Routledge, 2013.

Truman, Harry S, "Inaugural Address, January 20, 1949." http://www.herodote.net/20_janvier_1949-evenement-19490120.php.

Van Parijs, Philippe. "Internal Distributive Justice." In *A Companion to Contemporary Political Philosophy*, vol. 2, edited by Robert E. Goodin, et al. Oxford: Blackwell, 2007.

———. *Qu'est-ce qu'une société juste? Introduction à la pratique de la philosophie politique [What is a just society? Introduction to the practice of political philosophy]*. Paris: Seuil, 1991.

Verdross, Alfred. "La dignité humaine, comme base des droits de l'homme *[The dignity of the human being as the basis for human rights]*." Conférence donnée à Strasbourg, au Cercle International de Juristes, 22 avril 1977. In *Festschrift zum 70. Geburtstag von Kägi Werner*, 415–21. Zürich: Schulthess Polygraphischer Verlag, 1979.

Villey, Michel. *Le droit et les droits de l'homme [The law and the rights of Man]*. Paris: Quadrige-PUF, 1983.

Vujik, Jure. "La démocratie globale et les fondements postmodernes de la théologie politique [Global democracy and the postmodern foundations of political theology]." In *l'Etat, la religion et la laïcité [The State, religion and secularism]*, a text presented to the French National Assembly (2012), at a seminar organized by the Académie de Géopolitique de Paris. http://www.polemia.com/la-democratie-globale-et-les-fondements-postmodernes-de-la-theologie-politique/.

Wackernagel, Mathis, and William Rees. *Notre empreinte écologique [Our ecological footprint]*. Montréal: Ed. Ecosociété, 1999.

Walzer, Michael. *Sphères de Justice, Une défense du pluralisme et de l'égalité [Spheres of Justice. A defense of Pluralism and Equality]*. Translated by Pascal Engel. Paris: Seuil, 2013.

Weber, Max. "Le métier et la vocation d'homme politique [Politic as a vocation]." In *Le savant et le politique [The scientist and the politician]*. Translated by Julien Freund, 217–18. Paris: Département d'Univers Poche, 1963.

———. *L'éthique protestante et l'esprit du capitalisme [The protestant ethic and the spirit of capitalism]*. Translated by Mohr, (*Gesammelte Aufsätze zur Religionssoziologie [Collected essays on the sociology of religion]*). Paris: Plon, 1964.

Weissbrodt, Bernard. *"Aquaresponsabilité."* (Avril 2013). http://www.aqueduc.info/aquaresponsabilite.

———. "*Dakar sans eau, un fait divers*"*[Dakar without water, a news item]*. (October 2015). http://www.aqueduc.info/Dakar-sans-eau-un-fait-divers.

———. "*La Suisse et le droit à l'eau: du silence constitutionnel à l'engagement international [Switzerland and the right to water : from constitutional silence to international commitment]*." (April 2013). http://www.aqueduc.info/La-Suisse-et-le-droit-a-l-eau.

Wentworth Rinne, Katherine. *The Waters of Rome: Aqueducts, Fountains, and the Birth of the Baroque City.* New Haven and London: Yale University Press, 2011.

White, Lynn Jr. *Les racines historiques de notre crise écologique. [The Historical Roots of Our Ecologic Crisis]* In *Crise écologique, crise des valeurs? Défis pour l'anthropologie et la spiritualité [Ecological crisis, crisis of values? Challenges for anthropology and spirituality].* Edited by Dominique Bourg and Philippe Roch, 13–24. Genève: Labor et Fides, 2010.

Winkler, Inga T. "Respect, Protect, Fulfill: The implementation of the Human Right to Water in South Africa." In *Water Governance in Motion: Towards Socially & Environmentally Sustainable Water Law*, edited by Cullet et al., 415–43. New Delhi: Foundation, Cambridge University Press, 2010.

Wong, Baldwin. "*Reconstructing a Confucian Perspective on Global Distributive Justice: A Contractualist Approach.*" London School of Economics (LSE) (2011). papers.ssrn.com/sol3/papers.cfm?abstract_id=1902720.

Workshop for Water Ethics's colloquia 2011–2013. http://www.fiechter.name.

Woods, Kerry. *Human Rights and Environmental Sustainability.* Cheltenham: Edward Elgar, 2010.

World Health Organization (WHO)/United Nations Children's Fund (UNICEF) *Fast Facts about the 2013 JMP report concerning progress on sanitation and drinking water,* on the World Health Organization's website at http://www.who.int/water_sanitation_health/monitoring/jmp_fast_facts/en/.

———. *Updates report of the WHO/UNICEF Joint Monitoring Programme 2014 for Water Supply and Sanitation,* online (in English only) on the WHO website at http://www.unwater.org/publications/jmp/en/.

Xákmok Kásek. Indigenous Community v. Paraguay, Inter-American Court of Human Rights Series, 214, August 24, 2010.

Yang, Tongjin. "Towards an egalitarian global environmental ethics." In *Environmental Ethics* and *International Policy*, edited by Henk, A.M. and J. Ten Have. Paris: Unesco, 2006.

Ypsilantis, Nancy. *Ethique globale de l'eau.* Interviews of Evelyne Fiechter-Widemann, HE Benoît Girardin and Renaud de Watteville by Sarah Dirren. Babylone, broadcast on March 25, 2013, RTS (Radio Télévision Suisse). http://download-audio.rts.ch/espace-2/programmes/babylone/2013/babylone/20130325_full_babylone_1a43cd83-1988-4dc7-aab4-c560de2300b-128k.mp3.

Zeitoun, Marc. "*International Hydro-politics: Lessons for Water Diplomacy from the Jordan and the Nile.*" Actes du 3ème colloque interdisciplinaire organisé par le W4W, *Ethique globale de l'Eau.* http://www.ville-ge.ch/mhs/anima_2013_eau.php; in French: "Hydropolitique internationale: leçons à tirer du Jourdain et du Nil en matière de diplomatie de l'eau." (March 2013). http: www.fiechter.name.

Translator's Bibliography

Aquinas, Thomas. *The Summa Theologica of St. Thomas Aquinas.* Translated by Fathers of the English Dominican Province. New York: Benziger, 1917.

Arendt, Hannah. *The Human Condition.* Chicago: University of Chicago Press, 1958.

———. *The Life of the Mind. Thinking.* New York: Harcourt Brace Jovanovich, 1977.

Aristotle. *Nichomachean Ethics.* Translated by W. D. Ross, in Daniel C. Stevenson, *The Internet Classics Archive.* N.c.: Web Atomics, 1994–2009. http://classics.mit.edu/.

Berlin, Isaiah. "Two Concepts of Liberty." In Isaiah Berlin, *Four Essays on Liberty*. Oxford: Oxford University Press, 1969.

Bonhoeffer, Dietrich. *Ethics*. Translated by Neville Horton Smith, New York: Macmillan, 1955.

———. *Letters and Papers from Prison*. Edited by Eberhard Bethge. New York: Macmillan, 1971.

Calvin, John. *Commentaries on the Epistle of Paul the Apostle to the Romans*. Translated by Rev. John Owen, Grand Rapids: Christian Classics Ethereal Library, n. d. http://www.ccel.org/ccel/calfin/calcom38.i.html.

———. *Commentary on Acts*. Translated by Christopher Fetherstone. Edited by Henry Beveridge. Grand Rapids: Christian Classics Ethereal Library, n. d. 2 vols. http://www.ccel.org/ccel/calvin/, calcom36.html and http://www.ccel.org/ccel/calvin/calcom37.html.

———. *Commentary on Genesis*. Translated by Rev. John King, Grand Rapids: Christian Classics Ethereal Library, n. d. 2 vols. http://www.ccel.org/ccel/calfin/calcom01.html and http://www.ccel.org/ccel/calfin/calcom02.html.

———. *Commentary on Isaiah*. Translated by Rev. William Pringle. Grand Rapids: Christian Classics Ethereal Library, n.d. http://www.ccel.org/ccel/calvin/calcom14.html.

———. *Harmony of the Law*. Translated by Rev. Charles William Bingham. Grand Rapids: Christian Classics Ethereal Library, n.d. 4 vols. http://www.ccel.org/ccel/calvin/calcom03.html. http://www.ccel.org/, ccel/calvin/calcom04.html. http://www.ccel.org/ccel/calvin/calcom05.html and http://www.ccel.org/ccel/calvin/calcom06.html.

———. *Institutes of the Christian Religion*. Translated by John Allen, 6th ed. Philadelphia: Presbyterian Board of Christian Education, 1930.

———. *Sermons by M. John Calvin upon the Book of Job*. Translated by Arthur Golding, London: Binneman, 1574. https://archive.org/details/sermonsofmasterioocalv. Spelling modernized by Andrene C. Everson.

Calvo-Mendieta, Iratxe, et al. "Patrimonial Economics and Water Management: A French Case." In Schneier-Madanes, Graciela, ed. *Globalized Water: A Question of Governance*, New York: Springer Science and Business, 2014.

Camus, Albert. "Albert Camus—Banquet Speech" of December 10, 1957 (translation), Nobelprize.org, Nobel Media AB 2014. http://www.nobelprize.org/nobel_prizes/literature/laureates/1957/camus-speech.html.

Cicero, *De Republica, III, XII*. Translated by Clinton W. Keyes. In Cherif Bassiouni, *Crimes Against Humanity in International Criminal Law*. London: Kluwer Law International, 1999.

Cook, Walter Wheeler. "Hohfeld's Contributions to the Science of Law." *Yale Law Journal* 28 (1919) 727.

Cohen, S. Marc, et al. *Readings in Ancient Greek Philosophy, Fourth Edition, From Thales to Aristotle*. Indianapolis: Hackett, 2011.

Dilthey, William. *William Dilthey Selected Works Volume I: Introduction to the Human Sciences*. Translated by Michael Neville. Edited by Rudolf A. Makkreel and Frithjof Rodi. Princeton: Princeton University Press, 1985.

Dostoyevsky, Fyodor. *The Brothers Karamazov*. Translated by Constance Garnett, New York: The Modern Library, n.d.

Faruqui, Nasir I., et al., eds. *Water Management in Islam*, New York: United Nations University Press, 2001.

Global Water Partnership, Website. http://www.gwp.org/The-Challenge/What-is-IWRM/.

Grotius, Hugo. *Commentary on the Law of Prize and Booty.* Translated by Gwladys L. Williams. Indianapolis: Liberty Fund, 2006.

———. *The Rights of War and Peace, Book I.* Translated by John Morrice, et al., Indianapolis: Liberty Fund, 2005.

Gutierrez, Gustavo. *The Power of the Poor in History.* Translated by Robert R. Barr. Maryknoll, NY: Orbis, 1983.

Habermas, Jürgen. "Remarks on Discourse Ethics." In *Justification and Application: Remarks on Discourse Ethics.* Translated by Ciaran Cronin. Cambridge, MA: MIT Press, 1993.

Hegel, G. W. F. *Elements of the Philosophy of Right.* Translated by H. B. Nisbet. New York: Cambridge University Press, 1991.

Hobbes, Thomas. *De Cive (The Citizen): Philosophical Rudiments Concerning Government and Society.* London: Printed by J. C. for R. Royston, 1651, Chapter III §XXXIII. http://www.constitution.org/th/decive03.htm.

Hoyt, Randy. "The Fragments of Heraclitus." Published at http://www.heraclitusfragments.com/Fragments.html, "Greek Texts with English Translation" link, fragment DKB102.

International Committee of the Red Cross, "The Fundamental Principles of the Red Cross and Red Crescent," ICRC publication 0513, 1996. https://www.icrc.org/eng/assets/files/other/icrc_002_0513.pdf.

Jehle, Frank. *Ever Against the Stream: The Politics of Karl Barth, 1906–1968.* Translated by Richard and Martha Burnett. Eugene, OR: Wipf & Stock, 2002.

Jonas, Hans. *Das Prinzip Verantwortung: Versuch einer Ethik für die technologische Zivilisation.* Frankfurt am Main: Suhrkamp, 1984.

———. *The Imperative of Responsibility: In Search of an Ethics for the Technological Age.* Translated by Hans Jonas and David Herr. Chicago: University of Chicago Press, 1984.

Jung, C. G. (1971) *Psychological Types.* Collected Works 6. Princeton: Princeton University Press, n.d. Cited on Wikipedia, "Psyche (psychology)." https://en.wikipedia.org/wiki/Psyche_(psychology).

Kant, Immanuel. "An Answer to the Question: What is Enlightenment?" Translated by Mary J. Gregor in: *Practical Philosophy.* Cambridge: Cambridge University Press, 1996.

———. "Conjectural Beginning of Human History." Translated by Allen Wood in *Anthropology, History, and Education.* Cambridge Edition of the Works of Immanuel Kant in Translation. New York: Cambridge University Press, 2007.

———. *Groundwork of the Metaphysic of Morals.* Translated by H. J. Patton, New York: Harper Torchbooks, n.d.

———. *Immanuel Kant's Critique of Pure Reason in Commemoration of the Centenary of its First Publication.* Translated by F. Max Müller. New York: Macmillan, 1896.

———. *Kant's Introduction to Logic and His Essay on the Mistaken Subtilty of the Four Figures.* Translated by Thomas Kingsmill Abbott. London: Longmans, Green, 1885.

———. *The Metaphysics of Morals.* Translated and edited by Mary Gregor. New York: Cambridge University Press, 1996.

———. *Religion Within the Boundaries of Mere Reason and Other Writings.* Translated and edited by Allen Wood. New York: Cambridge University Press, 1998.

———. "Toward a Perpetual Peace: A Philosophical Sketch." Translated by Jonathan Bennett, n.c.: Earlymoderntexts.com, 2010–2015. http://www.earlymoderntexts.com/.

———. "What Does It Mean to Orient Oneself in Thinking?" Translated by Allen Wood in Wood, Allen and di Giovanni, George eds. *Religion within the Boundaries of Mere*

Reason and Other Writings. Cambridge Texts in the History of Philosophy. Cambridge: Cambridge University Press, 1998.

La Fontaine, Jean de. *Fables of La Fontaine*. Translated by Elizur Wright Jr. 3rd ed. Boston: Tappan & Dennet, 1842.

Leopold, Aldo. "Thinking Like a Mountain." In *A Sand County Almanac and Sketches Here and There*. New York: Oxford University Press, 1987.

Lévinas, Emmanuel. *Humanism of the Other*. Translated by Nidra Poller. Champaign: University of Illinois Press, 2003.

Mead, G.R.S. *Thrice-Greatest Hermes*. Vol. I. London: Theosophical Society, 1906.

Pascal, Blaise. *Pensées*. Translated by W. F. Trotter. New York: Dutton, 1958.

Rawls, John. *A Theory of Justice, Revised Edition*. Cambridge, MA: Belknap, 1999.

Rich, Arthur. *Business and Economic Ethics: The Ethics of Economic Systems*. Translated by Lutz, David and Wimmer, Albert. Dudley, MA: Peeters, 2005.

Ricoeur, Paul. "The Concept of Responsibility: An Essay in Semantic Analysis." In *The Just*. Translated by David Pellauer, Chicago: University of Chicago Press, 2000.

———. *Figuring the Sacred: Religion, Narrative, and Imagination*. Minneapolis: Fortress, 1995.

———. *From Text to Action: Essays in Hermeneutics, II*. Translated by Kathleen Blamey and John B. Thompson, Evanston, IL: Northwestern University Press, 2007.

———. "Love and Justice." Translated by David Pellauer in Ricœur, Paul and Kearney, Richard eds. *The Hermeneutics of Action*. London: Sage, 1996.

———. *Oneself As Another*. Translated by Kathleen Blamey. Chicago: The University of Chicago Press, 1992.

Rousseau, Jean-Jacques. *The Social Contract*. Translated by G.D.H. Cole, NY: E. P. Dutton, 1913.

Saint-Exupéry, Antoine de. *Wind, Sand and Stars*. Translated by Lewis Galantière, New York: Harcourt Brace Jovanovich, 1967.

Sartre, Jean-Paul. *Being and Nothingness*. Translated by Hazel E. Barnes. New York: Washington Square, 1992.

———. *Existentialism Is a Humanism*. Translated by Carol Macomber. New Haven: Yale University Press, 2007.

Sen, Amartya. "Capability and Well Being." In Hausman, Daniel, ed. *The Philosophy of Economics: An Anthology*. New York: Cambridge University Press, 2008.

———. *Commodities and Capabilities*. Amsterdam: North-Holland, 1985.

———. *Development as Freedom*. New York: Knopf, 2000.

———. *The Idea of Justice*. Cambridge, MA: Belknap, 2009.

———. *Inequality Reexamined*. Cambridge, MA: Harvard University Press, 1992.

Smith, Adam. "Report of 1762–3: Tuesday, March 29, 1763." In *Lectures on Jurisprudence*. Edited by R. L. Meek, et al. The Glasgow Edition of the Works and Correspondence of Adam Smith 5, Indianapolis: Liberty Fund, 1982. http://portalconservador.com/livros/Adam-Smith-Lectures-on-Jurisprudence.pdf.

———. *The Theory of Moral Sentiments*. London: Bohn, 1853.

———. *An Inquiry into the Nature and Causes of the Wealth of Nations Vol. II*. Edited by Edwin Cannan, London: Methuen, 1904.

Stiglitz, Josef. *Globalization and Its Discontents*. New York: Norton, 2002.

UNESCO, 2000. *The Ethics of Freshwater Use: A Survey*. COMEST Sub-Commission on the Ethics of Fresh Water (Lord Selborne, chairman).

UNDP, 1997, *Human Development Report,* New York. http://hdr.undp.org/sites/default/files/reports/258/hdr_1997_en_complete_nostats.pdf.

Weber, Max. "Politics as Vocation." In *From Max Weber: Essays in Sociology.* Translated and edited by H. H. Girth and C. Wright Mills, 77–128. New York: Oxford University Press, 1946.

White, Lynn Jr. "The Historical Roots of Our Ecologic Crisis." In *Dynamo and Virgin Reconsidered: Essays in the Dynamism of Western Culture.* Cambridge, MA: MIT Press, 1971.

Williams, James D. *An Introduction to Classical Rhetoric: Essential Readings.* Malden, MA: Wiley-Blackwell, 2009.

Wojtyla, Karol. *Love and Responsibility.* Translated by H. T. Willets. San Francisco: Ignatius, 1981.

Subject Index

adiaphoron/adiaphora, 17, 175, 273–75, 301, 324, 327, 334
alterity, xxvii, 29, 195, 199, 260, 277
axiological, 54, 63, 72, 80, 154, 225, 274
axiology, 80–81

beings, 220, 220n45, 221

Calvinistic ethic, 276
capabilities, 19, 19n21, 171, 197, 216, 218–19, 222, 224n64
care, 4, 18–19
carefulness, 279
categorical imperative, 37–38, 38n24, 48, 127–31, 136–37, 145, 204, 227–28, 254, 256, 338,
Christian ethic, 85, 182
city-state, 23, 132, 163, 331
civil society, xxv, xxix, 1, 9, 13, 23, 23n31, 44–45, 55, 57, 60, 112, 125, 131–32, 137, 171, 235, 243, 308, 331, 335
Cochabamba, 44, 132, 132n91, 166, 168–69, 243
collective respsonsibility, 211–12
conscience, xxvii, 83, 85n8, 101, 105–6, 117, 162, 162n23, 169, 199, 204, 209, 257–58, 275–76, 340
contingent justice, 40, 222, 224, 248
corporate social responsibility, 22, 23n34, 54n15, 236, 236n124
corrective justice, 32, 247, 324

deontological ethic, 125, 129, 324
difference principle, 214, 214n13, 253, 258, 258n60, 259, 339
dikaion physikon, 90, 333
distributive justice, 211, 247, 247n1, 248, 259, 324, 334
do no harm, 102, 122, 156, 228, 327, 334, 338
doings, 220, 220n45, 221
duties to respect, to protect, to fulfill, 226
Duty Bearers, 289, 291

economic development, 28–29, 92n17, 171, 191, 285, 291, 327
economic ethics, 176, 178n11, 325
economic liberalism, 186, 214
economy, 3, 5, 22–23, 30, 53, 174, 179–80, 185, 188, 191–92, 233, 264, 273, 280, 291, 336
economy of the gift, 257, 340
education, 20–21, 23, 32, 60, 96, 125, 157, 160, 164, 185n50, 219n40, 240, 280, 285, 287, 290, 302, 322, 327, 329, 345, 347–48, 351, 356
empowerment, 23, 171, 218, 222, 285, 289, 292, 356
endoxon/endoxa, 253
environment, xvii, 25n44, 31n19, 32, 53, 61, 65, 72, 207, 209, 241, 241n146, 272
environmental economy, 464
environmental ethics, 371
environmental sciences, 239
equity, xi, 32, 93, 107, 107n82, 108
ethic of conviction, 186, 209
ethic of responsibility, 186, 199, 209, 209n35,
ethical value, 301, 305–6, 326, 332,
eudaemonistic ethic, 29, 324

failed states, 43–44, 193n5, 238, 244, 336–38

geopolitics, xxvii, 10, 316
global justice, 4, 6, 159, 159n7, 211, 212n2, 213–15, 213n5, 214n10, 214n11, 241, 246, 301n50, 304n66, 317n112
global poverty, 4–7, 17, 81, 211, 213,
global responsibility, 4, 71, 181, 193, 210, 211, 224, 235, 242, 246
global water ethic, xxvii, xxxi, 48–9, 63, 157, 158, 242, 266, 280, 307, 324
globalization, 1, 3, 3n2, 4, 15, 19, 56, 64, 77, 142, 156, 202, 211, 235, 245, 279n76, 328, 330–31, 336
Golden Rule, xiii, 106, 156–57, 228–29, 248–50, 250n6, 251–61, 281, 324, 330, 338–40

389

Subject Index

governance, xi, xxix, 5, 10–11, 41, 44, 54–61, 66, 71, 103, 148, 157, 164, 175, 192, 287, 309, 313–16, 329, 333, 336–38, 350, 354
governmentality, 4–5

history, xi, xxvii, xxx–i, 7, 10, 24, 30, 33–35, 49n16, 55, 57, 69, 83, 97–99, 109, 112–13, 115–17, 121, 127, 137, 152, 185, 185n50, 186, 191, 195, 198, 201, 201n1, 205, 207, 208n31, 216n24, 230, 243, 260, 260n69, 266, 268, 271, 292
hominism, 39, 208
Human Development Index, 6, 218, 280, 285n11, 327,
human dignity, 33–40, 36n12, 43, 63, 81, 86–87, 104, 324, 332, 334–35
human rights, 11, xxvi, xxviii, xxx, 7–8, 10–11, 10n8, 35–36, 35n6, 39, 49, 49n16, 50, 72, 81n8, 83–87, 91–93, 92n15, 93n25, 95, 97, 102, 102n64, 104–5, 107–9, 113, 117, 123, 123n50, 125, 128, 130–33, 136–38, 142, 168, 174–75, 174n73, 214, 220, 224, 231, 232n108, 233n111, 240–41, 243, 259–60, 260n71, 261, 289, 302–3, 325, 331, 333, 336–37, 339
humanism, 35, 39, 39n28, 100, 148n24, 172, 172n62, 208, 209n34

impartial spectator, 169, 179
imperative of responsibility, 202–3, 205–7, 209, 234, 323, 328,
individual responsibility, 23, 193, 245
intergenerational responsibility, 32, 182, 193, 197, 201
intragenerational responsibility, 32, 182, 193, 197, 211
irenicism, xxix, 216n23
ius, 90n10, 91, 93, 94, 96n38, 97, 97n45, 226

legal corpus, 36, 136, 198, 260
legal responsibility, 198, 199
lex talionis, 251
liberal notion of democracy, 214

market, 5, 30, 60n32, 73, 77, 176, 180, 184–85, 215, 216n24, 221, 223, 233n114, 236, 241, 272n40, 298, 300, 305, 336
maximin principle, 258–59
money, 11, 27–30, 30n14, 103, 162, 174–75, 267, 319
moral philosophy, 167, 176, 180, 195, 273
moral responsibility, 198–99
moral value, 175, 274, 324, 334

nations-states, 55
natural law, 81, 83, 85n9, 86–87, 89–91, 93, 95–97, 99, 101, 103, 105–8, 108n89, 109–10, 113–19, 114n1, 119n24, 120–21, 123–26, 128, 133–38, 152, 177, 181, 202, 324–25, 332–34, 338
negative liberty, 217–18, 221,
neoliberalism, 4–5, 8, 245
NEWater, 25, 25n43, 147n20

objective respsonsibility, 198
oikonomia, 31
ombudsmen, 171
outcome respsonsibility, 212–13

phenomenology, 15, 15n1, 17, 143
philanthropy, 8, 81, 157, 159, 163–65, 164n28, 317, 336
philosophy, xii, xxvii, 7n22, 18–19, 35n6, 36n12, 47, 78, 83, 96–97, 115, 121, 136, 142, 150, 167, 172–73, 176, 176n1, 178n11, 180n21, 182, 195, 204, 207, 212, 225, 234n117, 254, 256–57, 273, 292, 330, 356, 359
physiocentrism, 269, 281
planned economy, 336
political economy, 30–31, 176n2
political ethic, 167
political liberalism, 186, 214
political philosophy, 173, 176, 176n1, 182, 212
political sciences, 236
political theology, 383
politics, xxvii, 7, 10, 30, 96, 98, 98n48, 112–13, 122, 139, 173, 173n65, 175, 185–88, 216n24, 234, 258, 307, 307n78, 330
pollution, xiii, 9–12, 40, 207, 323–24, 337,
positive liberty, 217–18, 223,
positive obligation for the State, 335
preferential option for the poor, 31, 224, 259, 295,
privatization, 28, 44, 67, 70–71, 73, 232, 234–39
prosopolepsy, 159, 159n9
Protestant ethic, 187–88, 242n49, 276, 325

reciprocity, 160, 164–65, 244, 252, 255–57, 259, 340
remedial responsibility, 212–13
repentance, xxix, 26, 54, 54n14, 273, 277–81, 277n63
resentment, 56, 81, 156–57, 165–71, 176, 189, 243n152
responsibility to protect, 214, 225, 228, 231–32, 262
reverse osmosis, 16, 25, 41, 221, 321

Subject Index

right to food, 28, 123, 240–41, 260n71, 335
right to water, xxv–xxx, xxviin12, 3, 47, 49, 51, 72n44, 79, 81, 83–84, 107–9, 113–14, 117, 123, 125, 132, 134, 136–38, 142–43, 157, 193, 197, 224–26, 226n72, 226n75, 226n78, 229–33, 238n138, 240–41, 243–45, 260n71, 261, 274, 299, 299n45, 301, 303, 323–25, 330–36, 338, 338n17, 339n33
Rights Bearers, 289–91
Rule of Law, 43, 60, 71, 92, 92n17, 104, 110, 131, 258, 335–36

scarcity of water, 9, 10, 40, 65–66, 73, 192, 239, 263, 296, 302, 305, 371
sciences, 15, 20, 115–16, 163, 202, 269, 286, 330
sham, xiii, xxviii, xxxi, 51, 331–32, 335, 338
social ethics, 176, 176n1
social notion of democracy, 224
social justice, 29
sociology, xxvii, 167, 225
solicitude, 138, 228, 247–49, 251, 253, 256–57, 259
sovereign State, 5, 122
sovereignty, 110–12, 116, 121–22, 124, 172–73, 183, 310, 312–13
State's definitions, 34, 185n50
State's duty, 13, 33, 36–37, 73, 73n47, 113, 335
state of nature, 55, 131, 184,
State under the Rule of Law (State of Law), 71, 92, 185, 185n50
State's social role, 23
Stoicism, 17, 119, 159
subjective respsonsibility, 198
supererogatory, xxix, 248–49, 340
sustainable development, 12, 25, 27, 31n20, 32–33, 55, 61–62, 65, 72, 204, 208, 235, 243, 338n27

teleological ethics, 48, 101–2, 125, 254
Ten Commandments, 29, 101–2, 106, 113, 133, 176

theological ethic, 182, 281
tragedy of the commons, 74, 74n58
transcendental, 7, 18, 86, 216–17, 224–25, 272, 332
transitional justice, 7

unequal access to water, xxv, xxvii
universal ethic, 87, 301
utilitarian ethic, 125, 324
utilitarianism, xxix, 33n29, 181–83, 182n34, 182n35,

virtual water, 52

waste water for reuse, 199
water
    as a common good, 10, 74, 305, 316n108
    as a human right, xii, xvii, xviin10, xxv, xxvn6, 1, 1n3, 13n18, 45, 62, 65, 66, 66n21, 73, 73n47, 187, 285, 324, 327, 330, 339n33
    as a public good, xvii, xxv, 1, 13, 45, 62–63, 66, 66n21, 67, 73, 73n47, 179, 187, 285, 324, 330, 339
    as a vital need, 16, 74n55, 241n147, 284n3, 294n28, 295n31, 297n37, 299n46, 301n50, 303n58, 304n66, 305, 308, 317–18, 317n112, 324, 326, 329
    as an economic good, 62, 71, 73, 239, 316n108, 324
    footprint, 52–53, 78
    prices, 44, 232, 244, 299
    rights, *see* right to water
    stress, 11, 41, 43, 53, 283, 286, 293, 296, 299, 305, 324
    synopsis table (water use and global water ethic), 324
welfare, 23, 54, 214–15, 215n15, 280, 359
well-being, xxviii, 17, 20, 23, 24, 28, 40, 47, 78, 102, 139, 165, 175–76, 181–83, 211, 216n24, 220, 220n45, 220n48, 221–22, 243, 261, 274, 280, 324, 334, 337

Scripture Index

Genesis

2:15	264
4:1–8	156
24:45–46	196
25:8	19

Exodus

20:1–17	29
23:10–11	265

Leviticus

19:18	252
24:17–21	251

Numbers

21:9	277

Job

26:8–14	364

Proverbs

23:23	137

Isaiah

30:23	264
50:4–5	xxxi

Matthew

5:3–12	17
7:12	149
25:14–30	276
25:35	281
28:19	158

Mark

5:22–23	17
5:25–34	17
5:35–43	17
10:14	326

Luke

6:31	250
6:32–35	257
10:25–37	253

John

4:11–19	196
11:1–46	17

Acts

3:6	17
10:34–35	159
20:35	157

Romans

2:14–15	85, 106
4:14	276
4:18	89
7:19	150
13:4	107
13:9	106
14:14	276

1 Corinthians

13:13	17, 340
14:3	xxxi

2 Corinthians

7:11	278

1 Thessalonians

1:8	244

1 Timothy

4:4–5	276

www.ingramcontent.com/pod-product-compliance
Lightning Source LLC
Chambersburg PA
CBHW081147290426
44108CB00018B/2464